W9-BUQ-707

FROM DESCARTES TO HUME

From
DESCARTES
to
HUME

---

*Continental Metaphysics and the
Development of Modern Philosophy*

LOUIS E. LOEB

CORNELL UNIVERSITY PRESS
Ithaca and London

CORNELL UNIVERSITY PRESS GRATEFULLY ACKNOWLEDGES A GRANT FROM THE
ANDREW W. MELLON FOUNDATION THAT AIDED IN BRINGING THIS BOOK TO
PUBLICATION.

Copyright © 1981 by Cornell University Press

All rights reserved. Except for brief quotations in a review, this book, or parts
thereof, must not be reproduced in any form without permission in writing
from the publisher. For information address Cornell University Press, 124
Roberts Place, Ithaca, New York 14850.

First published 1981 by Cornell University Press.
Published in the United Kingdom by Cornell University Press Ltd.,
Ely House, 37 Dover Street, London W1X 4HQ.

Passages from *The Philosophical Works of Descartes*, Vols. I and II, trans.
Elizabeth S. Haldane and G. R. T. Ross, are reprinted by permission of
Cambridge University Press.

International Standard Book Number 0–8014–1289–7
Library of Congress Catalog Card Number 80–69826
Printed in the United States of America
*Librarians: Library of Congress cataloging information appears
on the last page of the book.*

To Kay

CONTENTS

ACKNOWLEDGMENTS

In the course of writing this book, I have imposed upon the time of many professional colleagues. I am especially indebted to Wallace Anderson and Frederick Schmitt. Each read a draft, as well as various revisions, of the entire manuscript, and provided detailed written comments on each chapter. I am also indebted to a number of referees, whose identities are unknown to me, but whose challenging objections to aspects of my theory helped me to improve it.

An initial draft of most of this book was written during 1976–77, when I held a postdoctoral fellowship at the Ohio State University. The staff, graduate students, and faculty then associated with the Ohio State Department of Philosophy accorded me an extraordinary degree of social and philosophical hospitality, and created the climate that enabled me to make substantial progress toward the completion of this project. During that period, I benefited much from conversations with Steven Boer, Daniel Farrell, Alan Hausman, Robert Kraut, William Lycan, George Pappas, and Robert Turnbull. Subsequently, I have had valuable conversations or correspondence relating to the manuscript with John Bennett, Holly Goldman, David Hills, Stanley Kaminsky, Mark Kulstad, Ruth Mattern, Timothy McCarthy, Richard Rorty, Lawrence Sklar, and Margaret Wilson. I also want to thank several persons, with whom I had no prior acquaintance, for helpfully responding to written inquiries: Harry Bracken, James Collins, Maurice Mandelbaum, and John Passmore. I am grateful to Thomas Lennon and Paul Olscamp, and the Ohio State University Press, for access to new translations of Malebranche's *Search after Truth* and *Elucidations of the Search after Truth* in advance of their publication.

I acknowledge the support of the following organizations: the Graduate School of the Ohio State University, for a postdoctoral fellowship, 1976–77; the Department of Philosophy at the University of Michigan, for a leave of absence, 1976–77; the National Endowment for the Humanities, for a summer stipend, 1978; and finally the Rackham Graduate School of the University of Michigan, for a faculty research fellowship, 1978, and a faculty research grant, 1978–80.

All the superlatives one reads in acknowledgments notwithstanding, it is difficult to believe that anyone has ever had the help of a more splendid manuscript typist than Alice Gantt. And I am grateful to Patricia Berwald for supplying, apparently cheerfully, a vast amount of clerical assistance.

Acknowledgment is gratefully made to the following publishers for permission to quote copyright material: to Oxford University Press for passages from *Descartes: Philosophical Letters*, translated and edited by Anthony Kenny, © Oxford University Press 1970, and from *John Locke: An Essay Concerning Human Understanding*, edited by Peter H. Nidditch, © Oxford University Press 1975; to Thomas Nelson & Sons Limited for material from *The Works of George Berkeley, Bishop of Cloyne*, edited by A. A. Luce and T. E. Jessop, 9 vols.; and to D. Reidel Publishing Company for passages from *Gottfried Wilhelm Leibniz, Philosophical Papers and Letters*, translated and edited by Leroy Loemker.

L.E.L.

PREFACE

This book has its origins in difficulties I encountered when I began teaching the history of modern philosophy. I found that I could not, in good conscience, pass along much that I had been taught and much that I had read in the secondary literature. The vast majority of the critical and historical works to which I had been exposed operated, either explicitly or implicitly, within a common framework of claims about the fundamental relationships among the relevant philosophical systems. When I tried to provide my classes with detailed textual evidence to substantiate these claims, I found myself frustrated at every turn. I came increasingly to feel that the framework could be imposed upon the texts only by considerably distorting their content. It was as if I could put together a do-it-yourself kit I had acquired only by altering the size and shape of some of the parts, by substituting flexible materials for the more rigid ones provided, and so on.

The purpose of this book is twofold. The first is critical, to show that the common analytical framework grossly distorts and obscures the historical and philosophical relationships that obtained among seventeenth- and eighteenth-century figures. The second purpose is constructive, to offer a new overview of the relationships among the relevant philosophical systems.

The standard framework I reject involves three principal claims: first, that Berkeley, Descartes, Hume, Leibniz, Locke, and Spinoza are the most important figures of the period prior to Kant; second, that these figures divide into two competing schools, the Continental Rationalists and the British Empiricists; and third, that within each group successive figures apply the school's basic (Rationalist or Empiricist) principles with increasing rigor to a common body of problems, ultimately carrying them through to their "logical conclusion." This framework supports an elaborate body of associated theory.

All three components of the standard theory are examined critically in this book. In Chapter I, I argue that leading versions of the Continental Rationalism/British Empiricism distinction are broken-backed, and hence that the second component is not tenable. In Chapters II–VII, I develop a cumulative case to show that in any event Continental Rationalism and British Empiricism did not exhibit the substantial internal dialectical developments ascribed to these schools by the third component. In this connection, I focus on alleged progressions of thought regarding substance, the relationship between mind and body, and causation. In the course of a single book, I cannot adequately discuss all the topics that might be thought to exhibit the progressive structure described by the third component (a fuller list would include, for example, freedom, space and time, and universals). I believe, however, that the topics I do treat would have to play a pivotal role in any interesting version of the standard theory. The material in Chapters IV–VI suggests that the standard theory overestimates the importance of Spinoza and does not do justice to the importance of Malebranche, and hence that there are serious difficulties for its first component. In the course of the destructive arguments, the ingredients of my alternative theory emerge. I group together Descartes, Spinoza, Malebranche, Berkeley, and Leibniz as the leading representatives of a philosophical genre I call "Continental Metaphysics." This alternative overview is elaborated and defended in Chapter VIII.

Some will object that no serious scholar subscribes to the standard theory, that I am attacking a straw man. If this means that simple versions of the theory are not widely held today, I agree. Many scholars have documented problems and difficulties for aspects of the standard theory, but in a piecemeal way, scattered through various articles and books, and the reaction has generally been to attempt to preserve as much of the standard theory as possible, albeit with refinements, modifications, and qualifications. The standard theory continues to shape our thinking about the history of modern philosophy. Indeed, most of the historians who register substantial dissent continue to write within the shadow of its overall framework.

I approach the period from the perspective of an interest in dynamics, concerned to identify the sorts of forces which fueled the development of its philosophical systems. The standard theory is committed to a number of dialectical claims: British Empiricism arose *in philosophical opposition to* Continental Rationalism; the major figures are important, at least in part, because of their *philosophical influence upon* subsequent figures; and successive figures within a school provide *philosophical responses to* inconsistencies in the views of their predecessors, thereby developing the school's shared principles with increasing rigor. My own conclusion is that the standard theory imposes a much richer dialectical structure upon the developments within the period than is justified by the texts. The major differences between the systems are principally due to a variety of extraphilosophical factors, such as differing (and unargued) fundamental intuitions and various religious and theological motivations or interests. The apparent dialectical continuities are largely superficial.

In attempting to establish such results, I employ a recurrent pattern of argument which many historians of philosophy will find less than congenial. I begin by evaluating the arguments that a figure articulates in support of some central thesis; I show that these arguments are not just mistaken, but blatant failures; I suggest that under these conditions it is most implausible to suppose that the philosopher in question embraced the conclusion because of the availability of these arguments; to the contrary, the arguments must constitute his best attempt to support a position that he embraced for independent reasons. This leads me to attempt to identify what those reasons were. This project requires psychological speculations that many historians of philosophy would not consider proper to their subject.

When I began seriously to think about the history of modern philosophy, I did so without any prior commitment to the sort of methodology I have described. Quite the opposite—I assumed, as I was trained to assume, that a philosopher's articulated arguments constituted the grounds that led him to embrace his central theses. The quality of the arguments I encountered, however, undermined my confidence in this assumption. I became convinced that in many cases the argument was so weak that it could not possibly provide an adequate account of why a mind of the rank of Descartes' or Leibniz's committed itself to the argument's conclusion. Only at that point did I begin my search for extra-argumentative motivations—because it seemed to me the only method likely to be fruitful in gaining an understanding of why a figure committed himself to certain basic tenets. The justification for the methodology is to be found in the illumination it provides. The method might be far less productive if applied to other periods and figures. Indeed, even in connection with the philosophers I discuss, I believe it is much more useful in explaining their metaphysics than their epistemology.

There is an alternative methodology (apart from mere elucidation of the texts). Many historians, in the face of demonstrably weak arguments for important conclusions, prefer to provide contemporary "reconstructions" of the arguments in the historical texts. The idea is to refurbish the argument actually given by appeal to some recent philosophical developments (usually developments of the last two decades). If the point of reconstruction were simply to build the best possible argument for a philosopher's conclusion which is not incompatible with the texts, the activity would degenerate into a game or puzzle. Reconstructionists therefore find it necessary to suggest that the historical figure must have been "anticipating" the recent developments, and that the resulting argument must have been "in the back of his mind," at least in an embryonic form. The effect is to attribute to the historical figure an insight which, for lack of contemporary analytic tools and clarity, he failed to articulate. Such hypotheses require psychological speculation every bit as much as the ones I advance. The speculations of the reconstructionists, however, are preferred because they reassure historians of the richness and continuing philosophical relevance of the historical figures they study. Sometimes, of course, this approach has merit. But too often the arguments in the text are so weak, and so far removed in context and expression from contemporary discussions, that the approach seems hopelessly ahistorical.

Since I hold that the standard theory exaggerates the degree of philosophical development exhibited in the relationships among the philosophical systems of the period, it should come as no surprise that the alternative overview I offer is not nearly so rich in dialectical structure. In my scheme, Descartes, Spinoza, Malebranche, Berkeley, and Leibniz qualify as Continental Metaphysicians by virtue of their willingness to deny that some causal relation obtains between specified kinds of entities, different in each case. These denials typically generate large stretches of the fundamental structure of the metaphysics of each figure. Even if, however, we restrict our attention to the figures standardly classified as Rationalist, these denials are neither common responses to a single philosophical problem nor common consequences of a shared philosophical doctrine. Continental Metaphysics represents more of a philosophical genre or fashion than a philosophical movement.

Historians of philosophy may object that this overview is *philosophically* uninteresting. I am more than sympathetic. After my misgivings about the standard theory developed, I tried to teach the history of modern philosophy, in both surveys and advanced courses, in a way largely independent of the traditional framework. As time went on, however, I found my lectures progressively lapsing into the standard perspective. This occurred not because the theory seemed to me any truer than before, but because I came to appreciate its vast pedagogical virtues. The standard theory has a plot—leading from Rationalism to the Empiricist reaction and, in turn, to the Kantian synthesis—which is compelling and allows one to draw a variety of philosophical morals. But I do not assume that the history of philosophy must result in *philosophically* interesting history. This is not a book about how to teach the history of philosophy (I am not sure how to do so). It is a book about what actually happened, as best I can tell.

Most working historians of philosophy are, by training, predisposed to think and write about the history of philosophy in a way that attempts to maximize the philosophical interest of the material discussed. This is because most historians of philosophy have their principal advanced degree in philosophy, not history. There may be substantial justification for this institutional arrangement. Whether or not there is, the bias in our approach to the history of philosophy which results from our training is substantially reinforced by the network of rewards and incentives within the profession. As a consequence, historians of philosophy have generally been reluctant to draw upon the full range of historical considerations available to us.

Almost every new book in the field is devoted to a single figure, with the principle of organization following a predictable sequence of substantive topics (as they appear in the figure's "major" work). Discussions of the general intellectual climate and of individual biography are relegated to perfunctory introductory sections, if they are included at all. Research conforming to this model is restricted with respect to the sorts of historical understanding it can promote. The format is not adequate even for developmental studies of one thinker, much less for theorizing about the interrelationships among the philosophical views of different figures. My hope is that the ideas I present will help stimulate a greater variety of studies in the history of philosophy.

There are numerous possibilities, lines of research that can generate deeper historical insight, and consequently new overviews, interpretations, and evaluations. I suspect that prerequisites for real success here are a willingness both to consider the impact upon our thinking of the institutional arrangements (graduate programs, undergraduate curricula, journals, and societies) that circumscribe our profession and to inquire in more detail about the origins of prevailing theories. In other words, we have to take an interest in the sociology of philosophy and the history of the history of philosophy. And then we need to engage, without apologies, in research that takes seriously the range, depth, and complexity of the factors that influenced the development of modern philosophy.

Louis E. Loeb

Ann Arbor, Michigan

ABBREVIATIONS OF WORKS
AND EDITIONS

References to the works of Berkeley, Descartes, Hume, Leibniz, Locke, Malebranche, and Spinoza are incorporated into the text, using the abbreviations that follow. References are to volume (if there is more than one volume in the edition) and page number, unless otherwise noted.

AG   *An Early Draft of Locke's Essay, Together with Excerpts from His Journals.* Ed. R. I. Aaron and Jocelyn Gibb. Oxford: Oxford University Press, 1936.

Alc.   Berkeley, *Alciphron: or, the Minute Philosopher.* In Berk., below. References to dialogue and section numbers.

AT   *René Descartes, Oeuvres.* Ed. Charles Adam and Paul Tannery. 12 vols. Paris: J. Vrin, 1897–1913.

Berk.   *The Works of George Berkeley.* Ed. A. A. Luce and T. E. Jessop. 9 vols. London: Thomas Nelson, 1949–57.

CB   Descartes, *Conversations with Burman.* Trans. John Cottingham. Oxford: Oxford University Press, 1976. References to numbers of "pieces."

DCNR   Hume, *Dialogues Concerning Natural Religion.* Ed. Norman Kemp Smith. Indianapolis: Bobbs-Merrill, 1962. References to dialogue numbers.

Dia.   Berkeley, *Three Dialogues Between Hylas and Philonous.* In Berk., above. References to dialogue numbers, and to page numbers in Berk. II.

Disc.   Descartes, *Discourse on the Method for Rightly Conducting the Reason.* In HR, below. References to parts.

DM   Leibniz, *Discourse on Metaphysics.* Trans. Peter G. Lucas and Leslie Grint. Manchester: Manchester University Press, 1968. References to section numbers.

DMR   Malebranche, *Dialogues on Metaphysics and on Religion*. Trans. Morris Ginsberg. New York: Macmillan, 1923. References to dialogue and section numbers.

E   Spinoza, *Ethics*. Trans. W. Hale White and A. H. Sterling. Oxford: Oxford University Press, 1927. References to parts, by roman numerals, and, as appropriate, to preface (Pref.), definition (Def., followed by arabic numeral), axiom (A, followed by arabic numeral), proposition (P, followed by arabic numeral), demonstration (D, followed by arabic numeral if more than one demonstration), corollary (C, followed by arabic numeral if more than one corollary), and scholium or note (S, followed by arabic numeral if more than one scholium).

Eluc.   Malebranche, *Elucidations of the Search after Truth*. In LO, below. References to elucidation number.

Elwes   *The Chief Works of Benedict de Spinoza*. Trans. R. H. M. Elwes. 2 vols. New York: Dover, 1951.

Enq.   Hume, *An Enquiry Concerning Human Understanding*. Ed. L. A. Selby-Bigge. Oxford: Oxford University Press, 1902. References to section number.

Essay   Locke, *An Essay Concerning Human Understanding*. Ed. Peter H. Nidditch. Oxford: Oxford University Press, 1975. Capitalization and spelling have been modernized. References to book, chapter, and section. (Readers accustomed to other editions should note that the "Introduction" to Book I is properly a chapter, so that four chapters comprise Book I.)

HR   *The Philosophical Works of Descartes*. Trans. Elizabeth S. Haldane and G. R. T. Ross. 2 vols. Cambridge: Cambridge University Press, 1973.

IU   Spinoza, *On the Improvement of the Understanding*. In Elwes, above.

K   *Descartes' Philosophical Letters*. Trans. and ed. Anthony Kenny. Oxford: Oxford University Press, 1963.

L   *Gottfried Wilhelm Leibniz, Philosophical Papers and Letters*. Ed. Leroy E. Loemker. Dordrecht: D. Reidel, 1969.

LA   *The Leibniz-Arnauld Correspondence*. Ed. and trans. H. T. Mason. Manchester: Manchester University Press, 1967.

LC   *The Leibniz-Clarke Correspondence*. Ed. H. G. Alexander. Manchester: Manchester University Press, 1956. References to number and section of Leibniz's letters to Clarke, and to page number of Leibniz's letters to other correspondents.

LO   Malebranche, *The Search after Truth*. Trans. Thomas M. Lennon and Paul J. Olscamp. *Elucidations of the Search after*

	Truth. Trans. Thomas M. Lennon. Columbus: Ohio State University Press, 1980.
Locke	*The Works of John Locke*. 10 vols. London: Thomas Tegg, 1823.
M	Leibniz, *Monadology*. In L, above. References to section.
Med.	Descartes, *Meditations*. In HR, above. References to meditation number or page number.
Motu	Berkeley, *De Motu*. In Berk., above.
NE	Leibniz, *New Essays Concerning Human Understanding*. Trans. Alfred G. Langley. Chicago: Open Court, 1916.
NTV	Berkeley, *Essay towards a New Theory of Vision*. In Berk., above. References to section.
PAS	Descartes, *The Passions of the Soul*. In HR, above. References to part and article.
PC	Berkeley, *Philosophical Commentaries*. In Berk., above. References to numbered entry.
PHK	Berkeley, *The Principles of Human Knowledge*. In Berk., above. References to sections of the main body of the work.
PP	Descartes, *The Principles of Philosophy*. In HR, above. References to part and principle.
RDM	Descartes, *Rules for the Direction of the Mind*. In HR, above. References to the number of the rule preceding the relevant text.
S	Leibniz, *Monadology and Other Philosophical Essays*. Trans. Paul Schrecker and Anne Martin Schrecker. Indianapolis: Bobbs-Merrill, 1965.
Sir.	Berkeley, *Siris*. In Berk., above. References to section.
ST	Malebranche, *The Search after Truth*, in LO, above. This work is divided into six books; books 2, 3, and 6 are divided into parts; each part or book is divided into chapters; and some chapters are divided into sections. References to book, part (if any), chapter, and section (if any). For example: '2, 1, 1, 1' stands for bk. 2, pt. 1, ch. 1. sec. 1; '1, 1, 1' stands for bk. 1, ch. 1, sec. 1; and '1, 15' stands for bk. 1, ch. 15.
T	Leibniz, *Theodicy*. Trans. E. M. Huggard. London: Routledge & Kegan Paul, 1952. References to section number of the main body of the work.
Trea.	Hume, *A Treatise of Human Nature*. Ed. L. A. Selby-Bigge. Oxford: Oxford University Press, 1967.
TVV	Berkeley, *The Theory of Vision . . . Vindicated and Explained*. In Berk., above. References to section.
W	*Leibniz: Selections*. Ed. Philip P. Wiener. New York: Scribner's, 1930.

Wild   *Spinoza: Selections*. Ed. John Wild. New York: Scribner's, 1930.

Wolf   *The Correspondence of Spinoza*. Trans. and ed. A. Wolf. London: George Allen & Unwin, 1928. References to letter number.

FROM DESCARTES TO HUME

I

CONTINENTAL RATIONALISM
AND BRITISH EMPIRICISM

1. The Standard Theory

Most philosophers, historians of philosophy, and intellectual historians find themselves committed to a complex historical-philosophical theory about the interrelationships between the philosophical systems that developed in Western Europe during the seventeenth and eighteenth centuries. This theory has three major components.

First, certain figures are supposed to be more important than others. In alphabetical order, Berkeley, Descartes, Hume, Leibniz, Locke, and Spinoza are singled out as the most important philosophers of the period (prior to Kant). By contrast, such men as Arnauld, Bacon, Gassendi, Hobbes, Malebranche, Pascal—not to mention the "minor Cartesians" and the "Cambridge Platonists"— receive scant attention.

Second, among the figures deemed important, there is supposed to be a distinction between two schools, Continental Rationalism and British Empiricism, which reflects important differences in the philosophical views of their members. The labels "Rationalism" and "Empiricism" suggest that these differences are primarily epistemological, that they have something to do with competing accounts of the nature of human knowledge, of the standards, sources, structure, and extent of knowledge. There is a body of (Rationalist or Empiricist) epistemological principles or doctrines common to the members of the respective schools. A figure qualifies as a member of a particular school because he accepts the body of principles held to be characteristic of it. Descartes, Spinoza, and Leibniz, together with such less important thinkers as Malebranche, are the Continental Rationalists; Locke, Berkeley, and Hume are the British Empiricists.

Third, within a given school, there is supposed to be a dialectical development which results from applying the school's principles with increasing rigor to a common body of problems. On the one hand, Descartes' admission of causal interaction between mind and body, between two kinds of substances, was inconsistent with Rationalist principles; Malebranche's occasionalism, Spinoza's double-aspect theory, and Leibniz's preestablished harmony were successive attempts to solve the mind-body problem within a Rationalist framework. On the other, Locke's admission of material substance was inconsistent with Empiricist principles, and was rejected as such by Berkeley; Berkeley's admission of spiritual substance was likewise inconsistent with Empiricist principles, and was rejected as such by Hume. In both cases, the common body of problems is metaphysical. The principles which are applied to these problems, and which give rise to the alleged inconsistencies, are presumably epistemological: sense experience cannot provide us with the idea, or at least the knowledge, of material or spiritual substance; reason cannot determine how mind and body would interact if they did, or we cannot clearly and distinctly conceive of mind-body interaction. In sum, Continental Rationalism and British Empiricism are supposed to be not simply schools, but movements that exhibit significant internal developments resulting from successive applications of their shared principles through to their "logical conclusion."

Virtually the whole of the standard theory can be extracted from volumes 4 and 5 of the premier twentieth-century history of philosophy, that of Frederick Copleston (these volumes appeared in 1958 and 1959). (1) Copleston devotes from three to five chapters to each of the six "most important" figures (four or five chapters in all but one case); and no more than two chapters to any other figure (Hobbes). Here we have an implicit commitment to the first component of the standard theory. (2) Copleston writes: "It is customary to divide pre-Kantian modern philosophy into two main streams, the one comprising the rationalist systems of the Continent from Descartes to Leibniz and his disciple Christian Wolff, the other comprising British Empiricism down to and including Hume. This division has been adopted here." The custom can be justified "by referring to the problem of the origin of knowledge," and Copleston immediately proceeds to discuss Rationalist views on innate ideas and a priori knowledge. Here we have a statement of the second component. (3) With respect to Descartes' admission of causal interaction between mind and body, we are told that "if man consists of two clearly distinguishable substances, . . . it then becomes very difficult to account for the evident facts of psycho-physical interaction"; "the Cartesians who devoted their attention to the problem chose to retain Descartes' dualistic position and to deny that interaction does in fact take place. This heroic way of disposing of the problem . . . is associated above all with the names of Geulincx and Malebranche"; "in the system of Spinoza the problem of interaction was eliminated, because mind and body were regarded as two aspects of one reality. In the philosophy of Leibniz, however, the problem reappears in a somewhat different form." Here we have the centrality of (some form of) the problem of mind-body interaction to the development of Continental Rationalism. And here is Copleston's statement of the third component of the standard theory in its application to British Empiricism: "though he [Berkeley] eliminated material substance, he retained spiritual substance. Hume . . . , however, proceeded to eliminate spiritual substance as well."[1]

Who are the most important figures in the early development of modern Western philosophy? What are the important philosophical differences between groups of these figures? What are the important dialectical developments within a given group? The standard theory has answers for all these questions. I shall argue that that theory is radically deficient. It is not important for my purposes to show that leading scholars subscribe to the whole of the standard theory in the form in which I have presented it. Since I maintain that it is radically deficient, my method is to state the theory in a pure form and attempt to exhibit just how far removed it (or any natural variant of it) is from the truth. Even in its pure form, however, the theory is

[1]The quotations are from Copleston, 1958, pp. 12, 15, 16, 28, 177.

not historically or philosophically simplistic. Copleston's is a sophisticated, systematic history of philosophy. He can consistently subscribe to the three components of the standard theory while pointing out that "a rigid adherence to this scheme is apt to give the impression that continental philosophy and British philosophy in the seventeenth and eighteenth centuries moved on two sets of parallel straight lines, each developing in entire independence of the other. . . . This is an erroneous impression." Copleston's position is that "the old division into continental rationalism and British Empiricism is justified, provided that a number of qualifications are added."[2]

I believe that this is the posture adopted by virtually all contemporary historians. They feel that the standard theory is more right than wrong, even when they have serious reservations about it; and they subscribe to the bulk of a large body of doctrine associated with and supportive of it. They would certainly want to defend the distinction between Continental Rationalists and British Empiricists against the claim that "on the whole, the only basis for this grouping is geographical."[3]

It would be surprising to find many contemporary philosophers who do not subscribe to some version of the standard theory.[4] We

[2]Ibid., p. ix.

[3]Matson, 1968, p. 389. The quotation occurs in "A Note on Classification," an impassioned one-page assault on the second component of the standard theory. See also Matson's remarks at p. vii.

[4]A handful of historians, however, have in scholarly writings either criticized the standard theory on quite fundamental grounds or at least exhibited considerable independence of it. Popkin, 1959b, p. 544, wrote that "we have been shackled by a mythology about our philosophical heritage." Also see Popkin, 1959a, pp. 67–68. Norton, 1974, attacks all three components of the standard theory, especially as they relate to British Empiricism. Mandelbaum criticizes the third component in its application to British Empiricism (and more generally "the conventional view of philosophic traditions," which "regards each successive figure in a particular philosophic succession as being primarily concerned with emending the system of his predecessor"). See Mandelbaum, 1976, especially pp. 725–729 and 739–741, and 1977, especially pp. 565–567 (the quotation is on p. 566). Collins, 1972, in a remarkably innovative study, resists the temptation to write in the shadow of the standard theory; and he clearly feels that the theory's second component is weak (see, for example, pp. 112–114, 223, 228–229). Buchdahl, 1969, provides detailed criticisms of the second component. Leyden, 1968, does much to disrupt the litany of the standard theory simply by treating seventeenth-century philosophy thematically rather than chronologically, and by juxtaposing the views of Continental and

have all been reared on it. Copleston tells us that it is "customary" to distinguish Continental Rationalism and British Empiricism, that this is an "old division." This "custom" informs works as distant from each other in date and approach as Jonathan Bennett's recent *Locke, Berkeley, Hume: Central Themes* (1971) and C. R. Morris' *Locke, Berkeley, Hume* (1931).[5]

Institutionally, the standard theory is thoroughly entrenched, a fact reflected in almost all college and university catalogues. If an academic institution has any course offerings beyond a one-semester survey of the history of modern philosophy, the entries will inevitably include: "Continental Rationalism—an examination of the philosophical systems of Descartes, Spinoza, and Leibniz"; "British Empiricism—an examination of the philosophical systems of Locke, Berkeley, and Hume." We do not find such catalogue entries as: "Theocentric Metaphysics—an examination of the

British philosophers, major and minor. On the other hand, while Leyden would append substantial qualifications to the second component of the standard theory (cf. p. 67), he still retains the basic framework of that component. Compare the titles and contents of chapters I and II, and the relevant material at pp. 46, 51, 52, and 57. (Leyden does write of the rationalism-empiricism distinction that "it is a difference of degree rather than of kind, or alternatively, it is a difference of *tendency*," quoting approvingly the remark of Ryle, 1960, p. 135, that the controversy between rationalism and empiricism is a tug-of-war which "lacks a rope." But Leyden's reservations here are philosophical rather than historical. He writes that "the issues between the two rival schools of thought were neither so grave nor so clear-cut as they themselves assumed," this because of philosophical difficulties—which the figures did not recognize—in drawing an a priori-a posteriori distinction [p. 66].)

[5]Bennett, p. v, explains that his interests are not historical: "This book discusses three topics, in the company of three philosophers: meaning, causality, objectivity; Locke, Berkeley, Hume. . . . I do not aim to be scholarly, except in the limited sense that I sometimes attend closely to textual details. Nor are my concerns historical: they relate primarily to three topics, and only secondarily to three philosophers. . . . All I need is the assumption, for which I hope my own book is evidence, that the work of each of the three can be usefully related to the work of the others." My point is that it is owing to the prevalence of the standard theory that Bennett chooses to discuss these topics "in the company of" Locke, Berkeley, and Hume, to the virtual exclusion of, for example, Descartes and Leibniz. A similar point applies to the anthology *Locke and Berkeley: A Collection of Critical Essays* (1968), edited by C. B. Martin and D. M. Armstrong. The editors write that articles on Locke and Berkeley have been combined in one volume "partly because in discussing either philosopher it is profitable and almost inevitable to oppose him to the other" (p. 1). Why not *Malebranche and Berkeley: A Collection of Critical Essays* (see § 2 and Ch. VI)?

philosophical systems of Malebranche, Leibniz, and Berkeley." What we encounter is the uniform stamp of the standard theory.

This remarkable uniformity in course offerings is not a massive coincidence. Nor is it the result of each philosophy faculty independently coming to perceive one optimal course organization of the relevant historical material. The existing catalogue entries have been inherited. Their uniformity is to be explained, historically, in terms of some common causal antecedent. Some philosopher must have subscribed to the standard theory, at least in large measure. He must have been sufficiently prominent to influence the courses of study at a number of important institutions. His followers, in their academic careers, must have spread his influence. In order to attract such followers, our prominent philosopher must have been much more than a historian. He must have adhered to some comprehensive (nonhistorical) philosophical position. And that position must have affected his view of the history of philosophy. Had his perspective on the history of philosophy not been in the service of the philosophical position of his school, it would have carried no special weight. It is virtually certain that our prominent philosopher organized or structured the history of philosophy (in his teaching, any historical writings, and any curricular innovations) in a way suggestive of philosophical "morals" that supported his philosophical views. Consciously or unconsciously, he might even have distorted the historical record in the service of those views. This scenario, which is intended merely to be suggestive, has a number of obvious variations which would allow for the introduction of considerable historical complexity. What matters is that the standard theory served some philosophical school or broader philosophical movement, which bequeathed it to us. We are all saddled with that school's perspective on the history of modern philosophy.

I am not concerned to establish the identity of the school in question. Most likely, however, the relevant "movement" was Hegelian idealism in Germany and Great Britain in the second half of the nineteenth century. Thomas Hill Green was one prominent philosopher who probably played a pivotal role. In 1874 he published a three-hundred-page "General Introduction" to Hume as part of a four-volume edition of Hume's philosophical works edited with T. H. Grose. His purpose was overwhelmingly philosophical: to show that Hume's skepticism was the result of pursuing Locke's principles to their logical conclusion, and hence that such nineteenth-century empiricist successors to Hume as John Stuart Mill were engaged in a futile enterprise.[6] Green was a Fellow of Balliol from 1860 to 1882, and Whyte's Professor of Moral Philosophy at Oxford from 1879 to 1882. With distinguished former pupils teaching at major British universities, he was in just the right position to have his historical views influence courses of study.[7] Kuno Fischer was likely also an important figure. Fischer wrote of "the opposite trends of empiricism and rationalism" in *Descartes and His School*, the fourth volume of his history of modern philosophy, published in English translation in London in 1887. According to Fischer, empiricism was founded by Bacon, developed by Hobbes and Locke, and culminated in the work of Berkeley and Hume; the principal stages in the doctrine of rationalism were represented by Descartes (its founder), Spinoza, and Leibniz.[8] Filling out the development of the standard theory in any detail, from its ear-

[6]I owe the suggestion that Green contributed significantly to the status of the standard theory to Norton, 1974, pp. 3–7. See Green and Grose, 1874, especially the "Preface" and sections 1–5 of the "General Introduction." For brief discussions of Green's purposes there, see Norton, 1974, and Lemos, 1968, "Introduction." Writing one hundred years before Green, Thomas Reid had portrayed Hume's skepticism as the result of pursuing certain principles to their logical conclusion. Reid, however, located the source of those principles in Descartes (not Locke); he viewed Descartes, Malebranche, Locke, Berkeley, and Hume as stages in the development of a "common theory of ideas" or "common theory of perception." (Reid did contribute the view that Berkeley eliminated the material world from Locke, and that Hume in turn eliminated spirits from Berkeley.) See Reid, 1764, Essay II, §§ VII–XV, and 1785, "Conclusion."

[7]I have in mind such figures as Bernard Bosanquet, F. H. Bradley, Edward Caird, John Caird, R. L. Nettleship, David Ritchie, and William Wallace lodged at Glasgow, Oxford, and St. Andrews, together with other idealists at Cambridge and Edinburgh.

[8]John Passmore directed me to Fischer in the present connection. See Fischer, 1887, the chapter entitled "The Course of Development of Modern Philosophy," especially pp. 160–161. (In the same work, Fischer wrote that "Descartes, Spinoza, and Leibniz are the three greatest philosophers of modern times before Kant"—p. 491. Such statements may have introduced extraphilosophical considerations into the subsequent development of a contrast between *Continental* Rationalism and *British* Empiricism.) The second component of the standard theory, stated clearly in Fischer, of course had antecedents. Kant had contrasted noologists and empiricists in the final chapter of the *Critique of Pure Reason*. His only examples, however, were Plato and Leibniz on the one hand, and Aristotle and Locke on the other. And he classified Descartes and Berkeley together as idealists, problematic and dogmatic, respectively. See A854/B882 and A226/B274. For a discussion of Kant's view of his predecessors, see L. W. Beck, 1967.

liest sources to its twentieth-century textbook formulations, would require contributions from such subspecialties as the history of the history of philosophy,[9] and the history of the teaching of philosophy and of philosophy curricula.[10]

When we speak and write of "Continental Rationalism" and "British Empiricism," most of us are "buying into" at least large tracts of the standard theory. These commitments are an inheritance from a philosophical movement, most likely nineteenth-century idealism, which had a vested interest in the general perspective the theory provided. It is improbable that most working philosophers and historians of philosophy today share the philosophical position of that movement. The standard theory requires systematic reevaluation.

2. Existing Anomalies for the Standard Theory

I have been engaged in something of a "loosening up" exercise. The moral is that one should not have too much confidence in the standard theory, which we have inherited, in the absence of an independent evaluation of its components. In this section, I produce some concrete considerations leading to the same conclusion. I proceed by bringing together anomalies or puzzles for the standard theory which have already been identified. The scholarship of a number of historians of philosophy and historically minded philosophers has led to results that do not conform to the standard theory. The most serious anomalies that have surfaced affect principally the theory's second and third components in their application to Locke, Berkeley, and Hume.[11]

[9]For a discussion of the history of histories of philosophy, and numerous references, see Mandelbaum, 1976, Section I.

[10]Tipton, 1974, pp. 1–4, has emphasized the pernicious role of "the facts of course construction." Pedagogical requirements, however, explain only why there should be some distortions or other in the teaching of the history of philosophy, not why we should teach the standard theory in particular. There is a good psychological question here: to what extent do those of us who teach the standard theory on account of its pedagogical virtues thereby come to internalize that theory?

[11]Here and elsewhere in this and the preceding section I intentionally invoke the terminology of Thomas Kuhn, and emphasize Kuhnian points about the sociology and psychology of theory change (though not about the epistemological status of

(*a*) In 1937, the Locke scholar Richard Aaron complained that "in our own day . . . Locke is talked of as if he were a mere rationalist." A number of scholars have since maintained that Locke was not an empiricist. In 1958, Arthur Pap argued that "it is clear that modern empiricists cannot count the 'empiricist' Locke among their ancestors. . . . If the thesis of the analyticity of all a priori knowledge is part of what is meant by 'empiricism', then Locke was no empiricist at all." More recently, in 1971, R. S. Woolhouse asserted that "it is [Locke's] appeal to this notion [of a corpuscular real essence] in talking about natural laws which is in the end responsible for those elements in his views which leads me to dub him a 'rationalist' rather than an 'empiricist'."[12]

(*b*) Since at least 1933, a number of historians, including the Locke scholar John W. Yolton, have challenged the standard view that Locke subscribed to a representative theory of perception, or to any version of indirect realism on which the "immediate" objects of perception are something other than physical objects. These historians variously argue either that Locke was a direct realist, or that he had little interest in adjudicating between distinctively philosophical (as opposed to physical) theories of perception.[13]

(*c*) In 1934, A. A. Luce published his pioneering work, *Berkeley and Malebranche*, which argues that "Locke taught him [Berkeley], but Malebranche inspired him"; "the way to the heart of Berkeleianism lies through Malebranche"; "Malebranche did more than weaken the evidence for matter. He showed Berkeley, if I mistake not, how to construct a system dispensing with matter." Luce's thesis that Berkeley is more a Malebranchian than a Lockean became sufficiently credible and influential that by 1974 Harry Bracken could challenge Luce in the following way: "There are a number of characteristics which I take to mark a philosopher as

---

theories). The standard theory is a "paradigm" in Kuhn's sense. The reader will have to decide to what extent the theory is in "crisis." See Kuhn, 1962.

[12] Aaron, 1937b, p. 10; Pap, 1958, pp. 58, 61; Woolhouse, 1971, p. x.

[13] For the case that Locke did not subscribe to a representative theory of perception, see: Swabey, 1933, pp. 573–593; Woozley, 1964, pp. 24–35; Lewis, 1969, pp. 124–146; and Yolton, 1970, pp. 126–137. For a defense of the standard view on this point, see Matthews, 1971, and Mackie, 1976, pp. 37–41. For an exchange on the metaphysical status of "ideas" in Locke, see Greenlee, 1967, and Aspelin, 1967.

Cartesian. Just as there are a number of refinements which mark a philosopher as a Malebranchian. . . . I contend that Berkeley's philosophy and his philosophical goals are best understood as Cartesian. . . . He ought not to be thought of as a 'British Empiricist'." Bracken and Luce agree that Berkeley is best seen as a Continental figure, though they differ as to whether he is more akin to Malebranche or to Descartes.[14]

(d) In 1959, R. H. Popkin wrote an important article, entitled "Did Hume Ever Read Berkeley?", which seriously argues that the evidence for an affirmative answer to that question is slight. Well aware that Hume twice refers approvingly to Berkeley's views about abstract ideas (*Trea.* 17, *Enq.* 122), Popkin cites works by other writers which could have given Hume sufficient acquaintance with Berkeley's views to account for the content of these two passages. Because of the dearth of other evidence internal to Hume's philosophical works that he did read Berkeley, Popkin concludes that probably he did not, and that in any case he did not take Berkeley seriously.[15]

The cumulative threat of these difficulties for the standard theory is grave. According to the theory's second component, Locke, Berkeley, and Hume share a common body of "Empiricist" epistemological principles. Against this, a number of scholars have held (a) that Locke's epistemological principles were more rationalist than empiricist. According to the theory's third component, the successive Empiricist figures applied their common body of epistemological principles with increasing rigor to material substance (Berkeley) and spiritual substance (Hume). Against this, a number of scholars have held (b) that Locke did not hold the representative theory of perception which Berkeley attacked as a component of his argument against material substance; (c) that in any case Berkeley was developing the theories of Continental figures such as Descartes and Malebranche; and (d) that Hume did not take Berkeley suffi-

---

[14]Luce, 1934, pp. 7, 43, 83; Bracken, 1974, pp. 15–17.

[15]Popkin, 1959b. Popkin, 1964, concedes that Hume did read Berkeley's *Principles*, but he points out that the basic problem remains: "why is there so little trace of Berkeley in Hume's writings?" (p. 778). Passmore, 1968, p. 86, suggests that Hume "does not take Berkeley's central argument at all seriously."

ciently seriously to leave (in his philosophical works) any significant evidence that he even read Berkeley.

Nevertheless, many scholars who are aware of one or more of these difficulties have not abandoned the standard theory as it applies to British Empiricism. Substantial difficulties do not lead to abandonment of a perspective unless some new theory has emerged as an alternative. It is a source of intellectual discomfort to reject, in the absence of an alternative, a perspective that has as much theoretical power as does the standard theory. Even if an alternative is available, it is psychologically difficult to reject a theory which has been inculcated throughout one's education, and which has provided the framework for one's research and teaching. As a result, such difficulties are seen as "local" in their implications, raising problems for the standard theory which require that it be modified or qualified, but not that it be rejected outright. For example, many historians, even those prepared to label Locke a "rationalist" in some sense, would not want to deny that he was a "British Empiricist." Such historians would prefer to admit only to "rationalist elements" in Locke's philosophy. There is a nice example of this phenomenon in a recent survey of British philosophy. The author points to "three significant limitations to Locke's empiricism." In an attempt to preserve the standard theory in the face of these difficulties, he writes that "Locke's repudiation of rationalism . . . is less thoroughgoing *than he intended it to be*" (my emphasis).[16] The tendency to resist recognizing the collective force of various difficulties is even greater. My position is not that the standard theory is simply in need of local revisions, modifications, and retrenchment, but that it is radically mistaken.

The third component of the standard theory depends upon the second. If it is not the case that the members of the respective schools share some common body of epistemological principles, then it cannot be the case that there are internal dialectical developments within a school which result from applying some common body of principles with increasing rigor. While I will have much to say in other chapters about the third component as applied

[16]Quinton, 1967, pp. 379, 380.

to both British Empiricism and Continental Rationalism, most of the rest of this chapter examines the second component, the claim that there are bodies of Rationalist and Empiricist principles which are distinctive to the members of the respective schools. I believe that this claim, construed in any interesting way, is false; or at the very least that it considerably distorts the interrelationships of the epistemological theories of the period. Claim (a), that Locke was in some sense a Rationalist is especially relevant in this connection. The following section will expand on the grounds for this claim.

3. Epistemology in Descartes, Locke, and Berkeley

The principal thesis of this section is that if Descartes is a Rationalist, so is Locke. More specifically, I contend that most of Books III and IV of Locke's *Essay Concerning Human Understanding* constitutes an attempt to contribute to Descartes' epistemological program by establishing the theoretical possibility that both truths of morality and laws of nature can be known in a way which satisfies Descartes' standards for knowledge.

The strategy of the section will be to identify various features central to Descartes' epistemology, features which might be thought (individually or collectively) to qualify Descartes as a Rationalist, and to consider the degree to which Locke's epistemology shares these features. I will be principally concerned with Descartes' views with respect to the following issues: the standards for knowledge, the conditions true beliefs must satisfy in order to constitute knowledge; the sources of knowledge, the faculties employed in gaining knowledge; the structure of knowledge, the interrelationships of beliefs which constitute knowledge; and the extent of knowledge, the sorts of subject matter about which knowledge is possible. The standard theory would lead us to expect considerable divergence in the views of Descartes and Locke on these issues. This expectation is not fulfilled.[17]

---

[17]For other general discussions of Rationalist strains in Locke, and of the difficulty in making out the case that Locke was an empiricist, see: Ewing, 1937, pp. 33–34; and Odegard, 1965, pp. 185–196.

What, for Descartes, are the standards for knowledge, the conditions that true beliefs must satisfy in order to constitute knowledge? His principal standard for knowledge is certainty and indubitability. Thus he states in *The Rules for the Direction of the Mind*: "We should busy ourselves with no object about which we cannot attain a certainty equal to that of the demonstrations of Arithmetic and Geometry" (*RDM* II); "our inquiries should be directed ... to what we can clearly and perspicuously behold and with certainty deduce; for knowledge is not won in any other way" (*RDM* III). Locke seems to impose certainty as a condition for knowledge as well. In the correspondence with Bishop Edward Stillingfleet, he writes: "with me, to know and to be certain, is the same thing" (Locke IV, 145); and in the *Essay* proper, he explicitly equates "knowing" with "being certain of the truth of any proposition" (*Essay* IV.vi.3). Locke also provides an account of what he means by "certainty": "What we once know, we are certain is so: and we may be secure, that there are no latent proofs undiscovered, which may overturn our knowledge, or bring it in doubt" (*Essay* IV.xvi.3).

What, for Descartes, are the sources of knowledge, the faculties employed in gaining knowledge? In the *Rules*, he distinguishes intuition and deduction. He has less to say about the nature of intuition than one might hope, but the general picture is as follows (cf. *RDM* III, VII, XI): intuition is an act or operation of the mind in which a proposition is apprehended or perceived "in its totality at the same time and not successively," and so clearly and distinctly as to be certain or indubitable. Furthermore, it seems clear that propositions known by intuition are not only certain but self-evident (cf. *RDM* III, VII, XI). Truths known by intuition do not require argument of any sort.

Locke discusses intuitive knowledge at *Essay* IV.ii.1. Truths known by intuition have a degree of certainty which "every one finds to be so great, that he cannot imagine, and therefore not require a greater; for a man cannot conceive himself capable of a greater certainty.... He that demands a greater certainty ... , demands he knows not what. ..." The faculty which is the source of intuitive knowledge is "bare *intuition*," a faculty of the understanding. Exercise of this faculty requires "no pains" at all; the mind "perceives the truth, as the eye doth light, only by being directed towards it"; this sort of knowledge "forces it self immediately to be perceived, as soon as ever the mind turns its view that way." Truths known by intuition are self-evident (cf. *Essay* IV.vii.1–7), and therefore do not require any argument (cf. *Essay* IV.vii.19).

It is important to note that for both Descartes and Locke not all intuitive knowledge is a priori and general. For example, they both hold that we have intuitive knowledge of our own existence (*RDM* III; *Essay* IV.iii.21,ix.3). Such knowledge, where achieved via the Cartesian *cogito*, is not a priori relative to standard accounts of the a priori-a posteriori distinction. What is more, neither Descartes nor Locke places any premium upon, or assigns any pride of place to, intuitive knowledge that is a priori. Knowledge of one's own existence is Descartes' *first* example of intuitive knowledge: "*intuition is the undoubting conception of an unclouded and attentive mind. . . .* Thus each individual can mentally have intuition of the fact that he exists, and that he thinks; that the triangle is bounded by three lines only, the sphere by a single superficies, and so on" (*RDM* III). And according to Locke: "nothing can be more evident to us, than our own existence. . . . If I doubt of all other things, that very doubt makes me perceive my own *existence*" (*Essay* IV.ix.3). This is of course just Descartes' position in Part IV of the *Discourse on Method* and the second of the *Meditations on First Philosophy*.

Descartes has even less to say about deduction than intuition. The general picture, however, is again fairly clear. If a proposition is known by intuition, its truth is perceived "in its totality at the same time and not successively." This is the principal difference between intuition and deduction. Deduction "involves a sort of movement on the part of our mind when it infers one thing from another" (*RDM* XI); "Hence we distinguish this mental intuition from deduction by the fact that into the conception of the latter there enters a certain movement or succession, into that of the former there does not" (*RDM* III). Deduction is not a second mental operation supplementary to intuition; rather, it is best construed as a temporal sequence or series of intuitions. Further, truths known by deduction are certain but not self-evident (cf. *RDM* III, VII, XI). Whereas truths known by intuition do not require argument, truths known by deduction are established by arguments that are demonstrative—

"deduction" is characterized as "necessary inference from other facts that are known with certainty" (*RDM* III; cf. *RDM* XI, *HR* I, 45).

Locke discusses demonstrative knowledge at *Essay* IV.ii.2–13. If a proposition is known by intuition, its truth is perceived "presently" (*Essay* IV.ii.2), whereas in demonstrative knowledge "there must be a progression by steps and degrees" (*Essay* IV.ii.4). And *"in every step reason makes in demonstrative knowledge, there is an intuitive knowledge"* (*Essay* IV.ii.7). Or as Locke states, "Certainty depends so wholly on this intuition, that in the next degree of *knowledge*, which I call *demonstrative*, this intuition is necessary in all the connections" (*Essay* IV.ii.1). Further, demonstrative knowledge "though it be certain, yet the evidence of it is *not* altogether *so clear* and bright, nor the assent so ready, *as* in *intuitive* knowledge" (*Essay* IV.ii.4). In particular, truths known by demonstration are not self-evident; they require reasoning, that is, proof or demonstration (*Essay* IV.ii.2–3).

Thus far, the accounts of intuition and deduction or demonstration in Descartes and Locke are remarkably similar. Truths known by intuition are perceived "at the same time" or "presently," are self-evident, do not require argument, and are not restricted to a priori truths. Truths known by deduction or demonstration are perceived in a "succession" or "progression," are certain but not self-evident, and are established by arguments consisting of a series of intuitively grasped steps.[18]

Do intuition and demonstration exhaust the sources of knowledge? In the *Rules*, Descartes provides an explicit affirmative answer: "We have now indicated the two operations of our understanding, intuition and deduction, on which alone we have said we must rely in the acquisition of knowledge" (*RDM* IX; cf. III). Similarly, Locke states: "These two, (*viz.*) intuition and demonstration, are

[18]The similarity between Descartes' account of intuition and deduction and Locke's account of intuition and demonstration has been noted by a number of scholars: Gibson, 1917, p. 212; Aaron, 1937a, p. 29, and 1937b, pp. 220–227; Ware, 1950, pp. 226–227; and Smith, 1952, p. 70, n. 4. The point is stressed heavily in Roth, 1937, pp. 114–126. Curley, 1978, pp. 44–45, and n. 24, notes a similarity between an epistemological project recommended by Descartes in the *Rules*, and a project undertaken by Locke in the *Essay*.

the degrees of our knowledge; whatever comes short of one of these, with what assurance soever embraced, is but faith, or opinion, but not knowledge, at least in all general truths" (*Essay* IV.ii.14).

Locke agrees with Descartes not only in the details of his characterization of the nature of intuition and demonstration, but also in the claim that intuition and demonstration are the sole sources of knowledge, at least with respect to all general truths. (I will discuss the significance of this possible qualification below.) All Descartes' principal claims about intuition and deduction are to be found in Locke's discussion of intuitive and demonstrative knowledge, located in Chapter ii of Book IV of the *Essay*. The similarities of the two accounts are both wide and deep.

What, for Descartes, is the structure of knowledge, the interrelationships of beliefs which constitute knowledge? We have seen that Descartes claims that propositions known by intuition do not require argument. He makes an even stronger claim, that propositions known by intuition do not admit of argument, that they cannot be established by argument. Descartes' rules instruct us to proceed by accepting the absolutely simple or simplest and then progressively more complex propositions (*RDM* V, VI, VIII). Since "all facts can be arranged in certain . . . series, . . . in so far as certain truths can be known from others" (*RDM* VI), the simplest propositions must be those which cannot be established by appeal to other propositions. Not only do they not require argument, they do not admit of argument—they are incapable of being supported by appeal to other propositions. It is the simplest propositions, self-evident and known by intuition, which do not require nor even admit of proof, which constitute the "foundation" (cf. HR I, 140, 144) of all our knowledge. And we find the following in Locke: "intuitive knowledge neither requires, nor admits any proof, one part of it more than another. He that will suppose it does, takes away the foundations of all knowledge and certainty" (*Essay* IV.vii.19).

What, for Descartes, is the extent of human knowledge, the range of subject matter about which knowledge is possible? Taking seriously Descartes' claim in the *Rules* that we must rely upon intuition and deduction alone in the acquisition of knowledge, we can formulate the present question as follows: for Descartes, what sorts of subject matter contain propositions that can be established on the basis of intuition and demonstration alone? There is one especially important class of particular (as opposed to general) propositions which Descartes takes to be established on the basis of intuition alone: we can have intuitive knowledge of the content of our own present mental states. I have already noted that for Descartes and Locke not all intuitive knowledge is a priori and general; both hold that knowledge of one's own existence via the Cartesian *cogito* is intuitive. For the purposes of the *cogito*, we need be certain only that we are in some mental state or other, whatever. Descartes also holds that we can have intuitive knowledge of the contents of our own mental states at the time they obtain. This is explicit in the case of mental states that involve sensory experiences:

> I am the same who feels, that is to say, who perceives certain things, as by the organs of sense, since in truth I see light, I hear noise, I feel heat. But it will be said that these phenomena are false and that I am dreaming. Let it be so; still it is at least quite certain that it seems to me that I see light, that I hear noise and that I feel heat. That cannot be false; properly speaking it is what is in me called feeling; and used in this precise sense that is no other thing than thinking. [*Med. II*, HR I, 153]

The doctrine here, in more contemporary terminology, is that first-person beliefs about present mental states are incorrigible (a belief that a proposition is true is incorrigible just in case: necessarily, if a person believes the proposition is true, then it is true). In this terminology, Descartes holds that such beliefs as "I seem to see blue" are incorrigible. This doctrine is far from incidental to the overall strategy of the *Meditations*. Descartes holds that his arguments for the existence of God, including the "causal" arguments of *Meditation III*, are demonstrative (HR I, 133–135, 170). If so, they must consist of a series of intuitively grasped steps. Since it is a premise for the arguments of *Meditation III* that "I have an idea of God," this proposition must itself be known intuitively. It is just a special case of intuitive knowledge of the content of our present mental states.[19] This doctrine finds expression in Locke as follows: "There can be nothing more certain, than that the *idea* we receive

[19]Williams, 1978, pp. 79–81 and 87, is one commentator who has set out clearly both Descartes' views about first-person knowledge of present mental states and their importance.

from an external object is in our minds; this is intuitive knowledge. But whether there be any thing more than barely that *idea* in our minds, whether we can thence certainly infer the existence of any thing without us, which corresponds to that *idea*, is that, whereof some must think there may be a question made" (*Essay* IV.ii.14).

What, for Descartes, is the extent of intuitive or demonstrative knowledge of general truths? The textual evidence for the answer to this question is scattered through the *Rules, Discourse, Meditations*, and *Principles of Philosophy*. Descartes speaks specifically of wanting to establish a foundation for "the sciences" (HR I, 140, 144). In the *Rules*, he states that "the sciences taken all together are identical with human wisdom" (*RDM* I). In general, Descartes uses 'science' and 'philosophy' interchangeably. Science or philosophy is subdivided into arithmetic and geometry, metaphysics or first philosophy, natural philosophy or the natural sciences, and morals. (For the evidence for these claims, see *RDM* I, II, IV; *Disc.* I, V, VI; the "Author's Letter" introducing *PP*; and consider the overall titles of *PP* and *Med.* relative to their subject matter.) Descartes' view is that the sciences of metaphysics, natural philosophy, and morals are in principle susceptible to the same degree of certainty as arithmetic and geometry. Thus he states that "of all the sciences known *as yet*, arithmetic and geometry alone are free from any taint of falsity or uncertainty" (*RDM* II, emphasis added); and in the "Dedication" to the *Meditations* he states that the demonstrations "of which I here make use are equal to, or even surpass in certainty and evidence, the demonstrations of Geometry" (HR I, 135).

This view needs an explanation. What features are shared by mathematics, metaphysics, natural philosophy, and morals such that demonstrative knowledge is attainable with respect to all these subject matters? In other words, we want to know the conditions under which demonstrative knowledge is possible, and we want to be able to see that the various subjects satisfy these conditions. If Descartes said anything applicable to these matters, it is contained in his discussion of simple and complex natures in the *Rules* (*RDM* VI, VIII, XII). The basic idea is that there exist certain simple natures or essences (for example, those which are material—figure, extension, motion, etc.; those which are spiritual—thinking, doubting, volition, etc.; and those common to material and spiritual things—

existence, unity, duration, etc.). Some truths about these simple natures are known by intuition. In other cases, simple natures are united with each other necessarily, for example, figure is conjoined with extension. In such cases we can know by deduction that the necessary union obtains. This theory is far from thoroughly developed in the *Rules,* and references to it virtually disappear from Descartes' later writings.[20] The difficulties are obviously severe. Granted that "the union of these [simple natures] one with another is either necessary or contingent" (*RDM* xii, HR i, 42) how do we know in advance to what extent the unions are necessary and hence discoverable by deduction? And what are the simple natures relevant to the demonstration of morality?

Locke provides a much more developed or elaborate account of the conditions under which demonstrative knowledge is possible, and of what sorts of subject matter satisfy those conditions. This account is to be found in his views relating to real and nominal essence, located late in Book ii (beginning at section xxx) and in Books iii and iv of the *Essay*. His position can be summarized as follows: (1) all the properties of a kind of thing are deducible from statements about the real essence of that kind; (2) nominal and real essences coincide for all modes and relations; (3) mathematical and moral concepts are modes or relations; (4) in the case of substances, nominal and real essences need not coincide, and we do not (yet) know the real essences of substances. I will now sketch the theory embodied in these claims.

For Locke, words, in their primary and immediate signification, stand for ideas (*Essay* iii.ii); and general words or terms, in their primary and immediate signification, stand for abstract ideas (*Essay* iii.iii). Nominal essences are identified with the abstract ideas for which general terms stand (*Essay* iii.iii.16–17; cf. ii.xxxi.12). Since Locke holds that the meaning of a word is the idea for which it stands (*Essay* iii.iv.6), we can think of a nominal essence as a nominal definition. (Locke, however, has a slightly different use for the term 'definition'—see *Essay* iii.iii.10,iv.6.)

Some abstract ideas or nominal essences are real essences as well. What does this mean? It is not too helpful when Locke states that

[20]Drury, 1978, argues that the simple natures of the *Rules* reappear in Descartes' later writings as modes and attributes of substance.

real "*essence* may be taken for the very being of any thing, whereby it is, what it is" (*Essay* III.iii.15). Three sections later, he states that the real essence of something is "that foundation from which all its properties flow" (*Essay* III.iii.18). These two remarks are about all Locke provides by way of an explicit, general account of real essence. In order to understand them, and to cash the metaphors of a "foundation" from which properties "flow," we have to consider examples. The following is an instructive passage:

> The complex *ideas* we have of substances, are . . . certain collections of simple *ideas*, that have been observed or supposed constantly to exist together. But such a complex *idea* cannot be the real essence of any substance; for then the properties we discover in that body, would depend on that complex *idea*, and be deducible from it, and their necessary connexion with it be known; as all properties of a triangle depend on, and as far as they are discoverable, are deducible from the complex *idea* of three lines, including a space. But it is plain, that in our complex *ideas* of substances, are not contained such ideas, on which all the other qualities, that are to be found in them, do depend. The common *idea* men have of *iron*, is a body of a certain colour, weight, and hardness; and a property that they look on as belonging to it, is malleableness. But yet this property has no necessary connexion with that complex *idea*, or any part of it. [*Essay* II.xxxi.6]

Consider the abstract idea of a triangle as three lines including a space. There is, Locke maintains, a necessary connection between that abstract idea and all the properties of triangles in general; all the properties of triangles in general "flow" from this "foundation" in the sense that they are deducible from statements about this abstract idea. For example, we can deduce that the interior angles of a triangle sum to 180°. This abstract idea of a triangle as a three-sided closed figure is thus a real essence. It is when we know real essences that demonstrative knowledge is possible. Consider, by way of contrast, the abstract idea of a triangle as the geometrical figure pictured on page 1402 of my desk dictionary. From statements about this abstract idea, we cannot deduce the properties of triangles in general. Similarly, the abstract idea of iron as a body of a certain color, weight, and hardness is a mere nominal essence. It is not a real essence because there is no necessary connection between the other properties of iron, such as malleableness, and the properties in that abstract idea, and hence the properties of iron are not deducible from statements about that abstract idea.

Behind these distinctions there lurks a theory of definition. From an arbitrary nominal essence or nominal definition of a kind of thing, one cannot deduce all the properties of that kind of thing. But some nominal essences are also real essences, that is, in more traditional terminology, real or essential definitions. A real essence or real definition includes or sets out the properties that are essential to some kind. In addition, according to the theory it is possible to deduce from such a real essence or definition all the properties of that kind because there exists a necessary connection between them and that essence or definition.

There may be an element of this sort of theory in Descartes' view that we can deduce the necessary unions which obtain between two simple natures or essences. But the theory appears strikingly similar to one found in Spinoza. In *On the Improvement of the Understanding*, Spinoza states that "a conception or definition of a thing should be such that all the properties of that thing, in so far as it is considered by itself, . . . can be deduced from it" (*IU* 38). In a letter to Ehrenfried Walter von Tschirnhaus, he contrasts definitions of a circle and of God from which we can deduce all the properties of circles and of God, respectively, with definitions that are impotent for the purposes of such demonstrations (Wolf LX, January 1675). This theory of definition plays a crucial role in Spinoza's demonstration of Proposition XVI of Part I of the *Ethics*. He and Locke seem to share closely related doctrines to the effect that from an essential definition of a kind of thing all the properties of that kind can be deduced.

Locke's theory is that demonstrative knowledge depends upon knowledge of real essences. Which sorts of subject matter can satisfy this condition? Locke's answer to this question depends upon his distinction between three kinds of complex ideas: ideas of substances, modes, and relations. Against this background, Locke makes the following claims: nominal and real essences coincide in the case of all modes and relations (*Essay* III.iv.3,v.14,16); nominal and real essences need not coincide in the case of substances (*Essay* III.vi.3). His grounds for these crucial claims have to do with his theory of archetypes. He thinks that ideas signify or stand for archetypes, the "standards" or "patterns" which ideas "copy" or "represent" (*Essay* II.xxx,xxxi, III.passim., IV.iv); in the case of substances, the archetypes for our ideas, the standards or patterns that we attempt to copy or represent, are real substances existing in nature (*Essay* II.xxx.5,xxxi.3, IV.iv.5); in the case of modes and relations, the archetypes for our ideas are not entities really existing in nature, but rather our own ideas themselves (*Essay* II.xxx.4,xxxi.3, III.v.5,14,16, IV.iv.5). The suggestion seems to be that since our abstract ideas of modes and relations are framed without any intended reference to standards or patterns existing in nature, they must function as real essences because the modes and relations have no properties other than those we assign to them. This is a crucial doctrine.

According to Locke, ideas of figure, such as a triangle, are simple modes (*Essay* II.xiii.5–6); so too are ideas of numbers (*Essay* II.xvi.1–3). Since nominal and real essences coincide in the case of all modes and relations, demonstrative knowledge of geometry and arithmetic is therefore possible. To what extent is demonstrative knowledge possible outside of mathematics?

Consider morality. According to Locke, moral notions, such as obligation or moral good, are modes or relations (*Essay* II.xxii,xxviii). The nominal and real essences of moral notions therefore coincide, and demonstrative knowledge of morality is possible. Thus Locke states: "I am bold to think, that *morality is capable of demonstration*, as well as mathematics: since the precise real essence of the things moral words stand for, may be perfectly known" (*Essay* III.xi.16; cf. I.iii.1, IV.iii.18,iv.7–8).

Consider natural philosophy or natural science. Its subject matter is substances, material substances, such as iron, gold, hemlock. In these cases, nominal and real essence need not coincide. Locke identifies the real essence of a substance with its internal constitution (*Essay* II.xxxi.6, III.iii.15,17,18,vi.2–3,9), presumed to be the determinate primary qualities (together with the "texture" in the sense of configuration) of its insensible solid parts (e.g., at *Essay* II.xxxi.6). He emphasizes time and again that we do not know the determinate real essences of bodies because our senses are not sufficiently acute and our microscopes not sufficiently powerful (*Essay* II.xxiii.11–13, IV.iii.11,14,25–26,vi.7,14). But suppose we had stronger microscopes (or "microscopical eyes"), and did know the determinate real essence of bodies. Locke suggests, in that event, the following:

> I doubt not but if we could discover the figure, size, texture, and motion of the minute constituent parts of any two bodies, we should know without trial several of their operations one upon another, as we do now the properties of a square, or a triangle. Did we know the mechanical affections of the particles of *rhubarb, hemlock, opium,* and a *man,* . . . we should be able to tell before hand, that *rhubarb* will purge, *hemlock* kill, and *opium* make a man sleep. [*Essay* IV.iii.25]

> Had we such *ideas* of substances, as to know what real constitutions produce those sensible qualities we find in them, and how these qualities flowed from thence, we could, by the specific *ideas* of their real essences in our own minds, more certainly find out their properties, and discover what qualities they had, or had not, than we can now by our senses; and to know the properties of *gold,* it would be no more necessary, that *gold* should exist, and that we should make experiments upon it, than it is necessary for the knowing the properties of a triangle, that a triangle should exist in any matter, the *idea* in our own minds would serve for the one, as well as the other. [*Essay* IV.vi.11]

These passages are reminiscent of one in Descartes' *Rules:*

> If the question is, 'what is the nature of the magnet?'. . . . He who reflects that there can be nothing to know in the magnet which does not consist of certain simple natures evident in themselves, will have no doubt how to proceed. He will first collect all the observations with which experience can supply him about this stone, and from these he will next try to deduce the character of that inter-mixture of simple natures which is necessary to produce all those effects which he has seen to take place in connection with the magnet. [*RDM* XII, HR I, 47]

Whereas Descartes suggests that we could deduce the simple natures which are the constitution of the magnet from its effects or operations, Locke suggests that we could deduce the *operations* or properties of a substance from its internal microscopic constitution. In these passages, Locke is claiming that if we knew the real essences of substances we could deduce without experimentation or trial various properties of those substances.

There are two sorts of cases. First, if we knew the real essence of gold, we could deduce that gold is malleable. In other words, we could have demonstrative knowledge of "laws of natural kinds," laws of the form: whatever has characteristics $c_1, \ldots, c_i$ at time t also has c_j at time t. Locke calls knowledge of such laws knowledge of "co-existence" (*Essay* IV.iii.12) and knowledge of "necessary co-existence" (*Essay* IV.iii.14). Second, if we knew the real essences of two material substances, such as hemlock and human beings, we could deduce that hemlock causes persons to die. In other words, we could have demonstrative knowledge of causal laws. The trick in both cases is to construct an abstract idea or nominal essence of a substance which has for its components the determinate primary qualities of its insensible corpuscles rather than its macroscopic determinate primary and secondary qualities. This amounts to the claim that in principle we can have a priori knowledge of some laws, as follows (for the case of causal laws). Let 'ψ' stand for the complex description of the determinate internal microstructure that hemlock in fact has; and let 'ϕ' stand for the complex description of the determinate internal microstructure that human beings in fact have. In these terms, Locke's claim is that we could know without observation or experimentation that if anything has microstructure ψ, it would cause anything which has microstructure ϕ to die.

I hasten to add that it is not Locke's position that any law can be known a priori. We cannot even in principle have a priori knowledge of laws which formulate regularities involving secondary qualities. This is because the secondary qualities are nothing but the powers of material substances, by virtue of the primary qualities of their insensible corpuscles, to produce ideas or sensations in persons (*Essay* II.viii.10,22–23), and it is inconceivable how corpuscles in motion can produce anything but motion, and how they could produce any idea or sensation in particular (*Essay* IV.iii.6,13,28). Laws involving secondary qualities are therefore not grounded in necessary connections, but rather depend upon "the arbitrary determination" of God, and are not susceptible to demonstration (*Essay* IV.iii.28).

There is one passage which raises a serious difficulty for the present interpretation, on which physical laws can in principle be known a priori: "But the coherence and continuity of the parts of matter; the production of sensation in us of colours and sounds, *etc.* by impulse and motion; nay, the original rules and communication of motion being such, wherein we can discover no natural connexion with any *ideas* we have, we cannot but ascribe them to the arbitrary will and good pleasure of the Wise Architect" (*Essay* IV.iii.29). According to this passage, it is not only laws involving secondary qualities which depend upon God's arbitrary will; "the coherence and continuity of the parts of matter," and "the original rules and communication of motion" are not grounded in necessary connections either—they also depend upon God's arbitrary will. This would seem to rule out the possibility of an a priori physics. The passage at IV.iii.29 seems to be in direct conflict with the passages at IV.iii.25 and IV.vi.11 invoked to support the present interpretation.[21]

Can this apparent conflict be resolved in favor of one of the competing interpretations? To begin with, the relevant passages must be read against the background of Locke's epistemological apparatus or theory. The whole point of his doctrine of real essence is to explain the possibility of a priori knowledge. All the properties of a kind are deducible from statements about its real essence. And the real essence of a substance is identified with its internal constitution. Locke's position at IV.iii.25 and IV.vi.11, that if only we knew the real essences of substances we could deduce their properties, is the position his theoretical posture dictates. From this perspective, I believe that there is a strong presumption in favor of the present interpretation. This presumption can be sustained if we can go some way toward neutralizing the passage at IV.iii.29.

One point is that the passage is not strictly inconsistent with the thesis that an a priori physics is possible in principle. This is clear if we read it with the following emphases: the physical laws being "such, wherein *we* can discover no natural connexion with any

---

[21]Buchdahl, 1969, pp. 190–191, appeals to IV.iii.29 to document that Locke is sometimes tempted to deny that there are necessary connections in nature. Curley, 1972, p. 450, cites the same passage in support of the claim that "Locke appears to think of causal laws in Cartesian fashion, as depending on the arbitrary will of God (IV, 3, 29) and so, presumably, changeable in principle." In a more extended discussion, Wilson, 1979, esp. pp. 148–149, treats the passage as in conflict with Locke's Boylean mechanism and his ideal of an a priori deductive science of nature.

ideas *we* have, *we* cannot but ascribe them to the arbitrary will and good pleasure of the Wise Architect." A priori physics is possible "in principle" in the sense that it requires more acute senses and/or more powerful microscopes than are available to us. Locke makes this point in a picturesque way by introducing the "extravagant conjecture.... that spirits... can so frame, and shape to themselves organs of sensation or perception, as to suit them to their present design, and the circumstances of the object they would consider" (*Essay* II.xxiii.13); hence, "had we such a knowledge of that constitution of *man*, from which his faculties... and other powers flow... as 'tis possible angels have, and 'tis certain his maker has, we should have a quite other *idea* of his *essence*" (*Essay* III.vi.3). There may be other spirits who need not ascribe physical laws to God's arbitrary will, precisely because they are able to discover real essences.[22]

There is a second point, which requires lengthier discussion. Locke's claim that laws involving secondary qualities depend upon the arbitrary determination of God occurs at least five times in the *Essay* (II.xxx.2,xxxi.2,xxxii.14, IV.iii.28,29).[23] The statement that the same is true of some purely physical laws occurs only once, at IV.iii.29. The two purely physical examples Locke cites involve "the coherence and continuity of the parts of matter" and "the original rules and communication of motion," in other words, laws of cohesion and the communication of motion. At IV.iii.29, he offers no justification for the claim that we must ascribe these laws to God's arbitrary will. If there is any justification within the *Essay* for this apparent suggestion about the metaphysical status of these laws, it is to be found at II.xxiii.23–28, where Locke argues that both cohesion and communication of motion by impulse are unintelligible or inconceivable. He there provides an extended argument for the inconceivability of cohesion in particular. He argues, for example, that to explain the cohesion of parts in one body by refer-

---

[22]Wilson, 1979, pp. 147–148 (and n. 15), has moderately criticized the view that Locke's position even with respect to *laws involving secondary qualities* is that such laws are grounded in necessary connections, albeit not ones accessible to us. For the sorts of reasons which emerge below, I think that the view Wilson questions is much less plausible than the one I defend.

[23]I am indebted to Edwin McCann for some of these references.

ence to the pressure of another leaves the cohesion of parts of that
latter body itself unexplained. Locke does seem to find cohesion
genuinely problematic. However, it is the claim at IV.iii.29 that we
must ascribe the laws of communication of motion to God's arbitrary will which poses the central threat to the possibility of an a
priori physics.

For a number of reasons, I doubt that Locke takes his justification
for this claim seriously. First, whereas he devotes five full sections to
the inconceivability of cohesion (II.xxiii.23–27), the subsequent
discussion of the inconceivability of communication of motion by
impulse occupies only a single section (28). Second, the argument
is virtually nonexistent: in the most common case, "wherein as
much motion is lost to one body, as is got to the other, . . . we can
have no other conception, but of the passing of motion out of one
body into another; which, I think, is as obscure and unconceivable,
as how our minds move or stop our bodies by thought." Locke adds
that "the increase of motion by impulse, . . . is yet harder to be
understood." Third, in the one chapter of the *Essay* that is devoted
to the qualities of bodies and to physical theory, communication of
motion by impulse is treated as unproblematic: "The next thing to
be consider'd, is how *bodies* produce *ideas* in us, and that is man-
ifestly *by impulse*" (II.viii.11; cf. II.viii.12). Even in II.xxiii, Locke
writes of communication of motion by impulse as if it were not only
transparent but inevitable: "body cannot but communicate its motion by impulse, to another body, which it meets with at rest"
(*Essay* II.xxiii.18). It is odd indeed to find Locke stressing the inconceivability of communication of motion by impulse at
II.xxiii.28.

Why would Locke offer such a brief, unconvincing argument for
a claim which is destructive of his own favorite physical hypotheses?
I believe there is an explanation, one that should lead us to dismiss
the material at II.xxiii.28. The context in which the discussion of
the inconceivability of cohesion and the communication of motion
by impulse arises provides the key. The relevant chapter is titled "*Of
our Complex* Ideas *of Substances.*" A persistent claim throughout
that chapter is that our idea of spiritual substance or spirit is *as clear
as* our idea of bodily substance or body (II.xxiii.5,15,31). Why was
Locke concerned to emphasize this point? As I will argue in detail

below (§ 7), at II.xxiii and elsewhere in the *Essay* he sets out to demolish the view that there exist substances *in the sense of* substrata which "support" accidents or modifications (or in which accidents or modifications "inhere"), whether these substrata be material or spiritual. This is not a position that most religiously or theologically inclined readers would welcome, for how could spirits exist in any sense if not in the sense of spiritual substrata which support such mental operations as thinking and willing?

Locke's own position, as I argue in section 7, is as follows: material substances or bodies exist, even though they do not consist of material substrata supporting physical modifications (this is a mistaken account of the constitution of bodies); similarly, a spiritual substance or spirit need not consist of a spiritual substratum supporting mental modifications (some other account of the nature of spirits must be correct). Thus, Locke argues that our idea of spirit is as clear as our idea of body, in order to suggest that, since bodies obviously do exist, nothing in his critique of substrata tells any more against the existence of spirits than against the existence of bodies. His motivation is to contain and mitigate the apparently adverse consequences of his rejection of substrata for religion and theology.

Within this context, the discussion of cohesion and motion arises as follows. In order to show that our idea of spirit is as clear as our idea of body, Locke contends that there are "two primary qualities, or properties" which are peculiar, respectively, to body and to spirit: in the case of body, cohesion, and the power of communication of motion by impulse; in the case of spirit, thinking, and the power of exciting (or stopping) motion by volition (II.xxiii.17–18,22,30). Locke proceeds to argue at length that our idea of spirit, insofar as it involves thinking, is as clear as our idea of body, insofar as it involves cohesion, on the ground that cohesion of solid parts in a body is no more conceivable than thinking in a spirit (*Essay* II.xxiii.23–28). It is worth noting that the selection of cohesion for comparison to thinking seems quite artificial; extension and solidity, in the sense of impenetrability, are more likely candidates for this role. In any case, in order to complete the argument for the general claim that our idea of spirit is as clear as our idea of body, he must argue as well that our idea of spirit, insofar as it involves the power of exciting motion by volition, is as clear as our idea of body, insofar as it involves the power of communication of motion by impulse. It is for this reason only that at II.xxiii.28 we encounter the astounding claim that communication of motion by impulse is "as obscure and unconceivable, as how our minds move or stop our bodies by thought."

This rather frivolous argument at II.xxiii.28 provides the sole justification Locke has to offer for his subsequent suggestion about the metaphysical status of the laws of motion. Since this suggestion is in conflict with the whole burden of his doctrine of real essence as applied to substances, it seems unreasonable to let this one passage defeat the presumption in favor of the interpretation on which his considered view is that a priori physics is possible in principle. It seems the more unreasonable since the passage at IV.iii.29 can be read as claiming only that we humans must ascribe the laws of communication of motion to God's arbitrary will. This reading is consonant with Locke's ground for the principal conclusion of the *Essay*: "since our faculties are not fitted to penetrate into the internal fabric and real essence of bodies. . . . I think I may conclude that *morality is the proper science, and business of mankind in general*" (*Essay* IV.xii.11).

Locke distinguishes knowledge which is "experimental" or "historical" from knowledge which is (*a*) instructive (not "trifling" or trivially analytic), (*b*) certain, that is, at least demonstrative, and (*c*) general or universal (cf. *Essay* IV.iii.26,29,xii.10). The latter is "philosophical" or "scientifical" knowledge. For Descartes, "philosophy" or "science" includes mathematics, metaphysics, natural philosophy, and morals. In his final *"Division of the Sciences,"* Locke includes natural philosophy (of which mathematics is a part), morals, and the theory of signs (*Essay* IV.xxi). I believe that on the best overall interpretation, Locke's project in the *Essay* is to show that Descartes' standards for demonstrative knowledge can in fact be met in morals, and can in principle be met in natural philosophy (if only our perceptual faculties were more acute, or our microscopes stronger).[24] At the very least, the *Essay* is much more sympathetic

---

[24]The following commentators take Locke's view to be that a considerable demonstrative natural philosophy is in principle possible for human beings, or alternatively that there are necessary connections in nature: Kneale, 1949, p. 71; Pap, 1958, pp. 4–5, 53–62; Yolton, 1969, esp. pp. 183–190; Woolhouse, 1971, pp. x, 16–24; Ayers, 1970, pp. 39, 45; Mackie, 1976, ch. 3, esp. pp. 100–101; and most recently Ayers (again), 1977, p. 77 (at pp. 82–83, Ayers attempts to take into account Locke's occasional misgivings about even mechanical explanations).

toward the possibility of an a priori physics than we should expect
from Locke the empiricist.

To summarize this section thus far, Locke shares with Descartes
the following claims with respect to the standards, sources, structure, and extent of human knowledge: (1) certainty is a condition for
knowledge; (2) truths known by intuition are perceived all at once,
are self-evident, and do not require argument; (3) truths known by
deduction or demonstration are perceived in a succession or progression, are certain but not self-evident, and are established by
arguments consisting of a series of intuitively grasped steps; (4) intuition and deduction or demonstration are the sole sources of knowledge, at least with regard to all general truths; (5) not only do
propositions known by intuition not require argument, they do not
admit of argument, and in that sense they function as the foundation of all our knowledge; (6) we have intuitive knowledge of propositions about the content of our present sensory states; and (7) demonstrative knowledge of general or universal truths in principle extends well beyond mathematics, to morality and natural science
(and the theory about essential definitions which supports this claim
is Spinozistic). The range and depth of the agreement between
Descartes and Locke is striking. We do not encounter the sort of
divergence in epistemological positions that the standard theory
would lead us to expect. If it is one or more of the positions I have
enumerated which qualifies Descartes as a Rationalist, there is a
strong case to be made that Locke is a Rationalist as well.

In generating these results, especially (1–5) above, I have relied
heavily upon Descartes' epistemological theory as extracted from
the *Rules*. It might be objected that it would be a mistake to take the
Rules, an early work which was never completed, as representative
of Descartes' theory of knowledge. This objection is not to the point.
The *Rules* sets forth as Rationalistic an epistemology—as embodied, for example, in claim (4)—as is to be found in Descartes.
Whatever the precise extent of Locke's agreement with the epistemology of the *Rules*, we should expect no less agreement with a
more moderate Cartesianism that perhaps emerges in Descartes'
later works. And as we have seen, Locke's agreement with the epistemology of the *Rules* is extensive and striking indeed.

This raises the question of influence. Locke's *Essay* appeared in
1690. As Leon Roth has pointed out, the characterization of dem-

onstration as consisting of a series of intuitions does not appear in Draft B of the *Essay*, written in 1671. Locke spent the years 1675–80 in France, 1683–89 in Holland. He might have seen a copy of the Latin manuscript of the *Rules* (not published until 1701) in either country. And in any case, a Dutch translation was published in 1684, and he read Dutch.[25]

I have of course been emphasizing the affinities between the positions of Descartes and Locke with respect to the standards, sources, structure, and extent of knowledge. Am I not, however, simply distorting Locke's position, and ignoring the core of his Empiricism, by omitting any discussion of the third degree of knowledge, sensitive knowledge? As I noted earlier, the passage that seems to restrict all knowledge to intuition and demonstration takes note of a possible exception: "These two, (*viz.*) intuition and demonstration, are the degrees of our knowledge; whatever comes short of one of these, with what assurance soever embraced, is but faith, or opinion, but not knowledge, at least in all general truths." It is via sensitive knowledge, sensation or sense perception, that we are informed about "the *particular existence of finite beings* without us," that is, about the existence of particular material objects (*Essay* IV.ii.14). By contrast, it is the burden of Descartes' *First Meditation* that sense perception alone cannot yield knowledge of the external world. So does not Locke, unlike Descartes, hold that sense perception alone does yield knowledge of the existence of particular material objects? If so, have we not located a good sense in which Locke is an Empiricist and Descartes a Rationalist?

These are fair questions, though ones surprisingly resistant to the intended answer. The paragraph in which sensitive knowledge is introduced requires careful reading. The statement that intuition and demonstration are the sole sources of knowledge "*at least* in all general truths" does not commit Locke to the view that some particular truths are known in some other way; rather, it simply suggests that this may be the case. The next sentence reads: "There is, indeed, another *perception* of the mind, employed about the *par-*

---

[25]For a variety of suggestions as to how Locke might have become acquainted with the *Rules*, see: Gibson, 1917, pp. 211–212; Aaron, 1937b, p. 10; Roth, 1937, p. 117; L. J. Beck, 1952, pp. 8–9; Smith, 1952, pp. 70–71, n. 4; and esp. Curley, 1977, pp. 188–189. For a dissenting view, that Locke's doctrine of intuition was not borrowed from Descartes, see O'Kelley, 1971.

ticular existence of finite beings without us; which going beyond
bare probability, and yet not reaching perfectly to either of the
foregoing degrees of certainty, passes under the name of knowledge"
(*Essay* IV.ii.14). After some discussion of the sense in which sense
perception yields certainty, Locke concludes: "So that, I think, we
may add to the two former sorts of *knowledge,* this also, of the
existence of particular external objects, by that perception and consciousness we have of the actual entrance of *ideas* from them, and
allow these *three degrees of knowledge,* viz. *intuitive, demonstrative, and sensitive"* (*Essay* IV.ii.14). The language of this section is
carefully guarded: intuition and demonstration are the sole sources
of knowledge "*at least* in all general truths"; belief based upon sense
perception "*passes* under the name of knowledge"; and we may
"*allow* . . . three degrees of knowledge," which include sensitive
knowledge.

How are we to read the less than enthusiastic admissions of this
section? Is Locke a Rationalist, who agrees with Descartes with
respect to the epistemological theses I have enumerated, but who
allows as a matter of courtesy to those who may disagree that perceptual beliefs about the external world constitute knowledge?[26] Or is
he a budding or emerging Empiricist, who of course wants to say
that it is unproblematic that we have perceptual knowledge of the
external world, but remains in the psychological grip of Cartesian
epistemology?

I believe considerations can be brought to bear which weigh
against the Empiricist interpretation of Locke. First, he is definitely
unwilling to let knowledge based upon sense perception extend very
far: "when our senses do actually convey into our understanding
any *idea,* we cannot but be satisfied, that there doth something *at
that time* really exist without us. . . . But *this knowledge extends as
far as the present testimony of our senses,* employed about particular
objects that do then affect them, *and no farther"* (*Essay* IV.xi.9;
emphases in original). Second, recall that Locke equates knowing
and being certain without restriction, and his account of certainty is
such that "we may be secure, that there be no latent proofs undis-

---

[26]Quinton, 1973, pp. 131–132, has previously suggested that it is as a matter of
courtesy that Locke allows sensitive as well as intuitive and demonstrative knowledge.

covered, which may overturn our knowledge, or bring it in doubt." Note that he requires not only that there be no undermining evidence, but that the knower be secure that there is no such evidence. It is difficult to see how Locke could have thought that beliefs based upon sense perception could meet this standard. How could we possibly be secure, in the case of a particular perceptual belief, that there is no undiscovered evidence which could bring the belief in doubt? Locke seems aware of this point. He consistently describes the "certainty" of sensitive knowledge as a sort of moral certainty, quite sufficient relative to human concern for pleasure and pain, but distinct from the sort of Cartesian certainty described above (cf. *Essay* IV.ii.14,xi.8). Thus, I believe it relatively easy to explain why he should "allow" that a restricted class of beliefs based upon sense perception, beliefs which do not meet his own standards of certainty, "passes under the name of knowledge."

I have argued that Locke's project in the *Essay* is to provide a theoretical foundation for the constructive thesis that Cartesian standards for knowledge can in principle be satisfied with respect to truths of morality and natural philosophy. Locke's principal interest was in "scientifical" knowledge—knowledge that is instructive, certain, and general. Thus, in the chapter *"Of the Extent of Human Knowledge,"* he devotes eight sections to knowledge of coexistence, three long sections to knowledge of relation, and one section consisting of a single sentence to knowledge of real existence (*Essay* IV.iii.9–17,18–20,21, respectively). It would simply have been an irritation likely to alienate and distract the reader from Locke's constructive purposes if Locke had refused to allow that perceptual beliefs about external objects constitute knowledge. Thus, I believe that the balance of the evidence is that he extends the label "knowledge" to such beliefs as a matter of courtesy.

Suppose I am mistaken. Suppose Locke's view, however poorly expressed, is that it is of course unproblematic that we can have knowledge of the external world through sense perception alone. Nevertheless, to label him an Empiricist, in contrast to Descartes, on that account simply obscures the unmistakably Cartesian theses of Locke's epistemology: the emphasis on certainty; the claim that intuition and demonstration are the sole sources of knowledge of all general truths; the acceptance of a foundational picture of knowledge; and the claim that demonstrative knowledge of both morality and natural science is in principle possible. My own view is that all things considered, Locke is best seen as a Rationalist. It is sufficient for my purposes, however, if I have sustained the claim that the Continental Rationalist/British Empiricist distinction is broken-backed in the sense that Locke can be classified as an Empiricist only at the cost of considerably obscuring and distorting the Cartesian epistemology that is prominent in the *Essay*.

Why has the common epistemological ground between Descartes and Locke been so neglected? One reason (I will discuss another in the next section) is that historians have insisted upon approaching Locke's epistemology from the perspective of his famous dictum that "knowledge consists in the perception of the agreement or disagreement of any two ideas" (cf. *Essay* IV.i.2,ii.15,iii.1), together with the associated four sorts of agreement or disagreement: with respect to identity or diversity, coexistence or necessary connection, relation, and real existence (*Essay* IV.i.3).[27] The affinities with Descartes which I have discussed emerge most clearly when we examine Locke's discussion of the three degrees of knowledge. Historians' preoccupation with the four sorts of agreement and disagreement may be due in part to the fact that here we have a body of epistemological theory distinctive to Locke, not to be found in Descartes—this part of Locke's theory was innovative. I suspect, however, that this tradition in interpretation is more deeply rooted in efforts to criticize Locke's "Empiricism": how could Locke consistently have construed knowledge of *real existence* as the perception of the agreement or disagreement of any two *ideas*, short of equivocating on 'idea' as any perception in the mind and as any modification of matter (cf. *Essay* II.viii.7)? In any case, the Cartesian epistemological themes are by no means divorced from the treatment of knowledge as the perception of the agreement or disagreement of any two ideas (cf. *Essay* IV.vi.3,xvii.17).

If one finds the thesis that Locke was a Cartesian Rationalist, or at least not the Empiricist he is supposed to be, too counterintuitive or paradoxical, lines of resistance are, of course, available. For example, one could concede the mass of affinities between the epistemological theories of Descartes and Locke, but argue that surely,

[27]For a notable exception, see Woolhouse, 1971, pp. 3, 183–185, where the discussion of this dictum is relegated to an appendix.

as the first major Empiricist after Descartes, Locke need not have been the complete Empiricst—it would be quite enough if he initiated a movement more fully developed in Berkeley and Hume. Thus, for example, the willingness to "allow" that belief based upon sense perception "passes under the name of knowledge" is just what we might expect from an incipient Empiricism. This argument deserves comment.

Let us suppose that it might help preserve the view that Locke was an Empiricst. From this perspective, the expectation is that a more full-bodied Empiricist epistemology would emerge in the writings of Berkeley. Is the expectation fulfilled? The standard theory's insistence that Berkeley is an Empiricist is remarkable in light of the fact that it is virtually impossible to locate any explicit theory of knowledge in Berkeley's published works. To feel the force of this point, consider Locke's *Essay.* There we are provided with the following: two definitions of knowledge (in terms both of certainty and of the perception of agreement or disagreement of any two ideas), together with an extended account of four types of knowledge; an extended account, embedded in the discussion of the three degrees of knowledge, of the standards and sources of knowledge; and a view about the structure of knowledge. The contrast with Berkeley's principal work, *The Principles of Human Knowledge,* is glaring. There we do not encounter any explicit definition of knowledge, nor any explicit discussion of the standards, sources, or structure of knowledge. This may seem surprising in light of the work's title. But *The Principles of Human Knowledge* is no more a treatise on the theory of knowledge than is Descartes' *Principles of Philosophy.* As we have seen, for Descartes philosophy is simply identical with human wisdom or knowledge. Descartes' *Principles of Philosophy* and Berkeley's *Principles of Human Knowledge* both attempt to set out what it is that we know. The principal aim is not to provide a metatheoretical account of knowledge. Of course, Descartes' *Principles* does include some explicit epistemology, but one would be hard pressed to find such in the *Principles* of Berkeley. I am not claiming that there are no doctrines in the latter which could count as "epistemological," broadly construed, nor that no epistemology could be extracted from its pages. My point is that one does not find in Berkeley's published works any systematic epistemological theory; epistemology as such simply does not seem to have been of significant philosophical interest to Berkeley. Even if he subscribed to an Empiricist epistemological theory, doing so was not central to his philosophical enterprise.

But did Berkeley subscribe to an Empiricst epistemology? His most explicit epistemological remarks are found in the *Philosophical Commentaries*. The following are especially revealing:

> 80 I am more certain of ye existence & reality of Bodies than Mr Locke since he pretends onely to w^t he calls sensitive knowledge, whereas I think I have demonstrative knowledge of their Existence.
>
> 239 Metaphysiques as capable of Certainty as Ethiques but not so capable to be demonstrated in a Geometrical way because men see clearer & have not so many prejudices in Ethiques.
>
> 517a N.B. I am more for reality than any other Philosophers, they make a thousand doubts & know not certainly but we may be deceiv'd. I assert the direct Contrary.
>
> 547 We have intuitive Knowledge of the Existence of other things besides our selves & even praecedaneous to the Knowledge of our own existence. in that we must have Ideas or else we cannot think.
>
> 563 I am the farthest from Skepticism of any man. I know with an intuitive knowledge the existence of other things as well as my own Soul. this is w^t Locke nor scarce any other Thinking Philosopher will pretend to.
>
> 686a On second thoughts I am, on t'other extream I am certain of that wch Malbranch seems to doubt of. viz the existence of Bodies.
>
> 690 To demonstrate Morality it seems one need only make a Dictionary of Words & see which included which. at least. This is the greatest part & bulk of the Work.
>
> 705 God ought to be worship'd. This Easily demonstrated whn once we ascertain the signification of the word God, worship, ought.
>
> 719 Since I say men cannot mistake in short reasoning about things demonstrable if they lay aside words. it will be expected This treatise will Contain nothing but w^t is certain & evident Demonstration.
>
> 730 We may have certainty & knowledge without Ideas. . . .
>
> 755 Morality may be Demonstrated as mixt Mathematics.
>
> 813 I am certain there is a God, tho I do not perceive him have no intuition of him. this not difficult if we rightly understand w^t is meant by certainty.

These notebook entries contain a number of Cartesian epistemological themes. To what extent do these themes appear in Berkeley's later writings?

Consider our knowledge of "bodies." What is striking in the *Philosophical Commentaries* is that Berkeley is dissatisfied with Locke because "he pretends onely to w^t he calls sensitive knowledge." In the *Principles*, Berkeley claims to attain "self-evident or demonstrative knowledge of the existence of sensible things" (*PHK* 88). He achieves this result by construing "bodies" or "sensible things" as collections of ideas (*PHK* 1). His motivation for adopting this position was precisely the desire to satisfy Descartes' standards for knowledge. Locke was at least prepared to "allow" that belief in the existence of material substances based upon sense perception "passes under the name of knowledge." We should expect of his successor in an Empiricst movement an unhesitating relaxation of Cartesian standards for knowledge. Berkeley was unwilling to play this role.

Consider metaphysics. Berkeley writes in the "Preface" to the *Principles*:

> What I here make public has, after a long and scrupulous inquiry, seem'd to me evidently true, and not unuseful to be known, particularly to those who are tainted with skepticism, or want a demonstration of the existence and immateriality of God, or the natural immortality of the soul. . . . He must surely be either very weak, or very little acquainted with the sciences, who shall reject a truth, that is capable of demonstration, for no other reason but because it's newly known and contrary to the prejudices of mankind.

Similarly, the "Preface" to the *Three Dialogues between Hylas and Philonous* speaks of "a plain demonstration of the immediate Providence of an all-seeing God, and the natural immortality of the soul." The tone is virtually indistinguishable from that of Descartes in the "Dedication" to the *Meditations*:

> I have always considered that the two questions respecting God and the Soul were the chief of those that ought to be demonstrated by philosophical rather than theological argument. . . . The greater part of the reasons which have been brought forward concerning these two questions by so many great men are, when they are rightly understood, equal to so many demonstrations . . . , it will henceforth be evident to everybody that they are veritable demonstrations. [HR I, 133–134]

It is Berkeley's view that in the *Principles* he is providing demonstrative knowledge of any number of metaphysical claims: not only that God exists and that the soul is naturally immortal, but also that material substances, construed as objects which can exist independently of being perceived, cannot exist ("I think an intuitive knowledge may be obtained of this"—*PHK* 3), together with various theses about time and space, etc. In his mature works, Berkeley purports to provide certain and demonstrative knowledge in metaphysics. Finally, as to morality, he claimed to have lost in Italy a second part of the *Principles* which was to deal with that subject. But there is no reason to believe that he abandoned the claim made in the *Philosophical Commentaries* that morality is capable of demonstration.

In sum, taking into account the epistemological remarks found in the *Philosophical Commentaries*, together with evidence provided by the *Principles* and *Three Dialogues*, we find that Berkeley stresses certainty, the connection between certainty and knowledge, the virtue of intuitive and demonstrative knowledge, and the inadequacy of sensitive knowledge. And mathematics aside, demonstrative knowledge is possible for Descartes in metaphysics, natural philosophy, and morals; for Locke in natural philosophy and morals; and for Berkeley in metaphysics and morals. Berkeley was not much interested in systematic epistemology, but his views about the standards, sources, and extent of knowledge seem much more akin to those of Descartes than we might expect from the second in line of Empiricists.

4. Innate Knowledge and Innate Ideas

In the preceding section, I suggested that one reason why so much of the common epistemological ground between Descartes and Locke has been neglected is that historians have been preoccupied with Locke's definition of knowledge as the perception of the agreement or disagreement of any two ideas. Another reason is that Locke chose to begin the *Essay* with an entire book which sets out to demolish the doctrine that persons have innate knowledge of any "speculative" or "practical" principles. In Draft A of the *Essay*, innateness is not discussed until the forty-third of forty-five sections.[28] It is a good question whether Locke would standardly be

---

[28]Aaron, 1937a, p. 23. Swabey, 1933, pp. 574–575, has noted that it has proved misleading for Locke to open the *Essay* with the attack on innate knowledge.

viewed as something of Descartes' epistemological antithesis had the attack on innate knowledge been introduced late in the *Essay*.[29]

It is not at all clear even that Locke had, or so much as thought he had, Descartes for a target. John Yolton has shown that doctrines of innate knowledge, in various degrees of sophistication, were pervasive throughout the seventeenth century and well into the eighteenth. Appeals to innate knowledge were to be found in virtually every pamphlet dealing with morality and the existence of God in the early seventeenth century. Innate knowledge was invoked to provide a foundation for morality and religion. The idea was that God implants various "practical" (that is, moral) principles in the human mind, and these innate principles, quite independent of custom and upbringing, serve as the basis for morality. For example, Yolton quotes Sir Matthew Hale, writing in 1677, thirteen years before the publication of the *Essay:*

> I come now to consider of those rational Instincts as I call them, the connate Principles engraven in the humane Soul; which though they are Truths acquirable and deducible by rational consequences and Argumentation, yet they seem to be inscribed in the very *crasis* and texture of the Soul antecedent to any acquisition by industry or the exercise of the discursive Faculty in Man, and therefore they may be well called anticipations, prenotions, or sentiments characterized and engraven in the Soul, born with it.

Hale's examples of such truths include: "There is a God," "God is all powerful," "Promises are to be kept," "the obscene parts and actions are not to be exposed to publick view." As late as 1701, John Edwards wrote: "yet He hath Copied it [the truth] out into the Mind of Man, and hath imprinted the Figure of it on his Rational Nature. Humane Souls created after God's Image do in some manner contain in them This Transcript and Resemblance. There are in our Minds Natural Impressions & Inbred Notices of True and False, which are as it were Streams issuing forth from the Uncreated Everlasting Spring of Truth." Edwards' examples include: "We ought to venerate, love, serve, and worship the Supreme Being," "we must honour and obey our Parents," "we must not injure and harm any Person, but render to every Man his due." According to Edwards, these are principles "which every Rational Person agrees

---

[29]Cf. Swabey, 1933, pp. 574–575.

to without any help of arguing." Locke obviously had to attack this sort of doctrine at length in order to sustain the principle conclusion of the *Essay*, that the *demonstration* of morality is the proper science and business of mankind. His target was the widespread doctrine of the religious and moral pamphleteers.[30]

Why, then, would anyone think that Locke's attack on innate knowledge was directed at Descartes? Descartes certainly never suggests that we have innate knowledge of moral truths. He is at one with Locke in holding that morality is a science (HR I, 211). The possibility remains that Descartes held views relating to innateness which could be marshaled to support the widespread doctrine that Locke was attacking, and hence that Locke had his sights on Descartes as well. This suggestion requires evaluation.

In the section of the *Essay* which introduces the discussion of innateness, Locke writes: "I imagine any one will easily grant, that it would be impertinent to suppose, the *ideas* of colours innate in a creature, to whom God hath given sight, and a power to receive them by the eyes from external objects" (*Essay* I.ii.1). Descartes was involved in just this impertinence: "The ideas of the movements and figures are themselves innate in us. So much the more must the ideas of pain, colour, sound and the like be innate, that our mind may, on occasion of certain corporeal movements, envisage these ideas, for they have no likeness to the corporeal movements" (HR I, 443). Either Locke was unaware of this aspect of Descartes' position, or he was not concerned to attack it.[31]

Descartes does not always take the position that ideas of color, for example, are innate. In other writings, he distinguishes between innate, adventitious, and invented or fictitious ideas; ideas of color would fall in the adventitious category (cf. *Med. III*, and K 104). In such passages, Descartes casts the innateness net less widely. Those who held that there exists innate knowledge were committed to the existence of innate ideas. But one could believe in the existence of innate ideas without believing in the existence of innate knowledge of principles formulated in terms of those ideas. What was Descartes' posture?

[30]Yolton's discussion is much more extensive than my summary indicates. See Yolton, 1956, ch. II. The quotations are from pp. 34, 62–63.

[31]The point was made by J. O. Urmson, in a graduate seminar he conducted on Locke at Oxford in 1969.

One idea which Descartes considers innate is that of God: "It is innate in me. . . . God, in creating me, placed this idea within me to be like the mark of the workman imprinted on his work" (*Med. III*, HR I, 170). But it is not Descartes' position that we have innate knowledge of the proposition that God exists. His arguments in the *Third Meditation* purport to provide demonstrative knowledge of the existence of God: I have an idea of an all-perfect being, God; there must be at least as much formal reality in the cause of an idea as objective reality in the idea itself; therefore, there exists an all-perfect being which is the cause of my idea of God. It is a subsidiary conclusion of the argument that the idea of God is innate, because neither adventitious nor fictitious: "It only remains to me to examine into the manner in which I have acquired this idea from God; for I have not received it through the senses . . . nor is it likewise a fiction of my mind . . . and consequently the only alternative is that it is innate in me" (*Med. III*, HR I, 170). Descartes does not claim that the proposition that God exists is somehow placed within us, imprinted on us, and innately known. For Descartes, the idea of God is innate; knowledge of God's existence is not.

Does Descartes hold that there exists any innate knowledge? As we have seen, the sources of knowledge for Descartes are intuition and deduction, and deduction itself consists of a series of intuitively grasped steps. There may seem to be a third source of knowledge, in that Descartes often writes of truths which are known by "the light of nature," "the natural light," "the light of reason," or indeed an "innate light." He is not, however, contemplating some source of knowledge over and above intuition. In the *Rules* he states that "intuition . . . springs from the light of reason alone" (*RDM* III); and in the *Principles* he writes of "the light of nature, or the faculty of knowledge which God has given us" (*PP* I, 30). Particular intuitions are acts or operations of the God-given (and innate) faculty of the light of nature.

It might be argued that Descartes' reliance upon a God-given faculty of intuition is ultimately indistinguishable from some versions of dispositional accounts of innate knowledge, and hence that Locke's attack on innate knowledge does apply, and may well have been intended to apply, to Descartes.[32] Locke does attack disposi-

---

[32] I owe this suggestion to Ray Paul.

tional theories of innate knowledge (cf. *Essay* i.ii.5–23). He could not, however, have intended that this portion of his attack apply to Descartes. On Locke's own account, intuition is an act or operation in which "the mind perceives the agreement or disagreement of two *ideas* immediately by themselves" (*Essay* iv.ii.1); "The perception of the . . . agreement or disagreement, that there is between any of our *ideas*" is one instance of perception, an "act of the understanding" (*Essay* ii.xxi.5); the understanding is the "power" or "faculty" of perceiving or thinking (*Essay* ii.vi,xxi.6); and "the goodness of God hath not been wanting to men . . . since he hath furnished man with those faculties, which will serve for the sufficient discovery of all things requisite to the end of such a being" (*Essay* i.iv.12). Particular intuitions in Locke and Descartes are equally operations of God-given cognitive faculties. Nowhere does Locke even undertake to make out a case that Descartes' appeal to intuition collapses into a version of a doctrine of innate knowledge in a way that Locke's does not. It seems most unlikely that he saw Descartes as a target for his attack on innate knowledge.

The fact remains, of course, that insofar as Locke attacks the view that there exist any innate ideas (*Essay* i.iv), his arguments are applicable to Descartes. The standard view that Locke's principal target in Book i was Descartes probably results in part from A. C. Fraser's influential 1894 edition of the *Essay*. Fraser writes in his notes: "Locke does not name the 'men' of 'innate principles' whose 'opinion' he proceeds to criticise; nor does he quote their words. . . . From the first, Descartes, with whose writings he was early familiar, was probably in his view."[33]

I have argued that the Continental Rationalism/British Empiricism distinction is broken-backed. Locke, however, is an Empiricist in the sense that he denies the existence of innate knowledge and innate ideas. It might be suggested that a Continental Rationalism/British Empiricism distinction can be sustained if the schools are distinguished with respect to their members' positions relating to innate knowledge. Even if this suggestion is correct, however, it still seems to me that all things considered, Locke is best seen as a Rationalist. The fact that he adopts the Empiricist position on in-

[33]Fraser, 1894, n. 1 to Locke's chapter *"No innate speculative Principles."*

nate knowledge in no way gainsays the fact that he subscribed to the Cartesian epistemological claims I catalogued in the preceding section. But is it true that the Continental Rationalists and British Empiricists divide on the question of the existence of innate knowledge?

While Descartes writes of innate ideas and innate faculties, he does not write explicitly of innate knowledge. Why does he hold, apart from the special case of the idea of God, that there exist any ideas that are innate rather than adventitious or fictitious? This question has an answer which is intriguing historically but disappointing philosophically. The answer, I believe, relates to Descartes' curious doctrine that the "eternal truths," which include at least some truths of arithmetic and geometry, are dependent upon the will of God—were they not, there would exist a restriction on God's omnipotence. The following passages illustrate the doctrine:

> I do not think that the essence of things, and those mathematical truths which may be known about them, are independent of God; yet I think that because God so wished it and brought it to pass, they *are* immutable and eternal. [HR II, 226]

> God did not will to create the world in time because he saw that it would be better thus than if he created it from all eternity; nor did he will the three angles of a triangle to be equal to two right angles because he knew that they could not be otherwise. On the contrary, because he worked to create the world in time it is for that reason better than if he had created it from all eternity; and it is because he willed the three angles of a triangle to be necessarily equal to two right angles that this is true and cannot be otherwise; and so in other cases. [HR II, 248]

Descartes' view seems to be that, for example, the concept or definition of a triangle as three lines enclosing a space is insufficient to determine the essence of a triangle; the essence of triangles is dependent upon God, who might have willed that triangles have an essence such that their three interior angles do not equal two right angles. This is a hard saying.

But suppose we take it seriously. How could we possibly know, given only the concept or definition of a triangle, that its interior angles do equal two right angles? We would have to know the essence God has willed for triangles as well. Such knowledge would seem to be possible if we possess an innate idea of a triangle which is sufficiently rich to somehow convey or contain the essence God has willed to be associated with it. If this is correct, we should expect both that the ideas which Descartes considers innate are precisely those in terms of which eternal truths, dependent upon God's will, are formulated, and that these innate ideas do somehow convey or contain the associated essence. This is precisely Descartes' position. He writes to Marin Mersenne in 1641:

> I use the word 'idea' to mean everything which can be in our thought, and I distinguish three kinds. Some are adventitious, such as the idea we commonly have of the sun; others are constructed or factitious, in which class we can put the idea which the astronomers construct of the sun by their reasoning; and others are innate, such as the idea of God, mind, body, triangle, *and in general all those which represent true immutable and eternal essences.* Now if from a constructed idea I were to conclude to what I explicitly put into it when I was constructing it, I would obviously be begging the question; but it is not the same *if I draw out from an innate idea something which was implicitly contained in it but which I did not at first notice in it. Thus I can draw out from the idea of a triangle that its three angles equal two right angles,* and from the idea of God that He exists. [K 104; my emphases]

Note that the innate ideas are just those associated with the essences which underpin the eternal truths, and that these ideas implicitly contain the relevant eternal truths, which can therefore be drawn out from them.[34]

My suggestion is that, apart from the special case of the idea of God, Descartes would have had no use for innate ideas were it not for his peculiar doctrine that the eternal truths are dependent upon God-willed essences. Innateness is standardly thought of as a device to explain the possibility of a priori knowledge, but a priori knowledge has not seemed problematic for the quixotic reason that exercised Descartes. His appeal to innateness is therefore only superficially similar in function and motivation to, for example, that of Leibniz, who rejected Descartes' claim about the status of the eternal truths (*LA* 54–55; *M* 46; *T* 181, 185).

The case of Descartes aside, there are further difficulties for attempts to distinguish Continental Rationalists from British Empiri-

---

[34]The connection between Descartes' theories of innate ideas and eternal truths has also been noted by Rée, 1975, p. 144. The evidence Rée cites (HR I, 106 and K 11) all predates the *Meditations.*

cists with reference to innate knowledge. Spinoza is completely silent on the subject of innateness. Granted, he does not explicitly deny that there exists innate knowledge, but he does not affirm it either. While Hume, waiving the case of the missing shade of blue, denies innate ideas (*Trea.* 4–7, *Enq.* 13–17), at the same time he seems largely uninterested in the matter, and is prepared to label crucial aspects of the controversy "frivolous" (*Enq.* 17, note 1). Matters are worse in the case of Berkeley. In the *Philosophical Commentaries*, he writes: "There are innate Ideas, i.e. ideas created with us" (*PC* 649), and innate ideas are arguably treated with some sympathy in *Alciphron* and *Siris* (*Alc.* I.14; *Sir.* 308–310). Berkeley's Sermon x, "On the Will of God," written in 1751, establishes continuity with his earlier views, and leaves the matter beyond doubt.[35]

> But neither is the use of our reason, the only natural means, for discovering the will of God, the same being also suggested by a natural conscience, and inward feeling implanted in the soul of every man, previous to all deductions of reason. . . .
>
> That there are appetites and aversions, satisfactions and uneasiness, inclinations and instincts, originally interwoven in our nature, must be allowed by all impartial and considerate men. It is, I say, evident that the Soul is so constituted, in her original state, that certain dispositions and tendencies will not fail to shew themselves, at proper periods, and in certain circumstances; which affections, because they are universal not confined to any age or country, and not to be accounted for by custom or education, but alike in all nations and all times, are properly said to be natural or innate.
>
> Thus, for example, the fear of death and the love of one's children are accounted natural, and the same may be said of divers other instincts and notions, such as the apprehension of a superior being. . . . resulting from the natural make of our minds, inasmuch as, though they do not appear in our earliest infancy, yet in the growth and progress of the soul, they are sure to shoot forth to open and display themselves. . . . And all these natural tendencies and impressions on the conscience, are so many marks to direct and inform the mind, of the will of the author of nature. [Berk. vii, 130–131]

Berkeley writes mostly of certain feelings, but he extends the argument to various "notions, such as the apprehension of a superior

---

[35]The references to passages in Berkeley dealing with innate ideas are due to Bracken, 1974, p. 115.

being." This is an explicit statement of just the sort of position, as embodied in the quotations from Hale and Edwards, which Locke was concerned to attack in Book I of the *Essay*. What is more, Berkeley appeals to universality as proof of innateness, even though Locke had extensively attacked such moves in Chapter ii of Book I.

Perhaps the most important point, however, is that Berkeley's major philosophical works, the *Principles* and *Three Dialogues*, have nothing at all to say about innateness. If a controversy concerning innateness is taken to be central to the Continental Rationalism/British Empiricism distinction, Spinoza and Berkeley are simply not serious parties to the dispute. To the extent that they have positions (as Berkeley does) relating to innateness, the positions play no significant roles in their philosophical systems. It may seem incredible that this important aspect of the Continental Rationalism/British Empiricism distinction should prove so weak. My own suggestion is that this is but one symptom of the fact that the distinction is not a valid one.

5. Conclusion and Prospectus

In maintaining that the Continental Rationalism/British Empiricism distinction is fatally flawed, my point is not that it is impossible to locate a criterion such that Descartes, Spinoza, and Leibniz come out Continental Rationalists, and Locke, Berkeley, and Hume come out British Empiricists. I believe, however, that it is much more difficult to locate such a criterion than the sharp antithesis enshrined in the second component of the standard theory would suggest.

For example, there are difficulties in the cases of both Locke and Berkeley if we say that a figure is a British Empiricist just in case he holds that sensation or sense perception alone can yield knowledge of the existence of the external world. I have argued that Locke decides to "allow" that belief in the existence of particular material objects "passes under the name of knowledge" as a matter of courtesy and tactics, and not because he holds that such beliefs meet his standards for knowledge, strictly speaking. This is admittedly controversial. Matters are different with Berkeley. Is he an Empiricist, relative to the present criterion, because he holds that sensation alone yields knowledge, indeed certain knowledge, of the existence of bodies or sensible things? Surely not. The material objects of Descartes and Locke exist independently of being perceived; they are external objects, which cause ideas or sensory experiences. Berkeley holds that the existence of material objects in this sense involves "a manifest contradiction" (*PHK* 4). He claims to have knowledge of the existence of "bodies" or "sensible things" construed as collections of ideas or sensory experiences. As we have seen, Descartes agrees that we can have certain knowledge of the content of our sensory experiences. Descartes would agree that sensation alone yields knowledge of the existence of "bodies" in Berkeley's sense. The present criterion can enforce the result that Berkeley is an Empiricist, and Descartes a Rationalist, only by equivocating on the sense of 'external world'.

There is, however, room to gerrymander. Suppose a figure qualifies as a British Empiricist not by virtue of holding the constructive thesis that sensation or sense perception alone can yield knowledge of the existence of the external world, but rather by virtue of holding the negative thesis that reason alone (including intuition and demonstration) *cannot* yield knowledge of the external world. Relative to this criterion, Locke and Berkeley fall into place. Neither would be willing, for example, to follow Descartes through demonstrations of the existence of a nondeceiving God (*Med. III*) to the conclusion that there do exist corporeal objects on the ground that God has given us "a very great inclination to believe" that this is so, and hence would be a deceiver if corporeal objects did not exist (*Med. VI*, HR I, 191). Even this criterion faces a difficulty: Malebranche held that knowledge of the existence of the external world ultimately rests on revelation rather than reason (*Eluc.* VI, *DMR* VI.3), and would qualify as an Empiricist.

Another possible criterion distinguishes Continental Rationalists from British Empiricists with reference to figures' attitudes toward a priori arguments for the existence of God. Descartes, Spinoza, and Leibniz all argue that the existence of God can be established merely from consideration of God's essence. Even here, some careful tinkering may be required. Are we to say that Continental Rationalists accept some a priori argument for the existence of God, and that the British Empiricists reject all such arguments? It is far from clear that Berkeley holds that the ontological argument is fallacious. There is the following passage in *Alciphron:* "I am not to be persuaded by metaphysical arguments; such, for instance, as are drawn from the idea of an all-perfect being, or the absurdity of an infinite progression of causes. This sort of arguments I have always found dry and jejune; and, as they are not suited to my way of thinking, they may perhaps puzzle, but will never convince me" (*Alc.* IV.2). These words are put in the mouth of Alciphron rather than Euphranor, who speaks for Berkeley, but it is plausible to suppose that Alciphron is articulating the constraints Berkeley wants to set on himself in his argumentation for the existence of God. The passage seems to fall well short of rejecting the ontological argument on the ground that it is fallacious; the claim is that it fails to produce conviction. Further, in the discussion of absolute space in *De Motu,* there is the following comment: "By this argument the human mind is easily freed from great difficulties, and at the same time from the absurdity of attributing necessary existence to any being except the good and great God alone" (*Motu* 56). This is a surprising comment from someone who rejects as fallacious all "metaphysical arguments" for the existence of God; it is only via a cosmological or ontological argument that the conclusion that God is a necessary being could be established. It is possible that Berkeley thought the ontological argument cogent, but did not himself employ it. In section 28 below, I will offer an explanation of how this might have been the case. In any event, a little tinkering suggests that Continental Rationalists *employ* a priori arguments for the existence of God, whereas British Empiricists do not. Even here, I have two sorts of reservations.

The first is that while this may seem to be an important distinction to us, it would have been much less important to many of the figures in question. It is true that Berkeley does not employ the ontological argument, but he does employ what he considers to be demonstrative arguments for the existence of God. I have suggested (§ 3) that the epistemological distinction which matters to Descartes, Locke, and Berkeley is that between arguments (and hence knowledge) which are at least demonstrative, and arguments which are not. This does not coincide with the distinction between a priori and a posteriori arguments; some intuitive knowledge, and hence some demonstrative knowledge, is a posteriori. Further, I have pointed out that even Descartes places no premium upon, assigns no pride of place to, intuitive knowledge which is a priori. This point extends to demonstrative knowledge as well, and indeed to demonstrative knowledge of the existence of God. Descartes produces the a posteriori causal arguments for the existence of God in *Meditation III*, before providing the a priori ontological argument in *Meditation V*, and he describes the former as "the principal argument of which I will use in order to prove the existence of God" (*Med.*, "Synopsis"). Both arguments are demonstrative in Descartes' sense; the a posteriori premises for the causal arguments are about the content of a first-person mental state (I have an idea of an all-perfect being), and hence intuitively certain.

What is more, if one considers Descartes' epistemological purposes, it is easy to see why it was completely appropriate for him to prize a posteriori demonstrative arguments no less than a priori demonstrative arguments. One of his central concerns is to defeat the skepticism introduced in *Meditation I* on its own terms. The skeptical hypotheses of *Meditation I* have no tendency to impugn first-person beliefs about present mental states. I take it that the point of these hypotheses is to undermine any evidential link between justified beliefs about one's own sensory experiences and beliefs about the physical world.[36] Descartes' strategy is to defeat this skepticism by establishing the existence of a nondeceiving God, and arguing that God would be a deceiver, given our "very great inclination" to believe that material objects cause our sensory experiences (HR I, 191), if there were no material objects. Descartes need not beg the question against the form of skepticism introduced in *Meditation I* provided that his argument for the existence of a nondeceiving God does not proceed from any premise about the material world which is itself justified by appeal to sensory experiences. Neither the causal nor the ontological argument contains any such premise, and hence both are equally suited to Descartes' epistemological task.

---

[36]I follow Frankfurt, 1970, Part One, in holding that the skepticism of *Meditation I* extends only to perceptual knowledge of the material world, and not to a priori knowledge of mathematics and logic as well. But even if the early skepticism does extend to such knowledge, it would remain to show that it extended even to first-person knowledge of present mental states.

The causal argument does have an a posteriori premise (I have an idea of God), but such first-person beliefs about present mental states have not been called into question in *Meditation I*.[37]

Berkeley's arguments for the existence of God are also demonstrative (they are discussed in section 28 below) and thus fully meet the epistemological standards that mattered to Descartes, Locke, and Berkeley. Just as it was of no concern to Descartes that his "principal argument" for the existence of God is not a priori, Berkeley would not have thought it important that his arguments for the existence of God are not a priori. From this perspective, Berkeley's omitting to employ the ontological argument is of no special significance. So my first reservation is that a criterion which appeals to employment of a priori arguments for the existence of God is sustainable only at the cost of losing sight of the epistemological constraints that Descartes, Locke, and Berkeley considered to be at the heart of their enterprise. I suspect that the contemporary insistence upon viewing the whole of seventeenth- and eighteenth-century philosophy from the perspective of an a priori–a posteriori distinction is a post-Kantian imposition.

My second reservation applies to both the present criterion and that discussed earlier in this section. Can reason alone yield knowledge of the existence of the external world? Are a priori arguments employed to prove the existence of God? These criteria rest the Continental Rationalism/British Empiricism distinction upon a philosopher's epistemological posture toward a single proposition, rather than toward a range of subject matter, such as metaphysics, natural philosophy, and morality. Such narrowly focused criteria result from a retreat from others which are more sweeping (is all our knowledge, or all our knowledge outside of logic and mathematics, derived from reason alone?), but which fail to generate the intended results. Inevitably, therefore, such narrowly focused criteria do not cut very deep. To see the sense in which this is true, consider the

---

[37]Of course, if we take seriously the skepticism which seems to be introduced at *Meditation III* with Descartes' claim that until he has established the existence of a nondeceiving God "I do not see that I can ever be certain of anything" (HR I, 159), invoking first-person beliefs about present mental states would beg the question. But any argument whatsoever would beg the question against that form of skepticism.

fact that if one relies upon the second criterion, Kant comes out an Empiricist because he rejects the ontological argument. Labeling him on that basis does not begin to do justice to the complexities involved in any attempt to classify Kant one way or the other.

With sufficient ingenuity, one can doubtless specify criteria which will not have the untoward result that Malebranche is an Empiricist, or that Kant is an Empiricist, and so on. My point is that such an intellectual enterprise is wrongheaded; it cannot possibly do justice to the complex of epistemological similarities and differences which obtain among the various epistemological theories of the period. I have tried to bring considerable pressure to bear upon the second component of the standard theory.[38] To the extent that I have been successful, the appropriate response is not to look for some way to generate the standard distinction, but rather to recognize that the second component, in insisting upon a sharp distinction between two epistemological schools, is more obfuscating than illuminating.

The standard theory is not exhausted by its second component. Chapters II–VII will be devoted to developing the materials needed for evaluating the third component. Is it true, supposing that the Continental Rationalism/British Empiricism distinction can somehow be sustained, that within each school there is a dialectical development in which the school's principles are applied with increasing rigor to a common body of problems? Most, but by no means all, of my attention will be devoted to this component of the standard theory in its application to Continental Rationalism. In the process of developing my negative evaluation, a new theory of the historical and philosophical relationships between the philosophical systems of the time will emerge. This alternative theory will be discussed in Chapter VIII.

---

[38]It would be possible to pile on the difficulties: the Continental Rationalists are much more Empiricist than the standard theory allows. For example, Curley, 1973, p. 26, maintains that "the view that Spinoza was a rationalist . . . is not just mildly inaccurate, it is wildly inaccurate." For important recent discussions of Descartes' view of the role of experimentation in science see Garber, 1978, and Williams, 1978, ch. 9. For extensive references to literature which identifies Empiricist themes in the Continental Rationalists, see Curley, 1973, n. 3, and Garber, 1978, n. 1.

II

SUBSTANCE

6. Introduction

According to the standard theory, Descartes' admission of causal interaction between mind and body, between two kinds of *substances*, was inconsistent with Rationalist principles; Malebranche's occasionalism, Spinoza's double-aspect theory, and Leibniz's preestablished harmony were successive attempts to solve this mind-body problem within a Rationalist framework. In the case of British Empiricism, Locke's admission of *material substance* was inconsistent with Empiricist principles, and was rejected as such by Berkeley; Berkeley's admission of *spiritual substance* was likewise inconsistent with Empiricist principles, and was rejected as such by Hume. It is obviously impossible to undertake a serious evaluation of the third component of the standard theory without being attentive to conceptions of substance during the seventeenth and eighteenth centuries.

There are various ways to fail to give attention where it is due. One is to suppose that the conceptions of substance are so obscure, or so confused, or so medieval (in a pejorative sense) as to be useless for the purposes of significant philosophical discussion. Such a supposition may be correct. If so, most of the metaphysics of the period is infected by these difficulties. Substance plays a leading role in possibly the most distinctive metaphysical doctrines of various figures: for Descartes, I am a substance whose whole essence is to think; for Spinoza, there exists only one substance; for Berkeley, material substance does not exist; and for Leibniz, no two substances causally interact. If one is seriously going to explore the metaphysics of the period, one had better take substance seriously.

It is tempting to suppose, on the other hand, that taking substance seriously is not a difficult project, at least if one's attention is confined to the notion of substance as it appears in the metaphysics of the Continental Rationalists. For surely, one thinks, those philosophers shared some doctrine about substance, and at the very least some definition of substance, as common property—though the implications of the shared views may be drawn out with increasing rigor by successive figures. Such a perspective leads to a sort of grudging acquiescence to the importance of substance which instills patience and equanimity just sufficient for exposure to *the* Rationalist conception of it. Such an attitude does not take substance seriously enough.

Consider the supposition that the Continental Rationalists share some common body of doctrine about substance. As I have suggested, leading metaphysical doctrines of individual Rationalists (as well as Berkeley, whom we bracket for the moment) are formulated in terms of substance. The Continental Rationalists have this much in common: some doctrine about substance is central to the metaphysics of each of them. God exists and is a substance; each Continental Rationalist agreed to that. But this claim virtually exhausts their nominal agreement about substance. The range of nominal disagreement is much greater. It has two principal areas. The first is doctrines about the numbers and kinds of substances: for Descartes, there exists a plurality of thinking substances, and a different kind of substance, material substance, as well; for Spinoza, God is the only substance; for Leibniz, there exists an infinity of substances, and they are all of the same kind—they are all thinking or perceiving substances.[1] The second is doctrines about the interrelationships of substances. For Descartes, thinking substance and material substance, though they differ in kind, causally interact. The relevant views of Spinoza and Leibniz diverge in ways which

[1]According to the standard theory, Descartes was a dualist, holding that there exist two kinds of substances; Spinoza was a monist, holding that there exists a single substance; and Leibniz a pluralist, holding that there exists an infinity of substances. For difficulties in locating a question which Descartes answered "two" and Spinoza "one," see Bennett, 1965, pp. 379–380.

immediately raise prima facie puzzles for the standard theory. Descartes' position is supposed to be objectionable because he admits causal interaction between two different kinds of substances. For Spinoza, thought and extension are two attributes or aspects of a single substance, but he denies causal interaction between thought and extension nevertheless. For Leibniz, all substances are of the same kind, and yet he denies causal interaction between substances. In any case, the disagreements here appear to be serious. As we shall see, the Rationalists do not even define 'substance' in the same way. There is no single Rationalist conception of substance. The terrain is complicated, and one must be willing to investigate it.[2]

7. Descartes' Substance$_\text{S}$

Both Spinoza (in Pt. i of the *Ethics* through Prop. xv) and Leibniz (in sections viii–xv of the *Discourse on Metaphysics*, the correspondence with Arnauld, and sections 1–25 of the *Monadology*) have left us with extended, systematic treatments of their conceptions of substance. Despite the fact that there are systematic presentations of Descartes' philosophy in both the *Meditations* and the *Principles*, his remarks concerning substance are much more diffuse. It therefore may not be surprising that there seem to be (at least) two distinguishable (though not unrelated) strands in his conception of it.[3] I will label these 'substance$_\text{S}$' and 'substance$_\text{I}$' (the point of the subscripts will become clear).

A substance$_\text{S}$ is a subject or substratum in which qualities inhere. Descartes has two important general theses about the relationship between "qualities" and the "subject" in which they "inhere." These theses are asserted without argument, and appear axiomatic.

The first thesis emerges in the following passages:

> It is certain that no thought can exist apart from a thing that thinks; no activity, no accident can be without a substance in which to exist. [HR ii, 64]

---

[2]For a variety of theoretical functions for substance terminology, with special application to Leibniz, see Hacking, 1972. For an interesting discussion of views about substance during the seventeenth century, see Windelband, 1901, §31.

[3]The point that Descartes provides two different definitions of substance has been stressed by Curley, 1969, pp. 6–11.

From the mere fact that we perceive certain forms or attributes which must inhere in something in order to have existence, we name the thing in which they exist a *substance*. [HR II, 98]

It is very manifest by the natural light... that no qualities or properties pertain to nothing; and that where some are perceived there must necessarily be some thing or substance on which they depend. [*PP* I, 11]

It is clear from the first and especially the third of these passages that for Descartes it is necessarily true that any quality inheres in some substance$_S$. This thesis is in no way incorporated into the definition of "substance$_S$": "Everything in which there resides immediately, as in a subject... any property, quality, or attribute... is called a *Substance*" (HR II, 53). It is consistent with this definition that there are substances$_S$, subjects in which qualities in fact inhere, even though those qualities could exist without inhering in a subject. In that case, Descartes' first thesis would be false. It also seems clear from the language of the passages that his first thesis should be stated more precisely as follows: necessarily, any quality which exists at time t inheres in some substance at time t. Inherence would appear to be a noncausal relation that obtains between a particular quality and substance at a time. Most (familiar) causal relations obtain between objects, events, or states which are not simultaneous. I know of no evidence that Descartes thinks of inherence as a causal relation.[4] When he writes in the third passage that qualities "depend" upon a substance, the dependence in question is not causal.

[4]Bracken, 1964, pp. 129–136, has argued that for Descartes modes "inhere" in a substance in the sense that they are necessarily connected with it (pp. 132, 136). I am unsure whether Bracken would include any causal relations among these necessary connections, but in any case his interpretation is different from mine, and, if correct, he would have sustained his claim that Locke misunderstood Descartes' doctrine (pp. 129, 136). Bracken's case rests upon his reading of Descartes' discussion of the wax in *Meditation II* (p. 132). Bracken's reading, however, goes well beyond anything in the cited text, and at best supports a conclusion about material substance in particular. Bracken has done nothing to show that Descartes did not hold the view of thinking substance which Locke attacks. I believe that Bracken himself has some reservations about attributing the general "deductive" model of inherence to Descartes, since he states that Locke misunderstood "the Cartesians," and Malebranche "especially" (pp. 129, 137). I agree with Bracken, though not on the same grounds, that Descartes had at least moved away from the account of material substance which Locke attacks (see the close of this section).

If we know that some quality exists, then given the first thesis that necessarily any quality inheres in some substance$_S$, we can also know that some substance$_S$ exists. Is knowing that some quality exists the only way of knowing that some substance$_S$ exists? Descartes answers affirmatively:

> We do not apprehend the substance itself immediately through itself, but by means only of the fact that it is the subject of certain activities. [HR II, 64]

> We do not have immediate cognition of substances, as has elsewhere been noted. [HR II, 98]

> Substance cannot be first discovered merely from the fact that it is a thing that exists, for that fact alone is not observed by us. [*PP* I, 52]

Descartes' second thesis about substance$_S$ is epistemological: we cannot immediately apprehend, cognize, or observe substances$_S$ themselves; rather, we immediately observe only the qualities which inhere in a substance$_S$, and then infer (via the first thesis) that a substance$_S$ exists.[5] Descartes has more to say about particular kinds of substance$_S$, but his general theory about substance$_S$ is before us. A substance$_S$ is a subject in which qualities inhere. Necessarily, any quality inheres in some subject. We cannot observe substance$_S$ immediately.

No one has ever criticized the sort of doctrine which Descartes held about subjects, qualities, and inhesion more vehemently than Locke. It has been held that in his philosophy Locke retains a belief in substance$_S$ as a sort of scholastic hangover which he was unable to shake off.[6] The fact is that Locke persistently deprecates such a doctrine (*Essay* I.iv.18, II.xii.6,xiii.17–20,xxiii.1–2). The principal evidence to the contrary derives from the correspondence with Stillingfleet, where Locke does offer an account of the origin of the idea of substance$_S$ (Locke IV, 19–21). Just how much is he granting the bishop? Consider this passage in the *Essay*, bearing in mind Locke's double use of 'idea' as either a sensation or perception in the mind, or a quality of an object (*Essay* II.viii.8):

[5]Wilson, 1978, pp. 66–67, 198–200, suggests (without endorsing) the possibility of an alternative interpretation, on which Descartes' concern is to claim that we cannot observe substances "naked of attributes."

[6]For the view that Locke retains a doctrine of substance, see: Gibson, 1917, pp. 28, 96; O'Connor, 1967, pp. 73–84; Woolhouse, 1971, pp. 66–68, 127–135; and Mabbot, 1973, ch. 3. Also cf. Buchdahl, 1969, pp. 215–223.

I confess, there is another *idea*, which would be of general use for mankind to have, as it is of general talk as if they had it; and that is the *idea of substance*, which we neither have, nor can have, by *sensation* or *reflection*. . . . We have no such *clear idea* at all, and therefore signify nothing by the word *substance*, but only an uncertain supposition of we know not what; *i.e.*, of something whereof we have no [particular distinct positive] *idea*, which we take to be the *substratum*, or support, of those *ideas* we do know. [*Essay* i.iv.18]

The bracketed material was added in the fourth edition, after Stillingfleet raised his objections. In all editions, Locke states that we cannot have the idea of substance$_S$ either by sensation or reflection. Since sensation and reflection are our only sources of ideas (*Essay* ii.i.2–5), we cannot have an idea of substance$_S$ at all. Since Locke holds that a word or phrase (barring particles) is meaningful only if it signifies an idea (*Essay* iii.ii,iv.6), his official position is that the word 'substance'—in the intended sense, as in "substance$_S$," a subject in which qualities inhere, or a substratum which supports ideas—is meaningless.

In response to Stillingfleet, Locke allows that we have some confused (though no particular, distinct, positive) idea of substance$_S$. He also writes to Stillingfleet: "it is a complex idea, made up of the general idea of something, or being, with the relation of a support to accidents. For general ideas . . . are the creatures or inventions of the understanding" (Locke iv, 19). Of our complex ideas, some are "fantastical," and "have no foundation in nature, nor have any conformity with that reality of being, to which they are tacitly referred" (*Essay* ii.xxx.1). One example is our centaur-idea. In response to Stillingfleet, Locke allows that another example is our substance$_S$-idea. As of the *Essay*'s first edition, we have no idea of substance$_S$; 'substance' is meaningless and unintelligible. In deference to Stillingfleet, we have some idea of substance$_S$, but there are no substances$_S$ (just as there are no centaurs). Either way, Locke thought he demolished the sort of doctrine embodied in Descartes' conception of substance$_S$.[7]

I hasten to add that Locke of course had some use for the term 'substance'. We have seen that his distinction between ideas of substances, modes, and relations is central to his epistemological

---

[7]For discussions of Locke's posture toward substance, which advance a similar view, see: Mandelbaum, 1964, pp. 15–16, 31–34; and Bennett, 1971, pp. 59–63.

theory (§ 3). The term 'substance' is meaningful and has a good use when employed modestly to refer to "distinct particular things subsisting by themselves" (*Essay* II.xii.6), in contrast to modes which are "dependences on, or affections of substances" (*Essay* II.xii.4).

Locke focused on two difficulties for doctrines of substance$_S$, difficulties which might be viewed as grounds for his claim that we have no idea of substance$_S$. Here is a statement of the first:

> If any one will examine himself concerning his *notion of pure substance in general,* he will find he has no other *idea* of it at all, but only a supposition of he knows not what support of such qualities, which are capable of producing simple *ideas* in us; which qualities are commonly called accidents. If any one should be asked, what is the subject wherein colour or weight inheres, he would have nothing to say, but the solid extended parts: and if he were demanded, what is it, that solidity and extension inhere in, he would not be in a much better case, than the *Indian* . . . who, saying that the world was supported by a great elephant, was asked, what the elephant rested on; to which his answer was, a great tortoise: But being again pressed to know what gave support to the broad-backed tortoise, replied, something, he knew not what. [*Essay* II.xxiii.2]

Locke is exhibiting the difficulty of grasping what sort of entity a substance$_S$, in itself, is. Can we characterize such a subject without reference to its relations to qualities inhering in it? It may appear that this question is especially difficult for Descartes to answer in light of his first thesis, that *all* qualities inhere in some subject$_S$. Then does a substance$_S$ have *any* qualities other than the relational ones of having qualities which inhere in it? If it does not, what sort of entity is this subject—as with the Indian philosopher, something, Descartes knows not what? If it does, then for any given quality Descartes is committed (by the first thesis) to a subject in which it inheres, and a further subject in which the qualities of the first subject inhere . . . , and so on ad infinitum.

A good deal depends upon precisely what is to count as a "quality" for the purposes of Descartes' theory. Culling the quoted passages, one finds that where I formulate Descartes' theses about substance$_S$ in terms of "qualities," he writes more or less indifferently of "thoughts," "accidents," "activities," "attributes," "forms," "properties," and "qualities." Wherever Descartes uses any one or more of these, I have formulated his claim using 'qualities' as an umbrella term. Precisely what sorts of entities are these? We are not going to find in Descartes explicit definitions of each of the seven terms whose extensions I lump together as "qualities." I suggest we treat these passages (emphases mine) as clues:

> *Where some [qualities or properties] are perceived* there must necessarily be some thing or substance on which they depend. [*PP* I, 11]

> *We perceive certain forms of attributes* which must inhere in something in order to have existence. [HR II, 98]

> Everything . . . by means of which there exists *anything that we perceive*, i.e. any property, quality, or attribute, of which we have a real idea, is called a Substance; neither do we have any other idea of substance itself, precisely taken, than that it is a thing in which this *something that we perceive* or which is present objectively in some of our ideas, exists formally or eminently. [HR II, 53]

These passages are not decisive, but they suggest that Descartes' "qualities" are just those features of the universe which persons are constituted to perceive (either through sense perception or introspection). This yields a simple explanation of Descartes' second thesis, that substances$_S$ are not directly observable. Whatever features are observable or perceptible—that is, qualities—inhere in a subject or substance$_S$. If this is correct, Descartes' first thesis could be reformulated: all perceptible features inhere in some subject. It is then open to Descartes, provided he can motivate this thesis, to respond to Locke as follows: we can characterize a substance$_S$, without reference to the qualities which inhere in it, in terms of its own nonrelational and imperceptible features. Of course, it remains to specify what these imperceptible features are. Here Descartes would have to exercise more imagination than the Indian philosopher.

The second difficulty raised by Locke focuses not on the substance$_S$ or subject itself, but on its relation to qualities:

> They who first ran into the notion of *accidents*, as a sort of real beings, that needed something to inhere in, were forced to find out the word *substance*, to support them. . . . Whatever a learned man may do here, an intelligent *American*, who enquired into the nature of things, would scarce take it for a satisfactory account, if desiring to learn our architecture, he should be told, that a pillar was a thing supported by a *basis*, and a *basis* something that supported a pillar. . . . And a stranger to them would be very liberally instructed in the nature of books, and the things they contained, if he should be

> told, that all learned books consisted of paper and letters, and that
> letters were things inhering in paper, and paper a thing that held
> forth letters. . . . But were the Latin words *inhaerentia* and *substan-*
> *tia*, put into the plain English ones that answer them, and were
> called *sticking on*, and *under-propping*, they would better discover to
> us the very great clearness there is in the doctrine of substance and
> accidents, and show of what use they are in deciding of questions in
> philosophy. [*Essay* II.xiii.19–20]

Locke is objecting to the purely metaphorical characterization of the
relationship between a substance$_S$ and its accidents. Descartes variously claims that qualities "inhere in," "reside in," and "depend
upon" a substance$_S$. These are just metaphors which need to be
cashed if we are to understand the relation between qualities and
subjects.

It is important to note that Locke's attack on the doctrine of
substance$_S$ is completely general; he intends that his conclusions
should apply equally to the cases of material substance$_S$ and spiritual
substance$_S$. He nowhere restricts either his attack or his conclusions
to the special case of material substance$_S$. And there is substantial
direct evidence in *Essay* II.xxiii that Locke's position is that we have
no (particular, distinct, positive) idea of either material substance$_S$
or spiritual substance$_S$; in other words, the two ideas are equally
obscure. The point is explicit:

> For putting together the *ideas* of thinking and willing, or the power
> of moving or quieting corporeal motion, joined to substance, of
> which we have no distinct *idea*, we have the *idea* of an immaterial
> spirit; and by putting together the *ideas* of coherent solid parts, and a
> power of being moved, joined with substance, of which likewise we
> have no positive *idea*, we have the *idea* of matter. The one is as clear
> and distinct an *idea*, as the other: the *idea* of thinking, and moving a
> body, being as clear and distinct *ideas*, as the *ideas* of extension,
> solidity, and being moved. For our *idea* of substance, is equally
> obscure, or none at all, in both; it is but a supposed, I know not
> what, to support those *ideas*, we call accidents. [*Essay* II.xxiii.15]

Locke's claim in the final sentence is that either our ideas of material substance$_S$ and spiritual substance$_S$ are equally obscure, or we
have no idea of either. Then how are we to read the heading for this
chapter, "Idea *of spiritual substances, as clear as of bodily sub-*
stances"? This means that our ideas of material and spiritual sub-

stances, where 'substances' is taken in the modest, meaningful sense of "distinct particular things subsisting by themselves" (in contrast to modes), are equally clear. Locke maintains this, in part on the ground that insofar as these ideas include a substratum, that is, a substance$_S$, as a component, they are equally obscure.

Locke makes the point that there is complete parity between material and spiritual substances$_S$, and that we have no (clear and distinct) idea of either, in the following passage earlier in the chapter:

> Hence when we talk or think of any particular sort of corporeal substances, as *horse, stone, etc.* though the *idea*, we have of either of them, be but the complication, or collection of those several simple *ideas* of sensible qualities, which we use to find united in the thing called *horse* or *stone*, yet because we cannot conceive, how they should subsist alone, nor one in another, we suppose them existing in, and supported by some common subject; *which support we denote by the name substance*, though it be certain, that we have no clear, or distinct *idea* of that *thing* we suppose a support.
>
> The same thing happens concerning the operations of the mind, *viz.* thinking, reasoning, fearing, *etc.* which we concluding not to subsist of themselves, nor apprehending how they can belong to body, or be produced by it, we are apt to think these the actions of some other *substance*, which we call *spirit*; whereby yet it is evident, that having no other *idea* or notion, of matter, but *something* wherein those many sensible qualities, which affect our senses, do subsist; by supposing a substance, wherein *thinking, knowing, doubting*, and a power of moving, *etc.* do subsist, *we have as clear a notion of the substance of spirit, as we have of body*; the one being supposed to be (without knowing what it is) the *substratum* to those simple *ideas* we have from without; and the other supposed (with a like ignorance of what it is) to be the *substratum* to those operations, which we experiment in our sevles within. 'Tis plain then, that the *idea* of corporeal *substance* in matter is as remote from our conceptions, and apprehensions, as that of spiritual *substance*, or *spirit*; and therefore from our not having any notion of the *substance* of spirit, we can no more conclude its non-existence, than we can, for the same reason, deny the existence of body: It being as rational to affirm, there is no body, because we have no clear and distinct *idea* of the *substance* of matter; as to say, there is no spirit, because we have no clear and distinct *idea* of the *substance* of a spirit. [*Essay* II.xxiii.4–5]

When Locke writes here of "the substance of matter" and "the substance of a spirit" he is writing of substrata, or substances$_S$—we have no idea of either. He concludes that, even so, we have no right to conclude either that there is no matter or that there is no spirit.[8] Some distinctions will help to clarify Locke's point.

It is possible to believe in the existence of material substances=material objects without believing in the existence of material substances$_S$=substrata in which physical qualities inhere. The view that there exist material or corporeal substrata is a view about the nature or constitution of material objects. Similarly, it is possible to believe in the existence of spiritual substances=spiritual objects (rather than 'spirits' in order to maintain terminological parity) without believing in the existence of spiritual or thinking substances$_S$=substrata in which thoughts or mental operations inhere. The view that there exist thinking substrata is a view about the nature or constitution of spiritual objects. There are alternatives. For example, Hume rejected substance$_S$, whether material or thinking, but he provided a constructive account of the constitution of spiritual objects: a spirit or mind "is nothing but a heap or collection of different perceptions, united together by certain realtions" (*Trea.* 207; cf. I.IV.VI).

Locke rejected material substances$_S$=substrata supporting physical qualities as an account of the nature of material substances=material objects. In its stead, he appealed to real essences—the determinate primary qualities of microscopic corpuscles—as accounting for the constitution of material objects. Indeed, Locke had some inclination to suggest that his notion of real essence ought to supplant or replace the notion of substance$_S$ he attacks.[9] For while the Cartesian doctrine that qualities "depend" upon a substance in the sense that they stand in a noncausal relation of inherence to a substance is but a metaphor, Locke's doctrine that qualities "de-

[8] If one reads in isolation that "from our not having any notion of the *substance* of spirit, we can no more conclude its non-existence, than . . . ," it would at least be permissible to take the second possessive pronoun as referring to the substance of spirit, that is, to a substratum. It is clear, however, from the complete thought which follows, that Locke's point is that we have no right to conclude the nonexistence of spirit, as distinct from "the substance of spirit."

[9] For statements and developments of this perspective see: Mandelbaum, 1964, pp. 37–46; Yolton, 1969, p. 187, n. 1; Mackie, 1976, pp. 72–83; and Ayers, 1977, esp. pp. 80–96. For criticism, including an assessment of the views of Mandelbaum and Yolton, see Woolhouse, 1971, pp. 127–135.

pend" upon a substance causally is intelligible. At one point, Locke offers a dual characterization of "substratum": "we accustom our selves, to suppose, some substratum, wherein [ideas] do subsist, and from which they do result" (*Essay* II.xxiii.1). Qualities depend upon such a substratum both in that they subsist or inhere in it, and in that they result from or are caused by it. And Locke often writes that qualities of material objects "flow from," "depend upon," and indeed "result from" their internal constitutions or real essences— e.g., *Essay* II.xxiii.3, IV.iii.11.[10] So Locke's real essences assume one of the functions of substrata as characterized at II.xxiii.1. This dual characterization of a substratum nominally allows for the Cartesian conception, which Locke rejects, of an entity "wherein [ideas] do subsist," while Locke's own surrogate conception of an entity—an internal constitution—"from which [ideas] do result" provides his constructive alternative.

Locke also rejected thinking substances$_S$=substrata supporting ideas as an account of the nature of spiritual substance=spiritual objects. He was well aware of this sort of distinction, and when he wrote of "spirits" at *Essay* II.xxiii and elsewhere, he did not intend to commit himself to the existence of thinking substances$_S$. Thus he wrote to Stillingfleet: "Perhaps my using the word spirit for a thinking substance, without excluding materiality out of it, will be thought too great a liberty . . . because I leave immateriality out of the idea I make it a sign of. . . . But in the present case, I think, I have great authorities to justify me" (Locke IV, 34). While Locke gave no firm account of the nature of spiritual objects, he was

[10]Mandelbaum, 1964, p. 35, n. 68, writes of this same section: "It is . . . a confusion to speak as if the relation of 'inhering in' were equivalent to the relation of 'resulting from', as Locke does." Locke does not state that these notions are equivalent; he incorporates them both, conjunctively, into an account of substance. Of course, there is the potential for confusion insofar as the claim that qualities "depend" upon substance can be interpreted either causally or in terms of inherence. Thus Bennett, 1971, pp. 165–169, has argued that Berkeley was unaware of this ambiguity in his use of 'depend', an ambiguity which vitiates his passivity argument for the existence of God. Since there is ample evidence that the philosophers in question were more than aware of the difference between inhering in and being caused by, I am reluctant to suppose that these figures came to confuse these relations on account of their terminology (cf. my discussion of dependence in Descartes at section 8). I do believe, however, that they might have been prepared to exploit the ambiguity for expository and argumentative purposes.

prepared to write that it is "not much more remote from our com-
prehension to conceive, that GOD can, if he pleases, superadd to
matter a faculty of thinking, than that he should superadd to it
another substance, with a faculty of thinking" (*Essay* iv.iii.6). He
even wrote to Stillingfleet that "if God . . . should please to give a
system of very subtle matter sense and motion, it might, with
propriety of speech, be called spirit" (Locke iv, 36). Locke's point in
the quoted passage from ii.xxiii.4–5 is that just as his rejection of
material substances$_S$ in no way impugns the existence of material
objects, his rejection of thinking substances$_S$ on the same grounds in
no way impugns the existence of spiritual objects. He was concerned to press this point for the reason stated in section 3, in order
to mollify religious readers who would see (rightly) his general attack
on substance$_S$ as undermining doctrines of the soul.

Berkeley's response to the two difficulties raised by Locke for
doctrines of substance$_S$ was a bald denial of Locke's claim of parity
in the cases of material and spiritual substance$_S$. If there exists a
material substance$_S$, it is a subject that supports physical
modifications of bodies. For this, Berkeley has nothing but Lockean
ridicule: "It is said extension is a mode or accident of matter, and
that matter is the *substratum* that supports it. Now I desire you
would explain what is meant by matter's *supporting* extension. . . . It is evident *support* cannot here be taken in its usual or
literal sense, as when we say that pillars support a building: in what
sense therefore must it be taken?" (*PHK* 16). If there exists a
spiritual substance$_S$, and Berkeley believes there does, it is a subject
that supports ideas, that is, objects of introspective awareness (qualifications about "notions" are not necessary here). In the *Dialogues*,
Hylas objects, in good Lockean fashion, that Berkeley's position is
inconsistent, and that parity of reasoning demands that he reject
spiritual substance$_S$: "in consequence of your own principles, it
should follow that you are only a system of floating ideas, without
any substance to support them. . . . As there is no more meaning in
spiritual substance than in material substance, the one is to be
exploded as well as the other."

Philonous replies for Berkeley: "I know what I mean, when I
affirm that there is a spiritual substance or support of ideas, that is,
that a spirit knows and perceives ideas. But I do not know what is

meant, when it is said, that an unperceiving substance hath inherent in it and supports either ideas or the archetypes of ideas. There is therefore upon the whole no parity of case between spirit and matter" (*Dia. III*, Berk. II, 234). Berkeley's position is that whereas we cannot cash the metaphor of a material substance$_S$ "supporting" physical modifications of bodies, we can cash the metaphor of a spiritual substance$_S$ "supporting" ideas. A spiritual substance$_S$, Berkeley holds, "supports" ideas in the sense that it *perceives* ideas. This is his response to Locke's second objection, that the appeal to "inherence" is wholly metaphorical. In response to Locke's first objection, the challenge for some characterization of a substance$_S$ without reference to its relations to the qualities inhering in it, Berkeley states that *spiritual* substances$_S$ are perceiving, active, and simple, or indivisible (*PHK* 2, 27, 89).

When Berkeley attacks (*PHK* 16–17) the "received opinion" that there exist material substances$_S$=substrata ("It is said extension is a mode or accident of matter, and that matter is the *substratum* that supports it"), his target is a view which Locke had already demolished. And when Berkeley argues that there is "no parity" with the case of thinking substances$_S$=substrata, and that such entities do indeed exist, he is parting company with Locke. In so doing, Berkeley attempted to reinstate the Cartesian notion of a thinking substance$_S$ which Locke had already rejected. Berkeley even accepts Descartes' first thesis about substances$_S$ as applied to the special case of those substances$_S$ which exist and their qualities, that is, to spirits and ideas: necessarily, any idea inheres in (is perceived by) some spiritual substance (*PHK* 2, 4).

There is a further curiosity worth mentioning with respect to the vicissitudes of substance$_S$ among Locke, Berkeley, and Hume. Hume attacked substance$_S$, material and thinking, with complete generality, as follows: "Certain philosophers. . . . are the curious reasoners concerning the material or immaterial substances, in which they suppose our perceptions to inhere. In order to put a stop to these endless cavils on both sides, I know no better method, than to ask these philosophers in a few words, *What they mean by substance and inhesion?* And after they have answer'd this question, 'twill then be reasonable, and not till then, to enter seriously into the dispute" (*Trea.* 232). Berkeley thought he had answered this question. In the passage quoted from the *First Dialogue*, he insists: "I know what I mean, when I affirm that there is a spiritual substance or support of ideas, that is, that a spirit knows and perceives ideas." Hume does not proceed even to mention, much less consider, Berkeley's response that the "inhesion" of perceptions in thinking substance$_S$ consists in their being perceived. This is one way of raising Popkin's question (§2): did Hume even read Berkeley, and if so, did he take Berkeley seriously?

I have considered Locke's attack on substance$_S$, and Berkeley's claim that there is no parity between the cases of material substance$_S$ and thinking substance$_S$. Descartes anticipates the developments through Berkeley to the following extent: he is clearly committed to the existence of thinking substance$_S$; and while there is a nominal commitment to the existence of material substance$_S$, he resists treating it as quite analogous to thinking substance$_S$. Further, the claim that thinking substance$_S$, as distinct from thoughts, exists, is important to Descartes' metaphysics. It is less clear that the claim that material substance$_S$, as distinct from extended bodies, exists, is of any systematic importance in his work. (I will provide some evidence for this in section 13.) I therefore discuss Descartes' views about thinking substance$_S$ first.

A substance$_S$ is a subject in which qualities inhere. A thinking substance$_S$ is a subject in which a special class of qualities, thoughts, inhere. For us, 'thought' and 'thinking' have intellectual connotations. Descartes' use of such terms is much broader (see *Med. II, III; PP* I, 9, 32; and HR II, 52). A thought is any object of introspective awareness, or what Descartes calls "internal cognition" (HR II, 241). Thoughts are divided into two broad categories. First, there are volitions or operations of the will, including willing itself, feelings, emotions and passions such as desiring and aversion, and intellectual attitudes, such as affirming and doubting. Second, there are perceptions or operations of the understanding, including sensory experiences we have when we are dreaming or hallucinating, as well as those we have in the course of everyday, veridical sense experience. Because all thoughts are "perceptible" by introspective awareness, they are "qualities" in Descartes' sense. There is a simple Cartesian argument for the existence of thinking substance$_S$, as follows. We have intuitive knowledge that some thought exists. By

Descartes' first general thesis about substance$_S$, necessarily any quality inheres in some substance$_S$. By stipulation, a thought inheres in a thinking substance$_S$. It follows that some thinking substance$_S$ exists.[11]

I now turn to material substance$_S$. There are in Descartes passages which are strongly suggestive of the view that material substances$_S$ exist, and that they are subjects or entities, themselves unobservable, in which physical qualities inhere. Perhaps the clearest example is found in the discussion of the wax in *Meditation II*:

> Notice that while I speak and approach the fire what remained of the taste is exhaled, the smell evaporates, the colour alters, the figure is destroyed, the size increases, it becomes liquid, it heats, scarcely one can handle it, and when one strikes it, no sound is emitted. Does the same wax remain after this change? . . . All these things which fall under taste, smell, sight, touch, and hearing, are found to be changed, and yet the same wax remains. . . .
>
> When looking from a window and saying I see men who pass in the street, I really do not see them, but infer that what I see is men, just as I say that I see wax. And yet what do I see from the window but hats and coats which may cover automatic machines? Yet I judge these to be men. [HR I, 154, 155]

And in *Meditation III*, Descartes writes that "extension, figure, situation and motion . . . are merely certain modes of substance and so to speak the vestments under which corporeal substance appears to us" (HR I, 165). It is important to consider the contexts in which these passages appear. In *Meditation II*, Descartes is emphasizing the difficulty in knowing the wax in order to support his view of the priority of our knowledge of ourselves: "It may be that what I see is not really wax, it may also be that I do not possess eyes with which to see anything; but it cannot be that when I see, or . . . when I think I see, that I myself who think am nought" (HR I, 156). In *Meditation*

[11]The "simple Cartesian argument" for the existence of some thinking substance is not identical to the argument of *Meditation II* encapsulated in the literature as *"cogito, ergo sum."* However, the latter argument does need to be interpreted in light of Descartes' claim that any quality inheres in some subject and that we cannot observe substance$_S$ immediately. For a nice discussion of *Meditation II* in light of both Descartes' considered views about substance$_S$, and the relevant epistemological context, see Sievert, 1975.

III, he is explaining how we could have ideas of bodies without divine assistance in order to support his view that we could have the idea of God only with divine assistance. In neither case is the nature of material objects the principal topic of discussion. The existence of material objects is not even established until *Meditation VI*. Prior discussion of the nature of such objects should be viewed circumspectly.[12]

The analogies to persons in their clothes or vestments suggest, but I think only suggest, that material substance$_S$ stands to physical qualities as thinking substance$_S$ stands to thoughts—as an unobservable-substratum-in-which-qualities-inhere. It is relevant that in the conversation with Frans Burman, Descartes makes a related general point about the nature of substance$_S$, but chooses thinking substance$_S$ as his sole illustration: "Besides the attribute which specifies a species, there must in addition be conceived substance itself which lies under that attribute, as, since mind is a thinking thing, there is besides thought the substance which thinks, etc." (*CB* 25). He holds back from asserting that material substance$_S$ "lies under" physical qualities.

Descartes is concerned to make room for material substance$_S$ in a way which at least preserves some superficial parity to thinking substance$_S$. For example, he follows a definition of thinking substance$_S$ (which he calls "mind") with a definition of material substance$_S$ (which he calls "body"): "That substance in which thought immediately resides, I call *Mind*. . . . That substance, which is the immediate subject of extension in space and of the accidents that presuppose extension, e.g. figure, situation, movement in space etc., is called *Body*" (HR II, 53). The translation faithfully reflects differences in the Latin. Descartes' sensitivity to the fact that thinking substance$_S$ and material substance$_S$ are not on all fours is reflected in his unwillingness to write, "that substance in which extension immediately resides, I call *Body*." If he used that formulation, Locke's point—if one were "demanded, what is it, that solidity and extension inhere in, he would not be in a much better case, than the *Indian*"—would loom too close to the surface. The sorts of

---

[12]However, for sustained attempts to extract important theses about body from the discussion of the wax, see Curley, 1978, pp. 212–216; Williams, 1978, pp. 213–227; and Wilson, 1978, pp. 76–92.

difficulties which led Locke and Berkeley to reject material sub-stance$_S$ evidently caused Descartes at least some discomfort, evi-denced in his awkward definition of it.

There is a similar episode in the reply to *Objections III* to the *Meditations:* "it is certain that no thought can exist apart from a thing that thinks; no activity, no accident can be without a sub-stance in which to exist. . . . But there are *certain* activities, which we call *corporeal*, e.g. magnitude, figure, motion, and all those that cannot be thought of apart from extension in space; and the sub-stance in which they inhere is called *body*" (HR II, 64). Thoughts cannot exist "apart from" a thing that thinks; magnitude, figure, and motion cannot exist "apart from" extension in space. Here material substance$_S$ seems to be identified with "extension in space."[13] Mate-rial substance$_S$ is not identified with a subject in which extension itself somehow inheres. It was just such a position that Locke and Berkeley attack. Descartes himself was sensitive to the difficulties in it. Thoughts cannot exist "apart from" a thing that thinks because they require a perceiver. Magnitude and figure cannot exist "apart from" extension in space because nothing has a magnitude and figure unless it is extended. But it is not as if extension itself some-how inheres in a distinct entity which is not extended. Descartes does believe in the existence of thinking substance$_S$ which is unob-servable, which "lies under" thoughts in something like the way persons lie under their clothes. While he makes room for material substance$_S$ in some sense, it is not conceived on this sort of model. Insofar as he resists anything more than a nominal commitment to material substance$_S$, and suggests as an alternative that material substance be identified with extension in space, Descartes could agree with Berkeley that there is no parity in the cases of spiritual substance$_S$ and material substance$_S$.

8. Descartes' Substance$_I$

We now turn to the other strand in Descartes' conception of substance. I regard the following passage as formulating the core of

---

[13]For discussions of disanalogies in Descartes' treatments of thinking substance and material substance, see Keeling, 1968, pp. 129–130, including n. 1; and Williams, 1978, pp. 126–129.

his conception of substance$_I$: "Really the notion of *substance* is just this—that which can exist by itself, without the aid of any other substance" (HR II, 101). Substance$_I$ relates to the capacity for independent existence; an entity is a substance$_I$ provided that it is possible for that entity to exist by itself.[14]

One obvious difficulty is that Descartes' account of substance appears circular: a substance is that which can exist "without the aid of any other *substance*." One way to remove the circularity is to suppose that Descartes is defining 'substance$_I$' in terms of his conception of substance$_S$: an entity is a substance$_I$ provided that it is possible for it to exist independently of any other substance$_S$.

What sort of "independence" is in question? One way in which the existence of one entity can depend upon the existence of another is causally. For example, the existence of a valley depends causally upon a chain of previous geological events. The existence of one entity can also depend upon the existence of another entity non-causally. For example, the existence of a valley depends upon the existence of hills or mountains—"I cannot conceive . . . a mountain without a valley" (HR I, 181)—, but this dependence is not causal. We encountered a distinct variety of noncausal dependence in section 7: the dependence of qualities upon the substance$_S$ in which they inhere is not causal. We want to know whether Descartes is interested in causal or noncausal dependencies for the purpose of his conception of substance$_I$.

Here we must take a cue from the nature of the grounds he adduces for his claim that strictly speaking God is the only substance$_I$:

> By substance, we can understand nothing else than a thing which so exists that it needs no other thing in order to exist. And in fact only one single substance can be understood which clearly needs nothing else, namely, God. We perceive that all other things can exist only by the help of or the concourse of God. That is why the word substance does not pertain *univoce* to God and to other things, as they say in the Schools, that is, no common signification for this appelation which will apply equally to God and to them can be distinctly understood. . . .

[14]This seems to be the interpretation of Williams, 1978, pp. 124–125; and Curley, 1978, pp. 130–131.

> Created substances, however, whether corporeal or thinking, may be conceived under this common concept; for they are things which need only the concurrence of God in order to exist. [*PP* I, 51–52]

Entities other than God are not substances$_I$, strictly speaking, because it is not possible for them to exist without God's "concurrence." Descartes elaborates on this idea in his correspondence:

> It is much more certain that nothing can exist without the co-operation of God than that there is no sunlight without the sun. There is no doubt that if God withdrew his co-operation, everything which he has created would go to nothing; because all things were nothing until God created them and provided his co-operation. This does not mean that they should not be called substances, because when we call a created substance self-subsistent we do not rule out the divine co-operation which it needs in order to subsist. We mean only that it is a thing of a kind to exist without any other creature. . . . It is not the case that God would be showing the immensity of his power if he made things which could exist without him later on; on the contrary, he would thus be showing that his power was finite, since things once created would no longer depend on him. [K 115–116]

We need not worry whether Descartes is placing the burden of the argument upon considerations relating to God as creator and hence the initiating cause of existence, or God as sustainer and hence the sustaining cause of existence. In either case, entities other than God are disqualified as substances$_I$ in the strict sense on the ground that it is *not* possible that their existence does not depend *causally* upon the existence of any other substance$_S$. The sort of "independence" relevant to Descartes' conception of "substance$_I$" is causal independence, at least.[15] Perhaps some variety of noncausal dependence is relevant as well, but I know of no evidence for this.

I call Descartes' strict conception of substance$_I$ relative to which God is the only substance$_S$ 'primary-substance$_I$', and suggest that this be formulated as follows (where 'x' is any entity):

> (1) x is a primary-substance$_I$ just in case it is possible that:
> x's existence does not depend causally upon the existence of any other substance$_S$.

---

[15]Williams, 1978, pp. 126, 136, also takes it to be a specifically causal dependence which is of concern to Descartes.

Since Descartes grants that there is a sense in which created entities can property be called "substances," since it is possible for them to exist independently of any substance$_S$ other than God, we can formulate a definition of 'secondary-substance$_I$':

> (2) x is a secondary-substance$_I$ just in case it is possible that:
> x's existence does not depend causally upon the existence of any other substance$_S$ except God.

I have one dissatisfaction with these definitions. As we have seen, Descartes himself is not committed to the existence of material substances$_S$ fully analogous to thinking substances$_S$. Suppose that material objects exist, but that material substances$_S$ do not. In other words, suppose that it is false that material objects consist of an unobservable-substratum-in-which-qualities-inhere. In that event, if we employ (2) to determine whether some entity is a secondary-substance$_I$, any causal dependencies between that entity and material objects are irrelevant to the determination. We need only determine whether it is possible that the entity's existence does not depend causally upon the existence of any *substance$_S$* (other than itself and God). On this criterion, the entity could be a secondary-substance$_I$ even though its existence must depend causally upon the existence of material objects. It seems better to formulate a definition of 'secondary-substance$_I$' which does not presuppose the existence of material substances$_S$.

This sort of consideration may as well be generalized. Locke, Hume, and (I will suggest) Spinoza have no use either for material substance$_S$ or for thinking substance$_S$. It seems worthwhile to ask whether there is some core to Descartes' conception of substance$_I$ which can be captured in a definition that sets out a condition which is not vacuously fulfilled in case there are no substances$_S$. If so, we can so to speak liberate the heart of Descartes' conception of substance$_I$ from the unobservable-substratum-in-which-qualities-inhere metaphysics. The resulting notion of substance$_I$ would be potentially applicable in interesting ways to systems which do without substance$_S$. The required modifications are simple enough:

> (1') x is a primary-substance$_I$ just in case it is possible that:
> x's existence does not depend causally upon the existence of any other entity.

(2') x is a secondary-substance$_I$ just in case it is possible that:
   x's existence does not depend causally upon the existence of any
   other entity except God.

I have already introduced a simple Cartesian argument for the existence of some thinking substance$_S$. A simple Cartesian argument for the claim that a thinking substance$_S$ is a secondary-substance$_I$ is suggested by the following passage from *Discourse IV*: "examining attentively that which I was, I saw that I could conceive that I had no body, and that there was no world nor place where I might be; but yet that I could not for all that conceive that I was not. . . . From that I knew that I was a substance the whole essence or nature of which is to think, and that for its existence there is no need of any place, nor does it depend on any material thing" (HR I, 101). Descartes holds that it is conceivable (and hence, implicitly, possible) that a thinking substance$_S$ exists but no material object exists. If so, a fortiori it is possible that the existence of a thinking substance$_S$ does not depend causally upon the existence of any material object. This does not quite yield the conclusion that a thinking substance$_S$ is a secondary-substance$_I$, that it is possible that its existence does not depend causally upon the existence of any other entity except God. But the modest supplementation required is easy enough (at least if we suppose that the only entities which exist are thinking substances$_S$, their qualities, and material objects). Descartes need only claim that it is conceivable that a thinking substance$_S$ exists but that nothing else (no other thinking substance$_S$ nor any material objects) except God exists. Descartes himself makes this sort of point in the *Principles* (PP I, 60).

I stated earlier that the two strands in Descartes' conception of substance are distinct, though not unrelated. "Substance$_S$" and "substance$_I$" are obviously "related" at least in the sense that there are Cartesian arguments to show that a thinking substance$_S$ is a secondary-substance$_I$. In addition, I believe we can see a clear sense in which substance$_S$ and substance$_I$ are distinct strands in what is a unified conception of substance. In other words, I believe we can see why it is appropriate to use subscripted "substance" terminology rather than wholly different terms for the two strands discussed.

Both strands have to do with the capacity for independent existence, but the sorts of "independence" at issue are different in each case. Substance$_1$ relates to causal dependence, the possibility that an entity's existence does not depend causally upon the existence of certain other entities. Substance$_s$ realtes to one variety of noncausal dependence, the possibility that an entity's existence does not depend upon the existence of a substratum in which it inheres. Inherence is of course not the only variety of noncausal dependence. The existence of a valley depends noncausally upon the existence of mountains or hills, but the valley does not inhere in the mountains. The existence of a whole may, as Leibniz suggested (L 622), depend upon the existence of its parts, but the whole does not inhere in its parts. Substance$_s$ relates to inherence, a variety of noncausal dependence which is singled out for special treatment. (I am not claiming that Descartes confuses different sorts of dependencies, or that he equivocates between different senses of 'depends' or 'dependence', or that any of his arguments are vitiated by a failure to distinguish between different sorts of dependence. I claim only that Descartes' conceptions of substance$_s$ and substance$_1$ both reflect a concern for a capacity of independent existence of one sort or another.)

We have seen that Hume rejects substance$_s$ on the ground that 'substance' and 'inhesion' have no clear meaning. He also mounts a second attack on substance$_s$, and the strategy behind the attack applies to substance$_1$ as well. The strategy depends upon Hume's principles that all distinct ideas are separable from each other, and that whatever may be considered as existing separately may exist separately. These principles are applied to the case of substance$_s$ as follows:

> the definition of a substance is *something which may exist by itself* . . . this definition agrees to every thing, that can possibly be conceiv'd; and will never serve to distinguish substance from accident, or the soul from its perceptions. For thus I reason. . . . Every thing, which is different, is distinguishable, and every thing which is distinguishable, is separable by the imagination. . . . My conclusion . . . is, that since all our perceptions are different from each other, and from every thing else in the universe, they are also distinct and separable, and may be consider'd as separately existent, and may exist separately, and have no need of any thing else to support their existence. They are, therefore, substances, as far as this definition explains a substance. [*Trea.* 233]

If a substance$_S$ is an entity such that it is possible that its existence does not depend by way of inherence upon the existence of any other entity, even Humean perceptions or Cartesian thoughts are substances$_S$.

The same strategy is applicable to substance$_I$:

> 'Tis a general maxim in philosophy, that *whatever begins to exist, must have a cause of existence.*
>
> ... We can never demonstrate the necessity of a cause to every new existence, or new modification of existence, without shewing at the same time the impossibility there is, that any thing can ever begin to exist without some productive principle; and where the latter proposition cannot be prov'd, we must despair of ever being able to prove the former. Now that the latter proposition is utterly incapable of a demonstrative proof, we may satisfy ourselves by considering, that as all distinct ideas are separable from each other, and as the ideas of cause and effect are evidently distinct, 'twill be easy for us to conceive any object to be non-existent this moment, and existent the next, without conjoining to it the distinct idea of a cause or productive principle. The separation, therefore, of the idea of a cause from that of a beginning of existence, is plainly possible for the imagination; and consequently the actual separation of these objects is so far possible, that it implies no contradiction nor absurdity. [*Trea.* 78–80]

It is possible for any object to exist without any cause whatsoever. Hume does not explicitly relate this conclusion to the conception of substance$_I$, but its import is clear. If a substance$_I$ is an entity such that it is possible that its existence does not depend causally upon the existence of any other entity, every entity is a substance$_I$.

Here we have the foundation for one aspect of a Humean attack on substance$_I$. If every entity is a substance$_I$, this conception of substance is metaphysically indiscriminate—we are not dealing with a metaphysical notion which will help us draw any interesting discriminations between entities. Descartes would, of course, disagree with Hume's claim to have established the foundation for this attack. For the purposes of his causal arguments for the existence of God, he holds that necessarily an idea of an all-perfect being has an all-perfect being for a cause (*Med. III*). So this idea is not a substance$_I$. But whether or not the conception of substance$_I$ is of more general metaphysical interest remains to be seen.

There is a second aspect to the Humean attack on substance₁. As we have seen, Hume argues that every perception is a substance₁ in that it is possible that its existence does not depend causally upon the existence of any other entity. But a perception's existence might as a matter of fact depend causally upon the existence of some other entity. Indeed, this is precisely Hume's position:

> 'Twill first be proper to observe a few of those experiments, which convince us, that our perceptions are not possest of any independent existence. When we press one eye with a finger, we immediately perceive all the objects to become double, and one half of them to be remov'd from their common and natural position. But as we do not attribute a continu'd existence to both these perceptions, and as they are both of the same nature, we clearly perceive, that all our perceptions are dependent on our organs, and the disposition of our nerves and animal spirits. [*Trea.* 210–211]

What this "experiment" would seem to show is that the existence of perceptions in fact does depend causally upon the existence of other entities, our organs. This in no way rules out the claim that perceptions are substances₁. Hume's position is that while it is logically possible that perceptions have a causally independent existence, as a matter of empirical fact they do not. Here Hume sounds a second alarm. The fact that an entity is a substance₁ is not going to be of any help in determining the causal dependencies in which it in fact participates. The conception of substance₁ is not only metaphysically indiscriminate, but also, one might say, factually irrelevant.

9. Spinozistic Substance

In this and the following section, I locate the conceptions of substance of Spinoza (which I refer to as 'SP-substance') and of Leibniz ("monads") relative to that of Descartes. I want to specify the differences and similarities between substance ₛ together with substance₁ on the one hand, and both SP-substance and monads on the other.

Spinoza defines 'substance' at ₁Def. 3 of the *Ethics:* "By substance, I understand that which is in itself and is conceived through itself; in other words, that, the conception of which does not need the conception of another thing from which it must be formed." There are two ways to read this, depending upon whether the condition that the conception of substance does not need the conception of another thing is taken to be equivalent to the joint condition that a substance is in itself and is conceived through itself, or equivalent to the condition that a substance is conceived through itself alone. I will opt for the latter reading without argument.[16]

The serious interpretative issue is to determine what Spinoza means by the two conditions that an SP-substance is "in itself" and "conceived through itself." Here I follow the interpretation advanced by E. M. Curley.[17] For "conceived through itself," we get some help from a variant of Spinoza's definition of 'substance', provided at *E* IP8S2: "For by 'substance' would be understood that which is in itself and is conceived through itself, or, in other words, that, the knowledge of which does not need the knowledge of another thing." Here, the knowledge of substance does not need the knowledge of another thing; at *E* IDef.3 the conception of substance does not need the conception of another thing. Evidently, Spinoza uses 'conception' and 'knowledge' interchangeably. This is obscured in the Elwes translation of *E* IP8S2 which translates '*cognitio*' as 'conception' rather than 'knowledge', apparently in order to bring the passage here into accord with *E* IDef.3.[18] SP-substance is "conceived through itself" in the sense that it is known through itself, that is, the knowledge of SP-substance does not depend upon the knowledge of anything else. Further evidence for the interchangeability of 'conception' and 'knowledge' will emerge in section 19 when we examine Spinoza's arguments for *E* IIP6.

Whereas *E* IP8S2 provides a direct handle on "conceived through itself," there is no single passage which will so easily generate an interpretation of "in itself." At this point, I will be content to state Curley's interpretation, and to show that it has some initial plausibility. SP-substance is "in itself" in the sense that it is causally independent of anything else, that is, its existence does not depend causally upon the existence of anything else.

To see the plausibility of Curley's interpretation, we must improve our grip on the sense in which an SP-substance is "known

[16]This reading deprives me of an argument in support of an important point of interpretation. See §18, including n. 1.

[17]Curley, 1969, ch. I.

[18]Ibid., p. 163, n. 14.

through itself" by considering what constitutes "knowing" a thing for Spinoza. On this point, *E* 1A4 is reasonably explicit: "The knowledge of an effect depends upon and involves the knowledge of the cause." I do not know of any context in the *Ethics* which requires a distinction between a sense in which knowledge of an effect "depends upon," and a sense in which it "involves," the knowledge of its cause. I will therefore simplify *E* 1A4 as follows: "The knowledge of an effect depends upon the knowledge of its cause." The formulation need not be restricted to knowledge of *effects*. Spinoza holds: "For the existence or non-existence of everything there must be a reason or cause" (*E* 1P11D2). I assume that 'reason' and 'cause' are used interchangeably here, again on grounds that I do not know of any context in the *Ethics* where the argument requires a distinction. So for Spinoza, everything that exists has a cause, and hence everything that exists is an effect. This permits a generalization of *E* 1A4: the knowledge of anything that exists depends upon the knowledge of its cause.

Is Spinoza denying that I can have knowledge of something without knowing its cause? Suppose I enter a room and see a quite unfamiliar object *O* at time *t*. I may have no clue as to *O*'s cause, but surely I have knowledge of *O*, for example, that it exists, that it has a certain color, shape, etc. No doubt there is a good sense of 'knowledge' in which, in such circumstances, I do have knowledge of *O*. This is not the sense of 'knowledge' Spinoza has in mind. If I know nothing of *O*'s cause, I have no knowledge of *O* in Spinoza's sense of 'knowledge'. To remind ourselves that knowledge in his sense is different from, for example, knowledge by acquaintance, I will write of 'Spinozistic-knowledge', or 'SP-knowledge' for short.

SP-knowledge admits of degrees. In *On the Improvement of the Understanding*, Spinoza writes: "In reality, the knowledge of an effect is nothing else than the acquisition of more perfect knowledge of its cause" (IU, 36). An entity might be the effect of a number of (partial) causes which obtained at one time, where each of those causes is itself the effect of a number of (partial) causes at some previous time, and so on. What we might call 'perfect SP-knowledge' would require knowledge of the entire or complete causal history of the entity. (Of course, some objects might have, at least in part, causes which are atemporal or not in time. When I write of a "complete causal history," I do not exclude such a possibility. I simply mean a complete causal account or explanation, whatever its temporal features.) I suggest that when Spinoza writes of an entity's being "known," whether "through itself" or "through another," he has in mind perfect SP-knowledge. By 'SP-knowledge', I shall mean perfect SP-knowledge.

An SP-substance is "in itself" and "conceived through itself." We have seen that something is conceived through itself just in case it is known—in Spinoza's special sense of the term—through itself. We can say that SP-knowledge of SP-substance does not require the SP-knowledge of anything else. When we combine this with Curley's suggestion that an SP-substance is "in itself" in the sense that its existence does not depend causally upon the existence of anything else, we have:

> *x* is an SP-substance just in case
> (MC) *x*'s existence does not depend causally upon the existence of any other entity, and
> (EC) SP-knowledge of *x* does not require SP-knowledge of any other entity.

The first condition (MC) is metaphysical, the second (EC) epistemological. Curley's interpretation has the great merit of allowing us to see how these conditions are interrelated.

In particular, something is in itself if and only if it is conceived through itself; the metaphysical condition is satisfied just in case the epistemological condition is satisfied. First, suppose *x* is in itself. Then its existence does not depend causally upon the existence of anything else. But everything that exists has a cause (*E* 1P11D2). So *x* is its own cause. So SP-knowledge of *x* does not require SP-knowledge of anything else. Hence, *x* is known through itself. Second, suppose *x* is known through itself. But SP-knowledge of anything that exists depends upon knowledge of its cause (generalization of *E* 1A4). So *x* is its own cause. So *x*'s existence does not depend causally upon the existence of anything else. Hence, *x* is in itself.[19] Curley's interpretation succeeds in integrating the two conditions in Spinoza's account of substance into a neat epistemological and metaphysical package.

I am now in a position to locate the relationships between SP-substance and the Cartesian conception of substance. The

[19]Ibid., pp. 15–16, 17–18.

metaphysical component (MC) of Spinoza's conception of substance is obviously related to, but not identical with, substance$_I$.
Recall the Cartesian account of primary-substance$_I$:

    (1′) x is a primary-substance$_I$ just in case it is possible that:
          x's existence does not depend causally upon the existence of any
          other entity.

For Spinoza,

    x is an SP-substance only if
    (MC) x's existence does not depend causally upon the existence of
           any other entity.

(MC) differs from (1′) in the deletion of "it is possible that." Both
substance$_I$ and SP-substance are concerned, metaphysically, with
causal dependence exclusively. But x is a primary-substance$_I$ just in
case *it is possible that* x's existence does not depend causally upon
the existence of anything else; x is an SP-substance only if *it is true
that* x's existence does not depend causally upon the existence of
anything else. If an entity is an SP-substance, it is a primary-
substance$_I$. But an entity could be a primary-substance$_I$ without
satisfying (MC).

What about the epistemological component (EC) of Spinoza's
conception of substance? This might seem to contrast in an interesting way with Descartes' second general thesis about substance$_S$.
That thesis, too, is epistemological: we cannot immediately apprehend, cognize, or observe substances$_S$ themselves; rather we immediately observe the qualities which inhere in a substance$_S$, and then
infer that a substance$_S$ exists. This might be expressed by saying
that a substance$_S$ is not known through itself; it is known through
something else, its qualities. In other words, for Descartes knowledge of a substance$_S$ requires knowledge of something else, whereas
according to (EC), for Spinoza knowledge of SP-substance does not
require knowledge of anything else; SP-substance is known through
itself. It would be misleading, however, to view this as an interesting
point of contrast, and doubly so.[20]

[20]For the reasons which follow, I think it misleading when Curley, 1969, p. 15,
writes: "Spinoza has added a clause to his definition of 'substance' that disqualifies
most of the things Descartes would call substances from being so classified. An
entity whose existence must be inferred from the existence of something else,
whose knowledge requires the knowledge of another thing, . . . would not be a
substance in Spinoza's sense of the term."

First, to say that substance$_s$ is known through something else, whereas SP-substance is known through itself, obscures the fact that different kinds of knowledge are at issue. Descartes is concerned with "knowing" in the sense of knowing that something exists. Spinoza, as we have seen, is concerned with "knowing" in the sense of knowing the complete causal history of something that exists. Spinoza might admit that if there do exist substances$_s$ we could have "knowledge" of such substances$_s$ in the sense of knowing that they exist, without having SP-knowledge of those same substances$_s$.

And this leads to the second point. The account of SP-substance does not suggest any interest on Spinoza's part in any noncausal dependencies at all, and hence not in that species of noncausal dependence which obtains between qualities at time t and the subject or substratum in which they inhere at t. There is nothing in the account to suggest that Spinoza has any interest in Cartesian substances$_s$. Now this is controversial. According to one tradition of Spinoza interpretation, on Spinoza's conception a substance is something at least very much like a Cartesian substance$_s$. Curley has produced what I consider to be decisive arguments against this interpretation.[21]

10. Monads

Reading Leibniz is a good antidote for the belief that there is some single Continental Rationalist conception of substance handed down from one figure to another, or even for the belief that at least there must have existed considerable constraints with respect to the theoretical deployment of the term. At a very early stage in his development, Leibniz introduced the following definition: "I call *substance* whatever moves or is moved" (L 73). The degrees of freedom with respect to the term's use were considerable.

Leibniz offers the following remarks on Spinoza's definition of 'substance':

Definition 3. Substance is that which is in itself and is conceived through itself. This definition too is obscure. For what does 'to be in itself' mean? Then we must ask: Does he relate 'to be in itself' and 'to be conceived through itself' cumulatively or disjunctively? That is,

[21]Ibid., pp. 4–28.

does he mean that substance is what is in itself and also that substance is what is conceived through itself? Or does he mean that substance is that in which both occur together, that is, that substance is both in itself and conceived through itself? But then it would be necessary for him to prove that whatever has one property also has the other, while the contrary seems rather to be true, that there are some things which are in themselves though they are not conceived through themselves. And this is how men commonly conceive of substance. [L 196]

Leibniz seems genuinely puzzled: the expression 'in itself' is obscure; that aside, there is an ambiguity in the definition; and further, on one reading, the definition has the result that things which are commonly conceived as substances are not substances. This is not a commentary which suggests that Leibniz took over Spinoza's conception of substance. Apparently, he did not even fully understand Spinoza's definition.

Much later, Leibniz wrote to Burcher de Volder: "Now I admit that it is within your power to define the word 'substance' so that God alone becomes substance and everything else has another character. However, I fail to see how it is a suitable concept for the remainder of things or agrees with that of the general manner of speaking according to which all persons including yourself or myself are called substances" (W 173). This is not an early statement of the view that philosophy consists of linguistic analysis which focuses on "the general manner of speaking." Leibniz's point is that it is open to him to deploy the substance terminology for purposes he considers suitable. He uses the terminology to direct attention to individuals rather than to God.

Leibniz distinguishes between simple substances and compound substances. The former appear as "individual substances" in the *Discourse on Metaphysics* (1686) and the subsequent correspondence with Arnauld (1686–87), and as "monads" in the *Monadology* (1714). In section 33, I will discuss Leibniz's conception of substance as of 1686–87, and compare his position then to his later views. At this juncture, I will focus on the *Monadology*. There 'monad' is defined as a "simple substance," and 'simple' is defined as "having no parts" (M 1). So a monad is a substance that has no parts. Of course, this does not provide a definition of 'substance' itself, but it is an easy matter to extract one. The monad "enters into compounds" (*M* 1), and "the compounded is but a collection or an *aggregate* of simples" (*M* 2). Evidently, a substance is an entity that either has no parts (a simple substance), or is ultimately composed only of entities that have no parts (a compound substance). Monads or simple substances are just entities that have no parts.

Leibniz states that "it is necessary for monads to have some qualities, otherwise they would not even be beings" (*M* 8). The qualities monads have are "perceptions" (*M* 14). For Leibniz, 'perception' is a technical term. Suffice it to say that Descartes' "thoughts" are a subclass of Leibniz's "perceptions"—a subclass because some Leibnizian perceptions, but no Cartesian thoughts, are unconscious. So a monad, by definition an entity that has no parts, begins to look rather like a Cartesian thinking substance$_S$. Indeed, writing in 1692, Leibniz endorses at least Descartes' first general thesis about substance$_S$, that necessarily any quality inheres in some substance$_S$: "An accident . . . needs not only some substance in general but that very one in which it inheres" (L 390).[22]

In light of all this, it is not surprising to find that in his *New Essays Concerning Human Understanding* (1704) Leibniz is critical of Locke's attack on substance$_S$ (see *NE* 105, 148, 154, 225–227). On the other hand, while Leibniz asserts that consideration of substance "gives rise to many consequences of greatest importance in philosophy" (*NE* 227), it is far from clear that he is defending the Cartesian doctrine of a substratum in which qualities inhere. He claims weakly that "the idea of substance is not so obscure as you think" (*NE* 148). And his response to Locke's objection to such metaphors as "support" is this: "we conceive several predicates in one and the same subject, and these metaphorical words, *support* (*soutien*) or *substratum* mean only this; so that I do not see why it should cause any difficulty" (*NE* 225). Here Leibniz appears to be defending a conception of substance on the basis of considerations relating to predication, without drawing any ontological conclusions about the existence of substrata. His defense of substance$_S$ as envisioned by Descartes and attacked by Locke seems rather less than wholehearted.

[22]For additional handles on the relationships between Cartesian thinking substance$_S$ and monads, see Furth, 1967, §1.

As we have seen, Descartes argues that a thinking substance$_s$ is a secondary-substance$_I$. Recall the Cartesian account of this notion:

> (2') x is a secondary-substance$_I$ just in case it is possible that:
> x's existence does not depend causally upon the existence of any other entity except God.

Leibniz would hold that a monad's existence *does not* depend causally upon the existence of anything else except God, *not* simply that *it is possible* that a monad's existence does not depend causally upon the existence of anything else except God. But Leibniz holds as well that a monad does not even causally interact with anything else (this will be discussed in detail in section 30). To see that this is a much stronger thesis, consider billiard balls rather than monads. It might well be true (leaving aside bizarre cases that one could construct) that the existence of one billiard ball does not depend causally upon the existence of another billiard ball, even though the two billiard balls causally interact by bumping each other around.

11. Data for a Theory

Some of our principal results may be summarized as follows.

There are two strands in Descartes' conception of substance. Both have to do with the capacity for independent existence, but the sorts of "independence" are different in each case. Descartes' conception of substance$_s$ relates to inherence, a variety of noncausal dependence; it is not possible that a quality can exist without inhering in a substance$_s$. A substance$_s$ is an unobservable-substratum-in-which-qualities-inhere. In the *Essay*, Locke attempted to demolish substance$_s$, and Hume followed suit. Spinoza, who died before the *Essay* was published, appears to have had no use for substance$_s$. On the other hand, both Berkeley and Leibniz, writing after the *Essay* was published, reject Locke's attack on substance$_s$, at least in its full generality, and revive thinking substance$_s$ in particular in the guise of spirits and monads, respectively. Indeed, Descartes, Berkeley, and Leibniz agree on certain relationships between thoughts and thinking substances$_s$, ideas and spirits, and perceptions and monads. For example, necessarily, any thought/idea/perception inheres in some thinking substance$_s$/spirit/monad. But in the *New Essays*, Leibniz's defense of substance$_s$ against Locke is less than impassioned.

Descartes' conception of substance₁ relates to causal dependence, the possibility that an entity's existence does not depend causally upon the existence of certain other entities. Hume was eventually to suggest that this conception of substance is both metaphysically indiscriminate and irrelevant to establishing whether or not an entity's existence in fact depends causally upon other entities. For Spinoza, for something to qualify as a substance, it was not enough that it is possible that the entity's existence does not depend causally upon the existence of anything else. An SP-substance is such that its existence does not in fact depend causally upon the existence of anything else. Leibniz does not define his conception of a simple substance in a way which explicitly invokes causal notions, but it is perhaps his central metaphysical thesis that no two monads even causally interact, much less depend causally for their existence upon other monads (God aside).

Locke does allow the existence of substances in the sense of "distinct particular things subsisting by themselves," as contrasted with modes which are "dependences on, or affections of substances." The statement that modes are "dependences on" substances might suggest that Locke is interested in some sort of noncausal dependence other than that of inherence, which he of course attacks. And the statement that substances are things "subsisting by themselves" might suggest that he is interested in a notion of self-subsistence which has affinities with the conceptions of substance in Spinoza and Leibniz as well. But Locke's employment of his conceptions of substance and mode seem to be exclusively epistemological: nominal and real essences coincide for all modes, but not for substances (§ 3).

In my view, these results, together with some related points to be developed in subsequent chapters, constitute some preliminary data in need of a theory. How are we to account for the changing fortunes of substances? How are we to account for the shift of interest from the capacity for causally independent existence (Descartes), to interest in the fact of causally independent existence (Spinoza), to interest in the fact of a complete causal independence which precludes even causal interaction (Leibniz)? And how are we to account for the fact that Locke's conception of substance is principally epistemological in function? If we are to understand the metaphysics of the seventeenth and eighteenth centuries, we need a theory to explain this and related data. In order to develop such a theory, and to proceed with our evaluation of the third component of the standard theory, we will have to look in much more detail at the role of the various conceptions of substance, and their connections with claims about causation and causal dependence, in the principal metaphysical systems of the period.

III

DESCARTES' DENIAL THAT THE EXISTENCE OF MIND DEPENDS CAUSALLY UPON THE EXISTENCE OF BODY

12. Descartes' Claims about Minds

What I have called a "thinking substance$_S$," Descartes calls a "mind" or "soul" (HR II, 53). He tells us that he uses the latter two terms interchangeably (HR I, 141, 434). We find in Descartes at least the following claims about minds:

    (1) a thinking substance$_S$ or mind exists
    (2) (nonhuman) animals do not have minds
    (3) a mind's essence (at least in part) is to think
    (4) mind and body are really distinct substances$_S$
    (5) a mind's whole essence is to think
    (6) mind and body are essentially/entirely/absolutely distinct substances$_S$
    (7) mind and body are contrary or exclusive substances$_S$
    (8) no mind is a body
    (9) a mind's existence does not depend causally upon the existence of any body
    (10) mind and body causally interact
    (11) the mind functions immediately at the pineal gland, but is united to the entire human body
    (12) a human being consists of a mind and body so closely united as to constitute a single thing.

I stated a simple Cartesian argument for (1) in section 7. We have intuitive knowledge that some thoughts exists. By Descartes' first general thesis about substance$_S$, necessarily any quality inheres in some substance$_S$. By stipulation, a thought inheres in a thinking substance$_S$ or mind. It follows that (1) a thinking substance or mind exists. It remains to examine claims (2–12).

Consider (2). Descartes claimed with some persistence that (nonhuman) animals do not have souls or minds (HR I, 117–118; II, 103–104, 243–244; K 206–208, 243–245). This is equivalent to the claim that animals do not have any thoughts, since if animals did have thoughts, it would follow by his first thesis about substances that animals have minds. Thus he writes that "plainly the brutes do not possess thought" (HR II, 244). This claim is to be understood in light of Descartes' broad use of 'thought' (§ 7), such that "all the operations of will, intellect, imagination, and of the senses are thoughts" (HR II, 52); "not alone understanding, willing, imagining, but also feeling, are here the same thing as thought" (PP I, 9). Descartes is prepared to make verbal concessions: animals have "sensitive souls" (K 102) and "sensation, in so far as it depends on a bodily organ" (K 245). But "the souls of animals are nothing but their blood" (K 36), and animals do not feel pain (AT III, 85). Descartes' position is that animals do not have any conscious experiences.[1]

He produces an argument for this implausible thesis, but it is extremely weak. The basic idea is that humans differ from other animals in the creative use of language, and that this difference is to be explained by the hypothesis that humans have reason whereas animals lack reason (HR I, 116–117; K 244–245). As it stands, this sort of consideration at best supports the view that animals lack "reason" in an intellectual sense; the more general conclusion that animals lack "thought," where reasoning is just one species of thought, is completely unsupported. Even if Descartes has provided some reason for supposing that animals are not rational, he has provided none for supposing that they are not conscious. It may be that what appears to be a glaring non sequitur masks some suppressed premise, for example, that having any conscious experience, such as feeling pain, requires a conceptual apparatus possessed only by language users, or at least beings capable of using language. Thus Descartes asserts that "pain is only in the understanding" (AT III, 85). However, attributing the suppressed premise to Descartes may remove the non sequitur, but it hardly strengthens the argument—the premise would simply be rejected by anyone who holds that animals are conscious.

[1]For an extended discussion of Descartes' claim that nonhuman animals do not have minds or souls, and of the ensuing controversy, see Rosenfield, 1940.

Here we are confronted with a philosopher of obvious intelligence, appealing to an exceedingly weak argument in support of a grossly implausible conclusion. I suggest that under these conditions, whereas the argument constitutes the articulated grounds for the position, consideration of the argument did not lead its proponent to embrace the conclusion. We must distinguish between the articulated grounds for the conclusion, and the motive which led the philosopher to accept it.

In the present case, Descartes' motive is transparent, and was perceived, for example, by Locke:

> The usuall physicall proofe (as I may soe call it) of the immortality of the soule is this, Matter cannot thinke ergo the soule is immateriall, noe thing can naturally destroy an immateriall thing ergo the soule is naturally immortall.
>
> Those who oppose these men presse them very hard with the soules of beasts for say they beasts feele i.e. thinke and therefor their soules are immateriall and consequently immortall. This has by some men been judgd soe urgent that they have rather thought fit to conclude all beasts perfect machins rather then allow their soules immortality or annihilation both which seeme harsh doctrines. [AG 121]

And Leibniz offers a similar commentary:

> I believe that these vital principles are immortal and yet that they are everywhere. The common opinion holds instead that the souls of beasts perish, and according to the Cartesians, it is only man who truly has a soul and, indeed, who has perception and appetite—an opinion which will never receive general approval and into which they rushed only because it seemed necessary either to ascribe immortal souls to beasts or to admit that the soul of man could be mortal. [L 588]

It is not as if Descartes suppressed his motivation. The paragraph in the *Discourse* which argues that animals do not have minds is followed immediately by the following declaration: "I have here enlarged a little on the subject of the soul, because it is one of the greatest importance. For next to the error of those who deny God... there is none which is more effectual in leading feeble spirits from the straight path of virtue, than to imagine that the soul of the brute is of the same nature as our own, and that in consequence, after this life we have nothing to fear or to hope for, any more than the flies and ants" (HR I, 118). Similarly, Descartes writes to Henry More that animals most likely do not have thought because "it is more probable that worms and flies and caterpillars move mechanically than that they all have immortal souls" (K 244).

Descartes' difficulty is that all his arguments relating to human immortality appeal, as we shall see in the following section, solely to properties of all thinking substances$_S$. So if animals have minds, his conclusions about immortality will apply equally to them. Descartes' options were either to locate arguments supportive of human immortality which do not apply equally to animals, or to deny that animals have minds. He opted for the latter course, and the considerations relating to language use were the best he could find for this purpose.[2]

13. Immortality

What does Descartes believe can be established, by means other than revelation, about human immortality? At a minimum, he believes he can establish that (8) no mind is a body. This is a necessary condition for immortality. Thus Descartes asserts, in the

[2]Williams, 1978, pp. 82, 225–226, 284–287, grants that Descartes had an "external reason or motive for denying souls to animals" since for him "soul meant separable soul, and separable soul meant the possibility of immortality," but he treats this theological motivation as secondary. His suggestion is that Descartes' argument for the conclusion that animals lack conscious thought might have appeared tempting to him to the extent that he "was disposed to see all conscious experience as consisting of some kind of conceptual thought." The passages Williams cites as evidence that Descartes had the relevant disposition are from contexts where animal souls and immortality are directly at issue. He cites, for example, a letter to the physician Plempius, in which Descartes is responding to objections relating to the discussion of animal souls and immortality at the close of *Discourse* V. To establish that any disposition on Descartes' part to the view that consciousness requires self-consciousness is not itself to be explained as a by-product of the obvious theological motive, Williams would have to cite evidence that Descartes was so disposed quite independently of the demands of his position on immortality. There is a similar point to make with respect to the claim by Wilson, 1978, pp. 177–185 (esp. pp. 182–185), that if we are trying to understand why Descartes opted for dualism, "theological considerations cannot be regarded as fully explanatory"; rather, a reason for his dualism is to be found in "the perfectly creditable belief that human intelligence could never be accounted for on the available mechanistic models." However, the clearest passages which Wilson cites in order to show that Descartes held this belief occur at the close of *Discourse* V, where Descartes is arguing toward the conclusion that we have more to fear and hope for than the flies and ants.

Discourse, "our soul is in its nature entirely independent of body, and in consequence . . . it is not liable to die with it" (HR I, 118); in the "Synopsis" of the *Meditations, "the extinction of the mind does not follow from the corruption of the body"* (HR I, 141); and in a letter to Mersenne, the soul "is not bound by nature to die with" the body (K 87, cf. 130). At times, Descartes suggests that the fact of immortality can be established. The subtitle of the first edition claims that the *Meditations* provides demonstrations of both the existence of God and the immortality of the soul. This is altered in the second edition, "in which the Existence of God and the Distinction Between Mind and Body are Demonstrated" (HR I, 144). This alteration may simply be due to the fact that there is no argument for immortality in the *Meditations* proper. The original "Dedication" is retained. There Descartes states that "although it is quite enough for us faithful ones to accept by means of faith the fact that the human soul does not perish with the body, and that God exists, it certainly does not seem possible ever to persuade infidels of any religion . . . unless, to begin with, we prove these two facts by means of natural reason" (HR I, 133). The "Synopsis" provides a twofold explanation of Descartes' omitting to argue for immortality in the *Meditations: "I have not however dealt further with this matter in this treatise, both because what I have said is sufficient . . . to give men the hope of another life after death, as also because the premises from which the immortality of the soul may be deduced depend on an elucidation of a complete system of Physics"* (HR I, 141). In *Replies II,* Descartes offers something of a short route through such an elucidation to the conclusion that "the mind, so far as it can be known by aid of a natural philosophy, is immortal" (HR II, 47).

We have seen that Descartes embraces (2) in order to avoid the result that his position on immortality applies equally to nonhuman animals. My main purpose in this section is to show that his principal motivation for propounding not only (2), but all of (1–9)— though not (10–12), which are discussed in the following section— is his belief that these claims can be exploited in support of his position on immortality. I will defend and elaborate this suggestion in the course of examining these theses, and the use Descartes makes of them. We will also want to determine the role of his conceptions of substance$_s$ and substance$_I$ in the argumentation for (1–9).

Descartes claims that (3) a mind's essence (at least in part) is to think. In order to understand this, we need to determine how he uses the term 'essence'. There is no explicit definition, but Descartes does say this: "in my opinion nothing without which a thing can still exist is comprised in its essence" (HR II, 97). He holds that a property is essential to an entity only if it is impossible for that entity to exist without having that property. This states a necessary condition for a property's being essential. Presumably, if it is impossible for an entity to exist without having a certain property, then that property is essential to that entity. In sum, a property is essential to an entity if and only if it is impossible for that entity to exist without having that property.

There is a weak interpretation of this definition: a property is essential to an entity if and only if it is impossible for that entity to exist without having that property at least at some time or other. It will become apparent that Descartes has in mind the stronger and more obvious interpretation: a property is essential to an entity if and only if it is impossible for that entity to exist at any time without having that property at that time.

We now know how to understand (3): thought is essential to a mind in the sense that a mind cannot exist at any time without thinking at that time. It may seem that (3) is trivially true because a substance$_S$ is a subject in which qualities inhere, and by stipulation thinking substances$_S$ or minds are just those subjects in which thoughts inhere (HR II, 53); so a mind cannot exist without thinking. This stipulation, however, does not have (3) for a consequence. The force of the stipulation is that a substance$_S$ is a mind just in case it thinks at least at some time in its history. If a substance$_S$ persists over time, it is a mind just in case it thinks at least at some time. The stipulation guarantees that a mind cannot exist without thinking at some time or other. Put another way, the stipulation guarantees that thought is "essential" to minds in the *weak* sense of 'essence' stated above.

Descartes restricts his use of 'thought' to conscious mental episodes. For him, there are no unconscious thoughts: "By the word thought I understand all that of which we are conscious as operating in us" (PP I, 9); "*Thought* is a word that covers everything which exists in us in such a way that we are immediately conscious of it" (HR II, 52). If there are no unconscious thoughts, and if thought is essential to a mind in the sense that a mind cannot exist at any time without thinking at that time, then evidently the mind is conscious even during sound sleep and comas, and in the womb! This consequence might seem to count against either our claim that Descartes restricts 'thought' to conscious mental episodes, or our claim that the strong interpretation of 'essence' is correct, or both. But Descartes readily accepts the consequence in question.

Gassendi raises the present objection, pointing out that it is difficult to "*comprehend how you can think during a lethargic sleep, or while in the womb*" (HR ii, 141). Descartes replies:

> *You have a difficulty,* however, you say, *as to whether I think that the soul always thinks.* But why should it not always think, when it is a thinking substance? Why is it strange that we do not remember the thoughts it had when in the womb or in a stupor, when we do not even remember the most of those we know we have had when grown up, in good health, and awake? For the recollection of the thoughts which the mind has had during the period of its union with the body, it is necessary for certain traces of them to be impressed on the brain; and turning and applying itself to these the mind remembers. Is it remarkable if the brain of an infant or of one in a stupor is unfit to receive these residual impressions? [HR ii, 210–211]

It is explicit in a letter to Hyperaspistes (the name is a pseudonym for a supporter of Gassendi) that the force of the claim that the soul "is a thinking substance" is that thinking is essential to a soul:

> I had reason to assert that the human soul, wherever it be, even in the mother's womb, is always thinking. What more certain or evident reason could be wished for than the one I gave? I had proved that the nature or essence of soul consists in the fact that it is thinking, just as the essence of body consists in the fact that it is extended. Now nothing can ever be deprived of its own essence; so it seems to me that a man who denies that his soul was thinking at times when he does not remember noticing it thinking, deserves no more attention than a man who denied that his body was extended while he did not notice that it had extension. [K 111]

He repeats this defense in a letter to Guilliaume Gibieuf (K 125).

Descartes' stonewalling response to Gassendi's objection is unimpressive, and Locke took Descartes to task for his view. Locke agreed with Descartes that only conscious mental episodes are thoughts (*Essay* ii.i.10,19,xxvii.9), but he denied that thought is essential to the soul. He thereby avoids the consequence that the soul is conscious even during sound sleep or comas:

I know it is an opinion, that the soul always thinks, and that it has the actual perception of *ideas* in it self constantly, as long as it exists; and that actual thinking is as inseparable from the soul, as actual extension is from the body. . . .

I confess my self, to have one of those dull souls, that does not perceive it self always to contemplate *ideas*, nor can conceive it any more necessary for the *soul always to think*, than for the body always to move; the perception of *ideas* being (as I conceive) to the soul, what motion is to the body, not its essence, but one of its operations. . . . We know certainly by experience, that we sometimes think, and thence draw this infallible consequence, that there is something in us, that has a power to think: But whether that substance perpetually thinks, or no, we can be no farther assured, than experience informs us. [*Essay* ii.i.9–10; cf. AG 123]

Locke proceeds to ridicule Descartes' claim that the soul always thinks, e.g., during sleep, though it does not always remember its thoughts (*Essay* ii.i.13–15,18; cf. AG 121–122).

I have already noted the implausibility of Descartes' claim that (2) (nonhuman) animals do not have minds. In his claim that (3) a mind's essence (at least in part) is to think, we have a second implausible claim, susceptible to Gassendi's objections and to Locke's attack. Why did Descartes embrace this claim? I suggest that he wanted to establish (3), as well as (2), because of its potential for contributing to his position on immortality.

One point of connection is as follows. By stipulation, a substance$_S$ in which thought immediately resides is a mind, and a substance$_S$ in which extension immediately resides is a body (HR ii, 53). I have construed this to mean, in the case of a substance$_S$ which persists over time, that it is a mind if thoughts ever reside in it; similarly, it is a body if extension ever resides in it. Descartes points out that these stipulations leave it an open question "whether it is one and the same substance or whether there are two diverse substances to which the names Mind and Body apply" (HR ii, 53). Let us suppose that he holds a third thesis about substance$_S$ in general, namely, that necessarily any substance$_S$ has some quality that inheres in it at every time it exists. While it is difficult to find in Descartes an explicit commitment to this thesis (but cf. *PP* i, 52), it seems natural enough. In his commentary on Descartes' *Principles*, Leibniz holds that "a substance needs some accident" (L 389), and does not suggest that this might be a point of difference with Descartes. In any case, I will relax this assumption shortly. Since a mind is a substance$_s$, it would follow from this third general thesis that a mind must have some quality at every time it exists. Suppose further that minds and bodies are the only substances$_s$ there are, thoughts and modes of extension the only qualities there are. Then if at some time a mind has no thought, it must have some physical quality at that time, in which case it is a body. Thus Descartes' question "whether it is one and the same substance . . . to which the names Mind and Body apply" would be answered in the affirmative. If a mind is a body, and if bodies are corrupted, how could a mind be immortal?

Suppose, on the other hand, that Descartes did not hold the third general thesis about substance$_s$, that necessarily any substance$_s$ has some quality which inheres in it at every time it exists. In that case, an immortal mind could exist at times after the death of the body without having any qualities and a fortiori without having thoughts and being conscious; indeed, a mind could be immortal but never be conscious in the afterlife. Establishing the possibility or even the fact of immortality would be of slight relevance to a Christian conception of the afterlife. Locke, for one, was quite aware that if thought is not essential to the mind, arguments for immortality lose much of their force, and this was one of his reasons for wanting to deny that a mind's essence is to think (AG 122). In sum, if (3) is false, either minds are bodies and there is a serious threat to immortality, or the immortality which can be secured need not involve any consciousness.

Descartes' principal motivation for embracing (3), however, was doubtless to exploit it for the purposes of his direct argumentation for his position on immortality. In order to determine the contributions of (3), we must examine its interrelationships with his claims (4–9). Descartes frequently claims that (4) mind and body are "really distinct," or that there is a "real distinction" between mind and body (HR I, 142, 185, 244; II, 47, 59, 101–102, 211). He is quite explicit about the conditions under which this claim is justifiable: "we can conclude that two substances are really distinct one from the other from the sole fact that we can conceive the one clearly and distinctly without the other" (*PP* I, 60). Since Descartes holds that whatever we can clearly and distinctly conceive is within God's power (HR I,

190; ii, 59, 102), we should expect that two substances are really distinct just in case one can exist "without the other." This is precisely Descartes' position: "Two substances are said to be really distinct, when each of them can exist apart from the other" (HR ii, 53; cf. 32). This definition must be construed as an account of the conditions under which substances$_S$ are really distinct. Just prior to stating the definition of "really distinct substances," Descartes provides definitions of 'substance$_S$' ("everything in which there resides immediately . . . , or by means of which there exists anything that we perceive"), of 'mind' ("that substance in which thought immediately resides") and 'body' ("that substance which is the immediate subject of extension in space and of the accidents that presuppose extension").

In contexts relevant to the real distinction, Descartes writes that mind can exist "without," "apart from," "separately from," and "independently of" any body (HR i, 101, 190; ii, 32, 59, 102). What sort of "independence" is in question here? It is tempting to suppose that the sort of independence associated with substance$_I$ is at issue. Recall that x is a primary- (secondary-)substance just in case it is possible that: x's existence does not depend causally upon the existence of any other entity (except God). More generally, we could say that an entity is a substance$_I$ relative to certain other specified entities just in case it is possible that: x's existence does not depend causally upon the existence of those other entities. In these terms, a primary-substance$_I$ is a substance$_I$ relative to all other entities, a secondary-substance$_I$ is a substance$_I$ relative to all other entities except God. The temptation is to suppose that in claiming that mind and body are really distinct, Descartes is making the point that a mind is a substance$_I$ relative to body, that is, it is possible that a mind's existence does not depend causally upon the existence of any other entity which is a body.

I doubt, however, that this is correct. Descartes is going to want somehow to move from the possibility that minds are not bodies to the fact that (8) no mind is a body. It could be true, however, both that a mind is a body and that a mind is a substance$_I$ relative to body, i.e., that it is possible that a mind's existence does not depend *causally* upon the existence of any *other* entity which is a body. If a mind is a body, its existence depends noncausally upon the body with which it is identical. When Descartes claims that a mind can exist "independently" of body, his point is that it is possible that a mind exists even though no material objects exist; a fortiori, it is possible that no mind is a body (and a mind is a substance$_l$ relative to body).[3]

His argument for (4), construed in this way, is that we can clearly and distinctly conceive of a mind existing but no body existing; whatever we can clearly and distinctly conceive is within God's power and hence possible; therefore, it is possible that no mind is a body (cf. HR I, 101, 190). I do not contend that this crucial argument is cogent. In order to establish (4), Descartes has to show that it really is conceivable that a mind exists but no body exists, and that the sort of conceivability in question is sufficient to establish metaphysical possibility.[4]

By (4), mind and body are really distinct substances$_S$, that is, it is possible that a mind is not identical to any body. Against this background, Descartes has available a straightforward argument for the claim that (3) a mind's essence (at least in part) is to think, and in turn that (5) a mind's whole essence is to think. We need two assumptions. The first is that every substance$_S$ has some essential property (cf. *PP* I, 53). The second is that thought, extension, and their modifications are the only properties an entity can have. (For

---

[3]On my interpretation, two substances are really distinct if they can exist, if it is possible for them to exist, apart from each other. Here I part company with some commentators—such as Schiffer, 1976, p. 37, and Williams, 1978, p. 115—who take the language of the "real distinction" at face value. On their reading, two substances are really distinct only if they are distinct in reality or actually nonidentical; and hence, the claim that (4) mind and body are really distinct substances$_S$ entails that (8) no mind is a body. I do not see how this interpretation can deal with the explicit definitions at *PP* I, 60 and HR II, 53. Williams cites a letter to Elizabeth (K 142–143) in support of his interpretation. Descartes writes, in what I take to be the relevant passage, that "conceiving... the distinction... between body and soul" requires that we "conceive them as two things." However, this might mean simply that we can conceive of the possibility of their being two things. In addition, there is no explicit discussion within this letter of the *real* distinction between body and soul. It may well be that Descartes intentionally introduced technical terminology that has a natural reading which is much stronger than the technical meaning he assigns to it. For an interpretation of the real distinction congenial to my own, see Wilson, 1978, pp. 185–200.

[4]For difficulties in connection with the move from conceivability to possibility, see Hooker, 1978b, especially pp. 176–178, 182–183.

the purposes of both assumptions, we waive properties, such as existence and duration, which any entity must possess.) Since by (4) it is possible that a mind is not identical to any body, a mind's essential property cannot be extension. It follows immediately that a mind's essence, and indeed its whole essence, is thought.[5] It is worth noting that it is extremely difficult to find in Descartes any argument which is explicitly advanced in support of (3) as distinct from (5) (cf. HR I, 101, 138, 190; II, 97; K 34).

Descartes' claim that (4) mind and body are really distinct substances$_S$ is, I believe, different from his claim that (6) mind and body are "essentially," "entirely," or "absolutely" distinct substances$_S$ (HR I, 101, 118, 140, 190, 196; K 87). By (5), a mind's whole essence is to think. Extension is essential to body. This is a background assumption throughout (cf. *PP* I, 53). By (4), it is possible that a mind is not identical to any body, and hence thought is not essential to body. Again assuming that thought, extension, and their modifications are the only properties an entity can have, it follows that extension is the whole essence of body. If a mind's whole essence is to think, and if extension is the whole essence of body, then (6) mind and body are essentially/entirely/absolutely distinct substances$_S$, in the sense that their essences have nothing in common. Thus Descartes often asserts (6) after arguing for (5) (HR I, 101, 190).

What about the claim that (8) no mind is a body? Descartes writes that (8) follows from (4): "*I . . . am really distinct from my body and can exist without it. It is easy from this to pass to the following:— every thing that can think is a mind or is called mind, but, since*

---

[5]Williams, 1978, pp. 116–117, 120, has attributed a closely related argument to Descartes. Of course, there are other attempts in the literature to provide Cartesian arguments for (3) and (5). Schiffer, 1976, esp. §III, pp. 31–39, prefers a reconstruction which does not rely upon my first assumption (though he does make use of my second assumption). Schiffer's reconstruction depends upon eliminating the possibility that "something can be at one and the same time both a mind and a body"; his own view is that nothing could possibly count as there being just one thing which is both a mind and a body. Descartes could not have been relying upon such an insight. This is because he wants to exploit (3) in order to establish that (8) no mind is a body. This is, indeed, Schiffer's own procedure. The famous reconstruction by Malcolm, 1965, attributes to Descartes an argument that is confessedly invalid (pp. 333–338). For additional criticism of Schiffer and Malcolm, see Williams, 1978, p. 120, and Schiffer, 1976, pp. 29–30, respectively.

mind and body are really distinct, no body is a mind; hence no body can think" (HR II, 32). And it is "easy to pass" from (4) to (8), for the arguments of the last two paragraphs yield the conclusions that a mind's essence (at least in part) is to think—(3); a body's essence is not (even in part) to think—by (6); it follows that (7) mind and body are contrary or exclusive substances$_S$ in the sense that they have incompatible properties; therefore, by Leibniz's Law, no mind is a body. There are a number of obvious variants of this sort of argument.[6]

Descartes does have one line of argument in support of (7) and (8) which is quite independent of claims (3–6). The idea is to show that whereas the mind is indivisible, body is divisible. The argument is developed in the *Meditations*, beginning in the "Synopsis": "*we cannot conceive of body excepting in so far as it is divisible, while the mind cannot be conceived of excepting as indivisible. For we are not able to conceive of the half of a mind as we can do of the smallest of all bodies; so that we see that not only are their natures different but even in some respects contrary to one another*" (HR I, 141). (It is worth noting that if for Descartes a body were an unobservable substance$_S$ in which extension somehow inheres, it would not be at all obvious that a body is divisible. The present line of argument would collapse if a material substance$_S$, like a thinking substance$_S$, were an unobservable-substratum-in-which-qualities-inhere. This supports my suggestion in section 7 that Descartes does not seriously believe in the existence of material substance$_S$ fully analogous to thinking substance$_S$.) This argument begs the question against those who hold that the mind is a body, and hence do conceive of the mind as divisible. The basic idea is elaborated somewhat differently in *Meditation VI*, where Descartes writes: "when I consider the mind, that is to say, myself inasmuch as I am only a thinking thing, I cannot distinguish in myself any parts, but apprehend myself to be clearly one and entire; and although the whole mind seems to be united to the whole body, yet if a foot, or an arm, or some other

---

[6]For closely related arguments, see Schiffer, 1976, pp. 38–39; Hooker, 1978b, §II; and Williams, 1978, pp. 116–117. It is sometimes held that there is a yet more direct route from (4) to (8) via a controversial modal principle: if it is possible that *x* and *y* are not identical, *x* and *y* are not identical (where '*x*' and '*y*' are purely referential expressions). For difficulties with this as an interpretation of Descartes, see Curley, 1978, pp. 201–206, and Williams, 1978, pp. 121–124.

part, is separated from my body, I am aware that nothing has been taken away from my mind" (HR I, 196). Descartes should have considered the result of separating from his body some part of his brain rather than a foot or an arm before concluding so confidently that the mind has no parts and is indivisible. The considerations relating to indivisibility do not provide a promising route to (8). I conclude that Descartes' principal arguments for the claim that (8) no mind is a body do depend upon the claims (3–6) about the real distinction between, and the essences of, mind and body. So much for Descartes' attempt to establish this necessary condition for immortality.

As noted earlier, in the "Synopsis" of the *Meditations* Descartes maintains that to prove that the soul is in fact immortal would require *"an elucidation of a complete system of Physics."* When his views on immortality come under some pressure in *Objections II* (HR II, 29), he permits himself to provide considerations which fall far short of such an elucidation, but which are "sufficient to let us conclude that the mind, so far as it can be known by aid of a natural philosophy, is immortal" (HR II, 47).

Over and above the complaint that *"you say not one word [in your Meditations] about the immortality of the human soul,"* the authors of *Objections II* raise the following point: *"it does not seem to follow from the distinction you draw between it* [the soul] *and the body that it is incorruptible or immortal. What if its nature be limited by the duration of the life of the body, and God has granted it only such a supply of force and has so measured out its existence that, in the cessation of the corporeal life, it must come to an end?"* (HR II, 29). The authors of the objection are apparently contemplating the possibility that God might program each soul so that it ceases to exist at the same time as the body associated with it, even though the body's death does not cause the soul's extinction—a preestablished harmony between soul and body with respect to their duration. In his reply, Descartes admits that this is a suggestion which he cannot refute:

> I admit that I cannot refute your . . . contention, viz. that *the immortality of the soul does not follow from its distinctness from the body, because that does not prevent its being said that God in creating it has given the soul a nature such that its period of existence must*

terminate simultaneously with that of the corporeal life. For I do not presume so far as to attempt to settle by the power of human reason any of the questions that depend upon the free-will of God. . . . If the question, which asks whether human souls cease to exist at the same time as the bodies which God has united to them are destroyed, is one affecting the Divine power, it is for God alone to reply. [HR II, 47]

There is a closely related contention, however, which Descartes is prepared to refute: the hypothesis that the death of the body causes the extinction of the soul.

Natural knowledge shows that the mind is different from the body, and that it is likewise a substance; but that the human body, in so far as it differs from other bodies, is constituted entirely by the configuration of its parts and other similar accidents, and finally that the death of the body depends wholly on some division or change of figure. But we know no argument or example such as to convince us that the death or the annihilation of a substance such as the mind is, should follow from so light a cause as is a change in figure, which is no more than a mode, and indeed not a mode of mind, but of body that is really distinct from mind. Nor indeed is there any argument or example calculated to convince us that any substance can perish. But this is sufficient to let us conclude that the mind, so far as it can be known by aid of a natural philosophy, is immortal. [HR II, 47]

Descartes rejects the possibility that "the death or the annihilation of. . . the mind. . . should follow from so light a cause as. . . a change of figure." In other words, (9) a mind's existence does not depend causally upon the existence of any body.

What about the content of Descartes' argument for (9)? In *Discourse IV*, he argued that it is conceivable and hence possible that a mind exists but that no body exists. This supports the conclusion that (4) mind and body are really distinct substances$_S$, that it is possible that a mind is not identical to any body; and also that a mind is a substance$_1$ relative to body, that *it is possible* that a mind's existence does not depend causally upon the existence of any other entity which is a body. But this result cannot be parlayed into the claim that (9) a mind's existence does not depend causally upon the existence of any body. Descartes obviously neds some new resources if he is to establish (9).

The heart of his argument is as follows: "we know no argument or example such as to convince us that the death or the annihilation of a substance such as the mind is, should follow from so light a cause as is a change in figure, which is no more than a mode, and indeed not a mode of mind, but of body that is really distinct from mind." Descartes invites us to picture both minds and bodies as substances$_s$ in which accidents or qualities (thoughts and figures, respectively) inhere. Earlier, he has construed the death of body as a change (of a certain sort) in figure. From this perspective, the possibility that a mind's existence depends causally upon the existence of body requires that changes in qualities of material substance$_s$ could cause thinking substance$_s$ itself to cease to exist. But this, Descartes holds, could not be the case. Why not? A change in figure (the death of the body) is too "light" a cause to bring about the annihilation of a mind. After all, whereas a mind is a substance$_s$, figure is "no more than" a mode, and indeed a mode of a substance$_s$ (body) that is really distinct from mind. What this amounts to is the a priori claim that qualities of material substance$_s$ could not and hence do not cause thinking substance$_s$ to cease to exist. Descartes' point that mind and body are "really distinct" is pure rhetorical flair and plays no role in the argument. He has admitted that immortality does not follow from the "real distinctness" of mind and body. To show that the mind is immortal, he falls back on the a priori assertion that thinking substance$_s$ and qualities of material substance$_s$ are so different, have so little in common, that the existence of the former could not and hence does not depend causally upon changes in the latter.

14. Mind-Body Interaction

We turn now from Descartes' "immortality claims," (1–9), to his remaining claims about minds, (10–12), which serve an entirely different purpose. They are propounded in order to do justice to certain initially attractive theses about the relationship between human minds and bodies—mind and body causally interact—and about the nature of a human being—a human being is "a single thing" composed of a mind and a body.

I begin with Descartes' claim that (10) mind and body causally interact. Prior to philosophical scrutiny, at least, this is an attractive thesis. We are all inclined to think that sometimes states of or events involving bodies are among the causes of our thoughts (in Descartes' broad sense), and that sometimes our thoughts are among the causes of states of or events involving bodies. For example, the dentist's drilling is a cause of a severe pain, and the desire that the dentist stop drilling is a cause of the patient's informing the dentist of the pain. Here we seem to have two-way mind-body interaction; states of or events involving bodies are among the causes of our thoughts, and our thoughts are among the causes of states of or events involving bodies. In propounding (10), Descartes is claiming that there exists two-way mind-body interaction.

Descartes' account of the locus of the interaction between mind and body is well known. There are various nerves and sense organs in our limbs. Physical changes in these nerves and organs cause "animal spirits," that is, material bodily fluids of extreme minuteness (*PAS* I, 10), to flow around the pineal gland, located in the middle of the brain. These fluids move this gland in diverse ways. Depending upon how the gland is moved, certain thoughts are produced in the soul. Thoughts can in turn cause slight changes in the direction of movement of the pineal gland. These movements cause the fluids around the gland to move in certain ways, affecting the flow of fluids to the nerves and organs throughout the body, eventuating in some physical act such as raising one's hand (*PAS* I, 30–34).

The details of this account are sometimes read as an admission of some difficulty with respect to mind-body interaction, for example: "the Cartesians faced the puzzle of how a nonspatial, immaterial soul could exert an influence upon inert matter. . . . Descartes tried to make things easier for the soul by having it influence motions of very fine and light 'animal spirits' rather than have it directly move heavy lumps of matter."[7] The suggestion is that Descartes attempts to mitigate the alleged difficulty by supposing that the causal chain from mind to muscles and limbs is intermediated by minute amounts of bodily fluids. This reading of the relevant texts, however, is unsupportable: the causal chain from mind to body runs from the mind directly to the pineal gland, and only then to the

---

[7]Kim, 1979, p. 31. This reading of Descartes is not idiosyncratic to Kim. I find that it periodically emerges in conversation about the mind-body problem in Descartes.

fluids and on to the muscles and limbs—the causal chain from body to mind is just the reverse (see especially *PAS* I, 31, 34).

In claiming that thoughts cause changes in the movement of the pineal gland, Descartes sometimes seems to be taking the position that a desire, for example, is itself causally sufficient for these changes in movement. Consider the following: "the whole action of the soul consists in this, that solely because it desires something, it causes the little gland to which it is closely united to move in the way requisite to produce the effect which relates to this desire" (*PAS* I, 41). This suggests an extraordinarily strong form of interactionism on which some mental state or event taken alone is causally sufficient for some bodily event. In general, interactionists need claim only that mental states or events are nonredundant factors in or components of some complex condition, which includes the presence of physical states and events, and which is causally sufficient for some bodily event. But it may be that Descartes adopts the strong form of interactionism. This is a fine point of interpretation. While it need not be settled for the purposes of the material in this chapter, it will prove to be of some importance at section 19.

The claim that (10) mind and body causally interact is relatively clear with respect to its content. I turn to Descartes' more obscure claims than (11) the mind functions immediately at the pineal gland, but is united to the entire human body and that (12) a human being consists of a mind and body so closely united as to constitute a single thing. For Descartes, a mind is not itself a human being. A human being consists of a mind and a body which stand in a certain relation to each other. What is that relation? Negatively, Descartes states that a human being is not simply a mind making use of a body, not a mind lodged in a body as a pilot in a vessel (HR I, 118, 192; II, 102). Positively, a human being consists of a mind and body which are so closely (or intimately) united (or joined, intermingled) as to constitute a single thing (one whole, a substantial unity) (HR I, 118, 142, 190, 192; II, 102). Further, the mind is united to (is joined to, informs) the entire human body, but it has its principal seat in the pineal gland, where it exercises its functions immediately (*PAS* I, 31).

Given Descartes' claim that (10) mind and body causally interact, we can go a long way toward unpacking the metaphors in his account of the nature of a human being, of the relationship between a human being's mind and body. The key is to construe the metaphors causally. I begin with (11). Descartes was sensitive to a distinction between proximate and nonproximate causation (cf. *PAS* I, 29). The mind is "united" to the entire human body because the mind can cause physical movements throughout the human body. For example, a desire causes the raising of one's hand. The mind is not the immediate or proximate cause of this event—there is an intermediating causal process: the raising of one's hand is caused by changes in the nerves, in turn caused by the flow of fluids, in turn caused by changes in the movements of the pineal gland, in turn caused by a desire in the mind. The mind is the immediate or proximate cause of changes in the movement of the pineal gland; it causes such changes, or more precisely the initiation of such changes, without any intermediating causal process. The mind is never the immediate or proximate cause of any physical state or event except a change in the movement of the pineal gland. The mind is "united" to the entire body (including the pineal gland) because it is either a proximate or a nonproximate cause of physical states and events throughout the body; the mind is united "im-mediately" to, or has its "principal seat" in, the pineal gland in that it is a proximate cause of physical states and events involving that gland. Similarly, changes in the movements of the pineal gland are proximate causes of thoughts, but other physical states and events are only nonproximate causes of thoughts. Gassendi objects to Descartes' claim that the mind is united to the entire human body on the ground that the mind would then be divisible, whereas Descartes claims it is not (HR II, 198). Such objections are irrelevant since they construe the sense in which the mind is "united" to the body spatially. It is the causal construal of such metaphors which makes sense of Descartes' language.[8]

---

[8]It is needlessly unsympathetic for Williams, 1978, pp. 289–290 to write: "There is no one sense in which the soul is joined to every part of the body, but particularly connected with the gland. . . . In the supposed causal sense of 'joined', . . . the soul is joined to the body only at the pineal gland, and not anywhere else." The soul is "joined" in the causal sense to the entire body, though it is a proximate cause only with respect to the pineal gland. Mattern, 1978, esp. pp. 217–219, suggests that whereas in the *Meditations* and the *Principles* the union of mind and body "is really nothing more than certain special capacities of mind-

What about the claim that (12) a human being consists of a mind and body so closely united as to constitute a single thing? Mind and body are united in that they interact causally. This fact alone does not explain why a person's mind and body constitute a single thing or one whole. The bodies of two different people causally interact without constituting a single thing. Similarly, the mere fact that a mind and body causally interact does not explain why the relation of mind to body is not like that of pilot to vessel. Pilot and vessel causally interact without constituting a single thing. The fact of causal interaction provides a sense in which mind and body are united, but it does not in itself explain why they constitute a single thing.

Descartes was sensitive to such difficulties:

> It is not sufficient that it [the soul] should be lodged in a human body like a pilot in his ship, . . . but . . . it is necessary that it should also be joined and united more closely to the body in order to have sensations and appetites similar to our own, and thus to form a true man. [HR I, 118]

---

body interaction," in the correspondence with Elizabeth, Descartes holds that the mind is genuinely intermingled with, diffused throughout, coextensive with the body "in a manner irreducible to mere interaction." Mattern contends that what Descartes says in the correspondence "presupposes that the concept of union is not the same as the concept of interaction" and that this "is especially evident when Descartes writes that our concept of mind-body interaction depends on the concept of their union." But this is not quite what Descartes does write: "as regards soul and body together, we have only the notion of their union, on which depends our notion of the soul's power to move the body, and the body's power to act on the soul and cause sensations and passions" (K 138). It hardly follows that the concept of the union has any explanatory function. An alternative reading is simply that the mind's acting upon the body and the body's acting upon the mind are two species of the union. Mattern concedes that Descartes' view "appears to vacillate in a peculiar way, since the letters to Elizabeth followed the *Meditations* but preceded the *Principles*," and proceeds to attempt an explanation. She does not consider the obvious possibility that whatever hints there are in the correspondence with Elizabeth to the effect that the mind is genuinely coextensive with the body do not represent Descartes' considered position. One cannot simply ignore the fact that the 28 June 1643 letter to Elizabeth closes with the less than subtle suggestion that the princess would not be well advised to continue to pursue the principles of metaphysics. Wilson, 1978, pp. 211–213, argues that the view that the mind is coextensive with the body resurfaces in *The Passions of the Soul*. However, the passages she cites (PAS I, 30, 31) are easily neutralized by reference to the distinction between proximate and nonproximate causation.

But there is nothing which this nature teaches me more ex-
pressly . . . than that I have a body which is adversely affected when I
feel pain, which has need of food or drink when I experience the
feelings of hunger and thirst, and so on. . . .

Nature also teachers me by these sensations of pain, hunger,
thirst, etc., that I am not only lodged in my body as a pilot in a
vessel, but that I am very closely united to it, and so to speak so
intermingled with it that I seem to compose with it one whole. For if
that were not the case, when my body is hurt, I, who am merely a
thinking thing, should not feel pain, for I should perceive this wound
by the understanding only, just as the sailor perceives by sight when
something is damaged in his vessel. [HR I, 192]

It may be concluded also that a certain body is more closely united to
our mind than any other, from the fact that pain and other of our
sensations occur without our forseeing them; and . . . arise . . . in so
far as it [the mind] is united to another thing, extended and mobile,
which is called the human body. [*PP* II, 2]

In these passages, Descartes is in effect sketching a theory of the
conditions under which it is true that a given body is the body of
some particular mind or person. And he is sketching a "causal
theory" in particular. A crude causal theory would hold that a body
is (at least a part of) the body of some particular mind or person just
in case that body causally interacts with that person. This obviously
fails to provide a sufficient condition; there is causal interaction
between my body and the minds of other persons, but my body is
not theirs. Descartes' idea is that what makes a body mine is that my
mind experiences sensations such as pain in response to physical
states of that body[9]

[9]The theory which I attribute to Descartes is closely related to what Wilson,
1978, calls the "Natural Institution" theory of mind-body union: "On the Natural
Institution view, the difference between 'our' relation to 'our own' bodies, and our
relations to other bodies is that certain changes in our bodies . . . frequently result
in motions in our brains that, by God's institution, give rise to particular sort of
experiences in the mind that the mind tends to locate in the body itself" (pp.
210–211). The principal difference between a causal theory of the sort which I
attribute to Descartes, and the Natural Institution theory as characterized by Wilson, is that the latter builds into the theory the thesis that the relevant causal
connections are instituted by God. In support of this, Wilson quotes a passage
where Descartes states, "Of course the nature of man could have been so constituted by God that that same motion in the brain would exhibit something else to
the mind" (p. 208). This is a thin textual basis for emphasizing God's role since on
Descartes' view even the "eternal truths" (which include many intuitively necessary

Developing this idea into a precise criterion would be a difficult matter. My mind might experience a feeling of nausea upon seeing your hand cut, but your hand is not a part of my body. The pilot might feel nauseous upon seeing his ship disabled, but the ship is no part of the pilot's body. Descartes could attempt to exploit either of two features of such cases in order to develop a more adequate criterion. First, these cases involve *seeing* certain states of bodies, whereas this is not usually required when we experience sensations of our own bodies. In other words, in these cases the causal mechanism that results in the sensation is not of an appropriate sort. Second, the cases cited are relatively *occasional*. In other words, the sensations of a given mind depend in a much more regular way upon states of its own body than upon states of other bodies. (Indeed, the presence of causal mechanisms of the appropriate sort might insure such a regular dependence.) Descartes' fundamental claim is that a body is the body of a particular person just in case the body is causally connected in the appropriate way to that person or mind; and that when a mind and body are so connected, they constitute a single thing, one whole, or a unity—a human being.[10]

truths) are dependent upon God's will, as Wilson herself emphasizes (pp. 33–34, 120–131, 136). In any case, Wilson raises an objection to show "why it is not possible to ascribe to Descartes consistent adherence to the rather austere Natural Institution conception of embodiment" (p. 211), which, if correct, would apply equally to the causal theory of embodiment. The objection is that in a passage Wilson cites, "Descartes is surely saying that one has sensations of a certain sort, in response to changes in a certain body, *because* one is united with that body—not that having sensations of a certain sort, etc. is what *it is* to be united to that body" (p. 211). Descartes does characterize the sensations as "arising from the union." This need not present any difficulty: what *it is* to be united with a certain body is that "changes in our bodies... frequently result in motions in our brains that... give rise to particular sort of experiences in the mind"; this is not incompatible with saying of particular experiences or sensations that they arise *because* one is united to that body, that is, as a result of the operation of the mechanisms whose presence insures that the person is united to that body. Consider this analogy: what *it is* (we might say) for our telephones to be "united" is that there exist mechanisms which insure that my dialing a certain number frequently results in your telephone ringing; this is compatible with saying that when your phone rings on a particular occasion it is *because* of this union, that is, a result of the operation of those mechanisms.

[10]Beyond the need to work out the details, there is another difficulty for Descartes' sketchy theory. It might be objected that whereas Descartes places all the emphasis upon my ability to experience sensations as a causal consequence of a given body's being in a particular state, an important aspect of a body's being mine

Whereas Descartes typically states that a human being consists of a mind and body so closely united as to constitute a single thing or one whole, he occasionally states that the mind and body constitute a "substantial union" (HR II, 102; K 130). This flourish adds little content to the claim that mind and body constitute a single thing.[11] Consider the following passages:

> I do not ignore the fact that certain substances are popularly called *incomplete substances*. But if they are said to be incomplete, because they cannot exist by themselves . . . , I confess it seems to me to be a contradiction for them to be substances; i.e. for them to be things subsisting by themselves and at the same time incomplete, i.e. not capable of subsisting by themselves. But it is true that in another sense they can be called incomplete substances; viz. in a sense which allows that, in so far as they are substances, they have no lack of completeness, and merely asserts that they are incomplete in so far as they are referred to some other substance, in unison with which they form a single self-subsistent thing. . . .
>
> Thus, the hand is an incomplete substance, when taken in relation with the body, of which it is a part; but, regarded alone, it is a complete substance. Quite in the same way mind and body are incomplete substances viewed in relation to the man who is the unity which together they form; but, taken alone, they are complete. [HR II, 99]
>
> Likewise, just as one who said that a man's arm was a substance really distinct from the rest of his body, would not therefore deny that it belonged to the nature of the complete man, and as in saying that the arm belongs to the nature of the complete man no suspicion

---

is that I have a special ability to move it (as when I raise my hand because I want to). Typically, parts of a person's body satisfy both these conditions, but Descartes' theory ignores the latter. Descartes could respond that while this complication does suggest that his theory might be incomplete, to the extent that the objection is correct, it just strengthens the case for his fundamental approach, an attempt to provide a causal theory of a person's body. After all, he believes in two-way causal interaction. My ability to move parts of my body depends upon the fact that wants or desires of mine cause parts of my body to move. So if any adequate theory here would have to take into account both the fact that persons experience bodily sensations and that persons can move their bodies, any adequate theory wll be doubly causal. It will appeal to causal connections of an appropriate sort both between states of bodies and sensations and between mental states and bodily movements.

[11]Thus I agree with Williams, 1978, p. 280, that Descartes "says that the mind is 'substantially united' with the body . . . , but the surrounding explanations make it clear how little metaphysical weight Descartes gives to such formulations."

is raised that it cannot subsist by itself, so I think that I have neither proved too much in showing that mind can exist apart from body, nor yet too little in saying that it is substantially united to the body, because that substantial union does not prevent the formation of a clear and distinct concept of the mind alone as of a complete thing. [HR ɪɪ, 102–103]

Descartes' point is that the single thing, the human being, which consists of a mind and body united (causally connected) in the appropriate way is a secondary-substance$_I$. A human being is itself an entity such that it is possible that its existence does not depend causally upon the existence of any other entity except God. This is consistent with the claim that minds and bodies are themselves secondary-substances$_I$. A mind is a simple secondary-substance$_I$ in the sense that it has no parts which are secondary-substances$_I$. A human being is a compound secondary-substance$_I$ in the sense that it does have parts which are themselves secondary-substances$_I$.

This completes my exposition of claims (10–12), which I label the "interaction claims," for obvious reasons. They all relate to Descartes' views about mind-body interaction: (10) formulates the fact of interaction; (11) relates more specifically to the locus of interaction; and (12) captures the intuition that the interaction is of a sort appropriate to support the claim that a human being consisting of mind and body is a unity.

15. The Alleged Incoherence of Descartes' Interactionism

It is frequently maintained that Descartes was involved in an incoherence in his commitment to the claim that (10) mind and body causally interact, and a fortiori in his commitment to the remaining interaction claims, at least if the metaphor of the mind's "union" with the body is unpacked causally. The basis for the allegation of incoherence is potent enough to have led to one of the more curious episodes in the history of the history of philosophy. S. V. Keeling, convinced that there would have been a blatant incoherence in Descartes' position had he held (10), maintains, in what is otherwise a scholarly classic, that Descartes denied that (10) mind and body causally interact. He writes: "The conviction with which we ordinarily believe that mind interacts with body, and body with mind, is of the strongest; it is presupposed in all our daily behaviour, both reflective and involuntary. What Descartes denies, however, is not the strength of this conviction but its truth." There is some superficial terminological evidence for Keeling's position, that Descartes was (in some sense) an occasionalist.[12] But the fact remains that the whole of Part I of *The Passions of the Soul* is devoted to an account of mind-body interaction. The basis for the allegation of incoherence must have had such a strong hold on Keeling that he effectively ignored such evidence.

It is striking that whereas many philosophers and commentators subscribe to the allegation of incoherence, Descartes seems to find mind-body interaction both obvious and unproblematic. He wrote to Princess Elizabeth: "There are two facts about the human soul on which depend all the things we can know of its nature. The first is that it thinks, the second is that it is united to the body and can act and be acted upon along with it" (K 137). He writes to Arnauld, a philosopher rather than a princess and patroness: "That the mind, which is incorporeal, can set the body in motion—this is something which is shown to us not by any reasoning or comparison with other matters, but by the surest and plainest everyday experience" (K 235). And in response to Burman's query "But how can this be, and how can the soul be affected by the body and vice versa, when their natures are completely different?", Descartes responds that "here our experience is sufficient, since it is so clear on this point that it just cannot be gainsaid" (CB 44).

The striking discrepancy between the attitudes of Descartes and proponents of the allegation of incoherence cries out for explanation.[13] If Descartes' claim that (10) mind and body causally interact does generate some deep incoherence in his system, either his statements about interaction were disingenuous, or he was especially obtuse, blind, or thick-skinned when it came to recognizing that incoherence. Before opting for either explanation, we should attempt to locate the basis for the allegation of incoherence.

[12]For the quotation, together with the putative evidence for his position, see Keeling, 1968, pp. 154 and 156, n. 1.

[13]The discrepancy has been stressed previously by L. J. Beck, 1965, pp. 269–276.

Precisely why was Descartes involved in an incoherence in claiming that (10) mind and body causally interact? Our question is not whether or not it is true that mind and body causally interact. We want to know why it was objectionable in the context of his philosophical works, written in the first half of the seventeenth century, for Descartes to have put forward the claim that mind and body causally interact. In this section, I will discuss three aspects of Descartes' philosophy which might be thought to conflict with his claim that (10) mind and body causally interact: (i) his claim that (6) mind and body are essentially/entirely/absolutely distinct substances$_S$; (ii) his restrictions upon possible causal relations; and (iii) his doctrine of the freedom of the will.

(i) I believe that most philosophers and commentators who have held that there is an incoherence in Descartes' position have been principally troubled by the feeling that it was inconsistent for him to hold both that (10) mind and body causally interact and that (6) mind and body are essentially/entirely/absolutely distinct substances$_S$, i.e., that the essences of mind and body have nothing in common (since a mind's whole essence is to think, a body's whole essence to be extended).[14] For example, this is at least a good part of Keeling's concern when he writes: "The defining attributes of body and of mind being wholly different and mutually exclusive, direct causal interaction between them, he [Descartes] maintains, is necessarily impossible." Similarly, we have it from two Descartes scholars writing in the late 1960s:

> The fragmentation of the human being into two distinct substances presented Descartes with an acute and ultimately devastating difficulty: how to fit the pieces together again. . . . Since thought and motion have *ex hypothesi* nothing in common (motion presupposing extension), it is very hard to see how the translation of specific thoughts . . . into specific bodily motions, or of specific bodily motions into thoughts . . . can be rendered intelligible.

> On Descartes' principles it is difficult to see how an unextended thinking substance can cause motion in an extended unthinking substance and how the extended unthinking substance can cause sensations in the unextended thinking substance. The properties of the two kinds of substance seem to place them in such diverse categories that it is impossible for them to interact.

[14]One notable exception is Williams, 1978, pp. 288–292.

The general point behind these passages, I take it, is that the immense or radical qualitative difference between mind and body is such as to render interaction impossible—mind and body have too little in common for interaction to take place.[15]

It is somewhat shocking to see such objections raised after Hume, without any attempt to reinstate the notion that there must be some specific degree of qualitative similarity between cause and effect. And from a scholarly rather than philosophical perspective, such objections simply overlook Descartes' own foreshadowing of a Humean, constant conjunction, or regularity analysis of causation:

> There is no reason to be surprised that certain motions of the heart should be naturally connected in this way with certain thoughts, which they in no way resemble. The soul's natural capacity for union with a body brings with it the possibility of an association between thoughts and bodily motions or conditions so that when the same conditions recur in the body they impel the soul to the same thought; and conversely when the same thought recurs, it disposes the body to return to the same condition. [K 210]

Descartes sees no problem for the view that physical events cause mental events "which they in no way resemble." His position is that pointing to the qualitative difference between mind and body is insufficient to show that their causal interaction is impossible. Simply labeling the difference "immense" or "radical" does not magically preclude causal interaction. The critic must explain precisely why specific qualitative differences between mind and body render interaction impossible. Until such time, Descartes persists in a disarming reply to those who hold that an unextended thinking substance$_S$ cannot interact with body. While the mind is not "corporeal" in the sense of being "made up of the sort of substance called body," nevertheless there is a good sense in which the mind is corporeal: "If 'corporeal' is taken to mean anything which can in any way affect a body, then the mind too must be called corporeal in this sense" (K 112). So Descartes writes to Hyperaspistes; the point is repeated in correspondence with both Elizabeth and Arnauld (K 141, 236).

[15]The three quotations are from: Keeling, 1968, p. 153; Wilson, 1969, pp. xxix–xxx; and Kenny, 1968, pp. 222–223.

Descartes was simply unmoved by the sort of objection we are considering. He writes Claude Clerselier, in the *Replies:* "As for the two questions added at the end, viz.—*how the soul moves the body if it is not material? and how it can receive the specific forms of corporeal objects?* ... I declare that the whole of the perplexity involved in these questions arises entirely from a false supposition that can by no manner of means be proved, viz. that if the soul and the body are two substances of diverse nature, that prevents them of being capable of acting on one another" (HR II, 131–132). Descartes' position is that from the mere fact that two substances are "of diverse nature," that is, that they differ in nature or essence, it does not follow that they cannot causally interact. In other words, the fact that (6) mind and body are essentially/entirely/absolutely distinct substances$_S$ does not prevent interaction between them.

The principle that cause and effect must be similar in essence plays a crucial role in Richard A. Watson's *Downfall of Cartesianism, 1673–1712.* Watson purports to exhibit a "major defect" in Cartesianism, and to "show that not only is it a sufficient reason, it is also the actual cause of the downfall of Cartesian metaphysics." The defect (in large measure) is that a "Cartesian metaphysical system" holds, inconsistently, that mind and matter differ in essence; that mind and matter causally interact; and that "there must be essential likeness between a cause and its effect." In light of the passage from Descartes which I have just cited, it would be a mistake to suppose that Watson has located any inconsistency in *Descartes'* metaphysics. (It should be noted that Watson does not attribute his "causal likeness principle" to Descartes. He incorporates this principle into his formulation of "a late 17th century" Cartesian metaphysical system on the ground that "such a model Cartesianism" appears in "the polemical writing of Simon Foucher"; Foucher, as a consequence of *his interpretation* of Descartes, "assumed that a basic principle of Cartesianism" is that there must be an "essential likeness" between cause and effect.)[16]

[16]Watson, 1966, pp. 3, 29, 33, 34, 147. It should be noted that I am not here criticizing Watson; I am pointing out that nothing in his book tells against my position that there is no inconsistency here in the case of Descartes. For Watson, the downfall of Cartesianism is the downfall of "the basic metaphysical position" of "orthodox Cartesians," namely Rohault, La Forge, Régis, and Le Grand, and, to a lesser extent, Desgabets and Arnauld (p. 29). For a critical review of Watson on his own terms, see Sebba, 1970, pp. 251–262.

It might be objected that the passage from the letter to Clerselier should be treated more circumspectly. Have I not ignored overwhelming evidence that Descartes himself perceived some incompatibility between claims (10) and (6)? Did not Descartes claim that (12) a human being consists of a mind and body so closely united as to constitute a single thing, and indeed a substantial unity, precisely because he himself saw that two substances$_S$ which differ in essence could not causally interact? On this interpretation, the doctrine of the substantial union is an attempt to explain the possibility of mind-body interaction, in the face of the fact that they differ in essence, by bringing mind and body together within a single substance, in a substantial union.[17]

I reject this interpretation. First, it is uncharitable in the extreme, since from this perspective the doctrine of the "substantial union" would be more the name for a problem than for a solution. Second, Descartes simply does not appeal to the "substantial union" in contexts where he can reasonably be construed as attempting to explain the possibility of interaction between mind and body. The passages where he refers explicitly to a "substantial union" are few and far between. When he states in *Reply to Objections I* that mind and body are "substantially united" (HR II, 102), he is replying to the objection that his argumentation "proves too much" because it has the result that a human is "a spirit that makes use of a body" (HR II, 84); when he states in a letter to Henricus Regius that there is a "substantial union" between mind and body, he is responding to Regius' discomfort with Descartes' claim that a human being is an *ens per accidens* (K 130). In both contexts, Descartes is attempting to

---

[17]Here is a recent example of the widespread assumption that Descartes invokes the doctrine of the substantial union in order to explain the possibility of mind-body interaction: "what we have said shows that one need not interpret the notion of substantial union *in terms of* interaction of parts. Such a suggestion would help us to do justice to Descartes' claim that the notion of union is—in some as yet unspecified way—able to explain the fact or the nature of mind-body interaction" (Broughton and Mattern, 1978, p. 32). That Descartes had such an explanatory function in mind for the doctrine of the substantial union is by and large an unargued presupposition for this article. It is noteworthy that commentators (other than myself) who take at face value Descartes' frequent claims that mind-body interaction is a plain fact of experience, do not find an explanatory function in the doctrine of the substantial union, but rather interpret the doctrine along the lines I have suggested, as an attempt to do justice to the unity of the human being. See, for example, L. J. Beck, 1965, pp. 262–268.

do justice to the intuition that a human being is a single thing, one whole, a unity—better yet if he can say a human being is a substantial unity, albeit in the sense discussed in the preceding section. By contrast, in the letter to Clerselier, Descartes is responding specifically to such questions as "*how the soul moves the body if it is not material? and how it can receive the specific forms of corporeal objects?*", but there is no appeal to the *substantial* union of mind and body; and in the famous letter to Elizabeth of 28 June 1643, in which Descartes attempts to allay her qualms with respect to mind-body interaction, there is again no appeal to the *substantial* union. All this seems to confirm what I have stressed: that Descartes found mind-body interaction obvious on empirical grounds, and unproblematic. He simply does not recognize the problem that commentators have taken the doctrine of the substantial union as attempting to solve.

(ii) Descartes does not impose the restriction that there must be a likeness in essence between cause and effect. So the mere fact that mind and body differ in essence does not preclude causal interaction between them. But Descartes does impose other restrictions upon possible causal relations, and perhaps it is these, when coupled with differences between mind and body in particular, which generate some inconsistency. I have in mind in particular his assertion in *Meditation III*, for the purposes of his causal arguments for the existence of God, that "there must at least be as much reality in the efficient and total cause as in its effect" (HR I, 162). Descartes equates "reality" and "perfection" (HR I, 162; II, 56); so his principle is that the efficient and total cause must be at least as perfect as its effect. In other words, the cause must be "like" the effect in the sense that the cause is at least as perfect as the effect.

This principle can preclude interaction between mind and body only when coupled with some doctrine about the relative degree of perfection of various entities. It is clear that for Descartes a substance is more perfect than a mode, and an infinite and independent substance more perfect than a finite and dependent substance (HR II, 71). The latter point is of no relevance because neither mind nor body is infinite and independent. Whether or not there is an inconsistency would therefore seem to depend upon how Descartes construed his claim that (10) mind and body causally interact. There is no inconsistency if Descartes subscribes to any of the following models of mind-body interaction: (*a*) thinking substance causes material substance, and vice versa; (*b*) thinking substance causes modes of material substance, and material substance causes modes of thinking substance; (*c*) modes of thinking substance cause modes of material substance, and vice versa. An inconsistency arises only if (*d*) modes of thinking substance cause material substance itself (as distinct from its modes), and modes of material substance cause thinking substance itself (as distinct from its modes). With (*d*), we do have an apparent inconsistency—something less perfect (a mode) causing something more perfect (a substance). There is no reason to believe, however, that (*d*) was Descartes' model of mind–body interaction; and every reason to believe that it was not. It seems to require, for example, that thinking substances, that is, minds or spirits, are themselves caused by something material, rather than by God.

While it is conceivable that there is in Descartes some further set of doctrines about perfection which is relevant to the possibility of mind-body interaction, I believe that continuing to speculate along these lines is quite unnecessary. This is because Descartes' principle imposes a restriction only upon "the efficient and total cause." Descartes writes to Mersenne: "It is certain that there is nothing in an effect *which is not contained formally or eminently in its EFFI-CIENT and TOTAL cause*. I added these two words on purpose. The sun and the rain are not the total cause of the animals they generate" (K 91). In order to generate an inconsistency with Descartes' restrictions upon causation, one would have to show—whatever his model of mind-body interaction, whether (*d*) above or otherwise—that he held that the relevant causes are efficient and total causes.[18]

---

[18]Radner, 1978b, pp. 11–12, argues that Descartes cannot consistently hold that mind and body are entirely different in nature, and that mind and body causally interact, and that "a thing cannot communicate or impart to another what it does not possess in itself." Radner maintains that from this last principle "it seems to follow that the substance which acts and the substance acted upon must resemble one another, at least to the extent of being able to possess the same sorts of modifications." Her sole citation in this connection is HR I, 162. I have shown in the text that Descartes is committed only to the thesis that the efficient and total cause must be at least as perfect as its effect.

We have been considering Descartes' principle that the *cause* must be "like" the *effect* in the sense that the cause must be at least as perfect as the effect. He also holds that the *effect* must be "like" its cause. But in what sense? The principle emerges in the conversation with Burman (*CB* 24). Descartes states: "It is a common axiom and a true one that *the effect is like the cause.* Now God is the cause of me, and I am an effect of him, so it follows that I am like him." Burman objects: "But a builder is the cause of a house, yet for all that the house is not like him." Burman has not yet understood this common axiom, for Descartes replies: "He is not the cause of the house, in the sense in which we are taking the word here. . . . We are talking about the total cause, the cause of being itself. Anything produced by *this* cause must necessarily be like it. For since the cause is itself being and substance, and it brings something into being, . . . what is produced must at the very least be being and substance." The principle here is that the effect must be "like" its total cause in that both must be being and substance. This is not going to preclude mind-body interaction.

Descartes does impose restrictions upon possible causal relations, upon the extent to which the cause must be "like" the effect, and vice versa. Two points about these restrictions are worth noting. First, both principles apply only to "the efficient and total cause." Second, both are introduced in theological contexts. The principle that the cause must be "like" the effect is introduced for the purposes of proving the existence of God. The principle that the effect must be "like" the cause is introduced to show that Burman is wrong in his suggestion that surely God could have created humans not in his own image—we are and must be in the image of God, in the sense of "having some resemblance" with God, *qua* "being and substance." These points are not unrelated. Both principles are introduced for specifically religious purposes, to show that (roughly) if I have an idea of God, God must have caused me; and that if God caused me, I must be like God. Where the relevant cause is God, we are (presumably) dealing with a total cause. Descartes has no need to state either of his restrictions upon possible causal relations in a more general form (where they would apply to causes which are not "total"), and he refrains from doing so. I conclude that he does not impose any restrictions upon the extent to which cause and effect are like one another which would preclude mind-body interaction.[19]

(iii) It has been maintained that Descartes' claim that (10) mind and body causally interact is inconsistent with his doctrine of the freedom of the will. This sort of theme is to be found in Norman Kemp Smith, writing at the turn of the century: "Being always careful to respect, even in minor matters, the doctrines of the Church, he not only conforms to the theological doctrine of the freedom of the will in all its absoluteness, but insists on it in a way that shows his conformity to be complete. To it he is ready to sacrifice his most cherished convictions, even his rationalism." According to Bertrand Russell, Descartes' allowance that "a human soul could, by volition, alter the direction though not the quantity of the motion of the animal spirits . . . was contrary to the spirit of the system." Margaret Wilson makes the point fully explicit:

> Another aspect of the Cartesian problem of mind-body interaction has to do with the issue of free-will. One plausible motivation for introducing the notion of mental substance is to provide a locus for the operation of freedom or spontaneity within the clock-work universe of seventeenth-century physics. Descartes, in any case, claimed that freedom of the will is "self-evident". . . . But if the actions of mind have effects in the world of matter, it appears that ideterminacy in the former realm will infect the latter. . . . The motions of my body and their sequels in the material world . . . will also be irregular and indeterminate.

What are we to make of this suggestion? My own position is that Descartes did not hold, as is commonly assumed, that there is any indeterminacy in the realm of the mental.[20]

I agree with Wilson that one possible motivation for introducing the notion of mental substances derives from the desire to sustain a particular position with respect to free will and determinism. What I

[19]Wilson, 1978, p. 215, writes that Descartes' interactionism "is in apparent conflict with his various espousals of the 'like cause, like effect' principle." The context provides no reason to think that for Wilson the conflict is "merely" apparent. In any case, she provides no supporting argument.

[20]The quotations are from Smith, 1902, p. 112; Russell, 1945, p. 568; and Wilson, 1969, p. xxx. Williams, 1978. pp. 275–276 (cf. pp. 174–175), also holds that Descartes' views about the will commit him to indeterminism, though he does not offer this as a criticism.

have in mind is this. Consider the position of an "incompatibilist," who holds that if determinism is true, no human action is free, but who wants to insist that some human actions are free. One option is to embrace a straightforward indeterminist account of free action, on which an action is free just in case it is caused by a desire which is itself uncaused. (On a less plausible version, an action is free just in case it is itself uncaused.) One standard objection to this indeterminist account of free action is that if the desire causing an action is indeed uncaused, then it is not caused by the agent in particular; under these circumstances, it is unclear that the agent is responsible for the desire and the ensuing action, since the agent's possession of the relevant desire seems to be completely outside of his control.

This sort of consideration tends to push the incompatibilist away from the straightforward indeterminist account of free action, to the theory that desires are caused, not by preceding states or events of any sort, but by the agent or person himself, that is, by an object of a special sort. The theory hopes to avoid the objection against straightforward indeterminist accounts of free action in virtue of the hypothesis that the desire is caused by the agent and hence is within his control. But since the proponent of the theory holds that if determinism is true, no human action is free, some element of indeterminism is inevitably reintroduced. In particular, the theory hopes to avoid what the incompatibilist considers to be the pitfall of determinism in virtue of the additional hypothesis that the agent's causing the desire is not itself caused by preceding states or events of any sort. In other words, the self determines its desires, but is not itself causally determined to do so. This is the theory of "agent-causation" or "self-determination." On some versions of this theory, the agent is identified with the soul. Thomas Reid was an early proponent of the theory of self-determination, and Malebranche earlier yet (§ 23).[21]

Our question, then, is whether Descartes embraced some version of the theory of self-determination, invoking the soul "to provide a locus for the operation of freedom." I believe this question can be answered in the negative, on the ground that Descartes was in fact a

[21]See Reid, 1788, Essay IV, "Of the Liberty of Moral Agents."

"compatibilist" or "soft determinist," holding that free actions are those actions which are causally determined in a certain sort of way. If this is correct, Descartes would not have been tempted either by the straightforward indeterminist account of free action, or by the theory of self-determination spawned by objections to it. He certainly believed in "freedom of the will" (*Med. IV; PP* I, 41). At issue is what sort of account he would want to give of this notion.

There is substantial direct evidence that Descartes was a compatibilist. In *Meditation IV*, he attempts to explain how it is that an omniscient, omnipotent, nondeceiving God could allow humans to err or hold false beliefs. This is the epistemological variant of the traditional problem of evil. Descartes' response has something to do with free will or the power of judgment. But what? Consider the following passages:

> The faculty of will... consists alone in the fact that in order to affirm or deny, pursue or shun those things placed before us by the understanding, we act so that we are unconscious that any outside force constraints [*contraigne*] us in doing so. [HR I, 175]

> When I lately examined whether anything existed in the world, and found that from the very fact that I considered this question it followed very clearly that I myself existed, I could not prevent myself from believing that a thing I so clearly conceived was true: not that I found myself compelled [*forcé*] to do so by some external cause, but simply because from great clearness in my mind there followed a great inclination of my will. [HR I, 176]

These passages do not locate free will in the absence of causal determination, but rather in the absence of constraint or compulsion. In the second passage, Descartes is explicit that his belief or will *was* determined, by the clarity of his perception, though it was not compelled. This is the soft determinist position that actions are free just in case they are not "constrained" and not "compelled."

There is strong confirmation of my interpretation in a letter to Elizabeth:

> I turn to your Highness' problem about free will. I will try to give an illustration to explain how this is both dependent and free. Suppose that a King has forbidden duels, and knows with certainty that two gentlemen of his kingdom who live in different towns have a quarrel, and are so hostile to each other that if they meet nothing will stop them from fighting. If this King orders one of them to go on a certain

day to the town where the other lives, and orders the other to go on the same day to the place where the first is, he knows with certainty that they will meet, and fight, and thus disobey his prohibition; but none the less he does not compel them, and his knowledge, and even his will to make them act thus, does not prevent their fighting when they meet being as voluntary and as free as if they had met on some other occasion and he had known nothing about it. And they can be justly punished for disobeying the prohibition. Now what a King can do in such a case, concerning certain free actions of his subjects, God, with His infinite foresight and power does infallibly in regard to all the free actions of all men. Before He sent us into the world He knew exactly what all the inclinations of our will would be; it is He who gave us them. [K 188–189]

Here again, we have a distinction between unfree actions which are compelled, and free actions which are causally determined, but in a way which does not involve compulsion.

I believe that any doubt about Descartes' position can be removed on the basis of evidence in *Meditation IV*. This meditation is something of a case book containing many of the standard moves with respect to the problem of evil, albeit with special reference to epistemological evil or error. In the fourth paragraph, Descartes raises the possibility that error "is not a real thing . . . , but simply a defect" (HR I, 173); in the fifth paragraph, he rejects this solution. In the sixth paragraph, he raises the possibility that error has some final cause beyond his own knowledge, but he does not pursue this. In the seventh paragraph, he raises the possibility that the apparent imperfection of "one single creature" might be "found to be very perfect if regarded as part of the whole universe" (HR I, 173–174); Descartes does not reject this approach, though he points out that he has not yet established that there are any creatures other than himself and God.

It is in the eighth paragraph that Descartes begins his discussion of what has come to be called "the free will defense." The passages I have quoted which suggest that for him an action is free if unconstrained and uncompelled occur in the eighth and tenth paragraphs. But in the fifteenth paragraph, Descarts raises a serious difficulty: "I nevertheless perceive that God could easily have created me so that I never should err, although I still remained free, and endowed with a limited knowledge, viz. by giving to my understanding a clear and distinct intelligence of all things as to which I should ever have to deliberate; or simply by His engraving deeply in my memory the resolution never to form a judgment on anything without having a clear and distinct understanding of it" (HR I, 177–178). In this remarkable passage, Descartes states a leading twentieth-century objection to the free will defense. The objection is raised by those who believe that some compatibilist position is the only viable account of free action. They then ask: if God has brought it about that persons are sometimes causally determined freely to choose the good, why could not God have brought it about that persons are always causally determined freely to choose the good? The notion of being *causally determined freely to choose* the good may sound paradoxical, but if so that is from the perspective of indeterminist intuitions. The soft determinist position just is that free acts or choices are causally determined, but in a way which does not involve constraint or compulsion. Descartes asks the analogous question about belief: why could not God have brought it about that persons are always causally determined freely to believe the true?

For this question, Descartes has no answer. He immediately returns to the possibility raised in the seventh paragraph, that what is an imperfection in a part may be a perfection relative to the whole universe. Recall that earlier he did not reject this possibility; rather, he pointed out that for all he yet knew he and God were the only creatures. But now, after raising an objection to the free will defense which he cannot answer, he is prepared to write: "And it is easy for me to understand that, in so far as I consider myself alone, and as if there were only myself in the world, I should have been much more perfect than I am, if God had created me so that I could never err. Nevertheless I cannot deny that in some sense it is a greater perfection in the whole universe that certain parts should not be exempt from error as others are than that all parts should be exactly similar" (HR I, 178). Descartes' solution to the epistemological problem of evil is not to propound an indeterminist or agent-causation account of free action, but rather to declare that a universe composed of cognizers who vary in their degrees of success is more perfect than one in which all cognizers uniformly avoid error or false belief. This is the epistemic analogue of responses to the problem of evil which hold in the metaphysical case that a universe that contains, for example, physical deformities is better than one that does not, because of the diversity it affords.

I conclude that Descartes did not subscribe to any version of the straightforward indeterminist account of free will, or to the theory of self-determination. His own account of free will appears to be a soft determinist account. His ultimate explanation of the existence of error does not depend upon incorporating any indeterminist elements into an account of free will. Had he been an incompatibilist dissatisfied with straightforward indeterminism, he would have had a motivation "for introducing the notion of mental substance . . . to provide a locus for the operation of freedom." (Of course, he had sufficient independent motivation: to locate an entity which is a candidate for immortality.) But he was in fact a compatibilist. Descartes' account of free will does not conflict with determinism because it does not introduce any element of indeterminism.[22] Mind-body interaction, and the mind's having desires which result in its freely moving its body in particular (cf. *PAS* I, 41) is not in conflict with Descartes' determinism.

To summarize this section, Descartes' claim that (10) mind and body causally interact is not inconsistent with either: (i) his claim that (6) mind and body are essentially/entirely/absolutely distinct substances $_S$; (ii) his restrictions upon possible causal relations; or (iii) his doctrine of the freedom of the will together with his determinism. I cannot review every possible source of incoherence in Descartes (though I will introduce further relevant material at section 24), but I hope that I have established that it is surprisingly difficult to locate any incoherence in connection with his commitment to mind-body interaction. The discrepancy between the attitude of Descartes, who finds interaction obvious and unproblema-

----

[22]Descartes' position is possibly somewhat more complex than I have represented it. Kenny, 1972, pp. 17–31, argues that Descartes holds that free will sometimes consists in liberty of spontaneity (which is compatible with determinism), and sometimes in liberty of indifference (which is not). Even if this is correct, I do not think it damages my position. Kenny holds (p. 18) that on Descartes' view liberty of indifference, and hence indeterminism, is not essential to free will. As a consequence, free will would not seem to require any indeterminism. This is especially so since, according to Descartes, the liberty of indifference is "the lowest grade of liberty" (HR I, 175). For an account of Descartes' views on freedom which I find quite congenial, see Curley, 1975, pp. 163–167.

tic, and that of the proponents of the allegation of incoherence remains to be explained. I will be in a position to return to this question in section 20, after examining Spinoza's views on interaction.

16. Tensions

I have argued that Descartes propounds (1–9) because he believes they can be exploited in support of his position on immortality. Indeed, I would put this in a stronger form: he propounds these immortality claims to no metaphysical purpose except to support his position on immortality. He propounds (10–12), on the other hand, to do justice to the seemingly obvious facts of mind-body interaction and the consequent unity of the human being. Again, I would put this in a stronger form: he propounds these interaction claims to no metaphysical purpose except to do justice to these facts. Although I have argued that Descartes is not involved in any incoherence in claiming that (10) mind and body causally interact, I do believe that there are tensions between (10) and the claim that (9) a mind's existence does not depend causally upon the existence of any body, tensions with respect to both the content of these claims, and the supporting argumentation for them. In other words, I believe there are tensions between the strongest of the immortality claims and the weakest of the interaction claims.

In one passage, Descartes seems to suggest an outright incompatibility between these two sets of claims about minds: "It does not seem to me that the human mind is capable of conceiving at the same time the distinction and the union between body and soul, because for this it is necessary to conceive them as a single thing and at the same time to conceive them as two things; and this is absurd" (K 142). In this letter to Elizabeth, whether out of exasperation or deference, Descartes overstates his case. From the distinction of the mind and body, or the claim that (8) no mind is a body, it follows that a mind and a body are "two things" in the sense of numerically distinct entities. The union of mind and body, that is to say a human being, is "one thing" in the sense of a unity. There is no absurdity or contradiction here. A unity or single thing may have numerically distinct parts. The two halves of my brain together compose a single thing, though they are themselves numerically distinct, two things.[23]

I believe that Descartes' best account of the relationship between the immortality and interaction claims is contained in the preceding letter to Elizabeth:

> There are two facts about the human soul on which depend all the things we can know of its nature. The first is that it thinks, the second is that it is united to the body and can act and be acted upon along with it. About the second I have said hardly anything; I have tried only to make the first well understood. For my principal aim was to prove the distinction between soul and body, and to this end only the first was useful, and the second might have been harmful. [K 137]

Descartes suggests that emphasis upon mind-body interaction "might have been harmful" to his principal aim relating to immortality. He is sensitive to some tension in his views, but what is it? We have to tease the answer out of the texts.

Descartes holds both that (9) a mind's existence does not depend causally upon the existence of any body and that (10) mind and body causally interact. There need not be any incompatibility between the claim that x's existence does not depend causally upon the existence of y and the claim that x and y causally interact. For example, bizarre cases aside, it may be true both that the cue ball's existence does not depend causally upon the existence of the eight ball, and that the cue ball and the eight ball causally interact. Of course, there are other sorts of cases: the existence of a flame does depend causally upon the oxygen in its vicinity with which it causally interacts. Descartes claims that mind and body causally interact. Might they not interact in such a way that a mind's existence does depend causally upon a body's existence? I will argue that Descartes holds three theses which render this question particularly acute.

---

[23]Mattern, 1978, p. 220, argues that this interpretation "is unacceptable, in light of Descartes' clear commitments to the compatibility of mind-body distinctness and union in the rest of the letter." She prefers an interpretation on which "the problem arises in conceiving the union of mind and body and the *difference* between mind and body, that is, in conceiving mind and body as united and as two *different sorts* of things." We agree, however, that Descartes' view is that there is no incompatibility involved in the distinction and the union of mind and body, and that the passage in question at least suggests that there is.

He claims that (3) a mind's essence (at least in part) is to think, i.e., that a mind cannot exist at any time without thinking at that time. The existence of a thinking substance$_S$ depends upon the existence of some thought which inheres in it.[24] In *Meditation II*, Descartes writes: "I am, I exist, that is certain. But how often? Just when I think; for it might possibly be the case if I ceased entirely to think, that I should otherwise cease altogether to exist" (HR I, 151–152). He considers the claim that if a mind ceased entirely to think, it would cease to exist. In *Meditation II*, he claims this might possibly be true. His point is not that the claim is in fact false. Rather, its truth is not established until *Meditation VI*, where Descartes argues for (3). It is his position that if a mind ceased entirely to think, it would cease to exist. Thus he writes in a letter to Gibieuf: "I believe that the soul is always thinking for the same reason as I believe that . . . body, or extended substance always has extension, and in genral that whatever constitutes the nature of a thing always belongs to it as long as it exists. So it would be easier for me to believe that the soul ceased to exist at the times when it is supposed to cease to think than to conceive that it could exist without thought" (K 125).

[24]In section 8, I argued that Descartes' conception of substance$_S$ relates to inherence, a variety of noncausal dependence: a quality depends (noncausally) for its existence upon the existence of a substratum in which it inheres. But this cannot exhaust that conception. Given Descartes' commitment to (3), a mind or thinking substance$_S$ depends (noncausally) for its existence upon the existence of a thought which inheres in it. In other words, the dependence of thoughts upon thinking substances$_S$ and of thinking substances$_S$ upon thoughts appears symmetrical. Leibniz made this point: "I do [not] know whether the definition of substance as that which needs for its existence only the concurrence of God fits any created substance known to us, unless we interpret it in some unusual sense. For not only do we need other substances; we need our own accidents even much more. Therefore, since substance and accident depend upon each other, other marks are necessary for distinguishing a substance from an accident" (L 389). Leibniz has a constructive suggestion: among these other marks "may be this one: That a substance needs some accident but often does not need a determinate one but is content, when this accident is removed, with the substitution of another. An accident, however, needs not only some substance in general but that very one in which it inheres, so that it cannot change it" (L 389–390). The claim embodied in this last sentence, however, seems quite dubious. There is a better idea suggested earlier in the passage: that a substance, but not an accident, persists through time. Presumably, Descartes will have to fall back on some such point in order to justify bestowing the label "substance" on substrata rather than accidents.

I turn now to some of Descartes' empirical claims about the origin or genesis of thoughts. He uses a number of different criteria for classifying thoughts. One sort of criterion appeals to the causes of thoughts. The simplest statement of such a criterion is found in a letter to Elizabeth: "the term 'passion' can be applied in general to all the thoughts which are thus aroused in the soul by cerebral impressions alone, without the concurrence of the will, and therefore without any action of the soul itself, for whatever is not an action is a passion" (K 178). A passion is a thought caused by bodily states or events, and not by the will. Actions are those thoughts which "proceed directly from our soul, and appear to depend on it alone" (*PAS* I, 17). Descartes proceeds to point out that "commonly however, the term ['passion'] is restricted to thoughts which are caused by some extraordinary agitation of the spirits. For thoughts that come from external objects, or from the interior dispositions of the body—such as the perception of colours, sounds, and smells, hunger, thirst, pain and so on—are called external or internal sensations" (K 178). What Descartes calls "internal sensations"—hunger, thirst, pain, etc.—are a special case of "passions" in the initial, broad sense, and thus are caused by bodily states or events. In *The Passions of the Soul*, there is a more complicated cross-classification of thoughts with respect to their causes and other criteria. It is nevertheless clear that what Descartes has called internal sensations are a subclass of those thoughts which have the body as at least a partial cause (cf. *PAS* I, 19–24). Descartes' empirical claim is that there is a class of thoughts, passions (including the internal sensations), which are at least partially caused by bodily states or events and not by the mind alone. It follows from this claim that the existence of a certain class of thoughts, the passions (of which the internal sensations are a special case), depends causally upon the existence of certain bodily states or events (and hence upon the existence of certain bodies). I am not foisting this conclusion on Descartes. He points out in *Meditation II*: "Another attribute is sensation. But one cannot feel without body" (HR I, 151).

It is thought, in Descartes' broad sense of the term, which is essential to the mind. He nowhere argues that some particular subclass of thoughts is essential to the mind. This raises the possibility that at given times a mind's thoughts might be limited to some particular subclass of thoughts, and to internal sensations in particular. When Gassendi objected that if the mind's essence is to think, the mind must have conscious thoughts even in the womb, Descartes accepted this conclusion, which Gassendi saw as a *reductio* of his view. Descartes explained that while the mind is conscious in the womb, it does not later remember its thoughts. Even Locke granted that the fetus might experience sensations (*Essay* i.iv.2, ii.ix.5). Internal sensations seem a likely candidate for the sorts of thoughts the mind has in the womb. Descartes appeals to this natural candidate:

> I had proved that the nature or essence of soul consists in the fact that it is thinking. . . . Now nothing can ever be deprived of its own essence. . . . This does not mean that I believe that the mind of an infant meditates on metaphysics in its mother's womb; not at all. We know by experience that our minds are so closely joined to our bodies as to be almost always acted upon by them; and though in an adult and healthy body the mind enjoys some liberty to think of other things than those presented by the senses, we know there is not the same liberty in those who are sick or asleep or very young; and the younger they are the less liberty they have. So if one may conjecture on such an unexplored topic, it seems most reasonable to think that a mind newly united to an infant's body is wholly occupied in perceiving or feeling the ideas of pain, pleasure, heat, cold and other similar ideas which arise from its union and intermingling with the body. [K 111]

Not only does the fetus or infant experience pain, heat, etc.; probably it is "wholly occupied" by such thoughts. In other words, for extended periods of time, a mind's thoughts are limited to internal sensations.

Descartes holds the following three theses:

(A) There are periods of time (e.g., in the womb) when the mind's thoughts are limited to internal sensations.
(B) The existence of passions, which include internal sensations, depends causally upon the existence of certain bodies.
(C) If a mind ceased entirely to think, it would cease to exist—a consequence of (3).

The conjunction of (A–C) undermines Descartes' argument for the claim that (9) a mind's existence does not depend causally upon the existence of any body. Recall that he construes the corruption of a body as a change (of a certain sort) in its figure. His argument for (9) was this: "we know no argument or example such as to convince us that the death or the annihilation of a substance such as the mind is, should follow from so light a cause as a change in figure" (HR II, 47). On the contrary, his theses (A–C) provide the materials for just such an argument. Consider a mind in the womb. By (A), the mind's thoughts are limited to internal sensations. Suppose some medical mishap results in the corruption of the fetus' brain and pineal gland. Since by (B), the existence of internal sensations depends causally upon the existence of the brain, there might be no internal sensations in the ensuing moments. In that event, it appears that the mind might have ceased entirely to think, and thus by (C) have ceased to exist. It is easy to see, given (A–C), how the annihilation of a mind *could* follow from "so light a cause" as a change in figure which constitutes the corruption of the brain.

(Someone might object as follows. "In the imagined case, the corruption of the brain causes the cessation of all thought, but the cessation of thought does not *cause* the annihilation of the mind. Granted, the annihilation of the mind depends upon the cessation of all thought, but this dependence is noncausal—note that the mind's annihilation is simultaneous with the cessation of all thought. Thus, the corruption of the brain does *not cause* the annihilation of the mind." I grant everything to this objection except the conclusion. Consider this parallel argument. "My shooting Smith causes her to die, but her death does not *cause* her husband to become a widower. Granted, her husband's becoming a widower depends upon her death, but this dependence is noncausal—note that her husband's becoming a widower is simultaneous with her death. Thus, my shooting Smith did *not cause* her husband to become a widower." But this conclusion is clearly false. What these examples show is that it is often the case that if a is a cause of b, and c depends noncausally upon b, a is a cause of c as well.)

Descartes holds that (10) mind and body causally interact, and in particular that (B) the existence of passions, which include internal sensations, depends causally upon the existence of certain bodies. This admission, when coupled with (A) and (C), constitutes a threat to his claim that (9) a mind's existence does not depend causally upon the existence of any body. Here a tension emerges from the content of the immortality and interaction claims and directly threatens Descartes' argument for (9).

Another tension arises from his own arguments for the strongest of the immortality claims and the weakest of the interaction claims. Recall his argument to show that (9) a mind's existence does not depend causally upon the existence of any body: "We know of no argument or example such as to convince us that the death or the annihilation of a substance such as the mind is, should follow from so light a cause as is a change in figure, which is no more than a mode, and indeed not a mode of mind, but of body that is really distinct from mind" (HR ii, 47). This passage occurs in *Replies II*. In the letter to Clerselier following *Replies IV*, Descartes defends mind-body interaction, in part, as follows: "Those who admit the existence of real accidents, like heat, weight, and so forth, do not doubt that these accidents have the power of acting on the body, and nevertheless there is more difference between them and it, i.e., between accidents and a substance, than there is between two substances" (HR ii, 132). For the purposes of the defense of (9), Descartes construes the possibility that a mind's existence depends causally upon the existence of body as requiring that changes in *material qualities* could cause *thinking substance$_S$* to cease to exist. For the purposes of the defense of (10), he construes the possibility of mind-body interaction as requiring that *material substance$_S$* and *thinking substance$_S$* could causally interact. He then declares on the one hand that *material qualities* have *so little* in common with *thinking substance$_S$* itself that changes in the former *could not cause the latter to cease to exist*, but on the other hand that *material substance$_S$* and *thinking substance$_S$* have *enough* in common that they *could causally interact*. Of course, there is the problem of providing a justification for construing a mind's depending for its existence upon a body as requiring a causal relation between qualities and substance$_S$ while construing causal interaction between mind and body as requiring a causal relation between two substances $_S$. That aside, Descartes' bald assertions given that he construes matters this way are entirely *ad hoc*. How much do two entities need to have in common if the existence of one can depend causally upon the other? And how different do two entities have to be in order to preclude causal interaction between them? Descartes has no general theory to invoke in order to answer these questions. The body of doctrine about "efficient and total" causes is, as we have seen in the preceding section, too restricted in its application.

The tensions identified in this section hardly amount to incoherence. Since no one found Descartes' interactionism more incoherent than did Spinoza, an examination of the basis for Spinoza's vehement rejection of mind-body interaction may help us identify the basis for the allegation of incoherence.

IV

SPINOZA'S DENIAL OF CAUSAL INTERACTION BETWEEN MODES OF DISTINCT ATTRIBUTES

17. Spinoza's Informal Arguments against Mind-Body Interaction

Spinoza certainly found Descartes' interactionism incoherent: "What the will is, and in what manner it moves the body, every one is ignorant, for those who pretend otherwise, and devise seats and dwelling-places of the soul, usually excite our laughter or disgust" (E IIP35S). Similarly, in the long first paragraph of the Preface of Part v of the *Ethics*, Spinoza provides a summary of Descartes' position which is both accurate and unusually sensitive to some fine points in Descartes' views, but which reads as if Spinoza found Descartes' interactionism ridiculous on its face. What was the basis for Spinoza's denial that mind and body causally interact?

The *Ethics* contains two kinds of arguments against mind-body interaction. The first is formal argument, a priori in character, cast in the technical vocabulary ('attribute', 'mode') of Spinoza's metaphysics, and set out in geometrical fashion within the demonstrations proper of specific propositions (E IIP6, IIIP2). The second is informal argument, largely empirical, cast wholly in vocabulary not impregnated by Spinoza's metaphysics, and set out discursively in prefatory material and notes outside the demonstrations proper of the *Ethics* (E IIP35S, IIIP2S, vPref.). I begin with this latter body of argumentation.

First, Spinoza has a number of arguments designed to exhibit our ignorance of the means by which the soul moves the body. Descartes' appeal to the pineal gland is at best a sketchy hypothesis.

The details of the interaction (for example, how many degrees of motion the mind can impart to the pineal gland) are not spelled out (*E* vPref., cf. ⅢP2S). What is worse, at least some details of Descartes' hypothesis are empirically false; in particular, the pineal gland is not located in the middle of the brain, and not all the nerves extend to its actual location (*E* vPref.). The upshot is that no one knows the means or method by which the mind moves the body (*E* ⅡP2S). This ignorance has no tendency to show that there is no mind-body interaction. Often we know that some causal interaction obtains without knowing the means or method by which it takes place. We know that cigarette smoking causes cancer without knowing how it causes cancer. How it does so remains an open empirical question. Spinoza's arguments thus far at best show that it is an open empirical question how mind and body causally interact.

Second, Spinoza attempts to undermine the force of a consideration which might be produced in favor of mind-body interaction: we know from experience that many operations of the body depend upon the volitions of the mind—when the mind is not fit for thinking, the body is generally inert. Spinoza grants this, pointing out that experience "also" teaches that many operations of the mind depend upon the condition of the body. When the body is sluggish, the mind is not fit for thinking (*E* ⅢP2S). This reply is entirely wrongheaded for Spinoza's purposes. Descartes held that there exists two-way mind-body interaction: thoughts are among the causes of states of or events involving bodies, and states of or events involving bodies are among the causes of thoughts. Spinoza's reply is that if certain experiences show the dependence of bodily operations on the mind, other experiences equally show the dependence of mental operations on the body. This is no *reductio* from the viewpoint of the two-way interactionist. If Spinoza's point is construed to be that it cannot be the case both that "the body depends upon the mind and the mind depends upon the body," this is just simplistic. There may be a complex network of interdependencies.

Third, Spinoza contends that it may not be necessary to appeal to the mind in order to give a complete explanation of bodily functions. It remains to be shown precisely what the body can do on its own. If one considers brutes and sleep-walkers, it is obvious that the body can do a great deal without the direction of the mind. It is useless to object that architecture, painting, and the like could not be the causal product of bodily functioning without the direction of the mind, both because what the body alone can do remains to be determined, and because the human body itself is more complex than works of art, but is not itself caused by the mind (*E* ⅢP2S). These points do nothing to show that mind and body do not interact. They are simply reflections of a methodological program, an attempt to explain all bodily phenomena exclusively in terms of other bodily phenomena.

Fourth and finally, Spinoza objects that Descartes has provided no clear and distinct conception of what he understands by "the union of the mind and body" or of "thought intimately connected with a certain small portion of matter" (*E* vPref.). I have argued that Descartes does cash the metaphors of "union" and "intimate connection" in terms of causation and proximate causation, respectively (§14). The present objection therefore reduces to the claim that there is something obscure or objectionable about the notion of a thought being the proximate cause of a bodily state or event, and vice versa. None of the three considerations above tends to support so strong a position. This leaves us pretty much where we started, with ridicule and disgust. Spinoza finds mind-body interaction too obscure or objectionable to be acceptable, but the basis of, or source for, this viewpoint remains to be identified. I turn now to his formal argument.

18. Attributes and Modes

Spinoza's formal argument against the claim that mind and body causally interact is set out at *E* ⅡP6D and ⅢP2D. To follow it, we need to understand the technical vocabulary of 'attribute' and 'mode' in which it is cast. The argumentation of the *Ethics*, of course, comprises a closely knit structure set out in geometrical fashion. Since the argument against mind-body interaction does not appear until Part ⅠⅠ, will we not have to go through at least most of the argument of Part Ⅰ as background? Surprisingly, but fortunately, the answer is negative.

The central argument of the demonstration at *E* ⅡP6 invokes the terminology of 'attribute' and 'mode' defined at *E* ⅠDef.4 and

1Def.5, respectively; it appeals to *E* 1P10, which is itself proved solely by appeal to the definitions of 'substance' and 'attribute', *E* 1Def.3 and 1Def.4, respectively; and it appeals to *E* 1A4, "The knowledge of an effect depends upon and involves the knowledge of the cause." All the materials for the central argument of the demonstration at *E* 11P6 ultimately derive from the three definitions, *E* 1Defs.3–5, for 'substance', 'attribute', and 'mode', together with one axiom, *E* 1A4. Only one proposition (P10) of Part 1 contributes to Spinoza's argument against mind-body interaction. The remaining five definitions, six axioms, and thirty-five propositions of Part 1 intervene spatially, but make no contribution to the proof. I am not suggesting that if one simply picked up the *Ethics* and read *E* 1Defs.3–5, A4, P10D, and 11P6D, that one would readily understand the argument. The point is that much of Part 1 is not necessary for understanding the argument.

As we have seen (§9), Spinoza defines 'substance' at *E* 1Def.3, and provides an equivalent formulation at *E* 1P8S2: "By substance, I understand that which is in itself and is conceived through itself; in other words, that, the conception [knowledge] of which does not need the conception of another thing from which it must be formed." With respect to the serious interpretative issue of determining the force of the claims that SP-substance is "in itself" and "conceived through itself," I followed E. M. Curley in construing these as the following metaphysical and epistemological conditions, respectively:

> *x* is an SP-substance just in case
>   (MC) *x*'s existence does not depend causally upon the existence of any other entity, and
>   (EC) SP-knowledge of *x* does not require SP-knowledge of any other entity.

I formulated the notion of Spinozistic or SP-knowledge in light of *E* 1A4, "The knowledge of an effect depends upon the knowledge of its cause," together with Spinoza's claim that everything that exists has a cause (*E* 1P11D2). On my interpretation, (perfect) SP-knowledge of a thing requires knowledge of the complete causal history of the entity.

I now turn to Spinoza's conception of attributes and modes, attributes first. At *E* 1Def.4, he defines 'attribute': "By *attribute*, I mean that which the intellect perceives as constituting the essence of substance" (Elwes' translation). 'Attribute' is defined in terms of 'substance'. What is the precise relationship between attribute and SP-substance?

I begin by considering the phrase "constituting its essence." It is tempting to suppose that in this context Spinoza is using 'essence' in a technical sense. It might seem unlikely that he would use the term casually. But although I do not deny that 'essence' is being used in a technical sense at *E* IDef.4, I hold that understanding that passage does not require familiarity with Spinoza's technical sense of the term. My reason is that Spinoza does offer an explicit definition of 'essence', but not until Part II (Def.2). Surely, in defining 'attribute', he had his eye on his later definition of 'essence', so that his definition of 'attribute' would not require modification in light of the later definition of 'essence'. On the other hand, the definition of 'attribute' should be comprehensible without one's being familiar with the technical sense of 'essence'. The situation is this: an intuitive understanding of "essence" will do no harm early on, though reading into 'essence' its precise technical sense will lead to greater precision subsequently.

I am suggesting that we need not put a great deal of interpretative weight on the occurrence of 'essence' in *E* IDef.4. Whereas in that definition an attribute is construed as "constituting the essence of substance," there are various alternate formulations in the first half of Part I: each attribute "expresses the reality or being of substance" (*E* IP10S); each attribute "pertains to substance" (*E* IP19D). So attributes are variously said to constitute/express/pertain to the essence/being/reality of SP-substance. Although Spinoza often uses 'essence' and 'nature' interchangeably (cf. *E* IP8S2), this equivalence does not extend to 'being' and 'reality'.

Thus far we have: "By *attribute*, I mean that which the intellect perceives as constituting/expressing/pertaining to the essence/being/ reality of substance." This formulation places less weight on the technical term 'essence', but the question of the relationship between attribute and SP-substance remains. I suggest that (i) an SP-substance is a collection of attributes, and that (ii) any attribute is itself an SP-substance.

The evidence for (i) is as follows. (1) First, consider God. We have the following passages. (*a*) "By God, I understand Being absolutely infinite, that is to say, substance consisting of infinite attributes, each one of which expresses eternal and infinite essence" (*E* 1Def.6). (*b*) "God is eternal, or, in other words, all His attributes are eternal" (*E* 1P19). (*c*) "God is immutable, or (which is the same thing) all His attributes are immutable" (*E* 1P20C2). The suggestion in all these passages is that God consists of and is identified with the totality of His attributes. But God is a special case. Perhaps the SP-substance God is a collection of (infinite) attributes, but other SP-substances are not collections of attributes.

(2) Against this, there is evidence that any arbitrary SP-substance, and not just God, is a collection of attributes. According to *E* 1P4, "Two or more distinct things are distinguished from one another, either by the difference of the attributes of the substances, or by the difference of their affections." The demonstration reads in part: "There is nothing therefore outside the intellect by which a number of things can be distinguished one from another, but *substances or (which is the same thing by Def. 4) their attributes*[,] and their affections" (*E* 1P4D, emphasis added). The Latin has a comma after "attributes." Adding the comma correctly conveys the intended sense. Def. 4 is the definition of 'attribute', and it makes no reference to affections, that is, modes, which are introduced at *E* 1Def.5. It could not possibly follow from Def. 4, the definition of 'attribute', that SP-substances are the same as their attributes and their affections (modes). Spinoza is saying that by Def. 4 it follows that SP-substances are the same as, identical with, their attributes. SP-substances quite generally, and not God alone, are identified with collections of attributes. I will cite additional evidence for (i) below.

Given that (i) an SP-substance is a collection of attributes, it does not follow that (ii) any attribute is itself an SP-substance. But there is extensive evidence for (ii), a good deal of it from Spinoza's correspondence. (*a*) Recall the definition of SP-substance: "that which is in itself and conceived through itself; in other words, that, the conception of which does not need the conception of another thing." Spinoza writes to Henry Oldenburg: "I understand by attribute all that which is conceived through itself, and in itself; so that its conception does not involve the conception of some other thing" (Wolf II). Here 'attribute' is given the same definition as 'substance' in the *Ethics*. (*b*) Similarly, Spinoza writes to Simon de Vries: "*By substance I mean that which is in itself and is conceived through itself, that is, whose conception does not involve the conception of some other thing. I mean the same by attribute, except that it is called attribute with respect to the intellect, which attributes such and such a nature to substance*" (Wolf IX). Again, 'attribute' and 'substance' are defined in the same way. Letters II and IX are relatively early, written in 1661 and 1663, whereas the *Ethics* was largely complete somewhere around 1665–66.

There is evidence for (ii) in the *Ethics* also. (*a*) An SP-substance is in itself and conceived through itself. According to *E* IP10 (the only proposition, recall, utilized in the crucial argument at *E* IIP6), "Each attribute of a substance must be conceived through itself." According to the demonstration, this follows directly from the definitions of 'attribute' and 'substance': "For an attribute is that which the intellect perceives of substance, as if constituting its essence (Def. 4), and therefore (Def. 3) it must be conceived through itself." So an attribute is conceived through itself, and hence has at least one of the two defining characteristics of SP-substance.[1] (*b*) Further, we have seen (§9) that something is in itself if and only if it is conceived through itself. In the present case, an attribute is conceived through itself, i.e., SP-knowledge of an attribute does not require SP-knowledge of anything else. But knowledge of anything which exists depends upon knowledge of its cause (generalization of *E* IA4). So an attribute is its own cause. So its existence does not depend causally upon the existence of anything else. Hence, it is in itself. Of course, I rely on Curley's interpretation to generate the consequence that an attribute is in itself as well as conceived through itself. Granted that attributes have both these characteristics in Letters II and IX, can we be sure that Curley's interpretation is

---

[1]Some commentators hold that it follows immediately from *E* IP10 together with *E* IDef.3 that each attribute is an SP-substance. And they are correct, if one reads *E* IDef.3 in a particular way. Recall that "by substance, I understand that which is in itself and is conceived through itself; in other words, that, the conception of which does not need the conception of another thing from which it must be formed." If one takes the material following the semicolon as an alternative definition of 'substance', rather than a gloss on what it is to be "conceived through itself," then it does follow from *E* IP10 coupled with that definition that each attribute is an SP-substance. I am reluctant, however, to rely upon the reading of *E* IDef.3 required for this argument. Two commentators who do employ this argument in support of (i) are Gueroult, 1968, p. 48, and Sprigge, 1977, p. 425. The reading of *E* IDef.3 which I prefer has been endorsed by Jarrett, 1978a, p. 20.

correct, and that attributes have both these characteristics in the *Ethics?* (c) There is striking confirmation at E 1P29S: "by *natura naturans* we are to understand *that which is in itself and is conceived through itself, or those attributes of substance* which express eternal and infinite essence, that is to say . . . God in so far as He is considered as a free cause" (emphasis added).[2] This seems to be an unequivocal statement that each attribute of God is both in itself and conceived through itself.[3] Of course, as before, God is a special case, an SP-substance consisting of infinite attributes. Later in this section, I will show on the basis of evidence internal to the *Ethics*, that (ii) any attribute is itself an SP-substance. In the *Ethics*, attributes are not defined as SP-substances, but they take on the defining characteristics of SP-substance.

Before proceeding, I want to clarify (i) and (ii) in two respects. First, it may seem puzzling that (i) an SP-substance is a collection of (one or more) attributes, given the fact that (ii) any attribute is itself an SP-substance. For example, how could the SP-substance God consist of infinite attributes which are themselves SP-substances? We can answer that a single attribute is a simple SP-substance, and a set or collection of attributes is a compound SP-substance. This sort of distinction is to be found in both Leibniz, who distinguishes between simple substances or monads and compound substances (§10), and in Descartes, who requires a distinction between simple

---

[2]All the textual evidence to this point for (i) and (ii) is to be found in Gueroult, 1968, pp. 47–48, or in Curley, 1969, pp. 16–17, or in both. Neither commentator, however, distinguishes (i) and (ii) as carefully as he might. Gueroult's position is that "attribute and substance are interchangeable," which seems to be the conjunction of (i) and (ii); as a result, he does not distinguish between passages which support (i) or (ii) alone. And Curley cites, for example, the passage from Wolf II in support of the thesis that "Spinoza . . . does identify substance . . . with the totality of its attributes," that is, thesis (i); the passage, however, directly supports only (ii). The basic point goes back to Wolf, 1927, §2, where he argued that "Substance (or Nature or God) is the unified totality of Attributes." The thesis that (ii) any attribute is itself an SP-substance is endorsed by Jarrett, 1978a, p. 20. Friedman, 1978, p. 74, has protested against the view that (i) an SP-substance is a collection of attributes, but he provides no arguments in support of his position.

[3]This important passage was overlooked by Curley, 1969, though it was cited in the present connection by Gueroult, 1968, p. 48, n. 111. The availability of this passage nullifies the objection of Parkinson, 1970, p. 342, that "[Curley's] assertion that an attribute both is in itself and is conceived through itself does not seem to have any textual justification."

secondary-substances$_I$, such as a mind, and compound secondary-substances$_I$, such as a human being (§ 14). Second, in asserting (i), I am not claiming that a compound SP-substance is merely a set or collection of two or more attributes, or that any arbitrary set of two or more attributes constitutes an SP-substance. It may be that (i') an SP-substance is any attribute, or any set or collection of two or more attributes *related in an appropriate way*. For Descartes, for example, a compound secondary-substance$_I$ consists of other secondary-substances$_I$ which are causally connected in an appropriate way (§ 14). In Spinoza's case, it may be that a compound SP-substance consists of attributes whose modes exhibit the sort of parallelism which Spinoza invokes at *E* IIP7 ("The order and connection of ideas is the same as the order and connection of things").[4]

It might be objected, despite all this evidence, that God, at least, cannot consist of (infinite) attributes, however related, on the grounds that "substance absolutely infinite is indivisible" (*E* IP13) and/or that "God is one" (*E* IP14C1). I do not believe that either of these objections has any force. The assertion that God is one need mean no more than that God is a single thing, one whole, a unity. This is not incompatible with the claim that attributes are constituents of God. Many wholes have constituents: for Descartes, a human being is a single thing which consists of a mind and body (related in an appropriate way); or to take a perfectly ordinary example, an automobile is a single thing which consists of various constituents (related in an appropriate way). Similarly, the assertion that infinite substance is indivisible is not incompatible with the claim

[4]The position of Gueroult, 1968, pp. 184–185 and ch. VII, seems to be that God is a unified substance because the existence of each of God's attributes follows necessarily from God's essence as the most real or perfect being. Unfortunately, this sort of consideration does not have any explanatory value in light of the nature of Spinoza's principal argument for the existence of God at *E* IP11D. The argument that "God, or substance consisting of infinite attributes... necessarily exists" is based solely on the ground that God is a substance, and hence by *E* IP7 ("It pertains to the nature of substance to exist") necessarily exists. The fact that God is the most real or perfect being, or absolutely infinite, or consists of infinite attributes, plays no role in the demonstration. The form of demonstration at *E* IP11D could equally be used to show that any arbitrary substance, e.g., Ged, where we stipulate that 'Ged' is the substance consisting of the attribute of extension alone, necessarily exists. But then it is not the case that the nature of God need play any special role in explaining the reason or cause for the existence of the individual attributes.

that attributes are constituents of SP-substance, for the following reason. While it might be true that something is divisible only if it has parts, it is not true that if something has parts it is divisible. The parts may not be divisible, because, for example, they are necessarily constituents of a whole which itself necessarily exists. This is precisely the case here, since "God, or substance consisting of infinite attributes... necessarily exists" (*E* ıP11).

It remains to deal with Spinoza's conception of modes. The relationship between SP-substance and attributes was not obvious given their respective definitions. The relationship between SP-substance and modes, on the other hand, can virtually be "read off" the definitions of 'substance' and of 'mode'. Spinoza defines 'mode' as follows: "By mode, I understand [*a*] the affections of substance, or [*b*] that which is in another thing through which also it is conceived" (*E* ıDef.5). I have distinguished two definitions here, though they are obviously intended to be equivalent (the difference, however, will prove important at section 19). It is definition (*b*) which is immediately helpful. A mode is in another thing, through which it is conceived. An SP-substance is in itself, and conceived through itself. A given interpretation of "in itself" and "conceived through itself" in the definition of 'substance' forces an interpretation of "in another" and "conceived through another" in the definition of 'mode'. If an SP-substance is "in itself" in the sense that its existence does not depend causally upon the existence of anything else, and "conceived through itself" in the sense that SP-knowledge of SP-substance does not require SP-knowledge of anything else, then metaphysical and epistemological components of the definition of 'mode' fall out immediately:

> x is a mode just in case
> (MC) x's existence depends causally upon the existence of some other entity, and
> (EC) SP-knowledge of x requires SP-knowledge of something else (in particular, of whatever it is upon which x's existence depends causally).

It is worth noting that Spinoza does not simply define 'mode' as "that which is in another thing and conceived through another thing." Rather, a mode is "that which is in another thing *through which also* it is conceived." In other words, it is not simply the case that a mode is in another thing (say y) and conceived through another thing (say z, possibly not identical to y). A mode is in another thing and conceived through *that* thing. Curley's interpretation of "in itself" and "conceived through itself" explains this feature of the definition of 'mode'. We have seen (§9) that Spinoza uses 'conception' and 'knowledge' and the relevant cognates interchangeably. Further, we have the explicit axiom (E 1A4) that the knowledge of an effect depends upon knowledge of its cause. On Curley's interpretation, it is then obvious why a mode is "conceived or known" through that which it is "in." A mode is "in another" in the sense that its existence depends causally upon the existence of something else (say y). Knowledge of a thing requires knowledge of its cause. Therefore, a mode is known or conceived through that on which its existence depends, through that which it is "in" (through y itself).

In what I have called definition (a) and elsewhere, Spinoza writes of the modes or affections *of an SP-substance* (e.g., E 1P1, P4D, P5D, P6C). What does this mean? Since definitions (a) and (b) are treated as equivalent, a mode is a mode of an SP-substance just in case it is both in and conceived through that SP-substance. Further, it is easy to show that if a mode is in an SP-substance, it is conceived through that SP-substance: suppose mode M is in SP-substance S; then M's existence depends causally upon the existence of S; by E 1A4, knowledge of an effect depends upon knowledge of its cause; so SP-knowledge of M requires SP-knowledge of S; hence, M is known or conceived through S. Thus, we can simplify matters by focusing exclusively on the metaphysical commitments and say that a mode is a mode *of an SP-substance* just in case it is in that SP-substance, just in case its existence depends causally upon the existence of that SP-substance. Spinoza also writes of the modes of an attribute (e.g., E 11P6). Since (i) an SP-substance is a collection of attributes, it must be the case that a mode is a mode of *an attribute* just in case its existence depends causally upon the existence of that attribute.

Indeed, we are now in a position to confirm that Spinoza subscribes to (i). He maintains that since modes are affections of SP-substance, and since God is the only SP-substance, all modes are in God (E 1P15D). So the existence of modes depends causally upon the existence of the SP-substance God. (Spinoza writes indifferently of modes as being caused by, produced by, determined to existence by, and following from God). Now, if the thesis that for Spinoza (i) an SP-substance is a collection of attributes is correct, Spinoza should be prepared to write that all modes are modes of the attributes of God. For if all modes depend causally upon God, and God consists of infinite attributes, then all modes depend causally upon those attributes. And Spinoza does use the relevant locutions, writing of "affections of the attributes of God" (*E* 1P14C2) and of "affections or modes of God's attributes" (*E* 1P25C).

I can also provide an additional argument for the claim that (ii) any attribute is itself an SP-substance. According to *E* 1A1, "Everything which is, is either in itself or in another." At *E* 1P4D, Spinoza states that "everything which is, is either in itself or in another (Ax. 1), that is to say (Defs. 3 and 5), outside the intellect there is nothing but substances and their affections"; at *E* 1P15D, "but besides substances and modes nothing is assumed (Ax. 1)"; and again at *E* 1P28D, "besides substance and modes nothing exists (Ax. 1 and Defs. 3 and 5)." Spinoza, appealing to *E* 1A1, together with the definitions of 'substance' and 'mode', claims that nothing exists except SP-substances and modes. And this claim is correct. We have seen (§9) that an entity is in itself just in case it is conceived through itself, and in another just in case it is conceived through another. So it does follow from *E* 1A1 that everything which exists is either in itself and conceived through itself, or in another and conceived through another. In other words, everything which exists is either an SP-substance or a mode in the sense of definition (*b*). An attribute, then, must either be an SP-substance or a mode. *E* 1P10 states that any attribute is conceived through itself. According to definition (*b*) of 'mode', a mode is conceived through another. Therefore, no attribute is a mode. So any attribute is itself a (simple) SP-substance.[5]

This argument is virtually conclusive. What is clear on the basis of the passages cited is that since whatever exists is either an SP-

[5]This same argument has been produced by Gueroult, 1968, p. 48, though he does not consider the possibility I raise in the following paragraph. The argument has also been formulated by Jarrett, 1978a, p. 56.

substance or a mode, and since a mode is conceived through another, and an attribute is conceived through itself, then *if attributes exist*, they are SP-substances. But perhaps no attribute exists, objectively, in reality, outside the intellect or understanding; perhaps attributes exist only subjectively, in the mind, as creatures of the intellect or understanding. Thus we are led to the controversy between proponents of "objectivist" and "subjectivist" interpretations of the ontological status of the attributes.

I believe that subjectivist interpretations have few adherents today, and for good reason, given the burden of the literature on this issue.[6] I will therefore let the case rest with some brief observations. (1) I am trying to establish that (ii) any attribute is itself an SP-substance. This does not follow from the claim that (i) an SP-substance is a collection of attributes. However, it does follow from (i) that attributes exist outside the intellect in the same sense as SP-substance itself. For how else could SP-substance consist of attributes, unless SP-substance itself exists only subjectively? For this reason, all the evidence cited at pp. 161–162 for (i) is evidence for the objectivist interpretation. It should be noted that all this evidence is from Part I of the *Ethics*, rather than from the corre-

[6] For a subjectivist interpretation, see Wolfson, 1934, Vol. 1, ch. v, part IV. For criticism of the subjectivist interpretation, see the following (listed chronologically): Wolf, 1927, §2; Haserot, 1953; Kessler, 1971; and Martens, 1978, pp. 107–108. While Jarrett has recently argued for a "subjectivist" interpretation of the attributes, his point is not to challenge the objectivity of the attributes themselves, but rather the objectivity of the distinction between the attributes; he agrees that attributes exist. See Jarrett, 1977, especially pp. 448–453 (and cf. 1978a, pp. 56 and 64, n. 95). One recent commentator who does criticize the objectivist interpretation is Sprigge, 1977, pp. 442–444. He has three objections: that the objectivist interpretation (i) cannot explain the parallelism of the attributes, (ii) cannot explain how the attributes are related into a unified totality, and (iii) is inconsistent with Spinoza's claim at *E* IIP7S that "a mode of extension and the idea of that mode are one and the same thing." None of these carries much weight. (i) Whether or not Spinoza can provide any "explanation" for the existence of the parallelism of the attributes, he at least thought he could demonstrate that the parallelism must obtain (*E* IIP7). (ii) And it is that very parallelism which, for Spinoza, must confer a unity upon the attributes. (iii) This objection is irrelevant since, in terms of Jarrett's distinction, it counts at most against the objectivity of the distinction between the attributes, not against the objectivity, that is, the existence outside the intellect, of at least one attribute. In any case, the objection is countered by my observation (3), p. 170, an observation which also raises a problem for Jarrett, 1977 (above).

spondence, and that it is wholly independent of Curley's interpretation of "in itself/another" and "conceived through itself/another." Further, this evidence is not incidental to Part I. Some of it, for example, is located in the demonstration of *E* IP4. *E* IP4 is essential to the demonstration of *E* IP5, which is in turn utilized in the demonstration of many important propositions in Part I, e.g., *E* IP14, "Besides God, no substance can be nor can be conceived." (2) I have appealed to Spinoza's claim that "there is nothing therefore outside the intellect by which a number of things can be distinguished one from another, but substances or (which is the same thing by Def. 4) their attributes[,] and their affections" (*E* IP4D) in support of (i). Even if this can be read to mean something other than that SP-substance consists of attributes, surely the proper reading is that attributes (whatever their relation to SP-substance) and modes exist "outside the intellect." (3) Spinoza's claim that "the more reality or being a thing possesses, the more attributes belong to it" (*E* IP9) has too often been overlooked in the present context. It is difficult to see, on a subjectivist interpretation, why greater reality or (by *E* IIDef.6) perfection should entail more attributes. I conclude that attributes indeed exist outside the intellect, and hence that by the line of argument in the two paragraphs preceding (ii) any attribute is itself a (simple) SP-substance. The ultimate ontological constituents of Spinoza's metaphysics are attributes or simple SP-substances, and modes.

It might be objected that an interpretation which has the consequence that (ii) any attribute is itself an SP-substance must be mistaken. Perhaps the most plausible way to develop the objection is to point out that according to *E* IP14, "besides God, no substance can be nor can be conceived." Since God, by definition, consists of infinite attributes (*E* IDef.6), if each of these infinite attributes is itself an SP-substance, there do exist SP-substances "besides God," contrary to *E* IP14. This contradiction seems to me largely superficial. To resolve it, we need only construe *E* IP14 as asserting that there is no SP-substance which is not at least a constituent of God (the compound SP-substance consisting of infinite attributes or simple SP-substances); or alternatively, that there is no simple SP-substance which is not a constituent of God. Indeed, what is shown in the demonstration of *E* IP14 is that any attribute which exists is an attribute of God—and the attributes are precisely the simple SP-substances.[7]

19. Spinoza's Formal Argument against Mind-Body Interaction

The purpose of this section is to evaluate the formal argument at *E* iiiP2 against mind-body interaction. Since that argument depends crucially upon *E* iiP6, we will have to examine the argument there first. Before doing so, I must mention one result which Spinoza believes he has secured. He maintains that "whatever is, is in God" (*E* iP15). At *E* iP25C, he writes that "individual things are nothing but affections or modes of" God, citing only *E* iD5 and iP15 as evidence. Spinoza takes *E* iP15D to constitute a demonstration that whatever exists, including the individual things of our everyday experience, is in God.

It is worth noting that Spinoza has not established this result. The demonstration fails even if we grant him *E* iP14. I cite the complete demonstration, isolating three principal parts:

> Besides God there is no substance, nor can any be conceived (Prop. 14), that is to say (Def. 3), nothing which is in itself and is conceived through itself. [*a*] But modes (Def. 5) can neither be nor be conceived without substance; therefore in the divine nature only can they be, and through it alone can they be conceived. [*b*] But besides

[7]There are at least two other proposals as to how Spinoza could have subscribed to both (ii) and the thesis that God is the only SP-substance. Curley, 1974, pp. 240–241, treats Gueroult's account of the unity of God (see n. 4 above) as an attempt to show how we can subscribe to (ii) without having to "say that the attributes constitute an infinity of distinct substances rather than one substance," and discusses the resulting proposal sympathetically. Even if Gueroult's account of the unity of God is successful, this result cannot be exploited to remove the contradiction at issue. This is because the contrast between commitment to "an infinity of distinct substances *rather than* one substance is illicit," since it overlooks the possibility that one, unified substance itself consists of substances. Showing that God is a unified substance does not show that God's constituent attributes are not substances. The second proposal would have us attribute to Spinoza intuitions of "relative identity," such that it is true that thought and extension, for example, are different attributes, but the same substance. This suggestion is developed and defended by Martens, 1978; the basic strategy has been moderately criticized by Jarrett, 1978a, pp. 56–59.

substances and modes nothing is assumed (Ax. 1). [c] Therefore nothing can be or be conceived without God.

The difficulty is that for the purposes of the first two parts of the demonstration Spinoza utilizes both of the definitions of 'mode' at *E* ID5 (see p. 166). It is definition (a), on which modes are affections or modifications of SP-substance, which is required to sustain part (a) of the argument. Let us label modes so defined 'modes$_a$'. Given that God is the only SP-substance, and that modes$_a$ are by definition affections of SP-substance, the conclusion of part (a) of the argument, that modes$_a$ are in God, does follow. But it is definition (b), on which a mode is in another through which also it is conceived, which is required to sustain part (b) of the argument. Let us label modes so defined 'modes$_b$'. Given *E* IA1, the claim at part (b), that nothing exists except SP-substances and modes$_b$, does follow, via the argument produced at p. 168. The inference to the conclusion (c) then depends upon an equivocation: all modes$_a$ are in God; only God and modes$_b$ exist; therefore, everything which exists is in God. The equivocation generates a serious lacuna; as it stands, the argument overlooks the possibility that there exists some mode$_b$ that is not a mode$_a$. How could this be? One mode$_b$ could be in and conceived through a second mode$_b$, which could itself be in and conceived through a third mode$_b$, and so on ad infinitum. In other words, the universe might consist, in part, of an infinite series of modes$_b$, where each member of the series depends causally upon a prior member (Spinoza himself requires causal chains stretching back ad infinitum at *E* IP28), though the series does not depend causally upon God. Each mode$_b$ would be in another (in another mode, in particular) through which also it is conceived, and no mode$_b$ would be in God; hence no mode$_b$ would be a mode$_a$. This is not at all a Spinozistic picture. The point is that nothing in the demonstration of *E* IP15 rules out this possibility. The demonstration of what is perhaps the most famous proposition of the *Ethics* does not succeed.[8]

[8]I cannot see that Jarrett, in his "Logical Structure of Spinoza's *Ethics*, Part I" (1978a), has developed any resources for circumventing the fundamental difficulty. What I isolate as definitions (a) and (b) of 'mode' appear as Jarrett's "two requirements" for being a mode, requirements ii′ and iii′, respectively (p. 25), and later as definitions D5b and D5a, respectively (p. 50). Jarrett treats the claim that nothing

In any case, Spinoza holds that individual things are modes of God, that they are in God, and hence that their existence depends causally upon the existence of God. Since God is "substance consisting of infinite attributes" (*E* ıDef.6), the existence of individual things depends causally upon the existence of the attributes of God. What all of this means more precisely is this. Let 'A_1, A_2, . . . ,A_i, . . .' represent the distinct attributes of God. Since the existence of a mode depends causally upon the existence of God, and since God consists of A_1, A_2, . . . ,A_i, . . . , it follows that the existence of a mode depends causally upon the disjunction of the attributes of God, that is, upon A_1 and/or A_2, . . . , and/or A_i, ... Thus, I have noted Spinoza's willingness to write of "affections of the attributes of God" (*E* ıP14C2), and to state that "individual things are nothing but affections or modes of God's attributes" (*E* ıP25C). But this is all that follows: that the existence of a mode depends causally upon the existence of one or more of the attributes of God. The following question arises: is a given mode caused by all of these attributes together, or by some combination of the attributes, or by a single attribute?

Spinoza answers this question at *E* ııP6: "The modes of any attribute have God for a cause only in so far as He is considered under that attribute of which they are modes, and not in so far as He is considered under any other attribute." Since God consists of attributes, the references to God are eliminable, yielding: a mode of an attribute is caused by *that attribute* alone, and not by any other attribute. Spinoza's answer to our question is that any mode is caused by a single attribute. Consider a mode which is caused, at least in part, by attribute i. Let 'M_i' designate this mode of attribute A_i. M_i qualifies as a mode of A_i only because it is caused, at least in part, by A_i. Spinoza's claim at *E* ııP6 is that M_i is not also caused, even in part, by any attribute A_j other than (distinct from) A_i. In other words, the claim is that no entity is a mode of more than one

---

exists except substances and modes as a derived axiom, one derived from his D5a—my definition (*b*)—, but not from his D5b (p. 53). He indicates that the derivation of Proposition 15 will rely upon both his D5b and his D5a (p. 54). The difficulty is going to be that there is no way to show, short of just adding a suppressed premise, that an entity which satisfies the first requirement for being a mode also satisfies the second.

attribute; or alternatively, no mode is caused or produced by more than one attribute. Any mode is caused by a single attribute alone.

It is helpful to read the demonstration of *E* IIP6 against the background of Spinoza's distinction, in Part I, between infinite modes, both immediate and mediate, and finite modes (*E* IPs. 21–23,28). Infinite modes "must follow from the absolute nature of some attribute of God, either immediately (Prop. 21), or mediately through some modification following from His absolute nature, that is to say (Prop. 22), a modification which necessarily and infinitely exists" (*E* IP23D). So infinite modes follow, whether immediately or mediately, from the absolute nature of some attribute of God. Finite modes, by contrast, "could not be produced by the absolute nature of any attribute of God, for whatever follows from the absolute nature of any attribute of God is infinite"; rather, a finite mode must "follow or be determined to existence and action by God, or by some attribute of God, in so far as the attribute is modified by a modification which is finite" (*E* IP28D). So finite modes are caused by some attribute of God insofar as it is modified by finite modes, that is, finite modes are caused by other finite modes.

The demonstration of *E* IIP6 is short and superficially straightforward, appealing only to *E* IA4 and IP10:

> Each attribute is conceived by itself and without any other (Prop. 10, pt. 1). Therefore the modes of any attribute involve the conception of that attribute and of no other, and therefore (Ax. 4, pt. 1) have God for a cause in so far as He is considered under that attribute of which they are modes, and not so far as He is considered under any other attribute.

The structure of this demonstration seems clear enough:

(1) each attribute is conceived through itself and not through any other attribute (by *E* IP10);
(2) therefore, a mode of any attribute is conceived through that attribute and not through any other attribute;
(3) therefore (by *E* IA4), a mode of any attribute is caused solely by (the absolute nature of, or finite modes of) that attribute.

The parenthetical portion of (3) follows as a direct consequence of *E* IPs. 21–23,28, and is added for concreteness.

I have argued on the basis of *E* IP8S2 that Spinoza uses cognates of 'conceiving' and 'knowing' interchangeably (§9). *E* IIP6D confirms this equivalence, or, at the very least, the claim that 'conceiving' entails 'knowing'. We have seen that he uses 'knowledge' in a special sense brought out at *E* IA4. To SP-know a thing is to know its cause. And one entity is conceived through another just in case the conception of the one requires the conception of the other. The demonstration of *E* IIP6 is cogent only if conceiving an entity is identified with SP-knowing an entity, or at the very least if conceiving an entity entails SP-knowing an entity. Spinoza moves from

(2) a mode of any attribute is conceived through that attribute and not through any other attribute

to

(3) therefore (by *E* IA4), a mode of any attribute is caused solely by (the absolute nature of, or finite modes of) that attribute.

E IA4 would be irrelevant if conceiving a mode did not at the very least entail SP-knowing a mode.

Spinoza justifies (1) by appeal to *E* IP10: each attribute is conceived through itself. The justification is straightforward: an entity *x* is conceived through itself just in case SP-knowledge of *x does not* require SP-knowledge of anything else. An entity *x* is conceived through another just in case SP-knowledge of *x* does require SP-knowledge of something else. So *x*'s being conceived through itself and through another are mutually exclusive possibilities.[9] It follows that (1) each attribute is conceived through itself and not through any other attribute.

These preliminaries aside, we can proceed to an evaluation of *E* IIP6D. The first point to note is that Spinoza infers (2) from (1) immediately, without any explicit argument. Some sort of justification is surely needed. This is because (1) is a principle about attributes, which makes no reference to modes; (1) is justified by appeal to *E* IP10 ("Each attribute of a substance must be conceived through itself"), also a principle about attributes which makes no reference to modes; and *E* IP10 is itself justified (at *E* IP10D) solely by appeal to the definitions of 'substance' and 'attribute'. The claim at (1), and the argument for it, make no reference to the definition of 'mode', or to any axiom, proposition, or corollary about modes. The claim at (2), however, is a claim about modes, one which cannot possibly follow from (1), even taking into account its sources

[9]A different justification for (1) is provided by Jarrett, 1978a, p. 20.

in Part I of the *Ethics*. In other words, at E IIP6D Spinoza does not really supply an argument at all. What is needed is some principle relating modes to attributes which would license the inference from (1) to (2).

Suppose we think of the inference from (1) to (2) as involving a *reductio*, as follows:

> (1) Each attribute is conceived through itself and not through any other attribute. Now suppose it is false that (2) a mode of an attribute is conceived through that attribute and not through any other attribute. Then some mode of some attribute A_i is conceived through some distinct attribute A_j. But if a mode of A_i is conceived through a distinct attribute A_j, the attribute A_i itself is conceived through A_j. In that case, A_i is conceived or known through another attribute, in contradiction to (1). Therefore, (2) is true.

This *reductio* version of the demonstration brings to the surface a principle relating modes to attributes: if a mode of attribute A_i is conceived through a distinct attribute A_j, then A_i itself is conceived through A_j. The content of this principle can be brought out more clearly if it is reformulated in light of the claim that an entity x is conceived through another just in case SP-knowledge of x requires SP-knowledge of something else. This yields the principle: (P) if SP-knowledge of a mode of attribute A_i requires SP-knowledge of a distinct attribute A_j, then SP-knowledge of A_i itself requires SP-knowledge of A_j. This principle, if it can be sustained, will license the inference from (1) to (2). But Spinoza does not even state this principle, much less offer any argument for it.

I am fully cognizant that E IIP6D and the crucial principle (P) have more than an air of plausibility. Note that (P) is an immediate consequence of a more basic principle: (R) SP-knowledge of the modes of an attribute A_i is required for SP-knowledge of A_i itself. (R) entails (P): for if (R) SP-knowledge of the modes of an attribute A_i is required for SP-knowledge of A_i itself, and if SP-knowledge of a mode of A_i requires SP-knowledge of a distinct attribute A_j, then SP-knowledge of A_i itself requires SP-knowledge of A_j. I suggest that the demonstration of E IIP6D is seductive because (R) itself can seem quite plausible relative to certain models of the relationship between modes and attributes.

For example, suppose one thinks of an attribute as a property, and one thinks of a mode of an attribute as an instance of the relevant property. Suppose this model is coupled with a natural picture of concept formation, according to which general concepts are formed only as a result of consideration of particular instances of those concepts.[10] Then one generates the result that knowing or conceiving (some of) the modes of an attribute A_i is required for conceiving A_i itself. And this can easily be confused with the stronger principle that is actually required for the purposes of Spinoza's argument: (R) SP-knowledge of (all of) the modes of an attribute A_i is required for SP knowledge of A_i itself. (This principle is required because Spinoza wants his argument to apply to every mode of an attribute.) Alternatively, one might think of an attribute as a whole, and of modes of an attribute as its parts. Relative to this model, the principle that (R) SP-knowledge of (all of) the modes of an attribute A_i is required for SP-knowledge of A_i itself looks especially plausible.

Unfortunately, if—for whatever reason—we attribute to Spinoza the principle (R), contradiction results at the heart of his system. According to *E* ıP1, "Substance is by its nature prior to its affections." In what sense is SP-substance "prior to" its modes? The demonstration of *E* ıP1 is simply, "This is evident from Defs. 3 and 5," that is, from the definitions of 'substance' and 'mode'. We ought to be able to "read off" from these definitions the sense(s) in which SP-substance is prior to its modes, the two senses following from the metaphysical and epistemological components of the definitions of 'substance' and 'mode' respectively. SP-substance is *metaphysically prior* to its modes because whereas the existence of SP-substance does not depend causally upon the existence of anything else (and hence not upon the existence of modes in particular), the existence of modes does depend causally upon the existence of SP-substance. Further, SP-substance is *epistemologically prior* to its modes because whereas SP-knowledge of SP-substance does not require SP-knowledge of anything else (and hence does not require SP-

---

[10] Curley, 1973, §§ıı–ııı, suggests that in the *Ethics* Spinoza's view was that knowledge of the nature of an attribute is, taking the case of extension, knowledge of something common to all bodies, and that this knowledge is obtained from our experience of bodies.

knowledge of modes in particular), SP-knowledge of modes does require SP-knowledge of SP-substance. In sum, SP-substance is doubly "prior" to modes: both metaphysically (causally) and epistemologically.

We have established that (i) an SP-substance is a collection of attributes. So if SP-substance is epistemologically prior to its modes, it would seem that the collection of attributes which constitutes that SP-substance is also epistemologically prior to its modes.[11] It is clear that Spinoza accepts this result. Consider a portion of the demonstration of E 1P5, "In nature there cannot be two or more substances of the same nature or attribute":

> If there were two or more distinct substances, they must be distinguished one from the other by difference of attributes or difference of affections (Prop. 4). . . . If they are distinguished by difference of affections, since substance is prior by nature to its affections (Prop. 1), the affections therefore being placed on one side, and the substance being considered in itself, or, in other words (Def. 3 and Ax. 6), truly considered, it cannot be conceived as distinguished from another substance, that is to say (Prop. 4), there cannot be two or more substances, but only one possessing the same nature or attribute.

If the conclusion follows, it is because an SP-substance consists of a collection of attributes. And the argument requires that an SP-substance, which is "prior by nature to its affections" by E 1P1, be "truly considered" or "conceived" *by placing its affections on one side;* this to show that there cannot be two or more SP-substances possessing the same attributes. The procedure is unaccountable unless SP-knowledge of the collection of attributes which constitutes an SP-substance does *not* require knowledge of any of its modes. According to (R), however, SP-knowledge of the modes of an attribute A_i is required for SP-knowledge of A_i itself. When coupled with the assumption that SP-knowledge of a collection of attributes requires SP-knowledge of each member of the collection, attributing (R) to Spinoza yields an outright contradiction. And the contradiction would lie at the heart of the *Ethics,* since E 1P1 is essential to the demonstration of E 1P5, which is in turn utilized in the demon-

---

[11]Watt, 1972, p. 186, has noted this sort of result, pointing out that for Spinoza attributes appear to be "logically prior" to their modes.

strations of many important propositions in Part I e.g., *E* ıPl4: "Besides God, no substance can be nor can be conceived."

The argument thus far has relied upon Spinoza's position that (i) an SP-substance is a collection of attributes. He also holds that (ii) any attribute is itself an SP-substance. Since by *E* ıP1, SP-substance is metaphysically and epistemologically prior to its modes, it follows that any individual attribute is metaphysically and epistemologically prior to its modes, so that SP-knowledge of an individual attribute does not require knowledge of any of its modes. (R) is in direct contradiction to this. Any appeal to (R) in a reconstruction of the demonstration generates a contradiction between substantive theses required for Parts I and II of the *Ethics*, respectively. I will introduce an alternative construal of *E* ııP6D toward the close of this section.

How did Spinoza attempt to exploit *E* ııP6 for the purposes of his formal argument against mind-body interaction? Unlike his informal arguments (§17), his formal argument against mind-body interaction at *E* ıııP2 is cast in the technical vocabulary of his metaphysics, in the vocabulary of 'attribute' and 'mode'. To this point, I have explained and discussed the interrelationships between SP-substance, attributes, and modes without invoking the terminology of 'mind' or 'body'. It therefore remains to determine how Spinoza attempts to exploit the metaphysics of attributes and modes in order to generate conclusions about the relationship between mind and body, and his denial of interaction in particular. Put another way, the applicability of the metaphysics of attributes and modes to the minds and bodies of everyday experience remains to be explained.

Spinoza contends at *E* ıııP2 that since modes of distinct attributes do not interact causally, mind and body do not interact causally. In his words, "The body cannot determine the mind to thought, neither can the mind determine the body to motion nor rest, nor to anything else, if there be anything else." The argument for the claim that the body cannot determine the mind to thought is as follows:

> All modes of thought have God for a cause in so far as He is a thinking thing, and not in so far as He is manifested by any other attribute (Prop. 6, pt. 2). That which determines the mind to thought, therefore, is a mode of thought and not of extension, that is

to say (Def. 1, pt. 2), it is not the body. This is the first thing which
was to be proved.

The argument that the mind cannot determine the body to motion
or rest essentially proceeds *mutatis mutandis*.

To remind ourselves that this demonstration attempts to connect
the individual minds (or thoughts) and individual bodies of everyday
experience with the attributes and modes of Spinoza's metaphysics,
I will refer to the attributes of thought and extension as 'A-thought'
and 'A-extension' respectively, and to modes of thought and modes
of extension as 'modes-of-A-thought' and 'modes-of-A-extension' respectively. Then Spinoza's argument is as follows:

(1) By *E* IIP6, modes of an attribute are caused solely by (the absolute
    nature of, or finite modes of) that attribute, not by any other
    attribute.
(2) It follows as a special case that modes-of-A-thought are caused
    solely by (the absolute nature of, or finite modes-of-) A-thought,
    not by any other attribute.
(3) Therefore, modes-of-A-extension are not causes of modes-of-A-
    thought.
(4) Therefore, bodies are not causes of thoughts or minds.

At (2–3) Spinoza assumes that there exist attributes of thought
and extension. Given this assumption, (2) does follow from (1) as a
special case. But (3) follows from (2) only if (i) A-thought and
A-extension are distinct attributes. By *E* IIP6, a mode of an attribute
is caused solely by *that* attribute, not by any other attribute. It
follows that modes-of-A-thought are caused solely by A-thought,
not by any other attribute. So modes-of-A-extension are not causes
of modes-of-A-thought provided that A-thought and A-extension
are different attributes. Finally, (4) follows from (3) only if (ii) the
thoughts and bodies of everyday experience are modes-of-A-thought
and modes-of-A-extension respectively.

I doubt that Spinoza can even establish (ii). We have seen that his
argument at *E* IP15D for the identification of all individual things
(other than God) with modes of God is not successful. But suppose
we grant him the conclusion of that argument. Then the existence
of any individual thing depends causally upon the existence of one
or more of the attributes of God. Suppose we also grant the claim at
E IIP6 that if an entity is a mode of an attribute in the sense that it

depends causally upon the existence of that attribute, then that entity is caused solely by that attribute. Then Spinoza is entitled to the result that any individual thing is a mode of exactly one attribute. For by *E* iP15 any individual thing is a mode of at least one attribute; and then by *E* iiP6 an individual thing is a mode of exactly one attribute.

Now, suppose we also grant that (i) A-thought and A-extension are distinct attributes. Can Spinoza establish (ii)? Can he establish, for example, that a particular thought, given that it is a mode of exactly one attribute, is a mode-of-A-thought in particular? Spinoza, of course, thinks that he can establish this:

> *E* iiP1—Thought is an attribute of God, or God is a thinking thing.
>   Demonstr.—Individual thoughts, or this and that thought, are modes which express the nature of God in a certain and determinate manner (Corol. Prop. 25, pt. 1). God therefore possesses an attribute (Def. 5, pt. 1), the conception of which is involved in all individual thoughts, and through which they are conceived. Thought, therefore, is one of the infinite attributes of God.

E iP25C states simply that "individual things are nothing but affections or modes of God's attributes, expressing those attributes in a certain and determinate manner." Spinoza at best asserts that individual thoughts are conceived through the attribute of thought. We have seen that conceiving an entity at least entails knowing that entity, and that to know an entity is to know its causal history (§§9 and 19). So the assertion here is that individual thoughts are caused solely by (the absolute nature of, or finite modes of) A-thought. This assertion would hardly convince, for example, a body-mind epiphenomenalist, who holds that every individual thought has a causal history which consists exclusively of physical causes. Of course, even a Cartesian (in the sense of a strict follower of Descartes) would agree that individual thoughts are "conceived through" the attribute thought in the sense that thought is the principal attribute of minds, and every individual thought is one of the "many diverse forms of thinking" (*PP* i, 53). Individual thoughts are particulars of a certain type, or exemplify a certain property, that of thinking or thought. But a Cartesian need not and should not agree that individual thoughts are SP-conceived ("conceived" in Spinoza's sense of the term) through A-thought, as is required for the purposes of *E* iiiP2D. Spinoza does not even produce a reasonable *ad hominem* argument against Descartes.

This example of terminology potentially misleading to a Cartesian leads to a general point about Spinoza's strategy in attempting to refute Descartes' interactionism. At *E* iDef.4 Spinoza writes: "By attribute, I understand that which the intellect perceives as constituting the essence of substance." To a Cartesian, this might well look like familiar doctrine. According to Descartes, "*each substance has a principal attribute*" and "there is always one principal property of substance which constitutes its nature and essence" (*PP* i, 53). The Cartesian might feel that Spinoza's attributes are just Descartes' principal attributes. It emerges only subsequently that *E* iDef.4 is to be understood in such a way that it follows immediately that "each attribute of a substance must be conceived through itself" (*E* iP10). Even this is superficially similar to Descartes' doctrine, for "*we may have distinct conceptions of thought and extension, inasmuch as the one constitutes the nature of mind, and the other that of body*" (*PP* i, 63). The similarity is only superficial because it depends upon the supposition that Spinoza and Descartes think of "conceiving" an attribute in similar senses. But as we have seen, for Spinoza conceiving an entity entails knowing an entity, and to know an entity is to know its causal history. And it finally emerges, buried in the scholium to *E* iP29, that these Spinozistic doctrines are held to have the consequence that an attribute is not only conceived through itself, but is in itself, in the sense that its existence does not depend causally upon the existence of anything else, as well. Even if this were intelligible to a Cartesian, it would not be acceptable; for example, body, and hence presumably its principal attribute, extension, depend causally upon the existence of something else, God. Spinoza's fundamental strategy throughout is to stress the superficial terminological similarities, in the hope that the Cartesian will feel that *E* iiiP2, for example, shows that it is a consequence of the Cartesian conception of attributes that mind-body interaction cannot occur.[12]

---

[12]Curley, 1969, pp. 16–18, has pointed out that Descartes' use of the term 'attribute' was "highly idiosyncratic" in the sense that it involved fundamentally non-Cartesian elements. The differences between Descartes' conception of attributes and Spinoza's are so great that I doubt that Spinoza can even establish to the satisfaction of a Cartesian that (i) A-thought and A-extension are distinct attributes.

I want to mention one additional way of viewing the developments in *E* IIP6 and *E* IIIP2. To begin with, there is an alternative construal of *E* IIP6D. Perhaps we should construe the claim at (2) not so much as an intermediate conclusion in an argument, but rather as providing an implicit definition of 'mode of an attribute'. I will not develop this idea in detail, but what I have in mind is this. In section 18, I suggested that an entity is a mode of an attribute just in case its existence depends causally upon the existence of that attribute (i.e., that attribute is causally necessary for the existence of that entity). And in this section, I have assumed that the point of *E* IIP6D is to establish the substantive thesis that if an entity is a mode of an attribute in this sense, that if it is caused at least in part by that attribute, then that entity is caused solely by that attribute. But perhaps Spinoza's assertion that a mode of an attribute is conceived through that attribute and not through any other attribute (when coupled with the doctrine of *E* IA4 that to know an entity is to know its cause) amounts to the following stipulation: an entity is a mode of an attribute just in case its existence depends causally upon the existence of that attribute alone. In other words, in speaking of a 'mode of an attribute', Spinoza just means an entity which is caused solely by (the absolute nature of, or finite modes of) that attribute. This account of his procedure at *E* IIP6D, in which (2) is treated as an implicit definition rather than as a substantive thesis, has the advantage of explaining the absence of what is otherwise badly needed argumentation for (2).[13]

The interesting question is why Spinoza might have engaged in a stipulation according to which a mode of an attribute cannot be caused even in part by any distinct attribute. In section 14, I noted that there is evidence within *The Passions of the Soul* that Descartes held that a desire is itself causally sufficient for changes in the movement of the pineal gland (*PAS* I, 41). This would constitute an extraordinarily strong form of interactionism on which some mental

---

[13]There is also a disadvantage: on this construal, Spinoza is no longer entitled to the result that any individual thing is a mode of exactly one attribute (cf. pp. 180–181). By *E* IP15 every individual thing depends causally upon one or more of the attributes of God. There could, however, exist an individual thing which is a mode of God in this sense, but is not a mode of an attribute in the stipulated sense, because it depends causally upon more than one attribute of God. Spinoza would need some further argument to show that every mode of God is a mode of an attribute in the stipulated sense.

state or event taken alone is causally sufficient for some bodily event. I have also mentioned that Spinoza was unusually sensitive to fine points in Descartes' position. His summary at *E* vPref., for example, includes a reference to a specific article of *The Passions of the Soul*. Now, at *E* iiiP2S Spinoza mimics Descartes' language at *PAS* i, 41, writing of the view that "solely at the bidding of the mind, the body moves or rests, and does a number of things which depend upon the will of the mind alone." It is possible that Spinoza saw his task as that of defeating only this strong form of interactionism. The argument of three paragraphs preceding, *mutatis mutandis*, shows that he failed even in this. But if he did see the strong form of interactionism as his target, his arguments might well have appeared attractive. We have observed his willingness to equivocate between the claims that an entity is "conceived through" some attribute=exemplifies the relevant property and that the entity is a mode of that attribute=depends causally upon the existence of that attribute. Spinoza is prepared to move from the fact that a body is "conceived through" A-extension=exemplifies the property of being extended to the body's being a mode-of-A-extension. If the latter is taken to mean that features of the body are caused solely by the attribute of extension, the strong form of interactionism according to which the physical is caused by desires alone would appear to have been defeated.

Readers may be puzzled that I have omitted any discussion of the contribution of *E* iiP5 to Spinoza's formal argument against mind-body interaction. At *E* iiP5D, Spinoza argues that ideas or thoughts are caused by A-thought and not by any other attribute. Two arguments are supplied. The first of these either does not generalize to show that bodies are caused by A-extension and not by any other attribute, or does apply to bodies but so applied tends to show that they are caused by A-thought alone! The second argument is generalized at *E* iiP6D in a form which generates the denial of mind-body interaction, and this I have discussed in detail.

If I am correct, Spinoza's formal argument against mind-body interaction is a failure. This may be an unwelcome result; however, it is, I believe, entirely unsurprising given the quality of the argumentation for other central propositions of the *Ethics*. As Leibniz pointed out, there is a serious flaw in Spinoza's demonstration of *E*

1P5, a proposition employed in the subsequent demonstration of such important propositions as *E* 1P14.[14] I have shown above that the argument for Spinoza's most distinctive claim, "Whatever is, is in God" (*E* 1P15) is also a failure. The argument for the crucial proposition of Part 11, "The order and connection of ideas is the same as the order and connection of things" (*E* 11P7), has been demolished elsewhere in the literature.[15] There are many other examples of serious breakdowns in the argumentation of the *Ethics*.[16]

20. The Basis for Spinoza's Denial of Mind-Body Interaction

Spinoza reacts with laughter and disgust to Descartes' claim that minds and bodies causally interact. He joins in the allegation of incoherence (§15), but his formal arguments against mind-body interaction lend no support to this position, and his informal arguments hardly support so strong a posture. What, then, was the basis for Spinoza's denial of mind-body interaction?

There is a clue in the early sections of Part 1 of the *Ethics*:

A5. Those things which have nothing mutually in common with one another cannot through one another be mutually understood,

[14]Leibniz contends that Spinoza's appeal to indiscernibility fails to establish that "in nature there cannot be two or more substances of the same nature or attribute" (*E* 1P5). Leibniz's argument is that "two substances can be distinguished by their attributes and still have some common attribute, provided they also have others peculiar to themselves in addition. For example, A may have the attributes *c* and *d*, and B the attributes *d* and *e*" (L 198–199). Gueroult, 1968, p. 120, has come to Spinoza's defense. His point seems to be that Leibniz's substances do *not* have "the same nature or attribute" on the ground that the attribute of a substance is its whole essence; in this sense of 'attribute', A and B do differ in attribute. This does salvage the demonstration. Unfortunately, Spinoza's appeal to *E* 1P5 for the purposes of the demonstrations of *E* 1Ps.6,13,14 requires a stronger result. For example, at *E* 1P14D Spinoza argues that "there cannot be any substance excepting God" since, if there were, "two substances would exist possessing the same attribute, which (Prop. 5) is absurd." *E* 1P5, however, precludes only the possibility that there exist two substances identical in their whole essence; it does not preclude the possibility, for example, both that God exists and that there exists a substance whose whole essence is extension.

[15]See Barker, 1938, part 11, §4.

[16]For a taste of some further critical literature, see Taylor, 1937, and Barker, 1938.

that is to say, the conception of one does not involve the conception of the other.

Prop. III. If two things have nothing in common with one another, one cannot be the cause of the other.

Demonstr.—If they have nothing mutually in common with one another, they cannot (Ax. 5) through one another be mutually understood, and therefore (Ax. 4) one cannot be the cause of the other.

E IP3D is correct. By *E* IA5, if two things have nothing in common, neither is conceived through the other. But then by *E* IA4, neither is caused by the other, since to conceive a thing is to know its cause.

But *E* IA5 invites the question: Under what conditions is it the case that two things have nothing in common? A partial answer is at *E* IP2:

Prop. 2. Two substances having different attributes have nothing in common with one another.

Demonstr.—this is also evident from Def. 3. For each substance must be in itself and must be conceived through itself, that is to say, the conception of one does not involve the conception of the other.

Spinoza does not bother to complete the proof. We must add: therefore, by *E* IA5, two SP-substances have nothing in common with one another. If *E* IP2D is to work (as well as *E* IP3D), *E* IA5 must be read as a biconditional.[17] *E* IP3D requires:

A5a. If two things have nothing in common, then neither is conceived through the other.

E IP2D requires:

A5b. If neither of two things are conceived through the other, they have nothing in common.

What does *E* IA5 add to the *Ethics?* It permits Spinoza to argue as follows:

    (i) x and y are conceived through themselves;
    (ii) by *E* IA5b, they have nothing in common (at *E* IP2D);
    (iii) then by *E* IA5a, they are conceived through themselves;
    (iv) then by *E* IA4, neither is caused by the other (at *E* IP3D).

---

[17]Jarrett, 1978a, pp. 29, 32, has also made these points.

Since the contents of the claims at (i) and (iii) are identical, the appeal to *E* 1A5 is obviously eliminable in favor of:

    (i) x and y are conceived through themselves;
    (iv) then by *E* 1A4, neither is caused by the other.

The appeal to *E* 1A5 simply adds a superfluous argumentative loop.

This may seem astonishing, but I am not misdescribing Spinoza. He produces two demonstrations of *E* 1P6, the claim that neither x nor y can cause the other, where x and y are SP-substances. At the first demonstration he invokes, *inter alia*, *E* 1Ps.2–3. But he appends a second demonstration, which deduces *E* 1P6 directly from the fact that SP-substances are conceived through themselves (*E* 1Def.3) together with 1A4. The first demonstration appeals to propositions whose proofs appeal to *E* 1Def.3, 1A4, 1A5 (a and b), and more, whereas the second demonstration appeals to *E* 1Def.3 and no previous propositions; it relies upon *E* 1Def.3 and 1A4 alone.

At *E* 1P6D, Spinoza utilizes *E* 1A5 to show that no substance is the cause of another. He could equally use *E* 1A5 to show that no attribute is the cause of another. According to *E* 1P10, it follows from *E* 1Defs.3–4 alone that each attribute is conceived through itself. And given that at *E* 11P6D Spinoza moves from

    (1) each attribute is conceived through itself and not through any other attribute

to

    (2) a mode of any attribute is conceived through that attribute and not through any other attribute,

he could proceed to conclude by *E* 1A5b that modes of one attribute have nothing in common with modes of another, and that by *E* 1A5a they are therefore not conceived through one another, and by *E* 1A4 not causes of each other. Using *E* 1A5 in this way, in order to show that one thing is not the cause of another (as Spinoza does himself at *E* 1P6D), is rather like following a detour in order to get to one's present location. Further, this is the only "use" to which *E* 1A5 is put—*E* 1P3D is the only demonstration of the *Ethics* which appeals explicitly to *E* 1A5; *E* 1P2D is the only demonstration I know where it seems to be required, though not stated. What, then, is the function of the detour through *E* 1A5?

It seems to me that the basic function of E 1A5 is not so much to provide the materials for an argument as to ventilate a felt conviction. The conviction is that certain entities are so disparate or so unlike, have so little in common, that they could not interact causally. But it is not true, strictly speaking, that the entities (whether SP-substances, or attributes, or modes of distinct attributes) have *nothing* in common.[18] The conviction that they have so little in common that they could not interact, not itself an effective argument, gets converted into a stipulation—Spinoza stipulates that two entities "have nothing in common" just in case they cannot interact causally. This has the effect of giving the claim that two entities "have nothing in common" a particular theoretical force or bite. The detour through E 1A5 is a sort of pointer to the intuitions which guide Spinoza's conception of SP-substances and attributes. Attributes are conceived through themselves, and hence immediately by E 1A4 are not caused by anything else. What sorts of entities are conceived through themselves? Those that have so little in common, intuitively, that they could not interact causally (for example, A-thought and A-extension, and their respective modes). Arguments using E 1A5 are effectively monuments to a felt conviction for which no independent justification is provided.

Recall Descartes' bald assertions that qualities of material substance$_S$ have so little in common with thinking substance$_S$ itself that changes in the former could not cause the latter to cease to exist, but on the other hand that material substance$_S$ and thinking substance$_S$ have enough in common that they could causally interact. How much do two entities need to have in common if the existence of one can depend causally upon the other? And how different do two entities have to be in order to preclude causal interaction between them? Descartes had no general theory to invoke in order to answer these questions (§16). Spinoza was sure that minds and bodies had so little in common that they could not causally interact, but he too had no interesting theory on this matter. At E 1A5, he in effect announces (given E 1A4) that he will say that two entities "have nothing in common" just in case they do not causally interact.

[18]On this point, cf. ibid., pp. 29–30.

At the beginning of this section, I pointed to the discrepancy between Spinoza's attitude (laughter and disgust) toward Descartes' interactionism on the one hand, and the force of his informal and formal arguments against it on the other. I believe the basis of, or source for, the attitude reduces to the conviction that minds and bodies are too different, have too little in common, to interact causally. Both informal and formal argumentation is then marshaled, unsuccessfully, to support and justify this claim.

There may appear to be a sense in which Spinoza advances the discussion of the relationship between mind and body. Descartes' claims about the relationship between mind and body are entirely *ad hoc*, in the sense that they are not supported by an appeal to any more general theory. The question of the relationship between mind and body is treated as *sui generis*. By contrast, Spinoza treats the relationship between mind and body as a special case of the relationship between modes of any two distinct attributes. God consists of infinite attributes; by *E* IIP6, modes of any two distinct attributes do not causally interact; by *E* IIIP2, bodies or modes of extension and thoughts or modes of thought do not interact in particular. It looks as if Spinoza at least attempted a degree of theoretical or metaphysical generalization in his discussion of the mind-body relationship.

Possibly, however all we have here is the appearance of an attempt at theoretical advance. Spinoza seems to want to secure the result that there is a parallelism between modes of distinct attributes: "whether we think of nature under the attribute of extension, or under the attribute of thought, or under any other attribute whatever, we shall discover one and the same order, or one and the same connection of causes" (*E* IIP7S). This is supposed to follow from *E* IIP7: "The order and connection of ideas is the same as the order and connection of things." If the "things" in question are the modes of extension and nothing else, there will be one idea or mode of thought for every mode of extension, generating a parallelism between the modes of thought and the modes of extension, that is, a psychophysical parallelism. But if the "things" in question include not only modes of extension but modes of one or more other attributes as well, then the attribute of thought would seem to emerge as a "super-attribute" containing a mode (an idea) corresponding to each mode of every other attribute. In that case, the parallelism between modes of distinct attributes would seem to break down.[19]

It has been claimed that Spinoza avoids such difficulties because he uses 'infinite' to mean 'all' (so that God consists of infinite attributes in the sense that he consists of all the attributes there are), and he holds that in fact thought and extension are the only attributes.[20] This reinstates a parallelism between all the attributes, since thought and extension are the only attributes there are. Until this sort of interpretation has been defeated, it is possible that the appearance of theoretical advance in treating the mind-body relationship as but a special case of the relationship between modes of any two (of the infinity of distinct) attributes is nothing but window dressing. Spinoza may have purposely given the appearance of theoretical or metaphysical generalization where there was none. The relationship between mind and body, modes of thought and modes of extension, may have been for him the only case rather than a special case.

[19]The difficulties here are well known. See, for example, the discussion in Curley, 1969, pp. 144–153.
[20]See Wolf. 1927, § 5.

V

MALEBRANCHE'S DENIAL OF
CAUSES OTHER THAN GOD

21. Malebranche's Metaphysics

In discussing Malebranche after Spinoza, I depart from custom. Histories standardly treat Malebranche as preeminent among the "minor Cartesians" (a group usually taken to include John Clauberg, Gérauld de Cordemoy, Louis de la Forge, Arnold Geulincx, Pierre-Sylvain Régis, and others), not as a figure who ranks with either Spinoza or Leibniz.[1] This judgment with respect to Malebranche's relative philosophical merit and historical influence was not that of his times; it was Spinoza, not Malebranche, who was largely ignored or dismissed until late in the eighteenth century.[2]

The standard technique for justifying the prevailing historical judgment is to portray Malebranche as a transitional figure: his occasionalism is held to be simply a more consistent version of Descartes' philosophy on the one hand, and a mere way station en route to Spinoza's metaphysics on the other. For example:

> The principal findings of the Cartesian School were designed, some to complement, others to correct, certain deficiencies and errors in Descartes' metaphysics. From its earliest and most Cartesian phase that prolongation issues finally in a doctrine of complete Occasionalism. Then the introduction of certain new, non-Cartesian conceptions divides the main stream, on the one side toward pantheism, and on the other towards a form of spiritual pluralism. In its

[1] For a treatment of some of the minor Cartesians, see Balz, 1951.
[2] For a brief account, see Hampshire, 1951, pp. 26–28.

course, the chief moments of the whole movement are marked by
the transition from Régis to Malebranche, thence to Spinoza in the
one direction and to Liebniz in the other.[3]

In sections 24 and 25 below, I criticize the thesis that Malebranche's
occasionalism results from correcting deficiencies in Descartes' system. Here I want only to raise some questions about this account of
the relationship between the systems of Malebranche and Spinoza.

Malebranche's occasionalism is depicted as transitional to
Spinoza on the ground that occasionalism leads to pantheism. (In
addition, Malebranche's doctrine that there exists "infinite intelligible extension" in God is sometimes viewed as leading to
Spinoza's claim that extension is an attribute of God.) This sort of
picture presupposes a good deal of theoretical superstructure.
Malebranche emerges as a minor figure relative to Spinoza provided
that the theory of occasionalism was Malebranche's principal
philosophical contribution, and that occasionalism does lead in
some natural way to pantheism, and that Spinoza was a pantheist in
the relevant sense. Considerable interpretative and philosophical
work would be required to sustain these claims.[4]

Suppose, however, that these claims are correct. Even so, any
such dialectical relationship between the systems of Malebranche
and Spinoza was not mirrored in the historical relationships between these philosophers. The statement that the transition from
Malebranche to Spinoza was one of "the chief moments of the
whole movement" is simply mistaken if construed as a historical
account of the development of the relevant systems. While Spinoza's *Ethics* was not published until shortly after his death in 1677,
the work was substantially complete by 1665–66. Malebranche's
earliest published work, *The Search After Truth*, appeared in
1674–75, and the important summary of his system, *Dialogues on*

---

[3]Keeling, 1968, p. 218.

[4]It is interesting that the famous phrase "God or Nature," so often invoked in
support of a pantheist interpretation of Spinoza, does not (to my knowledge) appear
until Part IV of the *Ethics* (Pref. and P4D). Hampshire, 1951, pp. 39–55, is an
example of a commentator who interprets Spinoza as subscribing to a view which
identifies God with nature; he appeals to the phrase "God or Nature" without
textual citation (p. 39). For some difficulties for pantheist interpretations, see
Curley, 1969, pp. 41–43.

Metaphysics and on Religion, in 1688. Histories of philosophy typically suggest that Malebranche preceded and influenced Spinoza. This convenient picture, on which the chronological development mirrors the alleged dialectical relationship, is incorrect.

The portrayal of Malebranche as a historical transition to Spinoza might be a relatively harmless fiction, however, if Malebranche's occasionalism were the culmination of occasionalist trends that did influence Spinoza. The occasionalist systems of Cordemoy, La Forge, and Geulincx were published in 1665 and 1666, at precisely the time Spinoza was completing the *Ethics*. The occasionalist writings of Clauberg did appear as early as 1652, and occasionalism may have been "in the air" when Spinoza wrote. Whether Spinoza was conversant with such writings is another matter. Those who would see occasionalism as a transition or link between Descartes and Spinoza should not be heartened by the fact that occasionalism is not a subject of discussion in Spinoza's works.

I am not suggesting that, on the other hand, Malebranche was influenced by Spinoza. Malebranche's *Search* was written after the *Ethics* was composed, but before it was published. (Malebranche did come to know Spinoza's system, and late in his life had a correspondence on the subject with Dortous de Mairan, a disciple of Spinoza's.) Spinoza and Malebranche worked out their systems independently. Spinoza's system was fully developed somewhat earlier, though it appeared somewhat later. I treat Malebranche after Spinoza not because the latter influenced the former, but because Malebranche exerted much greater influence on the course of late seventeenth- and early eighteenth-century philosophy. We must consider his metaphysics on its own terms.

Any metaphysical theory includes at least two components: an account of the sorts of entities held to exist, and an account of the sorts of relations held to obtain between those entities. Malebranche's ontology is much more Cartesian than that of Spinoza. Cartesian substances$_S$, subjects or substrata in which qualities inhere, where inherence is a relation involving some sort of noncausal dependence, have no place in Spinoza's ontology. For Malebranche, there do exist Cartesian thinking substances$_S$ (*ST* 1, 1, 1; 1, 10, 1; *DMR* i.2), which include God and finite spirits. Malebranche's ontology also includes material or physical objects.

What sorts of relations obtain between these entities? I have already cited the noncausal relation of inherence between qualities and minds. Which of the entities are related causally? Malebranche was, of course, an occasionalist, denying the existence of causal relations between finite minds (and their qualities) and bodies. Physical states of bodies do not cause mental states. For example, "the point through which our hand is pricked does not cause the pain through the hole which it makes in the body" (*DMR* vi.3). Rather, the pain "is produced assuredly by a superior power. It is God Himself, who through the feelings with which He affects us reveals to us all that takes place outside us, I mean in our body and in the bodies of our environment" (*DMR* vi.3). Similarly, minds and/or mental states do not cause physical events. For example, "it is true that they [our arms] are moved when we will it, and that thus we are the natural cause of the movement of our arms. But *natural* causes are not true causes; they are only *occasional* causes that act only through the force and efficacy of the will of God" (*ST* 6, 2, 3). It is God who causes events in our bodies upon the occasion of mental events, and who causes mental states upon the occasion of physical events in our bodies.

Malebranche's occasionalism, however, is not simply a theory of the relationship between mind and body: "There is no relation of causality between a body and a mind. What am I saying? That there is no relation between a mind and a body. I am saying more. That there is no real relation between one body and another, between one mind and another. In a word, no created thing can act upon another by an activity which is its own. This I will prove to you presently" (*DMR* iv.11). Here Malebranche states not only that (created) minds and bodies do not interact, but also that no (created) mind interacts with any other mind, that no (created) body interacts with any other body. States of distinct minds (or bodies) do not interact.

This formulation leaves open the possibility that the state of a given body (or mind) at one time is a cause of states of that same body (or mind) at a subsequent time. Malebranche does not in fact countenance such interactions. States of the same body or mind do not interact. For example, in the case of a single mind, Malebranche writes: "I deny that my will is the true cause of my arm's movement, of my mind's ideas, and of other things accompanying my volitions" (*Eluc.* xv). One's volitions are not even causes of one's own mental life. He argues for a theory on which God is the only cause; no created entity has any causal efficacy—all created entities are completely impotent. This unqualified occasionalism is developed in *The Search after Truth*, Bk. 6, Pt. 2, Ch. 3, in the fifteenth of the *Elucidations* to the *Search*, and in *Dialogues on Metaphysics and on Religion*, Dialogue VII. The unqualified occasionalism amounts to this: of the physical and mental states of the created entities in the universe at one time, none are causes of any of the physical or mental states of any of the entities in the universe at the same or any subsequent time; it is God who is the cause of the total state of the created universe at any given time.

Malebranche's view is that God is the only cause in the universe; no created entity is ever a cause (not even a partial cause) of anything. (One exception will be noted in section 23 below.) When Malebranche contrasts *true, real* (*véritable, réele*) causes with *natural, occasional,* or *secondary* causes, and states that God is the sole real cause, whereas created entities are occasional causes, I understand this to mean that occasional causes are not (real) causes at all. On this interpretation, Malebranche's metaphysics is a structural analogue of body-mind epiphenomenalism. Think of body-mind epiphenomenalism as the position that bodies are a "base phenomenon" causally responsible for the states of minds which are causally inefficacious or a mere "epiphenomenon." Malebranche subscribes to a "God-created entity epiphenomenalism": God is the base phenomenon causally responsible for the states of created entities which are causally inefficacious or a mere epiphenomenon. Before turning to Malebranche's arguments for this position. I want to consider alternative interpretations of his occasionalism which attempt to locate at least some sense in which created entities are causally efficacious, some sense in which occasional causes are causes.

According to the first alternative, advanced by R. W. Church, it is God alone who is a proximate or immediate cause of the states of created entities, but created entities and their states are proximate causes of states of God (of God's volitions in particular), and hence are mediate or indirect causes of states of created entities. For example, a volition to move one's arm is not a proximate cause of motion in one's arm, or in one's pineal gland, or in any other part of one's body. But one's volition is the proximate cause of God's willing that one's arm move in a certain way. One's own volition occasions God's volition to move one's arm, and in that sense one's own volition is an occasional cause; it is the proximate cause of a volition of God's which in turn is the proximate cause of some physical state. On this interpretation, God is the sole real cause in the sense that God is the sole proximate cause of states of the created world. Occasional causes are proximate causes of God's volitions only.[5]

There is extensive superficial evidence for this interpretation, for example: "A natural cause is therefore not a real and true, but only an occasional cause, which determines the Author of nature to act in such and such a manner" (*ST* 6, 2, 3). Such statements must not be read at face value, for Malebranche argues:

> God is independent, hence He is unchangeable!
> ... there can be no effect or change without a cause. But God is independent of the activity of causes. Hence, if any change took place in God, He Himself would be the cause of it. But, although God is the cause and the principle of His volitions and decrees, He has never produced any change within Himself; for His decrees, though perfectly free, are themselves eternal and immutable....
> Understand, then, that in God there is no succession of thoughts and volitions, that it is by an eternal and immutable act that He knows all, and that He wills all that He wills. ... One and the same act of His will has reference to the different times which are contained in His eternity. God, then. ... cannot change because what He wills He wills without succession by a simple and invariable act. [*DMR* VIII.2]

Malebranche states that "God is independent of the activity of causes." This means at least that created entities are not causes of any of God's states. On the first alternative interpretation, a created spirit's volition, e.g., to move its arm, determines, occasions, or causes a volition of God, which in turn causes the arm to move. This is obviously not the position Malebranche adopts in the quoted passage. God's volition or decree that the arm move exists from eternity and hence predates any volitions of created spirits.

[5]See Church, 1931, chs. 3–4, esp. pp. 73–74, 102–106, 113–114.

I have relied upon a single passage which deals with God's independence and immutability in order to show that states of created entities are not causes even of God's volitions. Such evidence might be dismissed if it occurred in a work or letter dealing specifically with theological issues. At times, Malebranche might have made theological concessions inconsistent with his metaphysics. The passage I have quoted, however, occurs within the first few pages of Dialogue VIII of the *Dialogues,* and the theory of occasionalism is developed in Dialogue VII. It seems reasonable to interpret the occasionalist theory in light of the discussion of God's attributes which immediately follows.

According to the second alternative, advanced by Beatrice Rome, for Malebranche God is the sole true cause only in the sense that God alone has the power of creation; entities other than God do (directly) cause or act upon other created entities, though their causal efficacy is derivative from God's power and will rather than a consequence of their own essence.[6] Once again, there is extensive superficial evidence for this interpretation, for example: "*natural* causes . . . are only *occasional* causes that act only through the force and efficacy of the will of God" (*ST* 6, 2, 3). This seems to state that occasional causes do act, albeit via God's will.

Malebranche's statements that created entities do act upon each other should not be taken at face value, however. Granted, Malebranche often states that one created entity is the occasional cause of, acts upon, has power with respect to, or depends upon, another. The issue is how to interpret such claims. Consider the passage where he writes of "general laws in accordance with which God regulates the ordinary course of His Providence:—1. The general laws of the communication of motion, of which laws the impact of bodies is the occasional or natural cause. It is by the establishment of these laws that God has communicated to the sun the power to illumine, the fire the power to burn, and so on with regard to the other virtues or powers which bodies have for the purpose of acting upon one another" (*DMR* XIII.9). This certainly reads as if created entities have causal powers and act upon one another in a way which is derivative from God's will. But the direct continuation of

---

[6]See Rome, 1963, ch. IV, esp. §IV, pp. 209–242.

the passage immediately withdraws any such suggestion: "and it is by obeying His own laws that God produces everything which the secondary causes seem to produce." Secondary causes seem to be productive or efficacious, but they are not; they are not true causes. This passage is especially damaging to the second alternative interpretation because the sort of causation in question is the communication of motion. Rome holds that while bodies cannot create motion, they can and do impart motion.[7] Malebranche holds that bodies only seem to act upon one another in this way. His position is the same in the *Search*: "the collision of the two balls is the occasion for the Author of all motion in matter to carry out the decree of His will. . . . He does so by communicating to the second ball part of the motion of the first, i.e., to speak more clearly, by willing that the latter ball should acquire as much motion in the same direction as the former loses" (*ST* 3, 2, 3). Here again, it is God who "communicates" the motion; there is no causal interaction of any sort between the two balls.

Malebranche's theory that God is the only cause is, of course, paradoxical. This has perhaps led some commentators to attribute to Malebranche some mitigated version of occasionalism. Thus it has been suggested that created entities are mediate or indirect causes of natural states of affairs, and that created entities have derivative causal efficacy.[8] Malebranche himself, however, embraced the

---

[7]Ibid., p. 226.

[8]I find the interpretation of Radner, 1978b, ch. II, unclear. Insofar as I understand it, it seems to reduce either to a special case of the first alternative interpretation, or to a variant of the second alternative. Radner states persistently that "occasional causes determine the efficacy of God's general volitions" (p. 33). Precisely what does this mean? She provides a number of examples: "the small parts of the burning wood, coming into contact with the water on the linen, determine God to set the parts of the water in motion and to detach them from the linen in accordance with the laws of motion" (p. 35); "I determine God to move my arm . . . simply by having the desire" (p. 46); "Bodies determine God to move them . . . simply by colliding" (p. 46). In each case, some event or circumstance "determines" God to cause some motion. The most natural reading of these quotations is that the events or circumstances in question *cause* God to cause some motion. On this reading, we have a special case of the first alternative, an interpretation at odds with Malebranche's insistence that God is "independent of the activity of causes." I suspect that Radner would reply that the passages I have quoted are not representative, that it is not her view that any events or circumstances determine=cause God to do anything, and that in particular I have overlooked the role she assigns to "general volitions." "What distinguishes a general volition from a particular voli-

paradoxical results of his doctrine. He was content simply to find some way to do justice to our intuitions about interaction between created entities, and to the locutions of ordinary usage which capture those intuitions. God's volitions conform to certain regularities which Malebranche calls "natural laws," or "general laws," or "laws of conjunction," for example: "God has willed that my arm shall be set in motion at the instant that I will it myself." (*DMR* VII.13). Given this law of conjunction, we may say that my volition "causes" my arm to move, or "acts upon" my volition. But creatures

> cannot be in reciprocal dependence upon one another. One may, indeed, say that they are united to one another and that they depend upon one another. I grant this, provided that it is not understood in the ordinary and vulgar sense of the term, provided one agrees that they are so only in consequence of the immutable and ever effective will of the Creator.... God has linked together all His works, though He has not on that account produced in them entities charged with the function of union. He has subordinated them to one another without endowing them with active qualities. [*DMR* VII.13]

We may say that the motion of my arm *depends upon* my volition provided that we do not understand this phrase in its *vulgar* sense. Malebranche has no concessions to make to our intuitions about causation within the natural world.

---

tion is its conditional nature.... The volition that X should occur whenever something else Y occurs is a general volition" (p. 30). The idea seems to be that the presence of Y does not cause God to form the particular volition that X occurs. Rather, the presence of Y "determines the efficacy" of God's standing or persisting general volition. But what does this amount to? Whenever God's general volition is accompanied by the presence of Y, X occurs; if in a given case God's general volition had not been accompanied by the presence of Y, X would not have occurred. How could these conditions obtain unless the presence of God's general volition together with the presence of Y are joint causes of X? On the present reading, Radner's interpretation collapses into a variant of the second alternative, on which entities other than God are causes, albeit partial ones, of other entities in the world. The passages cited in the text do not allow for a division of causal labor between God's volitions on the one hand and occasional causes on the other. Radner holds that what is distinctive to her interpretation is that it is events or circumstances involving bodies or spirits (the having of some desire, the collision of bodies), rather than bodies or spirits *per se*, which are occasional causes (p. 46). But an interpretation which allows even that events or circumstances are either causes of God's volitions or acts, or partial causes of other events or circumstances, is too permissive.

22. Malebranche's Arguments

I turn to a review of Malebranche's arguments for unqualified occasionalism. He needs arguments which yield a dual result: first, that God is a cause; second, that no entity other than God is a cause; and hence that God is the sole cause. I discuss four arguments, in descending order of their importance to Malebranche.

(*a*) Throughout the first five books of the *Search*, Malebranche persistently draws upon occasionalist results, referring readers to a chapter of the final book for their demonstration. It is within this section (*ST* 6, 2, 3) that he produces his principal argument for occasionalism. A premise for the argument is that "a true cause . . . is one such that the mind perceives a necessary connection between it and its effect." Now, the idea of God is the idea of "an infinitely perfect and consequently all-powerful being," and hence one knows that "there is a necessary connection between the will of God and the thing He wills"; for example, "one knows there is such a connection between His will and the motion of all bodies, that it is impossible to conceive that He wills a body to be moved and that this body not be moved." What is more, "the mind perceives a necessary connection only between the will of an infinitely perfect being and its effects"; hence, God is the sole cause. I will briefly examine two lacunae within the argument.

The first difficulty is relatively minor. Let us grant Malebranche that necessarily, whatever an omnipotent being wills occurs. (Even this is not unproblematic, since some restrictions on the content of the being's volitions are required—what if, for example, the being wills that a square circle comes into existence? Unfortunately, the required restrictions are surprisingly difficult to state.) It does not follow that necessarily, whatever God wills occurs. This follows only if necessarily, God is omnipotent. There is an obvious route to this thesis available to any proponent of the ontological argument. If the ontological argument is cogent, it is necessarily the case that God exists, where God is that being than which none greater can be conceived, or the most perfect being. Suppose it is necessarily the case that having some specified property is a perfection. Then from the perspective of a proponent of the ontological argument, there can be no further question as to whether God has that property. So if it is necessarily the case that omnipotence is a perfection, and if the ontological argument is cogent, we have the result that necessarily, God is omnipotent. It is possible, however, that this route to the claim that necessarily, whatever God wills occurs was not available to Malebranche, since his posture toward the ontological argument is unclear (cf. *ST* 4, 11, 2–3). The matter is not worth pursuing, however, since Malebranche hardly needs to convince those who believe in God that God is a cause, and those who do not believe in God would not accept the ontological argument in any case.

The serious lacuna relates to the claim that the mind perceives a necessary connection *only* between the will of an infinitely perfect being and its effects. Granted that omnipotence might be one source of necessary connections between distinct events, it remains for Malebranche to show that it is the only source of such connections. It is difficult to see how the argument could proceed except eliminatively by consideration of cases. Thus he writes that "when we examine our idea of all finite minds, we do not see any necessary connection between their will and the motion of any body whatsoever. On the contrary, we see that there is none and that there can be none"; "it is clear that there is no necessary connection between our will to move our arms, for example, and the movement of our arms" (*ST* 6, 2, 3). What about the case of material objects? If they are causes, it is not by virtue of necessary connections between their volitions and distinct events. Malebranche must therefore argue in detail against the possibility of some sort of a priori geometrical science for moving bodies as envisioned by Descartes and subsequently by Locke (see §3, especially pp. 46–48).[9]

Such deficiencies aside, in drawing attention to one striking case of apparent necessary connections between distinct events—the connection between the volitions of an omnipotent being and their subsequent fulfillment—, Malebranche has perhaps thrown the burden of proof onto those who would find necessary connections elsewhere. His principal argument for occasionalism is an ingenious, breathtakingly swift attempt to exploit for his own purposes the thesis that causal relations obtain necessarily.

[9]Essentially the same point has been made by Lennon, 1974, p. 38.

(*b*) A second line of thought in support of the claim that no entity other than God is a cause emerges in the *Search,* and is elaborated in the *Dialogues.* The argument proceeds from the premise that as a matter of fact, whatever God wills occurs. (This presupposes only that God is in fact omnipotent, not that necessarily, God is omnipotent.) Malebranche makes the point as follows: "God created the world because He willed it: Dixit, & facta sunt" (*ST* 6, 2, 3); "God wills that a world shall come to be. His will being omnipotent, that world is at once an accomplished fact" (*DMR* vii. 7). We are invited to believe that since God's volitions are causally sufficient for the occurrence of what He wills, no other entity is a cause of the occurrence of what He wills. Even this conclusion falls short of the result that no entity other than God is a cause of anything whatsoever; for that, Malebranche requires the presmise that God wills the existence of the natural world in all its determinate detail.

Granting this point (but see § 23 below), we still find the difficulty that it simply does not follow from the fact that one state of affairs is causally sufficient for some effect that no other state of affairs is a cause of that effect. The present line of thought overlooks the possibility that God's volitions might be the initial members of a temporal chain of causes leading to the occurrence of what He wills. Malebranche invites us to form the following occasionalist picture. We can think of God's willing the existence of the natural world as a complex volition consisting of constituent volitions about the state of the natural world at each instant ("one and the same act of His will has reference to the different times which are contained in His eternity"—*DMR* viii.2). For any arbitrary time t_i, the constituent volition v_i about the state of the natural world at that time is the direct, unmediated cause of that state. Unfortunately, this simply overlooks the possibility that God realizes His volitions by causing an initial state of the natural world which, by virtue of the operation of genuine causal laws, is itself the cause of subsequent states of the natural world, which themselves cause later states, and so on.

Malebranche would object that on the present model created entities are (causal) "instruments" of God: "God needs no instruments to act; it suffices that He wills in order that a thing be, because it is a contradiction that He should will and that what He wills should not happen" (*ST* 6, 2, 3). The issue, however, is not whether God has need of instruments, but whether He in fact realizes some of His volitions through instruments. In the *Search*, Malebranche proceeds on two fronts. First, he falls back on argument (*a*), pointing out that we do not perceive any necessary connection between created entities themselves. Second, he produces some theological rhetoric: "those who claim that our power to move our arms is a true power should admit that God can also give to minds the power to create, annihilate, and to do all possible things; in short, that He can render them omnipotent" (*ST* 6, 2, 3).

(*c*) When a similar impasse is reached in the *Dialogues* (at the close of VII.7), a new sort of consideration emerges. Malebranche argues that a created thing "depends essentially" upon God (*DMR* VII.8). What does this mean? Malebranche's view is that *y* "depends essentially" upon *x* only if *y*'s continued existence depends upon *x*'s continued existence, only if *x*'s continued existence sustains the existence of *y*:

> To speak accurately, your house does not depend upon you. Why? Because it subsists without you. You can put it to flames whenever it pleases you, but you do not sustain it. This is why there is no essential relation of dependence between you and it. Thus, though God could destroy all created things whenever it pleased Him, so long as they could exist without the continual influence of the Creator, they would not be essentially dependent upon Him. . . . Suppose for a moment that God does not exist. The universe, according to your view, would not cease to exist. . . . Hence, if bodies are essentially dependent upon the Creator, they need, in order to exist, to be sustained by His continuous influence. [*DMR* VII.8]

Unfortunately, even if an entity *y* depends essentially upon *x* in the sense that *x* is a sustaining cause of *y*, it does not follow that *x* is the sole cause of *y*. For example, the continued existence of a flame might depend causally upon the continued presence of oxygen, but it does not follow that the presence of oxygen is the sole cause of the flame at a given time (another cause is the presence of sulphur). Similarly, it may be true that if God ceased to exist, the natural world would cease to exist, that God is a sustaining cause of the existence of the natural world. It does not follow that God is the sole cause of the existence of the natural world at a given time. Malebranche overlooks the possibility that a sustaining cause is but a partial use.

Malebranche's strategy is to show that the causal inefficacy of creatures follows from familiar properties of God relative to His creation, that God is "independent" and the created world "dependent." One can agree that the natural world depends upon God both as creator and sustainer, without being saddled with the result that God is the sole cause of the natural world at a given time. Of course, it is open to Malebranche to stipulate that the natural world "depends essentially" upon God in the strong sense that its continued existence depends causally upon God alone, but then argument, rather than mere exhortation, would be required to show that there does exist a God on whom the natural world "depends essentially" in this sense.

(*d*) Finally, I mention an argument that seems to have been of relatively little importance to Malebranche. There are a number of passages which suggest that he accepts the principle that one entity is a cause of another only if the former knows how to bring about the latter (*ST* 2, 1, 5, 1; *DMR* VII.13). This principle has the immediate consequence that no material object is ever a cause. And Malebranche does, at the passages cited, sometimes attempt to cast doubt on the claim that created spirits are causes, e.g., of the movement of their limbs, on the ground that they do not know how to move their limbs; they do not know the relevant anatomical and physiological facts. It would not be well advised to leave the argument there, since these are facts which someone could come to know, and Malebranche recognizes this himself: "But let us suppose that you know quite well what no one knows, about which even some scientists are not agreed, namely, that the arm can be moved only by means of the animal spirits, which flowing along the nerves to the muscles make them contract and draw towards themselves the bones to which they are attached. Let us suppose that you are acquainted with the anatomy and the action of your mechanism as well as a clockmaker is acquainted with his handiwork" (*DMR* VII. 13). Malebranche proceeds to argue on independent grounds that even if a spirit has such knowledge, the spirit does not cause the motion of its limbs. He is willing to appeal to the fact that we do not know the mechanisms involved in moving our limbs in order to prepare the ground for his conclusions, but he does not ultimately rely upon such considerations. The principle that a cause must have knowledge of the relevant causal mechanisms was utilized extensively by Arnold Geulincx (although it seems unlikely that Malebranche was familiar with his work), but not by Malebranche.[10]

Malebranche's four arguments for unqualified occasionalism appeal to (*a*) necessary connections grounded in omnipotence, (*b*) the sufficiency of God's will, (*c*) the "essential dependence" of created things upon God, and (*d*) a principle about causation and knowledge. Malebranche is unwilling to rely upon (*d*). Of the remaining arguments, (*b–c*) do not support his position. As for (*a*), if one grants the premise that cause and effect are necessarily connected, the argument is ingenious and even persuasive.

23. Some Complications and Difficulties

In order to make room for some sort of human freedom or liberty, Malebranche allows one exception to the claim that God is the sole cause. God wills that every created spirit has a general will or inclination toward the universal good (toward God himself); created spirits are free to apply or determine their will toward a particular object:

> There is a very significant difference between the impression of motion that the Author of nature produces in matter, and the impression or impulse toward the good in general that the same Author of nature continuously impresses in the mind. For matter is altogether without action; it has no force to arrest its motion or to direct it and turn it in one direction rather than another. . . . But such is not the case with the will, which in a sense can be said to be active, because our soul can direct in various ways the inclination or impression that God gives it. For although it cannot arrest this impression, it can in a sense turn it in the direction which pleases it, and thus cause all the disorder found in its inclinations, and all the miseries that are the certain and necessary results of sin.
>
> Consequently, I propose to designate by the word WILL, or capacity the soul has of loving different goods, *the impression or natural impulse that carries us toward general and indeterminate good;* and

[10]For the evidence that Malebranche was not familiar with Geulincx, see Church, 1931, p. 76, n. 1.

by FREEDOM I mean nothing else but *the power that the mind has of turning this impression toward objects that please us so that our natural inclinations are made to settle upon some particular object,* which inclinations were hitherto vaguely and indeterminately directed toward universal or general good, that is, toward God, who alone is the general good. [*ST* 1, 1, 2]

Malebranche's doctrine of liberty (elaborated at *ST* 4, 1, 3; *Elucs.* I and II) provides an exception to the general claim that no created entity is causally efficacious. Created spirits do have the freedom to cause or determine the content or object of their wills in particular volitions. Presumably, it is the soul itself which causes the volition; the soul does not do so by virtue of being in any particular mental state, since mental states themselves are only occasional causes. When Malebranche writes that "our soul can direct in various ways the inclination or impression that God gives it," or that "I have within myself a principle of my determinations" (*Eluc.* I), he is expounding a doctrine of "agent-causation" or "self-determination" (§15). Souls are causally efficacious in determining the content of their volitions.[11]

Malebranche attempts to mitigate the extent of this exception to what is otherwise an unqualified occasionalism. He points out, first, that minds "are incapable of willing anything unless God moves them toward good in general"; and second, since their thoughts and volitions are not themselves real causes, "one could always say that they are capable of nothing" (*ST* 6, 2, 3). The fact remains that souls do cause or determine the content or object of their volitions. This exception to the claim that God is the sole cause at once undermines the whole of Malebranche's argumentation for occasionalism and threatens some disastrous internal repercussions for the system.

[11]Keeling, 1968, p. 227, is mistaken in his claim that "for Malebranche, *none* of a self's states are caused by that self, its volitional acts are the effects of divine causation no less than changes of state or place in bodies." In taking as evidence a passage in which Malebranche denies that the volitions of created spirits are causally efficacious, Keeling confuses the claim that the volitions of created spirits are causally inefficacious with the claim that they are themselves caused by God. Malebranche accepts the former and denies the latter. Keeling's Malebranche may be more consistent than the historical Malebranche (see below), but Keeling's interpretation is mistaken.

The sorts of difficulties which the exception generates for Malebranche's arguments are obvious. His argument (*a*) depends upon the premise that causal connections are necessary connections. If this premise is to generate Malebranche's position, it must be the case that there somehow are necessary connections between souls and their volitions, but not, for example, between volitions and other mental states.

Or consider argument (*b*), which proceeds from the premise that whatever God wills occurs to the conclusion that God is the sole cause. I noted that the argument at best shows that if God wills particular determinate features of the natural world, God's will is the sole cause of the existence of those features. Just prior to deploying the argument in the *Dialogues*, Malebranche contends that God cannot will that a material object exist without also willing that it exist at a particular location and possessing a determinate velocity. Malebranche concludes that God is the sole cause of a material object's location and velocity as well as its existence (*DMR* vii.6). He has a target in the view that while finite spirits could not impart motion to material objects, they could affect or cause the direction of motion.[12] The admission of freedom is an embarrassment here. Malebranche argues that at a particular time a material object must either be at rest or in motion, and if in motion it must have a determinate velocity, and hence that God cannot will that a material object exists at a particular time unless it has a specified determinate velocity at that time. Parity suggests that at a particular time a created spirit either has no volition or some volition, and if some volition that it must have a determinate content or object, and hence that God cannot will that a created spirit exist at a particular time without willing that it has a specified determinate content or object. So God should be the sole cause of the volitions of minds as much as of the velocities of bodies. This would leave no room for freedom even in Malebranche's sense.[13] His claim that "there is a very significant difference between the impression or motion that the Author of nature produces in matter, and the impression or

[12]For a brief discussion of the position, see ibid., pp. 220–226.
[13]For some discussion of Malebranche's attempts to deal with this sort of difficulty, see Church, 1931, pp. 251–254.

impulse toward the good in general that the same Author of nature continuously impresses in the mind" is just special pleading.

The argumentation aside, the present exception to unqualified occasionalism threatens some disastrous internal repercussions. Apart from this exception, God is the sole cause, and He wills only that created entities have a general inclination or tendency toward the good. Although the soul causes or determines the content or object of its volitions, it is not causally determined to cause the particular volitions it does cause. Suppose that we freely will to move our arms, and that this free volition is the occasional cause of the motion of our arms. We have seen that God's volitions exist from eternity and hence predate the volitions of created spirits. So if God's willing that our arms move at the relevant time is not to prove fortuitous, He must have foreseen the content of the free volitions of created spirits. This is precisely Malebranche's position. He writes of

> the most inscrutable quality of the Divinity which is to foresee the free acts of a creature under all sorts of circumstances. According to my idea, God makes use just as readily of free causes as of necessary ones in the realisation of His designs. According to my idea, God does not form His wise designs blindly.... God gives them [free causes] a share in the glory of His work and of theirs, by allowing them to act freely according to their own nature, and in doing so He increases His own glory. For it is infinitely more difficult to realise His designs with certainty by means of free causes than by means of necessary or necessitated causes. [DMR xii.18]

I will not rehearse the difficulties which lead Malebranche to say, rightly, that the ability to foresee free volitions, where the agent is not himself causally determined to cause those volitions, is "most inscrutable." In the passage above, Malebranche attempts to turn this mystery into a virtue. What is interesting is that he must fall back upon Divine foreknowledge here if he is to retain central features of his occasionalism.

Suppose God lacked this quality. How would He bring it about that when at time t we will that our arms move, our arms do move at t', after some slight time lag? One possibility is that God "waits around" until t in order to see what created spirits freely will at t, and then He wills the next state of the natural world as appropriate. This is the sort of picture which the first alternative interpretation discussed in section 21 attributes to Malebranche: the volitions of created entities, at least, would seem to be proximate causes of states of God. This would be inconsistent with Malebranche's view that God's volitions predate those of created spirits, and would saddle Malebranche with the unwanted result that volitions of created spirits do cause or determine the will of God.

A second possibility avoids both of these results. Perhaps what God willed from eternity was the existence of irreducibly conditional laws, e.g., if in specified sorts of circumstances a spirit wills at t that his arm moves, his arm moves at t'. This is an "irreducibly" conditional law in the sense that it is not simply parasitic on regularities between completely determinate states of the natural world which God wills *ab initio*. God does not will for each instant a natural world that is completely determinate, including the content of created spirits' volitions. If the antecedent of such an irreducibly conditional law is satisfied, the consequent follows. It is then difficult to see any reason to deny that the conditional law is a causal law, and that the created spirit's volitions do cause its arm to move. Suppose not—then what did cause the arm to move? God did not will this *ab initio* (that would require inscrutable foreknowledge); He did not will it after seeing what the created spirit willed (that would reduce to the first alternative interpretation). So either the arm's moving has no cause, or the spirit's volition causes it to move. In other words, this second possibility collapses into the sort of picture which the second alternative interpretation attributes to Malebranche: the volitions of created entities, at least, are proximate causes of states of bodies.

The fact that Malebranche prefers to fall back upon the "most inscrutable" Divine foreknowledge rather than embrace either of the models contemplated by the alternative interpretations of his system is just further evidence that those interpretations are mistaken. On the other hand, Malebranche's appeal to agent-causation or self-determination as the locus of human freedom does create pressures in the direction of one or the other of these models. Malebranche relies upon God's foreknowledge in order to prevent the result that the volitions of created spirits are either proximate causes of God's volitions or proximate causes of subsequent states of the created world. The appeal to God's foreknowledge is his attempt to contain the repercussions of conceding some causal efficacy to created spirits.

It would be of no help to suppose that my interpretation of Malebranche's doctrine of freedom has gone astray, and that on his view volitions are "free" in the soft determinist sense. If this were his view, free volitions would be causally determined, albeit in the absence of constraint or compulsion, by preceding mental and/or physical states. These causes could not be exclusively states of God—such a position would be the unqualified occasionalism which prompts Malebranche to find some locus for human freedom in the first place. So at least some of these causes would have to be preceding mental and/or physical states of entities other than God, in which case exceptions to the claim that God is the sole cause, that created entities are not causes, would simply multiply.

24. Accounts of the Sources of Malebranche's Occasionalism in Descartes

It is often suggested that in embracing occasionalism Malebranche was simply recognizing that this is the position which results from the expulsion of some important inconsistency from Descartes' system. On this view, Malebranche was developing the philosophy of Descartes in a more consistent direction. This thesis was stated boldly by Norman Kemp Smith at the turn of the century: "The most extreme occasionalism is... the outcome of Descartes' metaphysics"; "Though Descartes thus inconsistently and vainly attempts to escape occasionalism, the inevitable consequences of his rationalism are one and all emphasized by his successor, Malebranche."[14] More recently, T. M. Lennon has argued for a somewhat guarded form of Kemp Smith's position: "My case here will be that his view [Malebranche's occasionalism] is the historical and logical dénouement of principles more or less explicit both in Descartes and in two of his lesser known disciples, LaForge and Cordemoy."[15] Daisie Radner holds the closely related thesis that Malebranche's philosophy is an attempt to solve problems inherent in Descartes' system.[16]

[14]Smith, 1902, pp. 74, 85.
[15]Lennon, 1974, p. 29.
[16]Radner, 1978b, ch. I.

I believe it a mistake to view Malebranche's occasionalism as an attempt to resolve difficulties in Descartes' philosophy. There are a number of versions of the sort of position I want to attack, depending upon where the inconsistency in Descartes' thought is located. Descartes' admission of causation by certain entities other than God has variously been held, in the present context, to be inconsistent with his claims (i) that conservation is continual re-creation, (ii) that motion is a mode of body, and (iii) that mind and body differ in essence.

(i) Kemp Smith's argument in connection with Descartes' views on conservation is relatively straightforward. He points out that for Descartes "persistence in existence . . . is in all essentials perpetual and unceasing re-creation," and "since persistence in existence is traced to God, so consistently must everything else."[17] I agree that for Descartes persistence in existence is unceasing re-creation, but I do not agree that persistence is unceasing re-creation by God. This needs explanation.

Descartes' claim that conservation is constant re-creation appears in *Meditation III*, in the *Reply to Objections II*, and in Part I of *The Principles of Philosophy*. In each case, the context is the same: Descartes is formulating the second of the two causal arguments for the existence of God contained in *Meditation III*. It cannot be a premise for such an argument that conservation is constant re-creation by God. What Descartes does say in the *Meditations*, and in the "geometrical" presentation of the same material in the *Replies*, is this:

> It is . . . perfectly clear and evident to all those who consider with attention the nature of time, that, in order to be conserved in each moment in which it endures, a substance has need of the same power and action as would be necessary to produce and create it anew, supposing it did not yet exist, so that the light of nature shows us clearly that the distinction between creation and conservation is solely a distinction of the reason. [*Med. III*, HR I, 168]

> In order to secure the continued existence of a thing, no less a cause is required than that needed to produce it at the first. [HR II, 56]

These passages suggest a "weak" re-creation principle: conservation of an entity requires continual re-creation by *at least as perfect an*

[17]Smith, 1902, p. 73. See also Ginsberg, 1923, pp. 51–52; and Leyden, 1968, pp. 17–18.

entity as that required to create it originally. In the *Principles*, there is this: "from the fact that we now are, it does not follow that we shall be a moment afterwards, if some cause—the same that first produced us—does not continue so to produce us; that is to say, to conserve us" (*PP* I, 21). This suggests a "strong" re-creation principle: conservation of an entity requires continual re-creation by *the same entity* as that which created it. The weak principle is sufficient for Descartes' purposes in the context of his second argument for the existence of God in *Meditation III*. In any case, it makes no difference to my argument against Kemp Smith whether Descartes would have preferred the weak or strong formulation. What matters is that neither of these principles states that conservation of an entity requires continual re-creation *by God*. That would be true only in the special case where it was God who originally created an entity.

If Descartes is to exploit the (strong or weak) re-creation principle in order to generate an argument for the (continued) existence of God, he has to locate an entity that was created by God. This is not difficult to do, since the second of Descartes' two causal arguments for the existence of God comes right on the heels of the first. There are a number of difficult questions concerning the relationships between the two arguments of *Meditation III*. I need only make the following points. The first argument moves from the premise that there exists an idea of God, an all-perfect being, together with the "causal principle" that there must be at least as much reality or perfection in the cause as in its effect, to the conclusion that God, an all-perfect being, exists. Now, in *Meditation III*, and in the *Reply to Objections II*, Descartes does not proceed to argue from the mere fact that he persists through time that God exists and conserves his existence by continually re-creating him. This would not follow from the mere fact that Descartes persists coupled with the re-creation principle. The most that would follow is that Descartes is conserved by the same entity which created him, where the question of the nature of that entity remains open. To answer that question in the way he wants, Descartes must rely upon the independent causal principle utilized in the first causal argument. Thus, in the course of formulating the second argument, he writes: "there must be at least as much reality in the cause as in the effect; and thus since I am a thinking thing, *and possess an idea of God within me . . .*"; "He to whom my conservation is due contains within

Himself formally or eminently everything that is in me. . . . But there exists in me the perception of many perfections that I do not possess, *as well as of the idea of God"* (HR I, 169, II, 58—emphases added). (In formulating the second causal argument in the *Principles*—Part I, 21—Descartes does write *"that the mere duration of our life suffices to prove the existence of God."* However, he is arguably presupposing the claim of the preceding section that we have an idea of God; and in any case the much lengthier formulations of the second causal argument in the *Meditations* and *Replies* deserve to be taken more seriously.) Conservation is re-creation by God, Divine re-creation, only in the special case where the original creation of the relevant entity was by God. The re-creation principle which Descartes requires and uses for the purposes of his second causal argument simply does not yield occasionalism as a result.[18] It may well be that, from Descartes' perspective, a variety of entities less extraordinary than a being who possesses the idea of God (e.g., such entities as clouds) are both brought into existence and conserved by entities other than God, but which are themselves at least as real or perfect as their effects. Hume, I think, got Descartes' position right: "Descartes insinuated that doctrine of the universal and sole efficacy of the Deity, without insisting on it" (*Enq.* 58, note 1).

Kemp Smith contends, however, that Descartes' views about the nature of time commit him to the thesis that conservation is Divine re-creation.[19] And Descartes of course does introduce his re-creation principles as "perfectly clear and evident to all those who consider with attention the nature of time." His position is that since the parts of time are not dependent upon one another, "from the fact that I was in existence a short time ago it does not follow that I must be in existence now," and he concludes that "some cause at this instant, so to speak, produces me anew, that is to say, conserves me" (*Med. III*, HR I, 168), or that "in order to secure the continued existence of a thing, no less a cause is required than that needed to

---

[18]Curley, 1978, p. 222, finds Descartes committed to continual re-creation by God ("We must acknowledge God as the universal cause of motion in general because He continuously creates the world") on the basis of *PP* II, 36. As far as I can see, however, the text cited states only that God conserves the quantity of motion in the world which He created.

[19]Smith, 1902, pp. 72–73, and 1952, p. 218.

produce it at the first" (HR II, 56). The most that follows from Descartes' view about time is that some cause, no less a cause than that required for an entity's creation, is required for its conservation. As before, conservation requires Divine re-creation only in a special case, e.g., the case of an entity that possesses an idea of an all-perfect being.[20]

In addition, there is a special difficulty since Kemp Smith is attempting to show that Malebranche emphasized the occasionalism implicit in Descartes. According to Kemp Smith, it is specifically Descartes' view that time is discontinuous which requires the view that conservation is continued re-creation. However, as Rome has pointed out, Malebranche did not accept this view of time: "For ultimately duration has no instants as bodies have no atoms; and just as the smallest part of matter can be infinitely divided, infinitely smaller and smaller parts of duration can be given, as is easy to demonstrate" (*ST* 1, 8, 2).[21]

In any case, even Descartes is not committed to the thesis that conservation is Divine re-creation. Kemp Smith attempts to saddle Descartes with this thesis as follows. He contends that the initial existence of finite and contingent entities is due to the arbitrary will of God. Then since continued existence requires no less a cause than initial existence, persistence consists specifically of Divine re-creation. The difficulty is that even if the existence of finite and contingent entities is ultimately due to the arbitrary will of God, it does not follow that God creates each finite and contingent entity. It may be that He creates some finite and contingent entities which in turn cause others to come into existence. Descartes can consistently hold that there are cases of conservation which are not re-creation by God.

(ii) I turn to Kemp Smith's argument in connection with Descartes' views relating to motion:

[20]L. J. Beck, 1965, p. 195, also tries to ground Divine re-creation in Descartes' views about time, though in a somewhat different manner: "Descartes is committed to the theory that time is discrete, that the moments of time are independent one of the other. Intrinsically discontinuous, they would not in fact form a succession of moments unless there were a God holding them together by a continuous act of creation, not of the moments of time but of the dependent substances which exist and endure." I see no philosophical warrant for the claim in the second sentence, and no textual warrant for the suggestion that this was Descartes' view.

[21]Rome, 1963, p. 223.

From the geometrical point of view (which is emphasized in his metaphysics) motion is mere transference from one place to another. So regarded it is a *mode* of extension. . . . Being a mode of the particular body moved, it cannot any more than other modes of that body be regarded either as transferable or as indestructible. Like figure, when it ceases to be in one particular body, it must cease altogether.

Descartes could not, however, consistently hold to that geometrical view of motion, as a *mode* of matter, since it would have forced him to adopt one of two disagreeable alternatives. Either, first, motion being as untransferable as figure, he would have had to ascribe to each particular body the power of creating new motion in other bodies on impact. Or secondly, he would have been forced to admit that body is incapable of acting on body, and that therefore God is the sole Mover.[22]

There is room for argument here on a number of points. First, it is far from clear that Kemp Smith's alternatives are really exhaustive. All that need be "transferred" is quantity of motion. Second, the criticism depends upon the picture of one particular body acting upon another where the two bodies are different substances—modes are untransferable between substances because necessarily any mode inheres in some substance (§7). Descartes is inclined toward a different view, that there is only one bodily substance, the whole of extension or of the physical universe (cf. *PP* II, 21–25).[23]

Suppose, however, that we grant the difficulty in connection with motion. Radner has suggested a problem which is in effect a generalization of this difficulty. She claims that for Descartes causal interaction between any two substances (e.g., a body and a mind, or two minds) is problematic. Her argument is that Descartes holds both that modes cannot pass from one substance to another, and that causation involves communication or impartment.[24] Radner provides no textual justification for this latter attribution, but suppose we grant this quite general difficulty as well.[25]

[22]Smith, 1902, pp. 75–76.
[23]The point is developed in Keeling, 1968, pp. 129–130, and Williams, 1978, pp. 126–129.
[24]Radner, 1978b, pp. 3, 11–12.
[25]The passages Radner does cite relate to the claim that "anything which acts as a cause must contain in itself what it produces in another thing" (1978b, p. 11). I have argued (§15) that Descartes did not hold this general principle. Even if he did, this principle does not itself commit one to the view that causation requires transmission.

These considerations do not have any tendency to preclude minds or mental states from being causes of subsequent mental states within a single individual. But as we have seen (§21), Malebranche denies causal interaction even between the mental states (for example, volitions and subsequent ideas) of a single created mind. The present accounts of the source or development of his occasionalism do not explain why Malebranche takes this further step.

Lennon has produced an account of the relevance of Descartes' view that motion is a mode which, if correct, would provide the needed explanation. He argues that it does follow from principles "more or less explicit... in Descartes" that "God is not only the first cause, but also the only real cause. ... at least as far as motion is concerned," and "that the case extends even to immaterial substance."[26] In the case of motion, where motion is a mode of bodies, the idea is this: "the Cartesian nominalism has as its consequence that to cause a new mode is to create a new substance—ultimately, no substance can remain identical through changes in its modes. If a thing is in motion to the extent that certain of its modes change over time, then motion must involve the creation of a succession of different substances, and hence there is none but a conceptual difference between moving a body and creating one."[27] Lennon has a further argument to show that in the case of motion this continued re-creation must be by God. He holds that "the case extends even to immaterial substance" as follows:

> There was a natural, and as we have seen, conscious extension of the analysis of the causation of motion to the causation of mental episodes. This was true also for Malebranche, who in his tenth *Eclaircissement* argues against the view that the mind produces its own thoughts: thoughts are modes or qualities of the mind; thought and will stand to the mind as do shape and motion to corporeal substance; as no body can move or shape itself, so no mind can give itself its own thoughts or volitions.[28]

Malebranche does treat thoughts as modes of the mind; however, to secure the result that conservation is re-creation in the case of minds, we need the additional principle that "to cause a new mode is to create a new substance—ultimately, no substance can remain

---

[26]Lennon, 1974, pp. 29, 35, 36.
[27]Ibid., p. 37.
[28]Ibid., pp. 36, 37.

identical through changes in its modes." Descartes did not himself subscribe to this thesis in its complete generality: *"the human mind . . . is a pure substance. For although all the accidents of mind be changed, although, for instance, it think certain things, will others, perceive others, etc., despite all this it does not emerge from these changes another mind: the human body on the other hand becomes a different thing from the sole fact that the figure or form of any of its portions is found to be changed"* (HR I, 141). Descartes' position is that a body does not persist through changes in figure; whatever the case with motion, he is explicit that minds do persist through changes in their modes. It is difficult to believe that Malebranche extended the argument to minds at the cost of denying that they persist through time. It is worth noting that the passages Lennon cites in support of his interpretation of Malebranche arise in the tenth of the *Elucidations* of the *Search*, whereas it is the fifteenth which is devoted to a defense of occasionalism.

(iii) According to perhaps the most popular account of the relationship between Malebranche and Descartes, Malebranche's occasionalism is a response to the mind-body problem. We are told, for example, that "the occasional causes of Malebranche, the parallelism of Spinoza, the pre-established harmony of Leibniz, are among the most famous attempts to solve the problem of how, once having accepted the radical separation of mind and body, some way can be devised to explain how they act the one upon the other."[29] And in the context of a more detailed study which extends to the minor Cartesians, we find this:

> These measures of de la Forge, Régis, and Clauberg, however, all leave untouched the original difficulty, viz. if mind and matter are wholly disparate, how is it possible for either to determine the character of a change in the other, any more than to cause the occurrence of a change in the other? Of this question, the three thinkers of our second group—Cordemoy, Geulincx, and Malebranche—take special account, and think to answer it by a doctrine of complete Occasionalism.[30]

---

[29]L. J. Beck, 1965, p. 269. It should be noted that Beck considers the problem a "pseudo-problem."

[30]Keeling, 1968, p. 224. Others who place considerable stress on the contribution of the mind-body problem are Ginsberg, 1923, pp. 52–53; Rodis-Lewis, 1963, p. 296; Leyden, 1968, p. 216; and Radner, 1978b, pp. 10–12.

Is there any good sense in which this is a correct picture?

I have already argued in detail (§15) that Descartes' claim that mind and body causally interact was not inconsistent either with his claim that mind and body are essentially/entirely/absolutely distinct substances$_S$, nor with any restrictions which he imposes upon the likeness of cause and effect. In other words, Descartes' interactionism was not inconsistent with his "radical separation of mind and body," even when coupled with any restrictions upon possible causal relations which he introduces. On the other hand, for many—including Spinoza—there is a perceived or felt difficulty for the claim that Descartes' mind and body interact. So there remains the issue as to whether Malebranche's occasionalism was a response to a perceived or felt mind-body problem. A number of considerations suggest a negative response to this question.

First, if the possibility of causal relations between mind and body is problematic, there is a clear sense in which Malebranche does not even address the problem—he leaves it untouched. To see what I have in mind, consider the following imaginary (very) minor Cartesian. Our Cartesian holds that Descartes' mind-body interactionism is "logically" or "conceptually" incoherent, perhaps on the ground that interaction between entities whose essences have nothing in common is inconceivable. Our Cartesian develops the following metaphysics: there exists an omnipotent being, God, who upon the occasion of appropriate mental states in finite minds causally interacts with certain bodies in order to produce changes in their states. Suppose God is itself a mind, unextended and immaterial. Then if mind-body interaction is logically or conceptually incoherent, God-body interaction is equally incoherent. Even if we grant that God is omnipotent, how can an omnipotent being achieve the logically or conceptually impossible? If there is a "mind-body problem," our imaginary Cartesian fails to address it; he obscures it by an appeal to divine omnipotence.

These considerations are applicable to Malebranche with some modification. It might be denied that the fact that x causes y to come into existence, or that x creates y, itself constitutes causal interaction between x and y. After all, prior to y's creation, y was not an existent entity available for interaction. This point need not be argued; we can stipulate that if x creates y, there is a "causal relation" between *x* and *y*, albeit not a causal interaction. Some causal relations are interactions, some creations. Now, suppose there is something problematic about the claim that a mind causally interacts with a body. It seems that it should be at least as problematic that a mind creates a body. Thus Descartes maintains that it is "a greater thing" to create a substance than to create its properties (HR II, 57). To interact with a substance just is (in most cases) to cause a change in its properties. Some quite specialized argument would be required to motivate the claim that a mind can create a body, but not interact with a body it has created. Put another way, arguments against mind-body interaction seem to militate a fortiori against mind-body creation. In Malebranche's metaphysics, there are no causal interactions, in the narrow sense, between any mind (including God) and any body. There are causal relations, creations, between God and bodies. But God is a mind, unextended and immaterial. If mind-body creation is logically or conceptually incoherent, God-body creation is equally incoherent. Granted that God is omnipotent, it is difficult to see how even an omnipotent being can achieve the logically or conceptually impossible. And it would seem uncharitable in the extreme to suppose occasionalism, perhaps the fundamental tenet of Malebranche's philosophy, nothing more than an attempt to obscure a mind-body problem in the shroud of Divine omnipotence.

Second, the suggestion that Malebranche's occasionalism is a response to the mind-body problem does not do justice to the character of his argumentation for occasionalism. I certainly do not want to deny that Malebranche felt that mind-body interaction is problematic. He did. What is significant is that he held that mind-body interaction is much more problematic than other forms of interaction, such as that between bodies. He writes, for example, that the belief that mind and body causally interact is "without the faintest plausibility," while the belief that bodies communicate motion to one another is at least "something having a certain plausibility" (ST 5, 1). This latter belief, however, is a "prejudice or error" (ST 5, 1), and for the proof of this position Malebranche refers the reader to Bk. 6, Pt. 2, Ch. 3 of the *Search*. Evidently, any considerations which might be thought to tell against the possibility of mind-body interaction would, on Malebranche's view, be less effec-

tive in telling against causal interaction within the physical (or mental) realm alone. The denial that any entity other than God is ever a
cause of anything will therefore require some special argument. For
these reasons, it should be no surprise that in the relevant section of
the *Search* (and in the *Dialogues* as well), Malebranche does not
attempt to show that occasionalism results, as it obviously does not,
from some generalization of the thought that entities whose essences
have nothing in common cannot interact. All of his principal arguments for occasionalism proceed from some consideration specifically about God: (*a*) that there is a necessary connection between
God's volitions and their realization. (*b*) that God's volitions are
sufficient for their realization, and (*c*) that creatures are essentially
dependent upon God.[31]

I have considered three distinct accounts of the sources of Malebranche's occasionalism in Descartes. According to the first, occasionalism is a consequence of Descartes' claim that conservation
is continual re-creation. Against this: Descartes did not hold, and
did not need to hold, that conservation is continual re-creation by
God; occasionalism is in any case such a trivial consequence of this
principle that Malebranche could not have argued for it on this
ground; and his arguments for occasionalism simply do not proceed
from such a principle. Lennon writes that the seventh dialogue
"contains . . . the logical foundation of all his attempts to prove that
only God can be a cause," namely, the Divine re-creation principle.[32] While Malebranche does state this principle, it is clearly
intended to be the conclusion of the independent argument (*b*),
which appeals to the sufficiency of God's will (*DMR* VII.7).

I believe that a hybrid theory, drawing upon the second and third
of the accounts above, would constitute the best defense of the thesis
that Malebranche's occasionalism results from attempts to resolve
difficulties or inconsistencies in Descartes. The hybrid theory need
not claim that Descartes was involved in any inconsistency in connection with his views relating either to motion or to mind-body
interaction. It need claim only that Malebranche was responding to
perceived or felt difficulties in both these areas: the perceived diffi-

[31]Lennon, 1974, p. 39, and Doney, 1967, pp. 142–143, have also taken the view
that Malebranche's occasionalism was not a response to any mind-body problem.
[32]Lennon, 1974, p. 38.

culties in connection with motion were thought to preclude interaction between bodies; and the perceived difficulties in connection with the radical difference between mind and body were thought to preclude mind-body interaction. Thus Kemp Smith supplements his argument relating to Descartes' view that motion is a mode with a statement of the intuitive mind-body problem.[33] Martial Gueroult is one commentator who holds much more explicitly that considerations relating both to motion and to the mind-body problem conspired in leading to Malebranche's occasionalism.[34]

The difficulty for the hybrid theory is that it leaves unexplained why Malebranche should deny all causation within a single (created) mind—with the exception (§23) of a mind's causing its own volitions. The hybrid theory yields the result that there is no causal interaction between any two bodies, and no causal interaction between any mind and any body. If we throw into the hopper Radner's generalization of the first difficulty, and suppose that causal interaction between substances requires the (impossible) transferrence of modes, we also have the result that there is no causal interaction between any two minds. But why did Malebranche take the further step of denying causation within a single mind?

We can imagine that with so much causation within the created world ruled out, considerations of tidiness or simplicity led to the elimination of all causation by entities other than God. I do not know of any passages suggestive of this sort of consideration. And the question would remain: why would Malebranche want to let considerations of "simplicity" lead him to the intuitively unwelcome view that it is not even the case that one causally determines large tracts of one's own mental life? Radner draws attention to a direct argument of Malebranche's: in order to create its ideas, the mind must already have the ideas, in which case it would be un-

[33]Smith, 1902, p. 81: "The states of the brain are but modes of matter and motion, and hence entirely different from the sensations and images which correspond to them in the mind. There can be no metamorphosis of the brain state. Dead unfeeling matter cannot hand over to the mind sensations ready made."

[34]More specifically, the theory is that Malebranche began with the conclusion of minor Cartesians such as Cordemoy that bodies are only occasional causes of motion, and transferred or generalized this conclusion in order to solve the mind-body problem. See Gueroult, 1959, vol. II, pp. 210–213.

necessary to create them.[35] This argument does not appear to be
responsive to any serious difficulty in the philosophy of Descartes.
The argument is also quite weak: it is at best relevant to the question
of how a mind first acquires an idea, whereas the issue that needs
addressing relates to the causes of the presence of an idea on particular occasions. Equally, the argument overlooks the possibility that a
mind's mental states are caused by its previous mental states, not by
the mind itself. It is difficult to believe that an argument along these
lines led Malebranche to conclude that there is no causation within
a single mind. There is a better explanation.

25. Malebranche's Motivations

Why indeed did Malebranche embrace occasionalism even to the
point of denying that mental states such as volitions are themselves
causes of subsequent mental states such as thoughts and emotions?
It should be obvious from my review of his arguments in section 22
that his metaphysics reflects his religious interests. Malebranche was
educated in theology at the Sorbonne, and ordained a priest in
1664. I do not believe that his religious interests simply guided his
selection of topics. It seems implausible, for example, that his religious interests led him to undertake an impartial philosophical examination of such topics as Divine omnipotence, an examination
which led him to conclude that God is the sole cause. Malebranche
had quite specific religious motivations, that is, his religious interests provided him with philosophical objectives, specific conclusions he wanted to establish. Two of these objectives virtually require his occasionalist position.

The first is explicit in the opening and closing portions of the
section of *The Search After Truth* where the arguments for occasionalism are developed. Malebranche maintains that the belief
that created entities are causally efficacious is the source of pagan
religion, of the worship of idols. In pagan religions, objects other
than God, such as the sun, are worshiped because they are thought
to have the causal power to affect our well-being. If God is the sole
cause, idolatry rests upon a false presupposition. I quote only sufficient material to communicate the flavor of Malebranche's position:

[35]Radner, 1978b, p. 24.

We therefore admit something divine in all the bodies around us when we posit forms, faculties, qualities, virtues, or real beings capable of producing certain effects through the force of their nature; and thus we insensibly adopt the opinion of the pagans. . . .

In the Sacred Scriptures, when God proves to the Israelites that they must adore Him, i.e., that they must fear and love Him, the main reasons He gives are drawn from His power to reward and punish them. . . . He forbids them to adore the gods of the pagans because they have no power over them and can do them neither good nor evil. He wants them only to honor Him because He alone is the true cause of good and evil, . . . because natural causes are not the true causes of the ill they appear to cause us, and because . . . it is God alone who acts in them. [*ST* 6, 2, 3]

Malebranche wants these points about idolatry to apply to all "natural causes," including persons, and not just to bodies alone: "philosophy . . . reveals to us that all secondary causes, or all the divinities of philosophy, are merely matter and inefficacious wills" (*ST* 6, 2, 3). One of his objectives in attempting to establish occasionalism is to undermine what he takes to be the source of pagan religion, a motive that has not been overlooked by his commentators.[36]

Malebranche, however, had a second and less obvious religious motivation for embracing occasionalism. In the opening paragraph of the "Preface" to the *Search*, he states that "the infinite distance between the sovereign Being and the mind of man does not prevent it from being immediately joined to it in a very intimate way." In the second paragraph he goes on: "I am not surprised that ordinary men or pagan philosophers consider only the soul's relation and union with the body, without recognizing the relation and union it has with God." We are told in the fourth paragraph that "this is not the place to adduce all the arguments and appeals to authority that might lead one to believe that it is more of the nature of the mind to be joined to God than to be joined to the body; these matters would lead us too far afield. To present this truth properly, it would be necessary to overthrow the fundamental principles of pagan philosophy." In order to demonstrate that the soul is united with God, and that it is more natural to the soul to be united with God than with

---

[36]See, for example, Church, 1931, p. 90; Doney, 1967, p. 143; and Lennon, 1974, p. 37.

the body, it is necessary to overthrow the fundamental principles of pagan religion. Why should this be the case?

These claims are inexplicable if one takes seriously the mystical connotations of the notion of "union" in religious contexts. If, for example, one construes Malebranche's doctrine of the soul's union with God to mean that human souls coalesce or merge with God, there is no apparent connection with pagan religion. The fundamental principle of pagan religion is that entities other than God are causes. To overthrow this principle is to show that God is the sole cause. This would have no tendency to show that souls somehow merge with God, or that it is more natural for the soul to merge with God than with the body.

If the overthrow of the fundamental principle of pagan religion is to be relevant to establishing Malebranche's position relating to the soul's union with God, and with the body, the union of the soul with another entity must be a causal relationship. Malebranche's claim that the soul is "immediately joined" to God and his writing of the soul's "union" with God should be reminiscent of Descartes' terminology in claiming that the mind is immediately joined or united to the pineal gland. I argued in section 14 that for Descartes the mind is immediately joined or united to the pineal gland in the sense that states of the mind are immediate or proximate causes of states of the pineal gland, and vice versa. Malebranche both interpreted Descartes' terminology in this way, and utilized the terminology in this sense himself. When Malebranche states that the soul is immediately joined to God, he means that there are proximate causal relations between the soul and God (of course, these proximate causal relations are in one direction only—God is the cause of states of the soul, though not vice versa); when Malebranche writes that it is more natural for the soul to be united to God than to the body, he means that there are no causal relations between the human soul and body. I do not think that I am foisting upon Malebranche the causal construal of the notion of "union." After writing of both the mind's union with God and the mind's union with the body, he adds a note about "the mind's two unions with God and the body": "For it is true that the mind can be immediately joined only to God, *i.e.*, it depends only on Him. And it is joined to, or depends on the body, only because the will of God is efficacious in establishing this union" (*ST*, "Preface"). To say that God has established the union of mind and body is just to say that God has established the relevant "laws of conjunction" between mind and body. Thus Malebranche writes that "only through the union it has with God is the soul hurt when the body is struck—as I have explained elsewhere" (*ST* 5, 5). His position is that, in metaphysical rigor, since God is the sole cause, there is a union between the mind and God in precisely the same (causal) sense that Descartes held that there is a union between mind and body. Malebranche takes this doctrine quite seriously. As we have seen, the objective of establishing the mind's union with God is announced in the earliest sections of the "Preface" to the *Search*. And just after arguing for occasionalism in the *Dialogues*, Malebranche states: "All creatures are united to God alone in an immediate union" (*DMR* VII.13). The importance of this to Malebranche is indicated by the headings which follow the formal title "Seventh Dialogue": "The inefficacy of natural causes or the impotence of created things—We are united immediately and direct to God alone." His first objective, to undermine pagan religion, is in the service of his second, to establish the union between the mind and God.

Malebranche's famous doctrine of "vision in God" or "seeing all things in God" (*ST* 3, 2, 6; *Eluc.* X; *DMR* II) is closely connected with the doctrine of the mind's union with God—the latter surfaces twice, explicitly, in the relevant section of the *Search*. Here I will be brief and somewhat dogmatic about a difficult matter of interpretation. If I am feeling depressed, God is the proximate cause of that emotional state, and I am thereby immediately united to God. In such a case, there is no vision in God. Vision in God is invoked in treating sense perception, and vision in particular. For Malebranche, God causes me to have a certain visual experience upon the occasion of appropriate changes in physical objects. This visual experience is a thought in the broad Cartesian sense, and inheres in my mind. But sense experience also involves an interpretative or conceptual element. In God's mind, there are ideas or archetypes either of particular physical objects, or of extension itself. Concurrently with the sense experience I have described, God causes me to see an idea or archetype in God's mind. Evidently, if one thinks of the idea or archetype as an object, Malebranche is a "direct realist" with respect to this vision in God. God does not cause me to have an experience which copies or represents the ideas or archetypes in His mind; rather, He causes me to see or be acquainted with those ideas or archetypes in the direct realist sense. Whether this "vision in God" or seeing the ideas or archetypes that exist in God's mind is simply concurrent with the "sense experience," or rather fused with, or partly constitutive of, or a condition for the possibility of, the sense experience or thought which does inhere in my mind, is somewhat obscure. But God's causing me to "see" his ideas or archetypes is a special case of the union with God. Here the motives are epistemological, to explain the interpretative or conceptual element in sense experience.

We have seen that it seems unlikely that consistent application of any one or more principles to be found in Descartes commits one to the denial of causation even between mental states within a single mind. Malebranche's religious motivations, on the other hand, explain why he should deny this. Apart from the special case of our volitions (which, in order to allow for human liberty, the mind determines itself), mental states are caused by God. It follows that there is a continuing union of the mind and God; and also that "philosophy . . . authorises only the love of God" since "we ordinarily love only things capable of doing us some good" (*Eluc.* xv). To say that Malebranche's occasionalism and his arguments for it were dictated by his religious motivations is not, however, to say that problems which were felt to infect Descartes' system were irrelevant to Malebranche's purposes.[37] To the contrary, Malebranche saw

[37]I find myself sympathetic with Church, 1931, p. 90: "Occasionalism is not proposed as the solution of a strictly philosophical problem." I am not prepared, however, to dismiss Malebranche's religious motivations as something less than "strictly philosophical." Gueroult, 1959, vol. II, p. 210, insists that Malebranche's "point of departure is not in theology, but in philosophy." Lennon, 1974, pp. 37, 29, concedes that the "dialectical motivation" which led Malebranche to his occasionalism is "ethico-theological," but he holds that at the same time the position "is the historical and logical *dénouement* of principles more or less explicit . . . in Descartes." It would have been quite fortuitous had Malebranche's position been overdetermined by his religious motivation on the one hand and some principles inherited from Descartes on the other. Radner, 1978b, pp. 132–133, notes that Malebranche's doctrine of freedom is incompatible with his occasionalism, and proceeds to suggest that whereas occasionalism is the metaphysics consistent with

that he could exploit the perceived or felt mind-body problem in particular in an effort to lend some credibility to his own position. Thus, in the *Dialogues*, it is Aristes who first introduces various intuitive difficulties for the thesis that bodies act upon the mind to produce sensations (*DMR* iv.5-7). Malebranche's spokesman, Theodore, then develops this theme (8–10), culminating in this statement: "there is no relation of causality between a body and a mind. What am I saying? That there is no relation between a mind and a body. I am saying more. There is no real relation between one body and another, between one mind and another. In a word, no created thing can act upon another by an activity which is its own. This I will prove to you presently" (*DMR* vii.11). The proofs are the arguments of *Dialogue VII* for occasionalism. The dialectic here is important. The interlocutor introduces difficulties for mind-body interactionism. To philosophers after Descartes, such intuitive difficulties were familiar. The thesis that mind and body do not or cannot interact did not require much argument. Malebranche could rely upon the reader to agree with, or at least be sympathetic to, or at the very least understand the grounds for, the denial of mind-body interaction. This provides a wedge. At section 11, Malebranche is saying: "The denial of interaction between mind and body is familiar enough; I go even further and deny interaction between any two created entities, between two minds, or two bodies. I realize this may sound extravagant. But you agree that there can be persuasive grounds for denying interaction between certain entities, minds and bodies. Read on, and I will show you that there are persuasive grounds for denying other interactions as well."

Malebranche's metaphysics is not a response to a "mind-body problem" which Descartes left to his successors, though it of course generates a position on the relationship between (created, finite) minds and bodies as a special case. The relationship between Descartes' interactionism and Malebranche's occasionalism is not that

---

the Cartesian ontology, the doctrine of freedom was required by the demands of religion. For this reason, "the problem Malebranche has with freedom is not a problem of reconciling two aspects of his metaphysics. It is a problem of reconciling his metaphysics with his religion." I suggest it is neither: it is a problem of reconciling two aspects of his religion.

of problem and response. Rather, the intuitive difficulties for Descartes' interactionism provided the opportunity for occasionalism to receive attention as a philosophical theory. The fact that the denial of mind-body interaction was familiar was a factor in making it possible for an occasionalist theory to be taken seriously.

Maurice Mandelbaum has suggested that the innovations of major philosophers do not usually have their roots in critical responses to the views of their predecessors, but rather in certain independent basic convictions or primary beliefs. And "the sources of a major philosopher's primary beliefs... are not to be found in his dissatisfaction with the ways in which his predecessors have developed their own views, but derive from religious, moral, or political problems," or from various other conflicts within the philosopher's life.[38] If we think of introducing innovations whose sources are such primary beliefs as a necessary condition for being a major philosopher, it is a condition that Malebranche satisfies.

[38]Mandelbaum, 1977, pp. 565–567.

VI

BERKELEY'S DENIAL OF
CAUSES OTHER THAN VOLITIONS

26. Berkeley's Metaphysics

The introduction of three modifications into Malebranche's metaphysics yields the basic structure of the metaphysics of Berkeley. First, eliminate material substances (in the sense of objects which exist independently of any perceiver). Second, allow that some volitions of created minds are causally efficacious (in particular, volitions of created minds can cause the movement of their own limbs, that is, can cause changes in those ideas which constitute their limbs). Third, deny that created minds are directly acquainted with anything except their own ideas and mental operations (thus, they are not directly acquainted with ideas in God). The system that results is Berkeley's metaphysics—a "trivial variant" of Malebranche's in the sense that the required modifications are so simple. In saying this, I do not mean to suggest that they are unimportant. Obviously, the elimination of material objects is not unimportant. Nor do I mean to suggest that the results of these modifications exhaust the metaphysical differences between Malebranche and Berkeley, although they do, I believe, comprise the most fundamental ones. Berkeley's is an occasionalist metaphysics in which God is the sole cause, except that certain volitions of created minds (when directed at their own limbs) are causally efficacious.

The intimate relationship between the metaphysics of Malebranche and Berkeley is no coincidence, and the importance of Malebranche's influence should not be underestimated. Locke had written a fifty-page essay, *An Examination of P. Malebranche's*

Opinion of Seeing All Things in God. In Berkeley's notebooks, called the *Commonplace Book* by A. C. Fraser, and renamed the *Philosophical Commentaries* by A. A. Luce, there are fourteen entries which refer to Malebranche by name. The notebooks were written when Berkeley was in his early twenties, in 1707–1708. They closely preceded the period of the publication of the main body of Berkeley's philosophical work: *An Essay Towards a New Theory of Vision,* 1709; *The Principles of Human Knowledge,* 1710; and *Three Dialogues Between Hylas and Philonous,* 1713. The *Philosophical Commentaries* are our best guide to the development of Berkeley's thought just prior to the publication of his system.

It appears that Berkeley accepted an unqualified occasionalism, the doctrine that God is the sole cause, early on. Notebook entry 107 reads: "Strange impotence of men. Man without God. Wretcheder than a stone or tree, he having onely the power to be miserable by his unperformed wills, these having no power at all." This is pure Malebranche: not even the volitions of created spirits are causally efficacious.[1] And as late as entry 433 we have: "One idea not the cause of another, one power not the cause of another. The cause of all natural things is onely God. Hence trifling to enquire after second Causes. This Doctrine gives a most suitable idea of the Divinity."

These two entries indicating Berkeley's early acceptance of Malebranche's occasionalism are both marked with an obelus or plus sign. A. A. Luce has shown that Berkeley used this symbol sometimes to indicate trivial or irrelevant entries, more often to indicate positions that he had come to modify or abandon.[2] It would be a mistake to suppose that Berkeley accepted Malebranche's occasionalism early on, and then came to reject it wholesale. In these cases, the obelus is used to indicate a previously held view which has come to be modified.

---

[1]Tipton, 1974, pp. 305–306, suggests that it is not possible to tell how seriously Berkeley took Malebranche's doctrine that volitions of created spirits are not causes, since Berkeley might simply be reporting Malebranche's position at *PC* 107. The subsequent entry at *PC* 433, which Tipton overlooks in this context, confirms that Berkeley did accept the view that God is the only cause.

[2]Luce, 1934, pp. 180–188.

The modification results from allowing that some volitions of created minds are causally efficacious: "We move our Legs our selves. 'tis we that will their movement. Herein I differ from Malbranch" (*PC* 548). Recall Malebranche: "It is true that they [our arms] are moved when we will it, and that thus we are the natural cause of the movement of our arms. But *natural* causes are not *true* causes; they are only occasional causes" (*ST* 6, 2, 3). At entry 548, Berkeley disagrees. (Of course, Berkeley's claim that we move our limbs must be construed in light of his immaterialism: our volitions are causally efficacious with respect to those collections of ideas which are taken to constitute our limbs—cf. *PHK* 1). After writing entry 548, Berkeley goes back and marks entries 107 and 433 with an obelus. This is a reconstruction, but a natural one. Berkeley has come to reject the view that without God man has only the power to be miserable by his "unperformed wills" (*PC* 107), and more generally the view that God is the only cause (*PC* 433). This is a modification of Malebranche. God is the only cause, except that volitions of created minds are causally efficacious with respect to their own limbs. Other volitions of created minds are not causally efficacious; and no idea is a cause of anything.

Berkeley is perhaps most famous for his immaterialism, for his rejection of material substances in the sense of objects which exist independently of any perceiver. This immaterialism is standardly portrayed as a reaction to the representative theory of perception. Characterized more fully, that theory is "causal representative indirect realism": "realism" because material objects are held to exist independently of any perceiver; "indirect" because it is ideas, rather than material objects themselves, which are the immediate objects of perception; "representative" because some ideas (those of the primary qualities) are held to resemble qualities of material objects; and "causal" because material objects are held to cause ideas in the perceiver. Berkeley's attack is well known: against the causal component, that material objects should cause ideas is inconceivable (*PHK* 19); against the representative component, ideas cannot resemble anything but ideas, and hence cannot resemble material objects (*PHK* 8); against the indirect component, if the immediate objects of perception are only ideas, we could never know that material objects exist (*PHK* 18); and against realism, the supposition that material objects exist independently of any perceiver is absurd and contradictory (*PHK* 3–5, 22–23). In light of Berkeley's systematic attack, it appears that it is difficulties for the representative theory of perception which lead him to immaterialism.

In disputing the representative theory, Berkeley would have had both Locke and Descartes in mind. In his criticism of the doctrine of abstract ideas, Berkeley is discussing Locke, since he explicitly cites sections of the *Essay*. By contrast, he does not associate the representative theory with a particular figure. The discussion simply begins: "But say you, though the ideas themselves do not exist without the mind, yet there may be things like them whereof they are copies or resemblances" (*PHK* 8). And one section later: "Some there are who make a distinction betwixt *primary* and *secondary* qualities" (*PHK* 9). Locke is not singled out (though some sections, such as *Principles* 13, attack doctrines associated with the representative theory which may be peculiarly Lockean). Descartes, as well as Locke, held the fundamental doctrines of the representative theory.[3] Thus, Berkeley complains that allowing that there are material substances, "tis impossible the mind should know or perceive them. the mind even according to ye materialists perceiving onely the impressions made upon its brain or rather the ideas attending those impressions" (*PC* 74). Berkeley would number Descartes and Locke both among the materialists: "Locke in his 4th book & Descartes in Med. 6. use the same argument for the Existence of objects viz. that sometimes we see feel etc against our will" (*PC* 790). In other words, both appeal to material objects as the hypothesis that provides the best causal explanation of features of sensory experience.

Berkeley's objections to the representative theory of Descartes and Locke did not, however, provide the principal impetus for his immaterialism. His attack on the theory must be read in the perspective of his familiarity with Malebranche, together with his early acceptance of Malebranche's occasionalism. Malebranche subscribed to something very much like the representative theory, ex-

---

[3]Descartes' version of the representative theory, however, may have been more sophisticated than Locke's. See Williams, 1978, esp. pp. 240, 285–286.

cept for its causal component.[4] He emphatically denied that material objects cause ideas; rather, it is God who causes ideas. Malebranche's materialism is much more suggestive of immaterialism than is materialism in the context of the representative theory. For a proponent of the latter, material objects cause ideas of sensation; because they cause ideas, one can argue for their existence as an explanatory hypothesis; and if they did not cause ideas of sensation, it is not clear how these ideas would be caused. In Malebranche's system, material objects are causally idle; because they do not cause ideas, their existence cannot be postulated in order to explain the existence of ideas; and it is clear how ideas are caused despite the inefficacy of material objects.

Berkeley was well aware of these features of Malebranche's system. First, since Malebranche's material objects are causally inefficacious or idle, they may as well be dispensed with altogether. In the *Philosophical Commentaries*, Berkeley writes "the sillyness of the Currant Doctrine makes much for me. they commonly suppose a material world ... according to their own confession to no purpose" (*PC* 476). He writes in the *Principles*:

> As to the opinion that there are no corporeal causes, this has been heretofore maintained by some of the Schoolmen, as it is of late by others among the modern philosophers, who though they allow matter to exist, yet will have God alone to be the immediate efficient cause of all things. . . . But then, that they should suppose an innumerable multitude of created beings, which they acknowledge are not capable of producing any one effect in Nature, and which therefore are made to no manner of purpose ... this I say, though we should allow it possible, must yet be a very unaccountable and extravagant supposition. [*PHK* 53]

And in the *Second Dialogue* Berkeley writes that "if it pass for a good argument against other hypotheses in the sciences, that they suppose Nature or the divine wisdom to make something in vain ... what shall we think of that hypothesis which supposes the whole world made in vain?" (Berk. ii, 214).

Second, precisely because his material objects are causally inefficacious, Malebranche was deprived of any causal argument for

---

[4]Malebranche's position is perhaps not exactly the representative theory minus the usual causal component, because he employs rather idiosyncratic conceptions of "representation," "idea," etc. Cf. Matthews, 1971.

their existence. Proponents of the representative theory, allowing that material objects are causes, could argue for the existence of material objects as an explanatory hypothesis, a hypothesis which provides a causal explanation of certain features of ideas of sensation. No such argument was available to Malebranche, who relies on Divine revelation (*Eluc.* VI, *DMR* VI.3). Berkeley was not impressed: "Scripture & possibility are the onely proofs with Malbranch add to these w^t he calls a great propension to think so" (*PC* 686); "Say Descartes & Malbranch God hath given us strong inclinations to think our Ideas proceed from Bodies. or that Bodies do exist. Pray w^t mean they by this" (*PC* 818). In the *Principles,* Berkeley criticizes those "who think, that though the arguments for the real existence of bodies, which are drawn from reason, be allowed not to amount to demonstration, yet the Holy Scriptures are so clear in the point, as will sufficiently convince every good Christian, that bodies do really exist" (*PHK* 82).

Third, Malebranche's occasionalism provides a causal account of ideas which is an alternative to the hypothesis that material objects cause ideas. In other words, since Malebranche's God is the cause of ideas, God usurps the causal function of material objects in the representative theory.

Looking at Malebranche's system, Berkeley saw that material objects were idle, that as a consequence no causal or explanatory argument for their existence was available, and that occasionalism provided a causal account of ideas which rendered the hypothesis that material objects cause ideas unnecessary. For these reasons, no metaphysics admitting material objects could have been more suggestive of a metaphysics dispensing with material objects than that of Malebranche. It must have been when reading or thinking about Malebranche that immaterialism first occurred to Berkeley.

We have seen that Berkeley accepted Malebranche's occasionalism early on. This is important. According to the representative theory, material objects cause ideas. Suppose there are no material objects. Then what does cause ideas or perceptual experiences? Malebranche's occasionalism delivered to Berkeley an answer to this question which he found acceptable, and (as we shall see) desirable. Imagine a philosopher reading a proponent of a representative theory without any familiarity with Malebranche.

Perhaps the philosopher is impressed by the difficulties. But if material objects are to be eliminated, how are ideas caused? There are various possibilities: ideas are uncaused, or we cause ideas ourselves, or ideas cause ideas (Leibniz, where the "ideas" appear as "perceptions"), or God causes ideas (Malebranche). Any of these are radical alternatives to the representative theory. While destructive argument against that theory would not have been difficult, a bold philosophical stroke would have been required to construct an alternative. Such was not required of Berkeley. Malebranche handed him a congenial alternative. Malebranche's metaphysics at once suggested immaterialism, and enabled Berkeley to construct an alternative to the representative theory.[5]

It is certainly possible that Berkeley preferred to be viewed as formulating a constructive alternative to the representative theory of perception rather than modifying Malebranche's system. In order to become important philosophically, one wants to maximize the appearance of originality. For the reasons I have been discussing, Berkeley's metaphysics looks much more original when viewed as a

[5]Luce, 1934 (and to a lesser extent, 1963), has argued in detail the case for Malebranche's influence on Berkeley. I agree with Luce's statements that "Locke taught him [Berkeley], but Malebranche inspired him"; "the way to the heart of Berkeleianism lies through Malebranche"; and "Malebranche did more than weaken the evidence for matter. He showed Berkeley, if I mistake not, how to construct a system dispensing with matter" (1934, pp. 7, 43, 83; cf. 1963, pp. 61–62). My principal disagreements with Luce, with respect to Malebranche's influence on Berkeley, are twofold. First, Luce overemphasizes Berkeley's genius in hitting upon immaterialism, pointing out, for example, that "thousands read Malebranche without dreaming of immaterialism. Norris and Collier, contemporaries of Berkeley, steeped themselves in Malebranche's philosophy, but originated little" (1934, p. 7). There is a difference between what a figure might have dreamed of and what he might have dared advance. In any case, Berkeley's immaterialism had already been advanced in the guise of the final skeptical hypothesis of Descartes' *First Meditation*, according to which there are no material substances, though an evil genius makes it appear otherwise; this just is Berkeley's metaphysics, though he prefers to call the evil genius "God." Second, I believe that Luce's claim that Berkeley "did not accept occasionalism" and "was not an occasionalist" (1934, pp. 43, 82) is extremely misleading. Luce's point seems to be that Berkeley did not accept Malebranche's doctrines of the intelligible extension in God and vision in God (1934, pp. 81–82). These doctrines, however, are independent of the fundamental occasionalist position that God is the only cause. Jessop, 1938, follows Luce, with whom he edited Berkeley's works, in stressing the differences between Berkeley and Malebranche. Wisdom's position on Berkeley's originality is also substantially similar to Luce's (Wisdom, 1953, pp. 49–52).

reaction against the representative theory rather than as a simple and straightforward modification of Malebranche.

It might be urged that while this consideration explains Berkeley's failure explicitly to acknowledge his debt to Malebranche, it does not fully explain why he should have gone so far positively to dissociate himself from Malebranche. In the *Principles,* there is no explicit reference to Malebranche, but Berkeley does criticize the modern philosophers who "suppose an innumerable multitude of created beings... not capable of producing any one effect in Nature" (*PHK* 53), together with the thesis that matter is some unknown occasion of ideas (*PHK* 69–70). In other words, he attacks Malebranche's materialism. By the time of the *Second Dialogue,* however, Berkeley mentions Malebranche by name. Philonous says, "Few men think, yet all will have opinions. Hence men's opinions are superficial and confused. It is nothing strange that tenets, which in themselves are ever so different, should nevertheless be confounded with each other, by those who do not consider them attentively. I shall not therefore be surprised, if some men imagine that I run into the enthusiasm of Malbranche, though in truth I am very remote from it" (Berk. II, 214).

What accounts for Berkeley's desire, as of the writing of the *Dialogues,* to dissociate himself from Malebranche in such strong terms? Upon publication of the *Principles,* Berkeley's affinity with Malebranche was immediately noted in both France and England.[6] As early as November, 1710, John Percival informed Berkeley that both Samuel Clarke and William Whiston took Berkeley to be a disciple of Malebranche or of Malebranche's British follower John Norris.[7] As Luce has pointed out, much more was at stake than Berkeley's perceived originality:

> It is curious that while obscure writers are named in the *Theory of Vision,* Malebranche receives neither acknowledgment nor mention. Possibly Berkeley was so conscious of the points of difference that he did not realize his debt. More probably his silence was prudence. In some quarters 'Malebranche' spelled enthusiasm, and enthusiasm was literally a sin. It was safe for Collier, settled in his

[6]See Bracken, 1965.
[7]Luce, 1934, p. 9.

Wiltshire rectory, to connect his system with that of Malebranche. It was another matter for the ambitious young Irish Protestant to do so. Only those who know the conditions can appreciate the point. Berkeley was absolutely dependent for promotion on the favour of Dublin Castle. A Roman Catholic monk who wrote bitterly of 'heretics', and who called the English 'those wretched people, those children of the world', attacking the English Crown, the Church, and the State, would not be the most profitable patron for Berkeley's first important venture in authorship. It seems certain that Berkeley deliberately avoided mentioning Malebranche.[8]

The prudential considerations Luce raises with reference to Berkeley's failure to mention Malebranche in the *Theory of Vision* also explain why Berkeley should have felt compelled, subsequent to the reception received by the *Principles,* to dissociate himself from Malebranche and religious enthusiasm.

The passage in the *Second Dialogue* where Malebranche is mentioned by name is prompted by Hylas' query: "Are not you too of opinion that we see all things in God? If I mistake not, what you advance comes near to it" (Berk. II, 214). Philonous responds:

> I shall not therefore be surprised, if some men imagine that I run into the enthusiasm of Malbranche, though in truth I am very remote from it. He builds on the most abstract general ideas, which I entirely disclaim. He asserts an absolute external world, which I deny. He maintains that we are deceived by our senses, and know not the real natures or the true forms and figures of extended beings; of all which I hold the direct contrary. So that upon the whole there are no principles more fundamentally opposite than his and mine. It must be owned I entirely agree with what the holy Scripture saith, *that in God we live, and move, and have our being.* But that we see things in his essence after the manner above set forth, I am far from believing. [Berk. II, 214]

Berkeley cites three principal differences, relating to abstract general ideas, material substances existing independently of any perceiver, and the vision in God. The first is something of a red herring. Perhaps Malebranche in some sense makes use of what Berkeley attacks under the heading of "abstract general ideas." But here the doctrinal dispute is with Locke. The remaining two differences cor-

[8]Ibid., p. 40.

respond to the first and third of the three modifications required to derive Berkeley's metaphysics from that of Malebranche: eliminate material objects (the points about skepticism are parasitic upon this), and deny acquaintance with ideas in God. The second modification, allowing that created spirits move their own limbs, is discussed within the next few pages of the *Dialogues*.

It is most significant that in the course of dissociating himself from Malebranche by rehearsing these points Berkeley states that "I entirely agree with what the holy Scripture saith, *that in God we live, and move, and have our being.*" Hylas charges that Berkeley holds that we see all things in God. Malebranche had closed the very section of the *Search* titled "That We See All Things in God" as follows: "let us believe with St. Paul, that He is not far from every one of us, and that in Him we live and move and have our being" (*ST* 3, 2, 6). Berkeley had already used this Pauline passage in the *Principles* (*PHK* 149), and it is invoked again in *Alciphron* (iv.14) and elsewhere.[9] He thereby acknowledges his debt to Malebranche, albeit in a way open to other explanations.

Berkeley's filiation with Malebranche was recognized by prominent historically-minded philosophers well after Berkeley's lifetime. Thomas Reid, in his *Essays on the Intellectual Powers of Man* (published in 1785), wrote, "We ought to do the justice to Malebranche to acknowledge, that . . . his system comes nearer to Berkeley's than the latter seems willing to own."[10] And Hegel, in his *Lectures on the History of Philosophy* (published in 1831) wrote that "Berkeley advocated an idealism which came very near to that of Malebranche."[11] And yet, Luce has said, quite rightly, that at the time he wrote *Berkeley and Malebranche* (published in 1934) "the view that Berkeley owed his 'immaterial hypothesis' to a French monk was a novelty to most readers."[12] How could Berkeley's debt to Malebranche, so widely recognized long before, have come as a novelty? The answer is that this debt is just not a point to be found in the writings of important idealist historians (cf. §1). Kuno Fischer allows that Berkeley "has a certain affinity with Malebranche," but

[9]The point about Berkeley's use of the Pauline passage is due to ibid., p. 82.
[10]Reid, 1785, ch. xi.
[11]Hegel, 1892–96, vol. iii, p. 364.
[12]Luce, 1934, p. vii.

his principal thesis is unmistakable: "Berkeley is... the consistent Locke. ... He rests upon Locke, as Hume rests upon him. Berkeley takes an historical and philosophical position between Locke and Hume, as the link in the series that marks a transition."[13] And there is no reference at all to Malebranche in T. H. Green's discussion of Berkeley for the purposes of his "General Introduction" to Hume's *Treatise*. Berkeley's debt to Malebranche had to be rediscovered in the 1930s.[14] Much recent Berkeley scholarship nevertheless proceeds in almost total disregard of Berkeley's relationship to Malebranche.[15]

Malebranche's contributions hardly account for the whole impact of Continental figures upon fundamental features of Berkeley's metaphysics. This is especially obvious if one considers Berkeley's positive views about the nature of the entities which have ideas. Here I note a number of doctrines that he shares with Descartes. (*a*) Berkeley believes in the existence of minds, souls, or spirits, entities

---

[13]Fischer, 1857, pp. 464, 454.

[14]Three historians made important contributions to the rediscovery of Berkeley's debt to Malebranche within a four-year period: Aaron, 1931; Hicks, 1932, pp. 229–236; and, most important, Luce, 1934. The influence had been recognized at the turn of the century by Smith, 1902, pp. 217–218: "By abolishing this superfluous material world Berkeley simplifies and develops the occasionalist theory." The point, however, was buried late in *Studies in the Cartesian Philosophy*.

[15]One example is Pitcher, *Berkeley*, 1977. There is no mention of occasionalism, and only two references to Malebranche. Neither has to do with philosophical substance. One arises in connection with the story that a conversation with Berkeley brought on Malebranche's death (p. 1); the other, in a footnote, identifies Malebranche as the author of the doctrine of the vision in God, a view referred to in one of Pitcher's quotations from Berkeley (p. 262). Pitcher views Berkeley's philosophy in precisely the way Berkeley would have desired, as arising from "conscious opposition" to "his predecessor" Locke (p. 91). This of course makes Berkeley appear bolder and more original than otherwise: "Berkeley seeks to rectify the faults he finds in Locke's system by the simple, but extraordinarily dramatic, expedient of eliminating all material substances" (p. 92). I have pointed out that this was not so simple, for lack of an alternative account of the cause of our ideas. On this point: "The positing of God as the cause of our ideas of sense cannot look, now, to be as reasonable a move as it does to Berkeley, living in the early eighteenth century, when God was a standard feature of world views" (p. 134). But Berkeley derived his occasionalism specifically from Malebranche, a nonstandard version of a religious world view. Pitcher writes that "Berkeley's metaphysics rises in the garden of British thought like some fantastic plant—beautiful and extravagant" (p. 4). This is not good philosophical botany; the extravagance had its roots in France.

which perceive ideas (*PHK* 2). He agrees with Descartes (§7) that there exist thinking substances$_S$ in which ideas inhere. (*b*) Berkeley holds in addition that it is necessarily the case that any idea inheres in some mind: "An idea cannot exist unperceiv'd" (*PC* 377); "certainly no *idea*, whether faint or strong, can exist otherwise than in a mind perceiving it" (*PHK* 33); "it is most evident [Hylas agrees], that *no idea can exist without the mind*" (*Dia. I*, Berk. II, 206). Berkeley agrees with Descartes' first general thesis about substance$_S$, that it is necessarily the case that any quality inheres in some substance$_S$, as applied to the special case of spirits and ideas (§7). (*c*) Berkeley holds that a spirit cannot exist at any time without having (perceiving) ideas at that time; "To say the mind exists' without thinking is a Contradiction, nonsense, nothing" (*PC* 652); "Some Ideas or other I must have so long as I exist or Will. But no one Idea or sort of Ideas is essential" (*PC* 842). This is Berkeley's doctrine that for spirits, to be is to perceive; the existence of a spirit consists in perceiving (*PHK* 139), that is, in having ideas (*PC* 301$_1$, 378$_{10}$; *PHK* 7). He agrees with Descartes that thinking (perceiving) is essential to a mind in the sense that a mind cannot exist at any time without thinking (perceiving) at that time (§12). (*d*) Finally, Berkeley believes that he can demonstrate that the soul is "naturally immortal" (cf. *PC* 814; *PHK* "Pref.", 141; *Dia.* "Pref.", Berk. II, 168; *Alc.* VI.11). In the *Principles*, the argument is that an indivisible, incorporeal, unextended entity is consequently incorruptible. In *Alciphron*, the argument is effectively Descartes': "when I consider that the soul and body are things so very different and heterogeneous, I can see no reason to be positive that the one must necessarily be extinguished upon the dissolution of the other." Berkeley follows Descartes in attempting to demonstrate the immortality of the soul (§13). He was aligned with Descartes on what might be called the metaphysics of minds or spirits.[16] (Of course, on many of these

---

[16]Bracken, 1974, pp. 114–115, has provided a somewhat similar inventory of doctrines to be found in both Descartes and Malebranche. Bracken indeed argues that Berkeley's philosophy is more akin to Descartes' than to Malebranche's (cf. pp. 15–18). I have no interest in addressing this question here. What matters, in either case, is that Berkeley was a Continental figure. At this level, I am entirely sympathetic with Bracken's claim that "the massive internal evidence which was once thought to bind Berkeley with the 'empiricists' Locke and Hume simply is not present. Berkeley is neither British nor empiricist" (p. 18).

points, Descartes was in agreement with Malebranche as well.) Berkeley's metaphysical views about the nature of minds derive from Descartes, and his views about the causation of the mind's ideas derive from Malebranche.

27. Berkeley's Motivations

If Berkeley's metaphysics derives from that of Malebranche in the simple and straightforward way I have suggested, we might expect to find at least some common motivation. I believe this expectation amply fulfilled. As general background, it should be borne in mind that Berkeley was ordained a deacon in 1709—at the age of twenty-four, one year prior to the publication of the *Principles*—and ordained a priest the year following.

I have suggested that Malebranche accepted occasionalism in order to achieve two principal objectives: to undermine a presupposition of pagan religion or idolatry, the belief that created entities are causally efficacious; and, more important, to establish that there is an immediate union between minds and God (§25). Berkeley was interested in both these objectives.

Berkeley was more than prepared to accept the result that persons are united to God. The doctrine, though not the terminology, is to be found in the *Principles*: "nothing can be more evident... than the existence of God, or a spirit who is intimately present to our minds, producing in them all that variety of ideas or sensations, which continually affect us, on whom we have an absolute and entire dependence, in short, *in whom we live, and move, and have our being*" (*PHK* 149). God is "intimately present to our minds." In later works, there is explicit reference to a "union." In *Alciphron*, Euphranor states: "I cannot comprehend why any one who admits the union of soul and body should pronounce it impossible for the human nature to be united to the divine" (*Alc.* VI.11). In *Siris*, Berkeley denies that God is united to the world in the way that the soul is united to the body, but only on the ground that an embodied spirit is "clogged by weight, and hindered by resistance," whereas a perfect being does not suffer any "weight or impediment" (*Sir.* 290).

Berkeley was also interested in undermining idolatry. Early in his notebooks, he writes: "ffall of Adam, rise of Idolatry, rise of

Epicurism & Hobbism dispute about divisibility of matter &c expounded by material substances" (*PC* 17). There is a further reference to idolatry as rooted in the denial of immaterialism at *PC* 411. This concern finds its way into the mature, systematic works. Berkeley writes in the *Principles*, "The existence of matter, or bodies unperceived, has not only been the main support of *atheists* and *fatalists*, but on the same principle doth *idolatry* likewise in all its various forms depend" (*PHK* 94). He cannot, however, leave an attack on idolatry quite in this form, since he denies the existence of material substances in the sense of objects which exist independently of any perceiver. He does hold that there exist material or sensible objects in the sense of certain collections of ideas. If collections of ideas were causally efficacious, there would be room to worship them. Thus *PHK* 94 continues: "Did men but consider that the sun, moon, and stars, and every other object of the senses, are only so many sensations in their minds, which have no other existence but barely being perceived, doubtless they would never fall down, and worship their own *ideas*; but rather address their homage to that eternal invisible Mind which produces and sustains all things." The point is made a second time in the *Principles*, and rather more clearly, that if "nature" means the things perceived by sense, there is no causal efficacy in nature: "if by *Nature* is meant only the visible *series* of effects, or sensations imprinted on our minds according to certain fixed and general laws: then it is plain, that Nature taken in this sense cannot produce anything at all" (*PHK* 150). The theme is taken up again in the *Third Dialogue*: "that which to you . . . seems so extravagant, is no more than what the Holy Scriptures assert in a hundred places. In them God is represented as the sole and immediate Author of all those effects, which some heathens and philosophers are wont to ascribe to Nature, matter, fate, or the like unthinking principle" (Berk. II, 236).

Although Berkeley takes idolatry seriously, his concern with it is more tempered by other interests than is Malebranche's. The point is best brought out by considering the attitudes of both toward ordinary causal locutions. According to Malebranche, creatures "cannot be in reciprocal dependence upon one another. One may, indeed, say that they are united to one another and that they depend upon one another. I grant this, provided it is not understood in the ordinary and vulgar sense of the term" (*DMR* vii.13). Contrast this with Berkeley: "it will... be demanded whether it does not seem absurd to take away natural causes, and ascribe every thing to the immediate operation of spirits? We must no longer say upon these principles, that fire heats, or water cools, but that a spirit heats, and so forth. Would not a man be deservedly laughed at, who should talk after this manner? I answer, he would so; in such things we ought to *think with the learned, and speak with the vulgar*" (*PHK* 51). The doctrines here are identical. For both Malebranche and Berkeley, fire (construed for Berkeley as a collection of sensible ideas) does not cause heat. For Malebranche, we *may* say that fire causes heat *provided that* we do not understand "cause" in the vulgar sense; for Berkeley, we *ought* to say that fire causes heat (speak with the vulgar) *while* thinking with the learned. The only difference is in emphasis. Malebranche stresses that ordinary causal attributions are mistaken; Berkeley emphasizes that ordinary causal locutions can be preserved if suitably reconstrued. Berkeley is fond of representing himself as aligned with "the Mob" (*PC* 405), a defender of common sense (*Dia. III*, Berk. ii, 244; *Alc.* vii.18). The present episode is illuminating. He wants an occasionalist metaphysics, which common sense would surely reject; the claim that we ought to speak with the vulgar while thinking with the learned is an attempt to cushion the blow.

Although there is a strong Malebranchian flavor to some of Berkeley's concerns, his interests in establishing the union of persons with God, and in attacking idolatry as based upon a false belief in the efficacy of sensible objects, are not nearly so prominent as Malebranche's. We must look further to identify the principal motivations for Berkeley's occasionalist metaphysics. A natural suggestion is that his fundamental objectives should emerge not in connection with the occasionalist orientation which he and Malebranche have in common, but rather in connection with the locus of their differences about causal efficacy, that is, in Berkeley's doctrine that we move our limbs ourselves. Luce has placed considerable emphasis upon this point of difference:

> Now here we have a main point at issue between Berkeley and Malebranche.... Here... was an inflammable matter, a point of acute difference.... Leaving matter out of account..., there is

little else to separate the two systems, as philosophies of ideas. This difference is no slight one. It is grave and far-reaching. Berkeley, loyal as ever to empirical fact, recognizes the reality of finite activity. He comes to terms with it, makes it indeed one of the poles on which his system turns. For if we move our legs ourselves, we make ideas ourselves. We make and unmake ideas (*Prin.* §28), as readily as we stretch and relax muscles.[17]

Do we really have here a "grave and far-reaching" difference that explains what is distinctive in Berkeley's occasionalist metaphysics and in his motivation for adopting it?

The claim that we move our limbs ourselves is important to Berkeley. It emerges in the *Philosophical Commentaries* (548), and recurs throughout his works: in the *Principles* (116, 147), the *Dialogues* (*Dia. III*, Berk. II, 237), eight years later (1721) in *De Motu* (25), and in the late work (1744) *Siris* (161). In an unqualified occasionalist system, God is the only cause, without exception. In Berkeley's occasionalism, God is the only cause, with the exception that the volitions of created minds cause movements in their "limbs." Why was Berkeley so insistent upon this exception?

If one thinks that Berkeley's claim that we move our own limbs results from some serious philosophical concern, his views relating to human freedom are the natural place to look. We know from notebook entry 508 that human freedom was to be a subject for discussion in a planned Part II of the *Principles*. Berkeley wrote to Samuel Johnson that he had lost a draft of this material in Italy (Berk. II, 282), and Part II never appeared. This leaves us two sources for his views on human freedom, the *Philosophical Commentaries*, and the relatively late (1732) work *Alciphron* (VII. 16–20).

In the *Philosophical Commentaries*, the strands of Berkeley's view are as follows. There is a general disinclination to place any positive construction on such terms as 'free'. Thus we have the following notebook entries: "We are imposed on by the words, will, determine, agent, free, can etc." (*PC* 627); "Man is free. There is no difficulty in this proposition if we but settle the signification of the word free, if we had an Idea annext to the word free & would but contemplate that Idea" (*PC* 626); "You tell me according to my Doctrine a Man is not free. I answer. tell me w^t you mean by the

[17]Luce, 1934, pp. 89–90.

word free & I shall resolve you" (*PC* 631); "Again. w^t mean you by determine?" (*PC* 654). Nowhere in the notebooks does Berkeley offer an account of freedom. If only the critic will state his definition, Berkeley will satisfy him.

In *Alciphron*, Berkeley goes somewhat further: "a man is said to be free so far forth as he can do what he will" (*Alc.* VII.19). Alciphron had wanted a deeper account: "This I admit to be true in the vulgar sense. But a philosopher goes higher and inquires whether a man be free to will" (*Alc.* VII.19). Euphranor declines the invitation to engage in further speculation:

> It is . . . evident that man is a free agent: and though, by abstracted reasonings, you should puzzle me, and seem to prove the contrary, yet, so long as I am conscious of my own actions, this inward evidence of plain fact will bear me up against all your reasonings, however subtle and refined. . . . If I . . . ask any plain untutored man whether he acts or is free in this or that particular action, he readily assents, and I as readily believe him from what I find within. And thus, by an induction of particulars, I may conclude man to be a free agent, although I may be puzzled to define or conceive a notion of freedom in general and abstract. And if a man be free, he is plainly accountable. But if you shall define, abstract, suppose, and it shall follow that, according to your definitions, abstractions, and suppositions, there can be no freedom in man, and you shall thence infer that he is not accountable, I shall make bold to depart from your metaphysical abstracted sense, and appeal to the common sense of mankind.
>
> The notions of guilt and merit, justice and reward, are in the minds of men antecedent to all metaphysical disquisitions. [*Alc.* VII.18–19]

It is difficult to avoid the conclusion that Berkeley is doing little more than attempting to make the absence of a theory look respectable. He certainly does not subscribe to the general thesis that metaphysical reasoning cannot overturn common sense. It is precisely metaphysical reasoning which shows that the common-sense view that fire causes heat is false. Why might not metaphysical reasoning show that the common-sense views that persons are free and accountable are false? The question is especially pressing since there is a substantive connection between issues relating to causation and freedom. For Berkeley, we are free to the extent that we can do what we will, that is, to the extent that we can cause what we will to occur. If metaphysics can and does show that the common-sense view that fire causes pain is mistaken, why should the common-sense view about freedom, which involves a causal claim, be immune to or protected from metaphysical criticism? Berkeley's unwillingness to engage in a metaphysical discussion of freedom is not a consequence of any consistently applied view about the interrelations of metaphysics and common sense.

Berkeley appeals to common sense in defending his views on freedom in the absence of any serious metaphysical theory. His position on freedom is neither systematic nor sophisticated. His view that we move our own limbs does not seem to be a result of considered philosophical reflection. In the notebooks, entry 548 formulates the departure from Malebranche. Only two earlier entries relate to freedom—508 announces the intention to discuss freedom in Part II of the *Principles*, and 423 attacks Locke's claim (*Essay* II.xxi.29–40) that it is a felt uneasiness which determines the will. There are sixteen entries later than 548 concerning freedom—most, but not all of these, deal with Locke. It appears that Berkeley first hit upon the departure from Malebranche, and subsequently devoted more attention to freedom—an issue raised immediately by the claim that we move our own limbs.

Why did, then, Berkeley depart from Malebranche in maintaining that we move our own limbs? Keep in mind that along with Malebranche before him, Berkeley, the priest, needs to locate human freedom somewhere. Then there are two obvious motivations. First, the modification was surely congenial. Of all the consequences of Malebranche's occasionalism, the result that we do not move our own limbs is perhaps the most repugnant to "common sense." (On the other hand, there is no philosophical advance since Berkeley leaves open the question of how our will is determined.) Second, in holding that we move our limbs ourselves, he introduces a modification which is clearly recognizable as such to anyone familiar with Malebranche. The departure allows Berkeley a way of dissociating himself from Malebranche. In the absence of any serious philosophical argument for his position, this difference does not seem important. The fact is that both Berkeley and Malebranche depart from an unqualified, uncompromising occasionalism in one way or another in order to allow for some sort of human freedom.

Berkeley locates freedom in the efficacy of volitions of created spirits in causing their limbs to move; Malebranche locates it in the efficacy of created spirits in causing their own volitions (§ 23). In either case, we have a departure from the view that God is the sole cause. It is misleading for Luce to write, in comparing Berkeley to Malebranche, that "Berkeley did not accept the full occasionalist doctrine of the divine operation; for he always recognized the finite spirit as a centre of real activity, but he agreed with part of the occasionalist creed."[18] Even Malebranche did not accept a full occasionalist position.

The fundamental differences between the occasionalist metaphysics of Berkeley and Malebranche lie not so much in matters of substance as in the *direction of the argument*. For Malebranche, God's existence is established on the ground that we have vision of God, some sort of direct, intuitive knowledge of God (*ST* 4, 11, 3; *DMR* II). Then, *given* the existence of a God with certain properties, Malebranche argues *for* his occasionalism, on various grounds: (*a*) there is a necessary connection between God's volitions and their realization; (*b*) God's volitions are sufficient for their realization; (*c*) created entities depend essentially upon God (§ 22). The existence of God is not proved on the ground that created entities are inefficacious. Rather, Malebranche argues *from* the existence of God *to* the conclusion that entities in the natural world are causally inefficacious. As we will see in the next section, Berkeley argues *from* the fact that entities in the natural world are causally inefficacious *to* the conclusion that God exists, a God who is continuously active in the natural world. Berkeley establishes the inefficacy of entities in the natural world quite independently of any appeal to the existence of God.

Berkeley was well aware of the sort of distinction I am emphasizing. In the *Second Dialogue*, there is this exchange:

> *Phil.* . . . as sure therefore as the sensible world really exists, so sure is there an infinite omnipresent spirit who contains and supports it.
>
> *Hylas.* What! this is no more than I and all Christians hold; nay, and all others too who believe there is a God, and that he knows and comprehends all things.

[18]Ibid., p. 118.

Phil. Ay, but here lies the difference. Men commonly believe that all things are known or perceived by God, because they believe the being of a God, whereas I on the other side, immediately and necessarily conclude the being of a God, because all sensible things must be perceived by him.

. . .

Phil. . . . is there no difference between saying, *there is a God, therefore he perceives all things:* and saying, *sensible things do really exist: and if they really exist, they are necessarily perceived by an infinite mind: therefore, there is an infinite mind or God.* [Berk. II, 212; Berkeley's emphasis]

A God who perceives or knows all things need not on that account be continuously active in the natural world. Berkeley makes the same point about the direction of argument with respect to a Malebranchian God who constantly re-creates the natural world. Samuel Johnson had raised some objections to Berkeley's view that God is continuously active in the world (Berk. II, 272–73). Berkeley replies: "Those who have all along contended for a material world have yet acknowledged . . . that the divine conservation of things is equipollent to, and in fact the same thing with, a continued repeated creation. . . . These are the common opinions of the School-men. . . . The Stoics and Platonists are everywhere full of the same notion. *I am not therefore singular in this point itself, so much as in my way of proving it*" (Berk. II, 280; emphasis added). What is distinctive about Berkeley's occasionalist metaphysics is his argumentation for it. Berkeley's strategy is to argue from the inefficacy of entities in the natural world to the existence of a continuously active God; his objective is to establish the existence of such a God.

28. Berkeley's Arguments for a Continuously Active God

Berkeley's best-known argument for the existence of God, sometimes called "the passivity argument," is an obvious example of his argumentative strategy.[19] The argument may be formulated as follows:

[19]The terminology is due to Bennett, 1971, p. 165.

(1) a succession of ideas of sense exists in my mind (*PHK* 26);
(2) these ideas have a cause: either (*a*) ideas, or a substance—(*b*) material or (*c*) spiritual (*PHK* 26);
(3*a*) ideas cannot cause ideas (*PHK* 25);
(3*b*) there are no material substances (*PHK* 3–7, 20–24); and if there were, they could not cause ideas (*PHK* 61);
(3*c*) I am not the cause of these ideas (*PHK* 29);
(4) therefore, some other spirit, God, is the cause of these ideas (*PHK* 29).

This argument appears, often in a much abbreviated form, in the *Philosophical Commentaries* (*PC* 499, 838), the *Principles* (*PHK* 25–29), the *Dialogues* (*Dia. II*, Berk. II, 214–215), and *The Theory of Vision . . . Vindicated and Explained* (13, 21). Although there are anticipations of the argument in Malebranche (*DMR* IV.8, V.5, VII.2), he does not explicitly propound it. The argument is not available to him because his principal arguments for the causal inefficacy of created entities (including ideas and material substances) are developed against the background of God's existence. As deployed by Berkeley, the passivity argument is a clear example of the strategy of arguing (at 3*a*) from the inefficacy of entities in the natural world to the existence of a continuously active God.

Berkeley's least-known argument for the existence of God, which I will call "the visual-language argument," provides a second example of this strategy. The argument may be formulated as follows:

(1) visible ideas (ideas of the sense of vision) suggest or signify other ideas (e.g., *NTV* 51, 64, 77, 140);
(2) signs are related to their signification either (*a*) by causation, (*b*) by necessity, (*c*) by similitude, or (*d*) arbitrarily (*TVV* 39–42);
(3) visible ideas are related to their signification neither by (*a*) causation (*TVV* 11–13, *PHK* 25–29), nor by (*b*) necessity (*NTV* 1–120), nor by (*c*) similitude (*NTV* 121–146);
(4) therefore, they are related arbitrarily (*NTV* 147, *TVV* 40, *Alc.* IV.10);
(5) a language is a system of arbitrary signs (*Alc.* IV.7, *TVV* 40);
(6) therefore, visible ideas constitute a universal language of the Author of nature (*NTV* 147, *Alc.* IV.10, *TVV* 40).

The visual-language argument shares two important features with the passivity argument. First, it leads to the conclusion that God is continuously active; He continuously speaks to us through the succession of ideas which constitutes a language. Second, the argument requires the premise (at 3*a*) that ideas do not cause ideas, that ideas are causally inefficacious.

The visual-language argument, whatever we may think of it, was a favorite of Berkeley's. His first published work, *A New Theory of Vision* (1709) contains all the apparatus leading to the conclusion that "the proper objects of vision constitute the universal language of nature" (*NTV* 147). He does not yet explicitly take the step of attributing the universal visual language to God. But he does so in the *Principles* in 1710: "It is, I say, evident from what has been said in the foregoing parts of this treatise, and in *Sect.* 147, and elsewhere of the essay concerning vision, that visible ideas are the language whereby the governing spirit, on whom we depend, informs us what tangible ideas he is about to imprint upon us. . . . But for a fuller information in this point, I refer to the essay it self" (*PHK* 44).

The full visual-language argument is employed in *Alciphron* (1732), Dialogue IV. In section 4, Alciphron states that he infers the existence of other rational spirits from their effects and operations. In section 5, Euphranor argues that there are many operations and effects of such a character (given their complexity) that they can be attributed only to God, rather than to finite spirits. Alciphron, holding out for atheism, decides that he is prepared only to infer the existence of a rational spirit from the use of language, defined by him at section 8 as "the arbitrary use of sensible signs, which have no similitude or necessary connection with the things signified." Enter the visual language. Euphranor proceeds to argue in section 10 to the conclusion that "it seems the proper objects of sight . . . form a language wonderfully adapted to suggest and exhibit to us the distances, figures, situations, dimensions, and various qualities of tangible objects: not by similitude, nor yet by inference of necessary connexion, but by the arbitrary imposition of Providence, just as words suggest the things signified by them." At section 12, Euphranor points out that on Alciphron's own principles there is "as much reason to think the Universal Agent or God speaks to your eyes, as . . . for thinking any particular person speaks to your ears." At section 14, a further participant, Crito, does Euphranor the favor of pointing out the antideistic implications: "Some philosophers . . .

did . . . imagine that he [the Creator] left this system . . . as an artist leaves a clock. . . . But this Visual Language proves, not a Creator merely, but a provident Governor, actually and intimately present."

New editions of *A New Theory of Vision*, containing one significant difference relevant in this context from earlier versions, were annexed to the two editions of *Alciphron* published in 1732. Whereas the first two editions of *A New Theory of Vision* (1709, 1710) had concluded only that "the proper objects of vision constitute the universal language of nature" (*NTV* 147), the later editions conclude that "the proper objects of vision constitute an universal language of the Author of nature." It is clear (cf. *PHK* 44) that Berkeley had this conclusion in view all along. We have seen that in section 44 of the *Principles* he had already claimed that it is evident on the basis of section 147 of *A New Theory of Vision* that there is a visual language attributed to "the governing spirit." What is more, in 1733, Berkeley published a second work on vision, *The Theory of Vision or Visual Language shewing the immediate Presence and Providence of a Deity Vindicated and Explained*. On the title page appeared the Pauline text familiar from Malebranche, "In Him we live, and move, and have our being." The very first section of *The Theory of Vision . . . Vindicated and Explained* states that "being persuaded that the *Theory of Vision*, annexed to the *Minute Philosopher* [*Alciphron*], affords to thinking men a new unanswerable proof of the existence and immediate operation of God . . . I think my self concerned . . . to defend and explain it" (*TVV* 1; cf. 2, 8).

The central conclusion of *A New Theory of Vision* just is that visible ideas constitute a universal language of (the Author of) nature, stated at 147.[20] The sections that follow (148–159) constitute a sort of appendix on the objects of geometry. Throughout the work (in sections 20, 32, 51, 64, 66, 73, 77, 140, and 143), Berkeley draws partial analogies between individual visible ideas and words, and between the system of visible ideas and language. But these are comparisons only. Berkeley, a master tactician, uses the series of

[20]Luce, 1934, p. 38, has also suggested that Berkeley "regarded this truth [*NTV* 147] as the net outcome of" *A New Theory of Vision*, though he does not argue for this thesis extensively.

analogies between visible ideas and a language to prepare the ground for the identification of the system of visible ideas with a language at 147.

It may seem implausible that the central conclusion of A *New Theory of Vision* should be that visible ideas constitute a universal language of (the Author of) nature. This thesis, however, allows us to account for the overall structure of the work, and to explain why Berkeley goes to great lengths to establish a particular claim. The claim is that there is a difference in kind, sort, or species between visible and tangible objects (*NTV* 111, 121, 127, 142), that visible and tangible objects are completely heterogeneous (*NTV* 108). I will call this "the heterogeneity thesis" (for visible and tangible objects). Previous commentators have been unable to provide an adequate explanation of the matter and import of the heterogeneity thesis.

The best clues to the interpretation of this thesis are to be gathered from the contexts in which it is stated. In section 44 of the *Principles*, Berkeley writes that "the ideas of sight and touch make two species, entirely distinct and heterogeneous"; the same section states that "visible ideas are the language whereby the governing spirit . . . informs us of what tangible ideas he is about to imprint on us." He states in sections 38 and 40 of *The Theory of Vision . . . Vindicated and Explained* that vision is the language of the Author of Nature; in 41 that the objects of sight and touch are "intirely different and heterogeneous"; and in 43 returns to the theme that vision is the language of the Author of nature. And in A *New Theory of Vision* itself, the conclusion at section 147 that visible ideas constitute a universal language of (the Author of) nature immediately follows twenty-six sections devoted entirely to proving the heterogeneity doctrine. The proximity in these three works of passages on the heterogeneity thesis and the visual-language argument strongly suggest that the two are intimately related. What is the relation?

Berkeley provides a sketchy characterization of what he means by a difference in kind, sort, or species, in a passage that has been largely ignored:[21] "When upon the perception of an idea I range it

_____
[21]One exception is Pitcher, 1977, pp. 50–51.

under this or that sort, it is because it is perceived after the same manner, or because it has a likeness or conformity with, or affects me in the same way as, the ideas of the sort I rank it under. In short, it must not be intirely new, but have something in it old and already perceived by me" (NTV 128). On this account, two ideas are included within the same sort if and only if either (i) they are perceived in the same manner, or (ii) they stand in a relationship of likeness, or (iii) they affect the percipient in the same way. Now, Berkeley wants to hold that visible ideas are arbitrary signs of tangible ideas. Recall that a sign is nonarbitrary (for Berkeley) just in case it is related to its signification (*a*) by causation (TVV 39); (*b*) by necessity (TVV 39); or (*c*) by similitude (TVV 39), resemblance (TVV 42), or likeness (TVV 14). However we explicate (i) and (iii), it is clear that if visible and tangible objects are heterogeneous, not included within the same sort, then they are not related in any of the ways (i–iii), and in particular it is false that (ii) they stand in a relationship of likeness. Berkeley defines heterogeneity—difference in kind, sort, or species—in a way that insures that if visible and tangible objects are heterogeneous, they are not related by resemblance. The heterogeneity thesis is tailor-made for this purpose.[22]

[22]I believe that Luce has badly missed the point and function of the heterogeneity doctrine. His position is that in *A New Theory of Vision* the substance of the heterogeneity doctrine is that the objects of sight and touch have a different metaphysical status, or differ generically, in that the former are "in the mind" whereas the latter pass for being external; the substance of the claim in later works, where the objects of touch are explicitly in the mind as well, is simply that objects of sight and touch are objects of different senses. If possible, we should avoid an account according to which the content of the heterogeneity doctrine changes so radically. In addition, Luce's overall view of *A New Theory of Vision* is incoherent because he holds jointly: that the heterogeneity doctrine is the principal and most distinctive thesis of the work; and that the doctrine is valid only on the more interesting reading where the objects of sight and touch differ in metaphysical status; and that in the first work on vision Berkeley does not state but only allows the reader to assume, what Berkeley in fact does not believe, that the objects of sight and touch do differ in metaphysical status since the objects of touch are external to the mind. The right step is to reject the second of these contentions. See Luce, 1934, pp. 25–30, 34; 1946, "Introduction"; Berk. I, pp. 147–153, 246; and 1963, pp. 51–53. Other commentators have held that Berkeley's point is that no word (such as 'round') has the same meaning when applied to objects of sight and touch. I would not claim that this is strictly mistaken, but it detracts attention from Berkeley's interest in questions about resemblance. See Warnock, 1953, pp. 39–45; and Armstrong, 1960, pp. 52–58.

The structure of A *New Theory of Vision* can now be seen to be guided by the demands of the visual-language argument. The bulk of the work is devoted to showing that visible ideas are not related to their signification by necessity—for distance in *NTV* 1–51, for magnitude in 52–87, and for situation in 88–120. In 121–146 Berkeley argues for the heterogeneity thesis, i.e., that visible ideas are not related to their signification by similtude. These are components (3*b*) and (3*c*) of the visual-language argument, respectively. (Obviously, we are concerned here with only the grosser structural aspects of the contents of the first work on vision.)

It emerges from this review that although the visual-language argument guides the structure of A *New Theory of Vision*, and makes an explicit appearance in the *Principles*, the argument comes into its greatest prominence in 1732–33, with the publication of *Alciphron*, the third edition of A *New Theory of Vision*, and *The Theory of Vision . . . Vindicated and Explained*. The passivity argument dominates Berkeley's early works, and the visual-language argument dominates his later ones, even though it was available from the beginning. It is curious that the visual-language argument does not appear in the *Dialogues*. There may well be a prudential explanation here, if one is willing to think of Berkeley's Divine visual language as a transmuted version of Malebranche's vision in God. For Malebranche, sensory awareness requires vision of ideas or archetypes in God; for Berkeley, in sensory experience we are acquainted with a visual language of God. Of course, these doctrines are not identical in content. On the other hand, the terminological similarities are not just coincidental, and both doctrines would invite the charge of enthusiasm. The prudential considerations cited by Luce (§26) might well have led Berkeley to downplay the visual-language argument in his early works; and since by the time of the *Dialogues* he was already defending himself against the suggestion that his views "run into the enthusiasm of Malbranche," the argument could not safely appear in that work at all.

In addition to the passivity and visual-language arguments, one further argument for the existence of God, sometimes called the "continuity argument," is often attributed to Berkeley:

(1) no sensible object can exist when not perceived by some spirit;
(2) sensible objects sometimes exist when not perceived by any finite spirit;
(3) therefore, there exists an infinite spirit, God, which perceives sensible objects (at least) when they are not perceived by any finite spirit.

This argument does not employ any premise about the inefficacy of created entities. As such, it may seem a threat to my claim that whereas Malebranche argues from God to the inefficacy of created entities, Berkeley argues from the inefficacy of created entities to God. Of course, I need not say that every one of Berkeley's arguments for the existence of God conforms to this procedure. It would be enough that two of the three have the inefficacy of created entities as a premise. In fact, however, the attention commentators have paid to the continuity and the visual-language arguments is inversely proportional to their importance. Berkeley did not employ the continuity argument in his serious philosophical moments. Jonathan Bennett has argued at length for this thesis,[23] and I will simply note two points. First, Berkeley advances the continuity argument at most twice (Berk. II, 230–231, 211–212) in his entire corpus. These passages occur in the third and first of the *Dialogues*, a popular work compared to the *Principles*. Second, where continuity is discussed in the *Principles* (PHK 6, 45–48), Berkeley's position is always that it does not follow from his principles that sensible objects have an intermittent existence—they are annihilated only if they are not perceived by any mind. He does not take the further step of arguing that since sensible things sometimes do exist when not perceived by any finite spirit, there exists an infinite spirit which perceives them (at least) at those times.

It is no surprise, in light of Berkeley's desire to prove the existence of a God who is continuously active, who operates immediately and is intimately present, that the ontological argument does not appear in his works. The ontological argument is ill suited to this purpose; even if it is cogent, it has no tendency to support the desired account

---

[23]Bennett, 1971, pp. 165–198. The terminology "continuity argument" is also due to Bennett.

of God's relationship to the world. I have pointed out (§5) that if Berkeley rejects the ontological argument, he does so on the ground that it fails to produce conviction; and that on one occasion he does write of the "necessary existence" of God. It is possible that he did not reject the ontological argument as fallacious, though he was not prepared to use it since it would require supplementation to yield an occasionalist account of God's relationship to the world.

29. Berkeley's Arguments against the Causal Efficacy of Ideas

Both of Berkeley's principal arguments for the existence of a continuously active God depend upon the premise that (3*a*) ideas are not causes of other ideas. He holds more generally that ideas are "*inefficacious perceptions*" (*PHK* 64, Berkeley's emphasis), that they are not causes of anything; and that material substances, if (*per impossible*) they were to exist, would not be causes (*PHK* 61). The only causes are the volitions of spirits, and derivatively spirits themselves. Before turning to Berkeley's arguments for these contentions, I want to consider in a general way what sorts of arguments are available to him.

There are two considerations which preclude his using any Malebranchian argument. First, whereas Malebranche holds that the only causes are the volitions of God, Berkeley holds more liberally that the only causes are the volitions of spirits, Divine or created. Second, whereas Malebranche argues from the existence of God to the inefficacy of created entities, Berkeley argues from the inefficacy of created entities (ideas) to the existence of God. Malebranche had argued that: (*a*) there is a necessary connection between God's volitions and their realization, but not between any other distinct events; (*b*) God's volitions are sufficient for their realization, so that nothing else is a cause of the effects of those volitions; and (*c*) creatures are essentially dependent upon God. The first consideration clearly prevents Berkeley from employing (*a*), unless he is prepared to argue that there is a necessary connection between the volitions of finite entities and their realization. The second consideration clearly prevents him from using any variant of (*b*) or (*c*), since for the purpose of these arguments God's existence must already have been established.[24]

Berkeley is also unable to invoke certain other arguments which had been used to support the denial of particular causal relations. Descartes, in attempting to show that the existence of mind does not depend causally upon the existence of body, had suggested that modes of material substances are so unlike or different from, have so little in common with, thinking substance that such causal dependence is impossible (§§ 13, 16). And Spinoza's attack on Descartes' mind-body interactionism seems to depend at bottom on the anti-Cartesian intuition that mind and body are too unlike, too different, have too little in common, to interact (§ 20). Whatever the merit of such "heterogeneity" considerations, they are not available to Berkeley. This is because the point that two entities have too little in common to interact yields symmetrical results; it shows, if it shows anything, that neither entity causally interacts with the other. Thus for Spinoza, modes of thought cannot cause modes of extension, and vice versa. Berkeley wants to show that ideas are not causes of anything (including volitions), while volitions are causes of ideas. Heterogeneity considerations cannot support such an "asymmetrical" denial of particular causal relations. In the first two editions of the *Dialogues*, Berkeley does argue that material substances could not cause ideas, on the ground that they do not have enough in common with ideas: "Yes, it is infinitely more extravagant to say, a

[24]Radner, 1978a, pp. 174–175, has suggested, however, that Berkeley's position does arise as a consequence of a critique of Malebranche's position on causation. Malebranche's "insistence upon a necessary connection between cause and effect stems from a misconception of the difference between an omnipotent being and a finite being. An omnipotent being is one that can accomplish all that it wills. A finite being cannot accomplish *anything* that it wills. To say that I am a being with the power to act is merely to say that I can do what I will. It is not to say that I cannot *fail* to do what I will." It is preposterous to suggest that Malebranche's requirement that there be a necessary connection between cause and effect arises from a misconception of the difference between an omnipotent being on the one hand and a finite being, as ordinarily understood, on the other. Surely, Malebranche did not misunderstand the difference between being able to do anything one wills and being able to do some things one wills. The passage Radner cites in order to show that this is a Berkelian response to Malebranche deals with free will, not causation.

thing which is inert, operates on the mind, and which is unperceiving, is the cause of our perceptions, without any regard to consistency, or to the old known axiom: *Nothing can give to another that which it hath not itself"* (*Dia. III*, Berk. II, 236). In the subsequent editions, he deletes the material following "perceptions." He must have come to see that appeal to the old known axiom threatened his own view that volitions cause ideas but not vice versa. since on his view, "the Will. . . . tis toto coelo different from the Understanding i.e. from all our Ideas" (*PC* 643).

Berkeley wants to deny the causal efficacy of ideas. The arguments of Malebranche and Spinoza for their denials of certain causal relations cannot be pressed into service. The constraints upon the argumentation available to Berkeley seem severe. Since the volitions of all spirits are causes, he cannot appeal to properties peculiar to God. Since he wants to rely upon the inefficacy of ideas in order to establish God's existence, he cannot appeal to arguments which presuppose the existence of God. Since volitions do cause ideas, he cannot argue that volitions and ideas have so little in common that they cannot interact. To put it bluntly, Berkeley had to find something new by way of argumentation.

What might we expect of him under these circumstances? Ideally, he should attempt to support some body of doctrine about the nature of causal relations, and then show that, given that body of doctrine, volitions stand in the requisite relation to ideas, but that ideas do not stand in the requisite relation to anything. Of course, this result might be held to count against the body of doctrine in question, but the force of this consideration would depend (in part) upon the strength of the original defense of that body of doctrine. The independent support might derive from an attempt to analyze the meaning of causal locutions (much as Berkeley himself attempts at section 3 of the *Principles* to unpack the meaning of 'exists' when applied to sensible objects). Or the independent support might derive from an attempt to diagnose or locate the features ideas are thought to have by those who think ideas are causes. It may be that the relations between ideas lack relevant features they are thought to have. What we should expect is some defense of a body of doctrine or principles about causal relations, coupled with an argument to show that only volitions are causes if that doctrine is correct.

We can trace the actual development of Berkeley's views on causation through the *Philosophical Commentaries*. There are the following notebook entries. Recall that the obelus is used to mark views that he has rejected or modified.

+461 The simple idea call'd Power seems obscure or rather none at all. but onely the relation 'twixt cause & Effect. W^n I ask whether A can move B. if A be an intelligent thing. I mean no more than whether the volition of A that B move be attended with the motion of B, if A be senseless whether the impulse of A against B be follow'd by ye motion of B.

+493 Power no simple Idea. it means nothing but the Relation between Cause & Effect.

499 What means Cause as distinguish'd from Occasion? nothing but a Being wch wills w^n the Effect follows the volition.

699 There is a difference betwixt Power & Volition. There may be volition without Power. But there can be no Power without Volition. Power implyeth volition & at the same time a Connotation of the Effects following the Volition.

850 I say there are no Causes (properly speaking) but Spiritual, nothing active but Spirit. Say you, this is only Verbal, tis only annexing a new sort of signification to the word Cause, & why may not others as well retain the old one, & call one Idea the Cause of another wch always follows it. I answer, if you do so, I shall drive you into many absurditys. I say you cannot avoid running into opinions you'll be glad to disown if you stick firmly to that signification of the Word Cause.

These entries are telling. At 461, Berkeley provides a disjunctive account of causation, or, more precisely, of the causation of motion—one clause applying to causation of motion by spirits, the other to causation of motion by sensible objects. At this juncture, he admits the possibility of communication of motion by impulse. In 499, he writes that a cause is "a Being wch wills w^n the Effect follows the volition." Since the clause allowing causation between sensible objects has been dropped, this entry appears to secure the result that only spirits are causes by brute force, by stipulation.[25] It is not certain, however, that this is the correct reading of the entry. The marginal signs that Berkeley uses in the notebooks include letters of

[25]Tipton, 1974, p. 307, writes that "the definition is very useful given Berkeley's purposes, and indeed suspiciously useful."

the alphabet in addition to mathematical symbols such as the plus sign. Entry 499 is marked "S," which means "Soul-Spirit" (Berk. I, 50). Now, Berkeley also had a letter indicating matter; he sometimes marked an entry with two letters (e.g., *PC* 472); and the earlier entries dealing with power and causation (*PC* 461, 493) are not marked with any letter at all. It therefore seems possible that at entry 499 Berkeley is stating the meaning of 'cause' in the case of spirits only, and that it is only subsequently that material causes are ruled out.

It is nevertheless clear from entry 850 that Berkeley is himself sensitive to the charge that he achieves his desired result by mere verbal stipulation. He replies that if one retains the older and broader significance of the term, one will be driven into absurdities and unwelcome consequences. Unfortunately, he never does produce any sort of *reductio* of a broader notion of causation. In the *Philosophical Commentaries*, there is no independently motivated body of doctrine about causation to which Berkeley appeals in order to support his position that spirits are causes but sensible objects are not. I want to make clear that I am not criticizing Berkeley's account of causation at 499 on the ground that it is susceptible to *post hoc ergo propter hoc* difficulties. Although that is true, it is just one symptom of the fundamental difficulty: that Berkeley lacks a considered, general account of causation which nontrivially yields the result that only spirits are causes. Of course, in the body of his work he has to produce something more than the general stipulation (if it is that) at 499, or the assertion (coupled with a challenge to those who think otherwise) that "there are no Causes... but Spiritual" at 850.[26] Does he have any argument to offer?

[26]Pitcher, 1977, p. 133, has suggested that Berkeley might have felt, with some justification, that the thesis that only volitions are causes did not need argument: "There is something altogether special about the causality of our own actions; we can just feel ourselves making them happen.... One is irresistibly drawn to the idea that here, with volitions, and only here, we experience real causality, real agency. Berkeley doubtless thinks that a truth as obvious as this needs no extended defense." For Pitcher, this is a charitable way to explain away the "regrettable" fact that Berkeley "does not work out and defend this position, so central to his whole philosophy." Even if it seemed obvious to Berkeley that volitions are the only causes, he was hardly entitled simply to help himself to this thesis. For both Descartes and Locke, the thesis is too restrictive, since they believe in the causal efficacy of physical objects; for Malebranche, the thesis is too liberal, since he does not believe in the causal efficacy of the volitions of created spirits.

Features of some later works should give pause to those who think he does. Even in the *Dialogues, Alciphron,* and *The Theory of Vision . . . Vindicated and Explained,* Berkeley seems content to maintain virtually without argument that ideas are not causes. Sometimes he simply asserts this position (*Dia. III,* Berk. II, 216; *TVV* 11); and sometimes the position is granted by courtesy of a participant in a dialogue in response to a rhetorical question (*Dia. III,* Berk. II, 231; *Alc.* VII.5).

In section 25 of the *Principles,* however, Berkeley clearly sets out to show that ideas are not causes. The result is invoked immediately in sections 26–30 for the purposes of the passivity argument for the existence of God. At section 102, he explicitly refers the reader to section 25 for the result that ideas are "perfectly inert." If Berkeley has a considered argument for this position, we should expect to find it at *Principles* 25. I believe that this section contains two distinct lines of argument.

The first argument comes at the beginning of the section:

> All our ideas, sensations, or the things which we perceive, by what-soever names they may be distinguished, are visibly inactive, there is nothing of power or agency included in them. So that one idea or object of thought cannot produce, or make any alteration in another. To be satisfied of the truth of this, there is nothing else requisite but a bare observation of our ideas. For since they and every part of them exist only in the mind, it follows that there is nothing in them but what is perceived. But whoever shall attend to his ideas, whether of sense or reflexion, will not perceive in them any power or activity; there is therefore no such thing contained in them. [*PHK* 25]

The natural reading to this point is that ideas are "visibly inactive" in the sense that they can be observed to be inactive—they are "perceived" by "bare observation" to be inactive. In the context, Berkeley's statement that "since they [ideas] and every part of them exist only in the mind, it follows that there is nothing in them but what is perceived," suggests that he holds that we cannot be mistaken about which properties our ideas have. The point is explicit in the discussion of the oar in the *Second Dialogue:* "his mistake lies not in what he perceives immediately and at present (it being a manifest contradiction to suppose he should err in respect of that) but in the wrong judgment he makes concerning the ideas he ap-prehends to be connected with those immediately perceived" (Berk. II, 238). In other words, Berkeley follows both Descartes and Locke in holding that beliefs about the content of first-person mental states (ideas) are incorrigible (§3). As we saw (§3), Berkeley emphasizes the virtues of intuitive and demonstrative knowledge, and holds that we have demonstrative knowledge of the existence of God in particular. Since each step of a demonstrative argument must itself be intuitive, he must hold that such incorrigible beliefs about our ideas constitute intuitive knowledge. The belief that ideas are inactive, when it arises in this way (by "bare observation" of our ideas), is an example of a posteriori intuitive knowledge.

The argument, however, is not strong on its own terms. The activity that Berkeley attributes to volitions, and denies of ideas, seems to be a phenomenological property. Phenomenologically, there is a sort of "activity" characteristic of volitions, but not of ideas. It is impossible to exploit such a difference in the absence of a body of doctrine about causal relations which explains why possession of this sort of activity should be a necessary condition for causation. The present line of argument seems to do little more than invite an equivocation between the claims that only volitions are active phenomenologically, and that only volitions are active causally. The most Berkeley has shown is that if ideas are causes, it is not by virtue of any volitional activity.

The first argument faces a more curious difficulty when considered in its argumentative context. Berkeley wants to appeal to the conclusion that ideas are not causes in order to prove the existence of God (*PHK* 26–30). The philosophical difficulty aside, the first argument is sufficient for Berkeley's purpose of providing demonstrative arguments for God's existence. However, as it stands, the most the argument can show is that those ideas which have been observed until now are inactive, ideas have until now been caused by God. We would at best have a probabilistic, nondemonstrative argument for the conclusion that ideas in the future will be caused by God. Surely, Berkeley wants a demonstrative argument for the conclusion that the succession of ideas of sense has and will be caused by God.

It should therefore be no surprise that the first argument of section 25 is followed immediately by an a priori demonstrative argument for the conclusion that it is "impossible" for ideas to be causes: "A little attention will discover to us that the very being of an idea implies passiveness and inertness in it, insomuch as it is impossible for an idea to do any thing, or, strictly speaking, to be the cause of any thing" (*PHK* 25). This is cryptic, but I believe Berkeley's idea is clear. Why should "the very being of an idea" imply passiveness and inertness? Perhaps because the being or "the existence of an idea consists in being perceived" (*PHK* 2; cf. *PC* 472, 656; *PHK* 3–4, 90; *Dia. III*, Berk. II, 230). The suggestion is that since for ideas, to be is to be perceived, ideas are by their nature dependent (upon a perceiver), passive, inactive, causally inefficacious. Unfortunately, an argument is needed if we are to accept each step here, an argument to show that the sort of dependence at issue is really incompatible with causal activity.

Does Berkeley have anything else to offer beyond the weak arguments of section 25? It is tempting to find a distinct line of argument three sections later:

> I find I can excite ideas in my mind at pleasure, and vary and shift the scene as oft as I think fit. It is no more than willing, and straightway this or that idea arises in my fancy: and by the same power it is obliterated, and makes way for another. This making and unmaking of ideas doth very properly denominate the mind active. Thus much is certain, and grounded on experience: but when we talk of unthinking agents, or of exciting ideas exclusive of volition, we only amuse our selves with words. [*PHK* 28]

This might be read to suggest that volitional activity is the paradigm of causal activity, and that other alleged examples of causation are too far removed from the paradigm to qualify. Alternatively, there is a stronger reading: that in volitions we have the experiential source of our idea or concept of "activity" or "causal activity"; and that any application of the concept beyond volitions is meaningless. In either form, the claims involved would have to be buttressed considerably. Attributing to Berkeley some argument along the present lines does put his views about causation in the best philosophical light possible.[27]

Unfortunately, section 28 does not provide any basis for attributing such an argument to him. Indeed, I do not think that at section

---

[27]For a commentator who places some emphasis upon *Principles* 28 in connection with Berkeley's argumentation for the thesis that ideas are not causes, see ibid., pp. 132–133.

28 Berkeley is even arguing that ideas are not causes. As we have seen, there are two arguments for this conclusion at section 25. The result that ideas are not causes is invoked immediately at section 26 for the purpose of showing, in route to the complete passivity argument, that "the cause of ideas is an incorporeal active substance or spirit." This leaves open the possibility that an agent is himself the cause of his ideas. At section 29, Berkeley argues against this possibility, concluding that "there is therefore some other will or spirit that produces them." The arguments at section 28 appear after Berkeley has shown that ideas are not causes; their role is to support the result at section 29. The point of section 28 is to lay the foundation for a contrast between those ideas which I can excite "at pleasure," by "no more than willing" and, at section 29, those ideas which "have not a like dependence on my will," as "when in broad day-light I open my eyes, it is not in my power . . . to determine what particular objects shall present themselves to my view." It is sensory ideas of this sort which must be produced by some other spirit. In section 28, Berkeley is not employing an argument from volitions as the paradigm of causal activity, or as the source of our concept of causal activity.

Berkeley does not produce any serious direct argument for his view that only volitions are causes. Beyond this, there is a serious gap in his views about what sorts of entities can be causes. When he "takes a survey of the objects of human knowledge," he distinguishes between the ideas which the mind has, and the "passions and operations of the mind" (*PHK* 1). The mind's operations explicitly include not only willing or volition, but also imagining and remembering (*PHK* 2) and such passions as loving and hating (*PHK* 27). The arguments at *Principles* 25 to show that ideas are not causes seem inapplicable in the case of the mental operations. Since the mental operations are precisely that, activities of the mind, it is difficult to see how they could be observed to be inert. (One suspects some equivocation which helps to blur the difficulty; the mind is active in that there are mental operations; and the mind is active in that its volitions are efficacious.) Since the existence of a mental operation does not consist in being perceived, it is difficult to see how the very existence of a mental operation could imply passiveness or inertness. Berkeley needs to provide some explanation of why mental operations other than volition cannot be causes of subsequent mental operations and/or ideas. It is interesting that whereas Descartes, Spinoza, Malebranche, Locke, and Hume at the very least take care to provide inventories and classifications of mental operations, and generally produce a considerable body of doctrine about the passions and other mental operations, such material is not to be found in Berkeley. He chooses to ignore further candidates for causally efficacious entities, rather than to proliferate unconvincing arguments and distinctions required to sustain his desired position.

What is worse, there is a serious internal threat to Berkeley's position that ideas are not causes. The difficulty arises in connection with his position on the conditions under which minds or spirits exist. Consider the following notebook entries:

429 Existence is percipi or percipere $\wedge$. the horse is in the stable, the Books are in the study as before.
$\wedge$ or velle i:e. agere

645 There can be perception wthout volition. Qu: whether there can be volition without perception.

646 Existence not conceivable without perception or volition not distinguish'd therefrom.

+659 Again if by is you mean is perceived or dos' perceive. I say nothing wch is perceived or does perceive Wills.

672a There is somewhat active in most perceptions i.e. such as ensue upon our Volitions, such as we can prevent & stop v.g. I turn my eyes toward the Sun I open them all this is active.

673 Things are two-fold active or inactive. The existence of Active things is to act, of inactive to be perceiv'd.

674 Distinct from or without perception there is no volition; therefore neither is there existence without perception.

791 While I exist or have any Idea I am eternally, constantly willing, my acquiescing in the present State is willing.

820 Qu: may not there be an Understanding without a Will.

821 Understanding is in some sort an Action.

833 It seems there can be no perception, no Idea without Will, being there are no Ideas so indifferent but one would rather Have them than annihilation, or annihilation than them.

841 It seems to me that Will & understanding Volition & ideas cannot be severed, that either cannot be possibly without the other.

842 Some Ideas or other I must have so long as I exist or Will. But no one Idea or sort of Ideas is essential.

At entry 429, Berkeley maintains that for a spirit, to be is to perceive *or* to act. The entries which follow constitute a prolonged attempt to find some way to reduce or compress this formula. At entries 672a, 791, and 833, he states the rudiments of a line of argument to the conclusion that there cannot be perception without volition. This, if correct, would justify a reduction to: for spirits, to be is to will. Other entries (674, 841, 842) assert that volition cannot exist without perception or ideas. Since "to have an idea is all one as to perceive" (*PHK* 7), this would justify a reduction to: for spirits, to be is to perceive. And this seems to be Berkeley's ultimate position, both in the *Philosophical Commentaries* and in the *Principles*: "a soul or spirit is an active being, whose existence consists... in perceiving ideas and thinking" (*PHK* 139).

Berkeley's reason for wanting to achieve such a reduction seems clear. He holds that a spirit or mind is simple, undivided, uncompounded (*PHK* 27, 141), and therefore immortal (*PHK* 141). Descartes could hold that the soul is simple, and that the soul's essence is to think, because he used 'thought' in a broad sense which included both perception and volition, *inter alia* (§§7, 13). Berkeley, however, insists on the complete heterogeneity of ideas and volitions or spirits (*PC* 643, 658; *PHK* 89, 139, 142; *Dia. III*, Berk. II, 231); his position is that these entities have nothing in common, no resemblance to each other, in part on the ground that ideas are inactive whereas volitions or spirits are active (*PHK* 137). Suppose Berkeley settled on the formula that to be is to perceive or to will. Apparently, we would be faced with an irreducibly disjunctive essence, since ideas and volitions or spirits have nothing in common. How are we to distinguish between a single, simple entity with a disjunctive essence, and two entities (which may or may not exist simultaneously), each with a single essence—to perceive and to will, respectively? This sort of concern would be reinforced by the Cartesian assumption that an entity has exactly one principal attribute or essence (§13). At this point, the doctrine of the simplicity of the soul would be considerably threatened. Berkeley's response is that ideas cannot be severed from volition. This enables him to hold that for spirits, to be is to perceive, since whenever we will we must have ideas, that is, we must perceive.

This doctrine that volition requires ideas in turn threatens Berkeley's position on causation. For if volitions require ideas, this at the least raises the suspicion that ideas are causally necessary for the realization of what is willed. For example, suppose that having a volition to move a limb requires having an idea of that limb moving. Is not the idea, partly constitutive of the volition, a likely candidate for a partial cause of the limb's moving? At this point, Berkeley needs to produce an elaborate account of the precise connection between volitions and ideas. No such account is forthcoming in the systematic works, and there is at best a handful of relevant entries in the *Philosophical Commentaries*.[28]

Berkeley's position on causation is feeble indeed. In the *Philosophical Commentaries*, there is little more than the assertion, and possibly the stipulation, that volitions are the only causes. In the systematic works, there is little advance. The arguments produced (for example, at *Principles* 25) do not begin to succeed. More promising lines of argument, which might be extracted from Berkeley's remarks (for example, at *Principles* 28), were in fact not pursued for the purpose of showing that volitions are the only causes. These deficiencies are serious since the thesis that ideas are not causes is a crucial premise for Berkeley's two principal arguments for the existence of God. The direct argumentation about causation aside, Berkeley is virtually silent about mental operations other than volitions, a class of candidates for causally efficacious entities which are not happily located on either side of the distinction between active volitions and inert ideas. Finally, in opting for the theses that volition requires ideas and hence that, for spirits, to be is to perceive, Berkeley introduces a serious internal threat to his position that ideas are not causes.

Perhaps these discouraging results are not really surprising. Berkeley's accounts of causation, freedom, the soul's essence, were dictated by a number of objectives: to establish an occasionalist metaphysics; to show in particular that since certain entities in the natural world are causally inefficacious, God is continuously active

---

[28]For an extended discussion, from a different point of view, of material relevant to the internal threat I have been discussing, see ibid., pp. 180–227.

in the world; to dissociate himself from Malebranche by allowing that finite spirits have a limited degree of causal power insofar as they execute their own wills; and to show that souls are simple, indivisible, and hence immortal. Berkeley's position on causation was the best he could muster in the face of the constraints imposed by these objectives.

VII

LEIBNIZ'S DENIAL OF CAUSAL INTERACTION BETWEEN MONADS

30. Some Arguments for the Claim That Nothing External Acts upon a Substance

The claim that nothing external acts (causally) upon an individual substance is perhaps both the most distinctive and the most central claim of Leibniz's metaphysics. In light of its prominence in his writings, we would expect that the precise reasons which led him to make it would be evident. We shall see, however, that this is far from the case.

It is clear that Leibniz did claim that nothing external acts upon a substance—subject, possibly, to two exceptions or qualifications: first, finite substances are created by God; and second, created substances depend upon God as sustaining cause of their continued existence. Leibniz's most famous statement of the claim is at section 7 of the *Monadology*: "Monads have no windows through which anything could enter or depart." The same metaphor had appeared almost thirty years earlier in section xxvi of the *Discourse on Metaphysics*: "Nothing ever enters into our spirit naturally from outside, and it is a bad habit that we have, to think as if our soul received certain messenger species and as if it had doors and windows." Substances "have no windows"; this was not Leibniz's only picturesque way of denying that anything external acts upon a substance. In the *Discourse* and the ensuing correspondence with Arnauld, Leibniz states that each substance "is like a world apart": "each substance is like a world apart, independent of any other thing save God"; "each individual substance or complete entity is like a world apart, independent of everything except God" (*DM* xiv, *LA* 64, cf. L 457). These passages do not mean simply that *for its existence* a substance does not depend upon anything else except God. That would leave open the possibility of causal interaction between substances. In the *Discourse*, Leibniz states unequivocally: "there is no external cause which acts on us except God alone" (*DM* xxviii).

Leibniz holds that everything that exists or happens has a sufficient reason or cause (for references, see §31). The states of a substance at a given time must therefore have some sufficient reason or cause. Since nothing external acts upon a substance, the only candidate for causes of states of a substance at one time are states of that same substance at previous times. This result is stated explicitly: "All our future thoughts and perceptions are *only* consequences... of our preceding ones"; "every present state of a substance... is *only* a consequence of its preceding state" (*DM* xiv, *LA* 51, emphases added). Leibniz frequently uses causal locutions in describing the relationship between earlier and later states or perceptions of substances: "the present state of a substance is a natural result of its preceding state"; "the soul is a most exact immaterial automaton"; "each preceding perception influences those which follow in conformity with a law of order"; "the creature [is] predetermined by its preceding state" (L 495, 496; LC v.91; T 47; cf. T 52).

The many passages where Leibniz writes of one substance *acting* upon another are not to be construed causally. Leibniz, in Berkelian fashion, is speaking with the vulgar while thinking with the metaphysically learned. We have this in the *Discourse*: "It could therefore be said in some sort, and in a good sense, although remote from *ordinary usage*, that a particular substance *never* acts on another particular substance, nor is acted on by it" (*DM* xiv, emphases added). Leibniz proceeds to add that we must "reconcile metaphysical language with practice" (*DM* xv). And he states in the Arnauld correspondence: "I maintain that one created substance does not act upon another, in metaphysical rigour, that is to say with a real influence" (*LA* 167). There are a number of similar passages (cf. L 457, 523). Leibniz made various attempts to reconcile ordinary ways of speaking with metaphysical rigor, attempts to give an account of *some* sense in which substances "act" upon each other which is consistent with the metaphysical truth that nothing external does act upon a substance (W 116–117; *T* 66; L 502–503; M 49, 52). For example, he sometimes holds that one substance "acts" upon another if it *expresses* the other more clearly than the other expresses it, where "expression" is a noncausal relation of representation or correlation (*DM* xv, LA 51–52, 64–65, 87). Here, as elsewhere, Leibniz tries, as his metaphysical theory requires, to explicate the sense in which one substance "acts" upon another entirely in terms of noncausal relations between those substances.

Nothing external acts upon a substance. Why did Leibniz embrace this thesis? Let us consider some of his arguments for it. He frequently states that it is *inexplicable* how anything could act upon a substance. For example, the following argument appears in the famous section of the *Monadology* where he states that "monads have no windows": "There is likewise no way of explaining how a monad can be altered or changed internally by any other creature, since nothing can be transposed in it, and we cannot conceive in it, as we can in composite things among whose parts there may be changes, that any internal motion can be excited, directed, increased, or diminished from without" (*M* 7). We know from sections 1 and 3 of the *Monadology* that monads are simple substances, that something is simple if it has no parts, and that where there are no parts there is no extension, figure, or divisibility. Monads have states or qualities (perceptions), but no internal structure. Leibniz proceeds to argue at section 7 that it is inexplicable how anything external could act upon a monad, on the ground that the monad has no parts which can be transposed. He provides no argument for his assumption that causal interaction requires changes in or transposition of parts. And this surely needs argument, unless the possibility of an immaterial mind (or the states of an immaterial mind) causing its subsequent states is to be excluded out of hand.[1] Indeed, we have seen that Leibniz holds that states of a substance are causes of subsequent states of a substance. Such causal interaction takes place without any changes in or transposition of parts. Leibniz's argument is too strong. If the reasoning were cogent, it would equally tend to

[1] Broad, 1975, p. 48, has made this same point.

show that the states of a monad are not causes of its subsequent states. Perhaps there is some reason why inter-monadic interaction requires changes in an internal structure whereas intra-monadic interaction does not, but then this becomes the point at issue. The argument of section 7 to this point is unimpressive.

Leibniz must have realized this, for he supplements the argument with an entirely new consideration: "Accidents cannot be detached from substances and march about outside of substances, as the sensible species of the Scholastics once did" (*M* 7). The point is that detached accidents are a metaphysical impossibility, since any accident needs some substance in which it inheres (L 390). For the purposes of this argument, Leibniz illicitly invites the reader to picture causal interaction as involving the transmission of accidents. It is far from obvious, however, that this is a plausible model even in the case of intra-monadic causation, where one set of perceptions can cause a markedly different set of perceptions at a subsequent time.

It is interesting, but unfortunate, that section 7 of the *Monadology* contains what is probably the most explicit argument Leibniz has to offer for the claim that nothing external acts upon a substance. There are a number of other passages where he asserts that it is "inexplicable" how anything external can act upon a substance, though not on the ground that monads have no parts. For example: "since our thoughts are only consequences of the nature of our soul . . . it is useless to require the influence of another particular substance, not to mention that this influence is absolutely inexplicable"; "I found no way of explaining . . . how a substance can communicate with another created substance" (*LA* 84, W 113; cf. *LA* 86, L 613). Are there any arguments lurking here distinct from that found in the *Monadology?*

The recurrence of the bald claim that it is "inexplicable" how anything could act upon a substance, without accompanying argument, suggests that Leibniz was unsure how to argue for this position. Nevertheless, we can try to locate some sort of argument by examining his scattered remarks concerning explanation. For Leibniz, "everything must be explained by its cause" (*LA* 43). Further, the causal explanation for material phenomena must be mechanical: "all the particular phenomena of nature can be explained mechanically if we explore them enough and . . . we cannot understand the causes of material things on any other basis"; "we agree . . . that the great globes of our system . . . attract each other. But . . . this can happen only in a way that has an explanation, namely, by the impact of more subtle bodies" (L 409, 663; cf. *NE* 61; L 478). Material phenomena are explicable just in case they can be accounted for mechanically. Since monads lack parts and hence are unextended and immaterial, the states of one monad are "inexplicable" in the present sense in terms of the states of another monad. But the states of one monad are equally "inexplicable" in terms of its own prior states.

When Leibniz has his eye on monads, rather than material phenomena, he gives a gloss to the notion of a "mechanical explanation" which does not require a physical mechanism: "*everything happens mechanically in nature*, that is, according to certain mathematical laws prescribed by God" (L 189). Each monad has an "internal principle," "indwelling law," "law of order," or "law of succession" that moves the monad from state to state. Leibniz compares such laws of succession to mathematical series: "to act uniformly is to follow perpetually the same law of order or of succession, as in a certain scale or series of numbers" (L 495; cf. 155). A monad's law of succession is a mathematical law, and thus a monad's states can be explained "mechanically" in the present sense, in terms of its own prior states. Thus Leibniz often speaks of a monad as a spiritual automaton. Further, each monad represents, mirrors, or expresses every other monad, where "one thing *expresses* another (in my terminology) when there exists a constant and fixed relationship between what can be said of one and of the other" (*LA* 144). This has the consequence that there will also be mathematical laws of succession relating states of one monad to states of other monads. It appears that inter-monadic and intra-monadic mechanical explanations, in the present sense, of a monad's states are equally available.

Leibniz does not succeed in providing a good sense in which it is "inexplicable" how anything could act upon a substance. The various constructions he places upon "explicability" either have the result that intra-monadic causation is precluded, or are consistent with inter-monadic causation.

31. Logic and Metaphysics: The
Russell-Couturat Thesis

The arguments I have reviewed for the claim that nothing external acts upon a substance are unimpressive. Bertrand Russell must have had such arguments in mind when he wrote:

> I found myself, after reading most of the standard commentators and most of Leibniz's connected treatises, still completely in the dark as to the grounds which had led him to many of his opinions. Why he thought that monads cannot interact; how he became persuaded of the Identity of Indiscernibles; what he meant by the Law of Sufficient Reason—these and many other questions seemed to demand an answer, but to find none.... At this point I read the *Discourse de Métaphysique* and the letters to Arnauld. Suddenly a flood of light was thrown on all the inmost recesses of Leibniz's philosophical edifice.[2]

Russell wrote this in the preface to the first edition of his *Critical Exposition of the Philosophy of Leibniz* (1900). In the body of that work, he claimed to locate in Leibniz a "purely logical argument" which "yields the whole, or nearly the whole, of the necessary part of Leibniz's philosophy—of the propositions, that is to say, which are true of all possible worlds."[3] This thesis, that Leibniz's metaphysics—including the claim that nothing external acts upon a substance—was derived entirely from his logic, was advanced by Russell and Louis Couturat at the turn of the century.

In the preface to *La Logique de Leibniz* (1901), Couturat wrote that "Leibniz's metaphysics is based solely upon the principles of his Logic, and arises entirely from them." Couturat attempted to establish this thesis "explicitly and in detail" in an article, "On Leibniz's Metaphysics" (1902). That article states: "In a word, all the metaphysical properties of the 'individual substance' derive, by virtue of the principle of reason, from the logical properties which the 'complete and singular' idea possesses." In his "Recent Work on the Philosophy of Leibniz" (1903), Russell stated that Couturat's book is "completely successful" in establishing that Leibniz's metaphysics rests solely upon his logic; and that in Couturat's arti-

---

[2] Russell, 1937, pp. xiii–xiv.
[3] Ibid., pp. 8, 9.

cle, "the general conclusion, that Leibniz's logic was the true foundation of his whole system, seems... to be once for all demonstrated." In the preface to the second edition of his book on Leibniz (1937), Russell maintained that the book's "principal thesis—namely, that Leibniz's philosophy was almost entirely derived from his logic—received overwhelming confirmation from the work of Louis Couturat." In *A History of Western Philosophy* (1945), Russell cited Parmenides, Plato, Spinoza, and Hegel as examples of philosophers for whom logic is the source of metaphysics. He added: "But none of these is so clear cut as Leibniz in drawing inferences from syntax to the real world." For Russell, "Leibniz, in his private thinking, is the best example of a philosopher who uses logic as a key to metaphysics."[4]

When Russell and Couturat write of Leibniz's "logic," they have in mind what I will call 'the subject-predicate theory of truth': in every true proposition, universal or particular, necessary or contingent, the concept (or notion) of the predicate is explicitly or implicitly (virtually) contained (or included, or involved) in the concept (or notion) of the subject (cf. W 94; LA 50, 63; S 13; L 226, 236–240, 263–264, 267–268). Sometimes Couturat states that Leibniz's metaphysics is derived from the principle of reason or of sufficient reason. Superficially, this complicates matters because the Leibniz corpus contains at least four *prima facie* distinct versions of "the principle of sufficient reason": first, everything that exists or happens has a sufficient reason or a cause (M 32; W 93–94, 436, 527; LC II.1; LA 71, T 44); second, for every true proposition (except those which are identical, immediate, or known *per se*), sufficient reasons can be given for its being true (M 32, S 13, W 94); third, for every true proposition (except, again, identities), there exists an a priori proof of its truth (W 94, L 226–227, LA 71, T 44); fourth, in every true proposition, the concept of the predicate is explicitly or implicitly contained in the concept of the subject (W 94, S 13). Fortunately, both Couturat and Russell (after the publication of Couturat's work) identify the principle of sufficient reason with the subject-predicate theory of truth, that is, they focus on the

[4]Couturat, 1901, pp. x–xi; Couturat, 1902, pp. 19, 23; Russell, 1903, pp. 366, 385; Russell, 1937, p. v; Russell, 1945, p. 595.

fourth version of the principle of sufficient reason. In evaluating the Russell-Couturat thesis, we therefore need not address the question of whether Leibniz's metaphysics derives from any of the first three versions, nor the question of the relationship of these versions to the subject-predicate theory of truth.[5]

When he writes of Leibniz's "metaphysics," Couturat includes at least the following theses: no two individuals can differ only numerically (identity of indiscernibles); there are no purely extrinsic denominations; every individual substance expresses (mirrors, represents) the entire universe from its own point of view; there is a preestablished harmony (concomitance) between all substances; there is a preestablished harmony (concomitance) between mind and body; and there is no causal interaction between substances. Russell does not provide such an explicit inventory of the theses Leibniz allegedly derives from his logic. He states that they include all those Leibnizian theses which are necessary, or true in all possible worlds, and it is clear that Russell includes among them the claim that nothing external acts upon a monad.[6]

Most criticism of the Russell-Couturat thesis proceeds from some overview of Leibniz's philosophy and takes on the thesis as a whole.[7]

---

[5]The positions attributed to Russell and Couturat are located in their writings as follows: Russell, 1937, pp. v, 10–11; Couturat, 1901, p. 209; Couturat, 1902, pp. 19–26; Russell, 1903, p. 373; and Russell, 1945, pp. 592–593.

[6]Couturat, 1901, pp. x–xi; Couturat, 1902, pp. 21–23; Russell, 1937, pp. xiii–xiv, 9.

[7]In my view, most previous criticism of the Russell-Couturat thesis has not been successful (but see notes 8 and 9 below). Although I am sympathetic with the following discussions, they are too brief, indirect, or unsystematic to achieve their purposes: Buchdahl, 1969, pp. 389, 393–394, 450; Joseph, 1949, esp. pp. 79–80; Loemker, 1973, esp. pp. 14, 18–19, 142–143, 159; and Gottfried Martin, 1964, p. 33. I find quite congenial the methodological broadside directed at Russell by Ayers, 1978, pp. 42–46, but this discussion too is overly brief. One sustained criticism is due to Parkinson. He argues that it is false that Leibniz deduces his metaphysics from his logic, if the "metaphysics" is construed as general propositions about the nature of what exists. Parkinson's point is that for Leibniz it is a contingent truth that God created any monads at all. Even if correct, this point leaves untouched the Russell-Couturat position formulated as the claim that certain hypothetical generalizations ("if more than one monad exists, no two monads causally interact") are deduced from Leibniz's logic. Parkinson also notes that he departs from Russell and Couturat in claiming that Leibniz's logic is not the sole source of his metaphysics. But so far as I can see, Parkinson finds extralogical sources only for the claim that monads exist, and not for any metaphysically necessary hypothetical generalizations (see Parkinson, 1965, esp. pp. 2–4, 123–124, 137–138, 150–151, 156–157, and 182–185).

By contrast, I will attack in detail the following specific subthesis, which both Russell and Couturat accept: Leibniz's claim that nothing external acts upon a substance is derived from his subject-predicate theory of truth.[8] I will argue that this subthesis in its intended sense, is false. Indeed, the truth is quite the opposite—Leibniz's "logic" was tailored to his metaphysics.[9]

In support of the subthesis, Russell and Couturat appeal to various passages—most notably from "First Truths" (ca. 1680–84), *The Discourse on Metaphysics* (1686), and the correspondence with Arnauld (1686–87)—where Leibniz states, or strongly suggests, that the denial of causal interaction between substances is a consequence of the subject-predicate theory of truth. Perhaps the clearest single example of such a passage is this: "when I refer to the concept I have of every true proposition, I find that every necessary or contingent predicate, past, present, or future, is included in the concept of the subject. . . . The proposition in question is of very great importance and merits a clear demonstration, for it follows that every soul is like a world apart, independent of everything except God" (*LA* 50–51;

[8]Although Ishiguro endorses the general Russell-Couturat posture on the importance of Leibniz's logic for his metaphysics, she combines this with the curious view that Leibniz does not deny causal interaction between monads. In other words, on her view, the denial of interaction is not derived from the logic because Leibniz does *not* deny the existence of what *we* (we Humeans) normally call causal relations, namely, regular concomitances or constant conjunctions. The point, as best as I can make it out, is this. Unlike ourselves, Leibniz holds that causal connections must obtain necessarily, but for Leibniz the preestablished harmony and the consequent inter-monadic laws are contingent. Unfortunately, for Leibniz the intra-monadic laws are also contingent—all laws of nature have the same metaphysical status. (For this point, see § 37.) Ishiguro, therefore, cannot explain how Leibniz could hold that the states of a monad do cause its subsequent states (see Ishiguro, 1972, esp. pp. 10, 111–114).

Broad, 1975, pp. 45–47, is perhaps the one commentator who attempts to show in some detail that the denial of causation between substances does not follow from the subject-predicate theory of truth. This takes place against the background of his insistence that "it is not easy to believe that any important ontological consequences could be entailed by such an extremely abstract logical principle alone. One is inclined to think that other principles must have been unwittingly combined with it in Leibniz's mind" (p. 24). Broad does not explicitly criticize either Russell or Couturat.

[9]Brody, 1977, esp. §§ II–III, has launched a promising attack in support of a similar conclusion. His position is that Leibniz argued for the relevant aspects of his "logic" on the basis of metaphysical assumptions and considerations. My argument against the Russell-Couturat thesis is based more upon the content of Leibniz's "logic." Brody's position, however, is more than congenial.

cf. *LA* 63–64; *DM* viii–ix). In addition, on the basis of passages in Leibniz, Russell and Couturat attempt to spell out the connection between the subject-predicate theory of truth and the denial of causal interaction between substances. Perhaps the most relevant passage is this:

> The predicate or consequent therefore always inheres in the subject or antecedent. . . .
> This is true, moreover, in every affirmative truth, universal or singular, necessary or contingent. . . .
> *The complete or perfect concept of an individual substance involves all its predicates, past, present, and future.* For certainly it is already true now that a future predicate will be a predicate in the future, and so it is contained in the concept of a thing. . . .
> It can be said that, speaking with metaphysical rigor, *no created substance exerts a metaphysical action or influence upon another.* For . . . it has already been shown that all the future states of each thing follow from its concept. [L 267]

And in a draft of a letter to Arnauld, Leibniz states: "Therefore, since our thoughts are only consequences of the nature of our soul, and are born in it by virtue of its concept, it is useless to require the influence of another particular substance" (*LA* 84). Russell's statement of the argument is as follows:

> Thus to say, all my states are involved in the notion of me, is merely to say, the predicate is in the subject. Every predicate, necessary or contingent, past, present, or future, is comprised in the notion of the subject. From this proposition it follows, says Leibniz, that every soul is a world apart; for every soul, as a subject, has eternally, as predicates, all the states which time will bring it; and thus these states follow from its notion alone, without any need of action from without.[10]

Russell's reading takes Leibniz's statement of the connection between the subject-predicate theory of truth and the denial of causal interaction between substances pretty much at face value. On Russell's reading, since the complete concept of an arbitrary substance S_i contains all the predicates which will ever be true of it, all the predicates of S_i follow from its complete concept alone, and hence all the states of S_i causally depend only on itself.

[10]Russell, 1937, pp. 10–11 and cf. pp. 43–44, 133–134.

In somewhat more detail, the argument attributed to Leibniz is as follows. (1) In every true proposition, the concept of the predicate is explicitly or implicitly contained in the concept of the subject. From this there follows as a special case: (2) in every true proposition about an individual substance, the concept of the predicate is contained in the concept of the subject (*DM* VIII, XIII). (3) If at some later time it will be true that an entity has a property, than it is already true that that entity will have that property. From this, Leibniz moves to what I will call "the complete concept principle": (4) the complete concept of an individual substance contains all of the substance's predicates—past, present, and future (*DM* XIII, L 268; *LA* 12, 47, 84). And Leibniz concludes that (5) all the states of an individual substance follow from its complete concept alone, and that therefore (6) all the states of an individual substance causally depend only upon itself. I will refer to this elaboration of Leibniz's remarks, pretty much taken at face value, as "the surface argument" for the denial of interaction.

One difficulty for attributing to Leibniz no more than the surface argument is that the move from (4) to (6) is clearly fallacious. To see this, apply the argument, *mutatis mutandis*, to a physical particle (suppose the particle's state at a time exhaustively characterized by a description of its momentum and spatial location). Then by (3), if at some later time it will be true that our particle has a particular momentum and is in a particular spatial location, then it is already true that the substance will have these properties. Thus (4′) the complete concept of a particle contains all of its predicates (past, present, and future). We proceed to conclude that (5′) all the states of a particle follow from its complete concept alone, and that therefore (6′) all the states of a particle causally depend only upon itself. But obviously, (4′) and (5′) may be true, but (6′) false—the momentum and spatial location of a particle at a time may be the result of causal interaction with other particles.[11]

It is no good to reply that in *that* case the complete concept of a particle would contain such predicates as 'has such-and-such state at *t*' caused in part by the state of another particle at *t*', and that therefore the states of a particle would not be causally dependent

[11] For a similar line of criticism, see Broad, 1975, pp. 45–47.

only on itself. Both (4–6) and (4′–6′) are arguments from the *mere* fact that a complete concept of a thing contains all the predicates of that thing (whatever these predicates may be) to the conclusion that the states of that thing causally depend only upon itself. If the existence of "causal predicates" true of the thing can undermine the argument, it would first have to be shown that there are no such predicates, which would of course beg the question.

A more plausible reply is that whereas individual substances have complete concepts, entities such as physical particles do not, and hence that (4′) is simply false. The difficulty is to see what the basis for denying that physical particles have complete concepts could be. Are there not true propositions about physical particles? And if so, does not the subject-predicate theory of truth require that in the case of these propositions the concept of the predicate is explicitly or implicitly contained in the concept of the particle? And is it not the case that at later times the particle will have various properties, and hence that it is already the case that the particle will have those properties? The argument attributed to Leinbniz seems powerless to prevent the result that physical particles do have complete concepts.

There are weak and strong interpretations of the Russell-Couturat thesis, depending upon whether these commentators are read as claiming that Leibniz validly derived his metaphysics from the subject-predicate theory of truth, or rather simply that Leibniz thought he validly derived his metaphysics from the subject-predicate theory of truth. Russell does state that in "the paper 'Primae Veritates'. . . all the main doctrines of the 'Monadology' are deduced, with terse logical rigour from the premiss. . ." that "always therefore the predicate or consequent inheres in the subject or antecedent." Although Couturat speaks of Leibniz "deducing" and "deriving" his metaphysics from the subject-predicate theory of truth, this could mean simply that Leibniz attempted such a derivation though possibly without success.[12] My point, however, is not simply that the strong thesis is false. Rather, the move from (4) to (6) is so obviously fallacious as to cast doubt upon the weak thesis. Charity suggests that we not attribute the surface argument to Leibniz if we can avoid it.

[12]Couturat, 1901, pp. x–xi; Couturat, 1902, pp. 19, 22, 23; Russell, 1937, p. vi.

There is, in addition, a serious internal difficulty if we attribute to Leibniz no more than the surface argument. In the very paper ("First Truths") in which the argument is stated most fully, Leibniz claims not only that *"the complete or perfect concept of an individual substance involves all its predicates, past, present, and future,"* but also (in the next paragraph) that *"every individual substance involves the whole universe in its perfect concept,* and all that exists in the universe has existed or will exist" (L 268–269). In both cases, 'involves' translates the same Latin word, *involvit.* Similarly, there is this passage in the Arnauld correspondence, taken from a letter Russell uses to support his interpretation: "it is in the nature of an individual substance to have such a complete concept, whence can be inferred everything that one can attribute to it, and even the whole universe" (*LA* 44). Here is an application: "Thus *all human events* could not fail to occur as in fact they did occur, once the choice of Adam is assumed; but not so much because of the individual concept of Adam, *although this concept contains them,* but because of God's plans" (*LA* 57, emphasis added; cf. *LA* 60). And as late as 1701, Leibniz writes to De Volder: "There is nothing in the whole created universe which does not need, for its perfect concept, the concept of everything else in the universality of things" (L 524). It appears that the complete concept of an individual substance involves or contains all the predicates (past, present, and future) of all other substances in the same way that it contains all its own predicates.

Russell and Couturat draw attention to Leibniz's recurrent claim that the complete concept of an arbitrary individual substance S_i contains or involves all of S_i's predicates. They overlook the fact that Leibniz also claims that the complete concept of an arbitrary individual substance S_i contains or involves as well all the predicates of any other individual substance S_j. It is now easy to see that to the extent that the surface argument is cogent, it proves too much. It is supposed to follow from the fact that the complete concept of S_i contains all S_i's predicates that all the states of S_i causally depend only upon S_i. Then why would it not equally follow from the fact that the complete concept of S_i contains all the predicates of S_j (distinct from S_i) that all the states of S_j causally depend only upon S_i? In that case, the substances S_i and S_j causally interact. Or the difficulty can be put slightly differently. The idea behind the surface argument is that if the complete concept of S_i contains all the predicates of S_i, then facts about S_i alone are causally sufficient for all its states. Then why would it not equally follow from the fact that the complete concept of S_j contains all the predicates of S_i (distinct from S_j) that facts about S_j alone are causally sufficient for the states of S_i? In that case, since the complete concept of every substance contains all the predicates not only of itself but of every other substance (including S_i) as well, the states of S_i would be multiply overdetermined.[13]

Of course, the surface argument could be supplemented to yield, for arbitrary substance S_i, a favorite substance to cause S_i's states. For example, God might be chosen as the favorite substance for any S_i, such that all the states of any S_i depend only upon God. This would yield occasionalism, which Leibniz of course rejected. Alternatively, as Leibniz wants, for every S_i the favorite substance could be S_i itself, such that all S_i's states causally depend only upon previous states of S_i. But the justification of the selection of some favorite substance then becomes the point at issue. Such a selection cannot be forced by the mere fact that the complete concept of S_i contains all S_i's predicates, for all S_i's predicates are also contained in the complete concept of every other substance.

To summarize thus far: From the fact that the complete concept of S_i contains all the predicates of S_i, it does not follow that all the states of S_i causally depend only upon itself—the surface argument is fallacious. Even if we suppose it cogent, since Leibniz holds that the complete concept of S_i contains all the predicates of every other substance, it would equally follow that the states of those other substances depend causally only upon S_i—the surface argument would prove too much. It is impossible to suppose that the surface argument, beset by such glaring difficulties, could have led Leibniz to embrace the thesis that nothing external acts upon a substance. I believe these considerations sufficient to cast substantial doubt upon the Russell-Couturat thesis. In the remainder of this section, I will provide an alternative account of what is going on in the passages where Couturat and Leibniz locate the surface argument.

[13]The "internal difficulty" that I discuss applies as well to a recent attempt by Campbell, 1976, pp. 83–84, to reconstruct what I have called "the surface argument."

Both the difficulties which beset the surface argument pretty clearly relate to the notion of "containment". I believe that if we press the sense in which, in a true proposition, the concept of the subject "contains" the concept of the predicate, the inadequacy of attributing the surface argument to Leibniz will be much clearer. Russell and Couturat are not as sensitive as one would hope to the problem of unpacking the metaphor of "containment" in Leibniz's statements of his subject-predicate theory of truth. Noting that for Leibniz the concept of the predicate is contained in the concept of the subject in every true proposition, they prefer to read 'contained' in a Kantian fashion and to conclude that Leibniz's subject-predicate theory of truth is equivalent to the thesis that every truth is analytic. Russell, however, does provide an account of the sense in which the complete concept of a subject contains all the predicates true of that subject: "Whatever happens to Socrates can be asserted in a sentence in which 'Socrates' is the subject and the words describing the happening in question are the predicates. All these predicates put together make up the 'notion' of Socrates."[14] On this interpretation of the complete concept principle, each predicate of an individual substance is contained in that substance's complete concept in the sense that it is a member of a conjunction or list, e.g.:

> substance 1 is in perceptual state 1 at t_1 (, and)
> substance 1 is in perceptual state 4 at t_2 (, and)
> substance 1 is in perceptual state 7 at t_3 (, and)
> . . .

On this "list" interpretation of 'contains', the surface argument is clearly beset by the two difficulties I have discussed.

I intend to construct a different interpretation of the sense in which a complete concept of an individual substance "contains" all its predicates. Leibniz's mature position on this matter is reasonably explicit in the Arnauld correspondence, and it is clearly anticipated in the *Discourse*. But to see fully the inadequacy of the list interpretation of 'contains', we must begin about seven years earlier with a group of writings in which the subject-predicate theory of truth emerged as an important theme in Leibniz's thought.

---

[14]Russell, 1945, p. 591; Rescher, 1967, pp. 23–25, also subscribes to this "list" interpretation of 'containment'.

In works dating from about 1679, Leibniz writes that in every true proposition, the concept of the predicate is "in some way" contained in the concept of the subject (L 226, 264). If a list had served as Leibniz's model of a complete concept, he need not have stated his theory of truth in such vague terms, and in any case he would have had no difficulty in spelling out the "way" in which concepts of predicates are "contained" in the concepts of subjects. In applying his subject-predicate theory of truth to general propositions, Leibniz states that "the concept of the subject, either in itself or with some addition, involves the concept of the predicate. . . . For example, some metals are gold. . . . In an affirmative particular proposition it suffices that the inclusion is successful when something is added to the subject. The concept of metal, viewed absolutely and in itself, does not involve the concept of gold; something must be added to involve it" (L 236–237). As of 1679, the concept of the predicate is only "in some way" or "in a sense" contained in the concept of the subject because the concept of the subject need not, in itself, contain the concept of the predicate.

In the *Discourse*, Leibniz writes of the "deduction" or "demonstration" of predicates from the concept of a subject (*DM* vii, xiii). This is consistent with the list model of the complete concept, but is a rather inflated or elevated way of referring to conjunction elimination. I suggest that the "deduction" or "demonstration" must be a somewhat more complicated affair.

Leibniz states in section viii of the *Discourse:* "the nature of an individual substance or of a complete being is to have a notion so complete that it is sufficient [in itself] to comprise and to allow the deduction from it of all the predicates of the subject to which the notion is attributed." Leibniz deleted 'in itself' from the first draft of the *Discourse*. In subsequent versions, he did not claim that a complete concept need in itself be sufficient for the deduction of all the predicates of a subject. Evidently, at this stage in his thought, the complete concept principle, the claim that the complete concept of an individual substance contains all of the substance's predicates, is an abbreviated (and misleading) statement of his position: the complete concept of an individual substance, either in itself or with some addition, contains all of the substance's predicates. If the deletion of 'in itself' is significant in the way that I have suggested, we should expect from Leibniz at least some account of the sort of addition to a subject's complete concept which is required for the deduction of its predicates.

Leibniz provides an account of the required addition in section XIII of the *Discourse*. There he is discussing the demonstration of certain predicates (e.g., 'resolved to cross the Rubicon') from the complete concept of Caesar: "it would be found that this demonstration of this predicate of Caesar is not as absolute as those of numbers or of geometry, but that it supposes the sequence of things that God has freely chosen and which is founded on the first free decree of God, the import of which is always to do what is most perfect, and on the decree which God made (following the first) with regard to human nature, which is that man will always do (although freely) that which appears to him best." The universal generalization that persons always do what appears to them best is required in addition to the complete concept of Caesar in order to demonstrate from that complete concept that Caesar resolved to cross the Rubicon. From this example, it appears that certain universal generalizations must be added to the complete concept of an individual substance in order to demonstrate that substance's predicates.

The position of the *Discourse* is significantly developed and modified in the Arnauld correspondence. Leibniz writes that in a true proposition the concept of the predicate is "in a sense" included in the concept of the subject (*LA* 63), and that predicates are "deduced" or "inferred" from complete concepts (*LA* 44, 48). As before, such phraseology suggests a more complicated account of 'contains' than that embodied in the list interpretation. The following passage removes any doubt on this matter: "all the predicates of Adam depend or do not depend upon other predicates of the same Adam. Setting aside, therefore, those which do depend upon others, one has only to consider together all the basic predicates in order to form the complete concept of Adam adequate to deduce from it everything that is ever to happen to him" (*LA* 48). The clear suggestion is that the basic predicates of Adam are a proper subset of all the predicates of Adam, and that a complete concept of Adam need not include the nonbasic predicates of him.

How could the nonbasic predicates of an individual substance be deduced from a proper subset of all its predicates, from its basic predicates? One or more generalizations will be required to license the inference from basic to nonbasic predicates. An example was provided in the *Discourse*. In the Arnauld correspondence, Leibniz writes: "For as there exists an infinite number of possible worlds, there exists also an infinite number of laws, some peculiar to one world, some to another, and each possible individual of any one world contains in the concept of him the laws of his world" (*LA* 43). In the *Discourse*, the complete concept together with universal generalizations—suppose they are laws—is sufficient for the deduction of the predicates of an individual substance. In the Arnauld correspondence, there is this modification: the complete concept includes laws as well as basic predicates. In the *Discourse*, predicates are deducible from complete concepts together with laws; in the Arnauld correspondence, predicates are deducible from complete concepts alone, but only because Leibniz there incorporates laws into the complete concept. The complete concept of an individual substance "contains" all the substance's predicates in the sense that all these predicates are deducible from the basic predicates and laws, which constitute a complete concept. The list model of a complete concept was not Leibniz's own. On the list model, all the predicates of an individual substance, but no laws, are explicitly included in a complete concept. On the present interpretation, some of the predicates and all laws are explicitly included. The inclusion of the laws yields an enriched interpretation of the complete concept principle. All the materials for this interpretation—the distinction between basic and nonbasic predicates, and the claim that complete concepts include laws—are contained in item IX of the correspondence, Leibniz's "Remarks upon M. Arnauld's Letter" of May 13, 1686.[15]

On the enriched interpretation of the complete concept principle, supported by the texts of the Arnauld correspondence, the

---

[15]Two commentators have previously constructed what I am calling "enriched" interpretations of the complete concept principle: Abraham, 1969, and Broad, 1975, esp. pp. 20–27. Whereas Broad's account is a speculative reconstruction ("I suspect the reasoning at the back of Leibniz's mind may be illustrated as follows"), Abraham draws attention to many of the passages I cite. The interpretation I have offered in the text differs in a number of details from those of both Abraham and Broad. And I have tried to make fully explicit the implications of the interpretation for the Russell-Couturat thesis.

complete concept of an arbitrary individual substance "contains" all of the substance's predicates in the sense that all these predicates are deducible from the basic predicates (a proper subset of the substance's predicates) and laws, which together constitute the complete concept. But this can be true only if the universe of substances is deterministic. In other words, a part of Leibniz's metaphysics has been built into the claim that a substance has a complete concept in the present sense. Think of the matter as follows. I have already said that, on the list interpretation, it does not follow from the fact that the complete concept of a substance contains all its predicates that all the states of the substance depend causally only upon itself. What is more, it does not even follow that the states of a substance are determined, much less causally determined, by that substance alone. On the list interpretation, the claim that the complete concept of a substance contains all its predicates is compatible with the claim that some of its states are uncaused. On the list model, there is nothing to prevent a particle some of whose states arise indeterministically from having a complete concept.[16] But on the enriched interpretation, the claim that the complete concept of a substance contains all its predicates entails that the states of the substance are, at least, determined.

Indeed, on the enriched interpretation, this claim entails that the states of a substance are determined in a specific way. The complete concept of a substance includes the laws of its universe. We know that for every individual substance there is an "internal principle," "indwelling law," "law of order," or "law of succession" which moves the substance from state to state. Leibniz states that it is the nature of an individual substance "to follow perpetually the same law of order or of succession, as in a certain scale or series of numbers" (L 495). Just as there is an arithmetical formula governing the arithmetical series "1, 4, 7, 10, . . .", there is a law of succession governing the sequence of perceptual states of an individual substance. We also know that Leibniz regarded an individual substance's law of succession as a causal law. For him, everything that exists, including the states of substances, has a sufficient reason or cause. The states of a substance have no external cause. Therefore

[16]Broad, 1975, pp. 27–28 and 46–47, has made this point.

they must be caused by other states of that substance (§ 30). So the law of succession governing the sequence of states of a substance must be a causal law. The terms 'internal principle', 'indwelling law', and 'law of order' are not used in the *Discourse* or the Arnauld correspondence, but the concept of such a law is clearly present in these works. In the *Discourse*, Leibniz states that "the perceptions... of all substances mutually correspond, ... each carefully following certain reasons or laws which it has observed agrees with the other doing the same" (*DM* XIV). In item X of the Arnauld correspondence, the letter from Leibniz to Arnauld for which item IX served as a draft, Leibniz writes of soul and body as "each one obeying its laws" (*LA* 65; cf. 146, 147, 161). Later in the correspondence he writes more explicitly "that each of these substances contains in its nature the law by which the series of its operations continues" (*LA* 170). So the complete concept of a substance includes certain basic predicates of that substance together with the laws of its universe, one of which is a causal law of succession for that substance. Since all the predicates of a substance can be deduced from its complete concept, it is natural to suppose that the basic predicates characterize the initial perceptual state of the substance. Thus Leibniz states that "everything occurs in every substance as a consequence of the first state which God bestowed upon it when he created it" (*LA* 115).

The upshot is this: from a statement of the initial perceptual state of a substance together with a statement of that substance's causal law of succession (both of which are included in the substance's complete concept), we can deduce statements of all subsequent perceptual states of that substance. This means that a substance's initial perceptual state *alone* is causally sufficient for its subsequent perceptual states. To see the force of this, reconsider our physical particle. Suppose that from statements exhaustively characterizing its initial state together with statements of the laws of nature, we could deduce statements of all subsequent states of that particle. Then the particle's initial state *alone* is causally sufficient for its subsequent states. Thus, waiving causal overdetermination, we see that all the states of the particle causally depend only upon itself. Of course, this is not the situation for any known physical particle— external causes do act upon physical particles as we know them. In other words, Leibnizian complete concepts do not exist for physical particles. But from the claim that there do exist Leibnizian complete concepts for substances it does follow that a substance's initial perceptual state *alone* is causally sufficient for its subsequent perceptual states. Thus the claim that a substance has a complete concept—now construed to include basic predicates of that substance but not other initial conditions, together with the laws of its universe, which include the substance's causal law of succession—entails that all the states of the substance are causally determined by other states of that substance. Thus, waiving causal overdetermination, we see that all the states of a substance depend causally only upon itself. And Leibniz does waive causal overdetermination on the ground that it would be "superfluous" and not in accord with God's wisdom (*LA* 84, 87; L 269, 613). In other words, if causal overdetermination is waived, the conclusion of the surface argument does follow from the claim that a substance has a complete concept. But now this claim is no longer trivial. The relevant aspects of Leibniz's metaphysics have been built into it. At this point the argument is valid, but no longer cogent, because the claim that a substance has a complete concept does all the work.

On the enriched interpretation of the complete concept principle, the claim that nothing external acts upon a substance does follow from the claim that a substance has a complete concept. What about Leibniz's contention that a substance's complete concept not only contains all its predicates but all the predicates of all other substances as well? This generated an internal difficulty for the list interpretation. On the enriched interpretation, a substance's complete concept contains the predicates of all other substances in that they can be deduced from the basic predicates of the one substance together with the laws of the universe. Since each substance expresses the universe in the sense that there exists a constant and fixed relationship between the states of different substances, the laws will include inter-monadic laws of coexistence, noncausal laws relating the simultaneous states of different monads. Thus the states of one substance determine, but noncausally, the states of all other substances. This result depends upon building into the complete concept noncausal laws of coexistence. Leibniz did not explicitly "enrich" complete concepts to this extent. But only if this is done can he block the result that all the states of one substance depend causally upon another substance. Once again, the argument is not cogent, because the claim that a substance has a complete concept in the required sense does the work.

We have seen that the surface argument is fallacious, and that in any case it cannot explain why the states of a substance should depend causally only upon itself rather than some other substance which also contains its predicates. Surely we cannot attribute the surface argument to Leibniz. Looking beneath the surface, we find an enriched interpretation of complete concepts. Here Leibniz's views emerge somewhat gradually. In his early writings the complete concept of a substance contains all its predicates only if some additions are made. These additions initially include the principle of the best. Subsequently, the additions are all the laws of the substance's universe, and these laws are incorporated into the complete concept. One such law that emerges is the substance's law of succession. At this point, it has become apparent that a complete concept need include only a proper subset of the substance's predicates. What we observe in the texts is not a deduction of the claim that nothing external acts upon a substance from the subject-predicate theory of truth construed in a Kantian manner. Rather, we observe the gradual enrichment of complete concepts toward the point of fully building the relevant metaphysical theses into the claim that a substance has a complete concept. In other words, Leibniz gradually tailors his conception of a complete concept to fit his metaphysics. The metaphysical horse is pulling the "logical" cart, and not the other way around.[17]

Russell notes that the "purely logical argument" which, in his view, led Leibniz to hold that nothing external acts upon a substance is pretty much confined to the *Discourse* and the correspondence with Arnauld. He proceeds: "That Leibniz did not repeat, in his published works, this purely logical argument, is explained, in view of his invariable habit of choosing the reasons most

---

[17]Here I am in complete sympathy with Loemker, 1973, p. 18: "the purely logical argument" located by Russell "was not an argument . . . but the arbitrary imposition of a logical doctrine upon a metaphysical one"; and with Ayers, 1978, p. 43: "it may be argued that Leibniz did not derive an ontology from a logic independently regarded as indispensable, so much as hammer out a logic appropriate to an ontology or world-view which attracted him for other reasons."

likely to convince his readers."[18] This statement is not convincing—
it does nothing to explain why the argument does not find its
way into subsequent, unpublished, serious, philosophical correspondence—with, for example, Bartholomew des Bosses and
De Volder. An alternative explanation is that Leibniz came to see
clearly that the surface argument was fallacious, that certain defects
could be overcome by enriching his notion of complete concepts,
but that the resulting argument was not cogent because the claim
that complete concepts exist then did all the work. In 1715, Des
Bosses invited Leibniz to explain in detail the grounds for his denial
of interaction between substances: "I ask whether or not there be
possible any system similar to the present world with respect to all
phenomena but in which substances act upon each other. If you
deny this, show me why" (L 612). Here is Leibniz's showing: "I do
not believe a system is possible in which the monads act upon each
other mutually, for there seems to be no possible way to explain
such action. I add that influence is superfluous, for why should one
monad give another what it already possesses? It is the very nature of
substance that the present is great with the future and that everything can be explained out of one" (L 613). Leibniz simply fails to
produce any sort of sustained argument in response to Des Bosses'
query. In section 34, I will construct an alternative account of the
factors which led Leibniz to the claim that nothing external acts
upon a substance. At that point, I will have completed my case
against the claim that the surface argument led him to this crucial
thesis.

32. The Mind-Body Problem and the Denial of Interaction

I believe that if we persist in looking for some argument which led
Leibniz to the thesis that nothing external acts upon a substance we
will remain, as Russell found himself, "completely in the dark as to
the grounds" for this view. If we look at Leibniz's motivations rather
than his arguments, the ground for this thesis might seem obvious,
as follows. There are straightforward relationships between Leibniz's

[18]Russell, 1937, p. 8.

claim that nothing external acts upon a substance and his claim that there exists a preestablished harmony between all substances. The preestablished harmony, in its intended sense, entails the denial of interaction. Leibniz views interactionism, preestablished harmony, and occasionalism, as mutually exclusive alternatives (cf. L 459–460, 494). A direct argument for the preestablished harmony would have the denial of interaction as a consequence. But tactically it is better to argue independently for the denial of interaction in order to prepare the way for the preestablished harmony as a constructive alternative. This is the natural argumentative strategy. For example, at *Ethics* IIP6 Spinoza argues against interaction between modes of distinct attributes, and at *E* IIP7, the very next proposition, he argues for his parallelism ("The order and connection of ideas is the same as the order and connection of things"). Similarly, in "First Truths," the paragraph in which Leibniz argues for the denial of interaction is followed immediately by the paragraph in which he asserts the preestablished harmony (L 269), the former preparing the ground for the latter. And the preestablished harmony—the hypothesis of concomitance, or of agreement—is Leibniz's solution to the mind-body problem. Is not the ground or motivation for the denial of interaction then obvious?

This simple and obvious account of the motivation for Leibniz's denial of interaction cannot be correct, however. It must be wrong because in Leibniz's mature metaphysics there are no bodies of a sort which generate any mind-body problem—there is no mind-body problem in need of the preestablished harmony or any other solution. Since the preestablished harmony is commonly thought of as Leibniz's contribution to the mind-body problem, this needs some explanation.

In what I am calling Leibniz's "mature metaphysics," the sole ultimate constituents of reality are monads and their qualities or affections, perceptions. Beginning in 1704, there are repeated, explicit statements of this mature metaphysics. In the philosophically serious correspondence with De Volder, he wrote: "Indeed, considering the matter carefully, it may be said that there is nothing in the world except simple substances, and, in them, perception and appetite" (L 537). And in the same letter: "the principle of change. . . . consists in the progress of the perceptions of each monad, *the entire nature of things containing nothing besides*" (L 538, emphasis added; cf. L 539). Again, writing to Des Bosses eight years later: "It is true that things which happen in the soul must agree with those which happen outside of it. But for this it is enough for the things taking place in one soul to correspond with each other as well as with those happening in any other soul, *and it is not necessary to assume anything outside of souls or monads*" (L 605, emphasis added; cf. L 614, *NE* 148). In a 1715 letter to Nicolas Remond, Leibniz writes that "absolute reality rests only in the monads and their perceptions" (L 659).

Well before 1704, he characterized monads as lacking parts (L 504). It is an immediate consequence that monads are unextended (cf. *M* 1, 3). But then if in metaphysical rigor nothing exists except monads, which are unextended, and their perceptions, what becomes of matter? Leibniz's position, in the mature metaphysics, is that matter is a phenomenon founded in the perceptions of monads. Thus, Leibniz writes in the letter to De Volder of 1704 cited in the paragraph above: "Accurately speaking, however, matter is not composed of these constitutive unities but results from them, since matter or extended mass is nothing but a phenomenon grounded in things . . . and all reality belongs only to unities. . . . Substantial unities are not parts but foundations of phenomena" (L 536). And in the same letter: "Matter and motion . . . are not so much substances or things as they are the phenomena of percipient beings, whose reality is located in the harmony of the percipient with himself (at different times) and with other percipient beings" (L 537). Again, writing to Des Bosses eight years later in the letter already cited: "I consider the explanation of all phenomena solely through the perceptions of monads functioning in harmony with each other, with corporeal substances rejected, to be useful for a fundamental investigation of things. . . . Certainly monads cannot really be in an absolute space, since they are not really ingredients but merely requisites of matter" (L 604; cf. 600). In a dialogue from the same period, Leibniz's views are reported as follows:

> There is even good ground for doubting whether God has made any other things than monads, or substances without extension, and whether bodies are anything but the phenomena resulting from these substances. My friend, whose opinions I have detailed to you, gives

evidence enough of leaning to this view, since he reduces everything
to monads or to simple substances and their modifications, along
with the phenomena which result from them and whose reality is
established by their relations. [L 625]

The position that matter is a phenomenon founded in or resulting
from the perceptions of monads is reiterated in two letters to Remond and one to the Abbé Conti written in 1714–15 (L 656, 659;
LC 185).

In Leibniz's mature metaphysics, the sole ultimate constituents of
reality are monads and their perceptions. The claim that nothing
external acts upon a substance reduces to the claim that no monad
(or its perceptions) acts upon another monad; the preestablished
harmony is a relationship which obtains between monads. But all
monads lack parts; no monad is extended or material—no monad is
a body. It is therefore impossible, in the context of Leibniz's mature
metaphysics, to construe the preestablished harmony as a solution
to the mind-body problem; there is no mind-body problem because
the relationship between two monads is always a relationship between two unextended, immaterial substances. If there ever was a
mind-body problem, it had something to do with the fact, in Descartes' terminology, that mind and body are essentially, entirely,
absolutely distinct, or, in Spinoza's terminology, that the attributes
of thought and extension have nothing in common. There is no
such qualitative disparity between any two monads.

Leibniz was fully aware that the mind-body problem was not even
formulable in his mature metaphysics. De Volder had raised the
objection that "nothing prevents substances of the same nature from
acting upon each other." De Volder's point is that since all monads
are unextended and immaterial, there is no reason why they should
not interact, and hence no need for the preestablished harmony.
Leibniz's reply, in 1704, is instructive. I insert numerals to isolate
three strands within it for subsequent reference.

[1] But you know that philosophers have rather denied any action
between similar beings. [2] And what is there that prevents substances which differ in nature from acting upon each other? When
you have explained this, you will see that your explanation prevents
all finite substances from influencing each other—[3] not to mention
the fact that all substances are different in nature, and there are no
two things in nature which differ in number alone. [L 534]

The first point to note is that Leibniz does not reply that at least some monads do differ in nature because though some are immaterial, others are extended. There just is no mind-body problem formulable in the mature metaphysics. His reply is also instructive because the substance of his response is a clear indication of his difficulties in arguing for the denial of interaction in the context of the mature metaphysics. Consider the three strands of the reply.

(1) Leibniz notes that some philosophers have denied interaction even between similar substances. This amounts to nothing more than an attempt to put De Volder in a frame of mind which might make him more receptive to Leibniz's position. Leibniz is pointing out that his denial of interaction between monads is a familiar sort of philosophical thesis in that other philosophers have denied interaction between entities similar to each other. This hardly constitutes an argument for such a position. Further, if the philosophers Leibniz has in mind are occasionalists (who else?) such as Malebranche, his point will inevitably be turned into an embarrassment. Granted, for an occasionalist finite spiritual (or material) substances do not interact. But the ground for this is the claim that God is the sole cause, yielding the result that the states of a finite spiritual (or material) substance do not even cause its own subsequent states. Leibniz, however, rejects occasionalism, and holds that the states of a monad do cause its subsequent states. So the arguments available to the philosophers he most likely has in mind are not available to him.

(2) Leibniz invites De Volder to believe that the grounds for denying interaction between substances differing in nature, e.g., mind and body, would preclude interaction between substances of the same nature as well. This, if true, would be important. It is difficult to believe that Leibniz's confident tone—he does not spell out the argument, but rather assigns it to De Volder as an exercise—is anything more than a bluff. The argument which he invites De Volder to believe exists is not, after all, stated anywhere in the Leibniz corpus.

(3) Finally, Leibniz appeals to the identity of indiscernibles to show that all substances differ in nature or essence, concluding that no two substances can interact. The suppressed Cartesian premise is that substances which differ in nature or essence cannot interact.

This argument would hardly convince De Volder. Two qualitatively different billiard balls would differ in nature or essence in the same sense that two monads differ in nature. De Volder would not be prepared to conclude that the billiard balls cannot interact. For De Volder, it is true that substances which differ in nature cannot interact when 'differ in nature' is taken in Descartes' sense of differing in essence or principal attribute. Two qualitatively distinct billiard balls, or monads, do not differ in nature in this sense. Of course, it may be true that Leibniz identifies an entity's nature or essence with its complete concept rather than its principal attribute. But De Volder would not grant that entities which differ in nature in this Leibnizian sense cannot interact. Leibniz cannot carry the day by coopting De Volder's terminology. Further, the argument Leibniz suggests is useless as it stands because successive perceptual states of a single monad do not differ in number alone, and hence they are dissimilar. Parity suggests that earlier perceptual states therefore cannot cause subsequent ones.

In response to De Volder's objection that there is nothing to prevent interaction between monads, Leibniz has nothing to offer except a grab bag of responses in the hope that De Volder will feel persuaded by one or more of its points. Such is Leibniz's defense, in serious philosophical correspondence, of what was perhaps the most central and distinctive feature of his metaphysics. In his mature metaphysics, the preestablished harmony and the attendant denial of interaction did not function as a solution to the mind-body problem; and for lack of a formulable mind-body problem, he was unable to produce any serious argument for these central metaphysical theses.

Leibniz persisted, after the mature metaphysics was developed, in writing of the preestablished harmony as the best explanation (as opposed to interactionism and occasionalism) of the union of the soul and the body, that is, as the best solution to the mind-body problem. How am I to explain this in light of my claims that the mind-body problem is not even formulable in the mature metaphysics, and that Leibniz himself recognized this fact?

The mind-body problem, construed as concerning the relationship between unextended thinking substances on the one hand and unthinking extended substances on the other, is not, I insist, formulable in the mature metaphysics; and the preestablished harmony cannot, therefore, be construed as a solution to it. But Leibniz did construct a metaphysical analogue to certain bodies. He held that monads stand in a relationship of dominance to an infinity of other monads. He attempted to unpack the relationship of dominance noncausally. For example: "in the monads themselves, domination and subordination consist only in degrees of perfection" (L 605). The details of his attempts to unpack the dominance relationship are unimportant for my purposes. We are then told, as of 1714, that "each outstanding simple substance or monad which forms the center of a compound substance (such as an animal, for example), and is the principle of its uniqueness, is surrounded by a mass composed of an infinity of other monads which constitute the body belonging to this central monad" (L 637). All the monads dominated by a given monad "constitute the body" of that monad. Thus Leibniz constructs, within the mature metaphysics, a metaphysical analogue to a living body, for short, an "analogue body." The mind-analogue body relationship is, then, the relationship between one unextended monad and an infinity of other unextended monads. While the question of the nature of the mind-analogue body relationship can be raised, there is no mind-analogue body *problem* comparable to the mind-body problem; the relationship is simply a special case of the preestablished harmony that obtains among the members of any set of monads.

By constructing metaphysical bodies, Leibniz has placed himself in an enviable tactical position. He believes that in metaphysical rigor there are no bodies—bodies are only phenomenal. It was unlikely that any of his readers or correspondents would be prepared to accept his official ontology according to which nothing exists except monads and their perceptions. So he constructs metaphysical bodies. When he writes that "the preestablished harmony is the best explanation of the union of mind and body," most readers, committed to a dualist ontology, will take the claim at face value. Leibniz himself has a relatively private reading of this claim which is consistent with his official ontology: the preestablished harmony is the best explanation of the union of mind and analogue body.

Consider the tactical advantages. First, the mind-body problem was one of the outstanding philosophical issues of the day. In Leibniz's official ontology, the problem is not even formulable. Few readers would be prepared to accept such a radical "solution." The construction of metaphysical bodies allows Leibniz to write of the nature of the union of the soul and body, thereby maintaining a superficial (verbal) continuity with the ontological framework within which this outstanding philosophical problem arose.

Second, while we normally associate such theories as epiphenomenalism and the preestablished harmony with a particular ontology, we can reserve such terminology for application to structural hypotheses which are of potential applicability to a variety of ontologies. We have seen, for example, that Malebranche's occasionalism can be viewed as structurally identical to mind-body epiphenomenalism, where God is the base phenomenon and created entities the epiphenomena (§21). In writing of the preestablished harmony as the best explanation of the union of soul and body, Leibniz might at least convince the reader of the attractiveness of the preestablished harmony as a structural hypothesis. To this extent, the reader would be sympathetic to "part" of Leibniz's metaphysics, though he would not thereby have moved closer to Leibniz's ontology.

Third and finally, if he could subsequently convince a reader to accept the official ontology, Leibniz might be in a position to exploit a commitment to the preestablished harmony in order to induce the reader to "buy into" both the ontology and the structure of Leibniz's metaphysics. All of this would be somewhat dishonest, rather than just extremely misleading, if Leibniz did not believe that the preestablished harmony *is* the best explanation of the union of soul and body *in a dualist ontology*. Otherwise, he could not honestly commend the preestablished harmony to readers likely to construe his remarks within a dualist framework. Suppose Leibniz was not being dishonest. Then he believed that the preestablished harmony is the best structural hypothesis both for a dualist ontology and for the system of monads. In hoping that a reader might eventually transfer a commitment to the preestablished harmony from its application to a dualist ontology to its application to the system of monads, Leibniz may have been envisioning for the reader a process of development which he had experienced himself.

The emerging suggestion is that while in the mature metaphysics the preestablished harmony does not function as a solution to the mind-body problem, Leibniz's assertion of the preestablished harmony, and the attendant denial of interaction, had something to do with the mind-body problem. In particular, prior to the development of the official ontology, he proposed the preestablished harmony as the best structural hypothesis within an ontological framework of minds and bodies. Subsequently, after he consigned bodies to a purely phenomenal status, the preestablished harmony is applied to the official metaphysics. I will document this account of the development of Leibniz's metaphysics, and flesh out the details, in the following two sections.

33. The Development of Leibniz's Mature Metaphysics

We will never understand why Leibniz denies interaction between monads if we persist in viewing the mature metaphysics statically.[19] I have stated that beginning in 1704 he made repeated, explicit statements of the mature metaphysics. But the position that nothing is real except monads and their perceptions, and that matter is a phenomenon founded in the perceptions of monads, was a long time in the making.

Leibniz began working within a dualist framework of minds and bodies. There were as many minds and souls as sentient creatures or animal bodies, and no more. Metaphysical and physical considerations then led to a proliferation of minds, or mindlike entities—souls, spirits, substantial forms, entelechies, substances, monads—through matter.

Some early statements (1676–84) of the metaphysical considerations are as follows:

> The identity of the mind is not destroyed by any modifications and therefore is not destroyed by anything—as can easily be shown. I

---

[19] In this and the following section, I employ what Castañeda, 1974, §1, has called Darwinian (evolutionary) rather than Athenian (static) methodology in the history of modern philosophy. I agree with Castañeda that this methodology is especially fruitful in connection with Leibniz.

therefore believe that solidity or unity of body comes from the mind and that there are *as many minds* as vortices, as many vortices as there are solid bodies. [L 162]

For the substance of bodies there is required something which lacks extension; otherwise, there would be no principle to account for the reality of the phenomena or for true unity. There would always be a plurality of bodies, never one body alone; and therefore there could not, in truth, be many. By a similar argument Cordemoi proved the existence of atoms. But since these have been excluded, there remains only something that lacks extension, something like the soul, which was once called a form or species. [L 270]

Without soul or forms of some kind, body would have no being, because no part of it can be designated which does not in turn consist of more parts. Thus nothing could be designated in a body which could be called 'this thing', or a unity. [L 278–279]

In these passages, drawn from a number of sources including "First Truths," there is a proliferation of minds through matter in an attempt to account for the unity of material objects.

Such metaphysical considerations were fully explicit by the time of the Arnauld correspondence. According to Leibniz, a substance is a real thing; a real thing is a true unity; a true unity is either itself without parts, indivisible (a simple substance), or bears some appropriate relationship to such simple substances (in which case it is a compound substance). Since any portion of matter is actually divided into smaller portions *ad infinitum,* no portion of matter is a simple substance, and any material object is a mere collection or aggregate (cf. *LA* 88–95). In the passages above, Leibniz proliferates minds through bodies in an attempt to allow that material objects are compound substances, true (nonsimple) unities, real things, because they bear the appropriate relationship to simple substances which are themselves indivisible. In the last of the quotations, there is the suggestion that a body need only have some true unity as a part, or associated with it, to qualify as a substance. In the first quotation, Leibniz seems to require that there be as many minds as bodies, minds assigned to bodies one on one. On the former picture, it would suffice to associate a single mind with, say, a rock; on the latter picture, minds would have to be assigned to each physical part of the rock, *ad infinitum.*

These suggestions can be summarized as follows: a portion of matter is a compound substance if one or more minds are associated with it or distributed through it. Any position of this sort is clearly unsatisfactory, for consider a portion of matter distinct from the minds associated with it. Is *that portion of matter* a compound substance? It would appear not. If the reality or substantial character of a portion of matter is parasitic upon that of associated minds, there will inevitably remain the residual problem of the metaphysical status of a portion of matter considered on its own. At this point, there are three options: more or less ignore the difficulty, simply declaring that portions of matter are (compound) substances because minds are distributed through them; maintain that portions of matter are "second-class" substances, "imperfect substances"; or hold that portions of matter are not substances or real things after all—they are only "phenomena." Leibniz finally arrives at this third position, but only after a period of uncertainty and vacillation.

Such wavering is readily documented within the *Discourse* and the Arnauld correspondence. Bracketed material was deleted:

[I do not yet undertake to determine whether bodies are substances, to speak with metaphysical rigour, or whether they are only *true* phenomena, like the rainbow, nor consequently whether there are substances, souls, or substantial forms, which are not intelligent.] Supposing that bodies... are substances and that they have substantial forms.... [DM xxxiv]

For assuredly Spirits [are either the only substances which are present in the world, in which case bodies are only real/true phenomena, or they are at least] the most perfect substances.... [DM xxxv]

If the body is a substance and not a simple phenomenon like the rainbow, nor an entity united by accident or aggregation like a heap of stones, it cannot consist of extension, and one must necessarily conceive of something there that one calls substantial form, and which corresponds in a way to the soul. [LA 66]

... one would have to be sure that bodies are substances and not merely true phenomena like the rainbow. But once this is granted, I believe that bodily substance does not consist of extension or divisibility.... the substance of a body, if bodies have one, must be indivisible; whether it is called soul or form does not concern me. ... I do not know if the body, when the soul or substantial form is left aside, can be called a substance. [LA 88–89]

... In my opinion our body in itself, leaving the soul aside, i.e. the corpse, cannot be correctly called a substance. [LA 93]

... if I am asked for my views in particular on the sun, the globe of the earth, the moon, trees and similar entities, and even on animals, I cannot declare with absolute certainty if they are animate, or at least if they are substances or even if they are simply machines or aggregates of many substances. But at least I can say that if there are no bodily substances such as I can accept, it follows that bodies will be no more than true phenomena. [LA 95]

... every entity through aggregation presupposes entities endowed with a true unity, because it obtains its reality from nowhere but that of its constituents, so that it will have no reality at all if each constituent entity is still an entity through aggregation; or one must yet seek another basis to its reality.... One must... arrive either at mathematical points from which certain authors make up extension, or at Epicurus' and M. Cordemoy's atoms (which you, like me, dismiss), or else one must acknowledge that no reality can be found in bodies, or finally one must recognize certain substances in them that possess a true unity. [LA 120–121]

We have here a record of uncertainty and vacillation with respect to the status of bodies from the winter of 1685–86, when the *Discourse* was written, through April 30, 1687, the last letter to Arnauld cited. Leibniz begins by working within a dualist framework. The *Discourse* and correspondence with Arnauld reflect the attempt to account for the unity of bodies by distributing minds through bodies.[20] This leads to considerable embarrassment over the status of bodies considered apart from the minds associated with them. These developments culminate in this passage from a letter to Arnauld of October, 1687:

As for the other problem that you raise, Sir, namely that the soul joined to matter does not make an entity that is truly one, since matter is not truly one in itself, and that the soul, in your view, gives it only an extrinsic denomination. I answer that it is the animate substance to which this matter belongs which is truly an entity, and the matter considered as the mass in itself is only a pure phenomenon or a well-founded appearance.... Extended mass considered without entelechies... is not bodily substance, but an entirely pure

[20]In at least two passages, Leibniz suggests that it is also necessary to distribute minds through bodies in order to account for the persistence of bodies over time. See *DM* xii and *LA* 60.

phenomenon like the rainbow. . . . Only indivisible substances and their different states are absolutely real. [LA 152–153]

In this letter we have the first statement of Leibniz's mature metaphysics, the view that in metaphysical rigor only monads and their perceptions are real.

Should we date Leibniz's mature metaphysics from October, 1687? This is a complicated matter. My position is that although this letter to Arnauld contains a (programmatic) statement of the mature metaphysics, nevertheless the mature metaphysics is stabilized as Leibniz's considered view only as of the letter to De Volder of June, 1704.[21] This claim, however, is not essential to the subsequent argument of the chapter. I will therefore deal with it relatively briefly.

In 1687, Leibniz claimed that only indivisible substances and their states are absolutely real. How confident could he be about this? He had long held that any portion of matter is divisible. He therefore had to account for the metaphysical status of bodies in terms of "indivisible substances and their different states." Until such an account was in hand, Leibniz could hardly be confident that his claim that only indivisible substances and their states are absolutely real could be sustained. Perhaps a metaphysics which attempts to account for all the features of our experience by appeal to true unities (entities without parts) and their states cannot succeed, in which case the premise that "a real thing is a true unity" might have to be abandoned. In other words, there was a programmatic element to Leibniz's position: he had to show how to account for bodies in terms of indivisible substances and their states.

As of 1687, Leibniz had said little more than that mass "is only a pure phenomenon or a well-founded appearance . . . an entirely pure phenomenon like the rainbow." Do we have anything here beyond a nice metaphor? It is exceedingly tempting to read this letter as a statement of *phenomenalism*, or a theory on which physicalistic statements are equivalent to statements about sense data, or in Leibniz's metaphysics, perceptions. I believe this tempta-

[21]Broad, 1975, pp. 73–74, 87–92, has previously suggested that while Leibniz entertained the mature metaphysics in the correspondence with Arnauld, he adopted this ontology only at the time of the correspondence with De Volder.

tion should be resisted. Leibniz was writing without benefit of A. J. Ayer's *Foundations of Empirical Knowledge*, or J. S. Mill's *Logic*, or even Berkeley's *Principles* or *Dialogues*, published about a quarter century after the correspondence with Arnauld. In working toward a phenomenalistic theory, he was a pioneer. In stating, in 1687, that matter is a phenomenon or appearance, he locates matter with respect to an "appearance/reality" distinction. But the work remains to be done. If matter is an appearance, of what is it an appearance, and to whom? The sorts of answers which are obvious to us were not yet obvious to Leibniz. We expect that bodies will be identified with sets of perceptions. In the end, I believe, this was Leibniz's theory; it was not his position in 1687. In the interim, he contemplated other alternatives.

In the Arnauld correspondence, subsequent to the letter of October, 1687, Leibniz states that "the body is an aggregate of substances" (*LA* 170). This suggestion is repeated in "On the Method of Distinguishing Real from Imaginary Phenomena" (L 365). Writing to De Volder as late as 1699, Leibniz states that active, substantial principles are "constitutive of the extended itself, or of matter" (L 520). Such statements suggest a reduction of bodies to aggregates of indivisible substances. Of course, it is difficult to see how an extended body could be reduced to unextended entities. Leibniz's idea, however, may well have been not that an extended body is an aggregate of indivisible substances, but rather that such aggregates somehow appear as extended bodies to perceiving beings. In other words, the phenomenon or appearance of extension would be founded in the aggregate of indivisible substances, and in that sense a body could be identified with such an aggregate. This was not Leibniz's final position.

Often he writes more obscurely of bodies as aggregates "resulting from" substances (L 411, 520, 529, 577–578). In precisely what sense do phenomena "result from" substances? Leibniz has the basic structure of his answer in the June, 1704, letter to De Volder: "Matter and motion, however, are not so much substances or things as they are the phenomena of percipient beings, *whose reality is located in the harmony of the percipient with himself (at different times) and with other percipient beings*" (L 537, my emphasis). It is at this time, I believe, that Leibniz sees the basic structure of an account of bodies in terms of indivisible substances and their states. Bodies are to be reduced to sets of *harmonized* perceptions of *different* substances *over time*. This was a breakthrough. Leibniz relies upon the harmonized perceptions of different substances over time to capture both the intuitive *interpersonal objectivity* and *temporal stability* or persistence of objects. Of course, we are still far short of the details of such a phenomenalistic construction. But in June, 1704, Leibniz sees how to exploit the preestablished harmony (long maintained for entirely different reasons—see the next section) in the service of a reductive account of bodies.[22] At this juncture, he could be much more secure with respect to the claim that bodies are not absolutely real, and rather are to be accounted for in terms of substances and their states. He writes to Des Bosses in 1712: "I consider the explanation of all phenomena solely through the perceptions of monads functioning in harmony with each other" (L 604). As we have seen (§ 32), after 1704 there are repeated, explicit statements of the mature metaphysics—to De Volder, Des Bosses, Remond, and Conti. With the basic structure of a phenomenalistic account of bodies in hand, the mature metaphysics is stabilized as Leibniz's view.[23]

In the previous section, I claimed that after 1704 Leibniz relied upon a metaphysical analogue of a body, an analogue body, for

[22] Furth, 1967, § 3, has also noted both Leibniz's shift from attempts to reduce bodies to aggregates of monads to attempts to reduce bodies to aggregates of perceptions, and his originality in suggesting the phenomenalistic reduction. Furth points out, insightfully, that since for Leibniz every perceptual "point of view" is represented by some monad (there is no "metaphysical vacuum"), Leibniz can deliver the full intuitive content of material object statements without any appeal to possible perceptions, or to the perceptions a monad would have were it appropriately situated. For this reason, certain familiar obstacles to a successful phenomenalistic reduction did not confront Leibniz. I find this point more than congenial. Even under these favorable conditions, it took Leibniz considerable time to formulate the basic strategy for a phenomenalistic reduction. This just helps to see how difficult pioneering steps in this area were to take.

[23] Furth, 1967, § 3 (including n. 30), cites a number of passages from the period 1706–11 which suggest that during that time Leibniz continued to contemplate the reduction of bodies to aggregates of monads. This may be, but we find the first of the repeated, explicit statements of the mature metaphysical view (that the sole ultimate constituents of reality are monads and their perceptions) in the same letter that the phenomenalistic reduction to perceptions is formulated. It should also be noted that in at least one of the passages Furth cites, Leibniz is explicitly discussing organic bodies. For the significance of this, see the next paragraph in my text.

tactical purposes, enabling him to write as if the preestablished harmony functioned as a solution to the mind-body problem which arises within a dualist framework. Such a metaphysical body was constituted by the infinity of monads dominated by some central monad. Was not this dishonest, since Leibniz had abandoned the view that bodies are aggregates of monads in favor of the view that bodies are to be reduced to sets of perceptions? This is a good question, but I believe there is a good answer. We need a simple distinction. The view Leibniz comes to reject is that any body = material object whatsoever can be reduced to an aggregate of monads. The view he relies upon for tactical purposes is that any body = living body or organism has a metaphysical analogue. The mind-body problem concerns the relationship between a mind and *its* body, a living organism. It is only living bodies or organisms which need a metaphysical body for Leibniz's tactical purposes. Thus, the position is as follows: all material objects (including living bodies or organisms) are susceptible to a phenomenalistic reduction to sets of perceptions; additionally, living bodies or organisms (but not any other material objects) can be construed as constituted by an infinity of monads dominated by some central monad. The substantive claim here which needs to be made out is that "dominance" can be unpacked in such a way that metaphysical analogues to living bodies, but not to other material objects, can be constructed. In any case, Leibniz must have been pleased with these distinctions and doctrines. All material objects can be construed phenomenalistically, and living bodies in particular have a real, metaphysical grounding. They are aggregates of true unities, and hence in a straightforward sense compound substances, whereas mere material objects are not. Leibniz often states that nature is full of creatures or of living things. He does not mean simply that reality ultimately consists of monads. He attempts to locate a "dominance" relationship which will permit the construction of living bodies, but no other material objects, as aggregates of true unitites.

I have attempted to explain how the mature metaphysics could have failed to stabilize until well after 1687. In addition, I believe there is substantial direct evidence that in fact it did not stabilize until late in Leibniz's career. For several years after 1687, Leibniz seems to appeal to physical considerations in support of proliferating minds through matter in a way that is intelligible only if he was working within a dualist framework. An early version of such considerations appears in 1671: "If bodies are devoid of mind, it is impossible for motion ever to be eternal" (W 91). After Leibniz discovered that it is quantity of "force" rather than "motion," as Descartes held, which is conserved, the physical considerations had to do with force rather than motion. He writes in the *Discourse*:

> For motion . . . is not an entirely real thing. . . . But force or the proximate cause of these changes is something more real, and there is enough ground for attributing it to one body rather than another. . . . Now this force is something different from size, figure and motion, and one can judge thereby that all that is conceived in a body does not consist uniquely in extension and its modifications. . . . Thus we are further obliged to re-establish certain beings or forms which they have banished. [*DM* xviii]

This passage is intelligible because, at the time, Leibniz was working within a dualist framework. His idea seems to be that we could account for the existence of physical force only by the distribution of minds, active entities, through matter. In the framework of the mature metaphysics, where matter is nothing but a phenomenon founded in the perceptions of monads, the existence of physical force could hardly constitute an argument for the proliferation of active minds—no more than the existence of red objects would constitute an argument for the existence of red minds. It is therefore significant that Leibniz seems to rely upon physical considerations to generate an argument for the proliferation of minds well after 1687. He writes to Arnauld in 1688:

> Motion in itself separated from force is merely relative. . . . But force is something real and absolute, and since its reckoning is different from that of motion . . . one must not be surprised that nature preserves the same quantity of force and not the same quantity of motion. However, it follows that there is in nature something other than extension and motion, unless one refuses things all force or power, which would be to change them from substances, which they are, into modes. [*LA* 167]

The following passages date from 1691 to 1698, a period during which Leibniz devoted a great deal of attention to dynamics:

> All of this shows that there is in matter something else than the purely Geometrical, that is, than just extension and bare change.

And in considering the matter clearly, we perceive that we must add to them some *higher or metaphysical notion, namely, that of substance, action, and force.* [W 101]

For in addition to extension and its variations, there is in matter a force or a power of action by which the transition is made from metaphysics to nature and from material to immaterial things. [L 409]

There is something besides extension in corporeal things; indeed . . . there is something prior to extension, namely, a natural force everywhere implanted by the Author of nature. . . . It is certainly necessary that this force be produced by him within bodies themselves. Indeed, it must constitute the inmost nature of the body, since it is the character of substance to act. . . . *Primitive force* . . . is in all corporeal substance as such, since I believe that a body entirely at rest is contrary to the nature of things. . . . Primitive force, which is nothing but the first entelechy, corresponds to the *soul* or *substantial form.* [L 435–436]

For it must be admitted that it is impossible for mere extension, which involves geometric concepts, to be capable of action and passion. . . . We show, therefore, that there is in every substance a force of action. [L 444–445]

I have had many disputes on that score with some able Cartesians, and have shown them by mathematics itself that they do not have the true laws of nature, and that to obtain them we must consider not only matter but also force in nature, and that the old forms or *Entelechies* are nothing but forces. . . . And it will be found that nothing is more suited to encourage the consideration of spiritual causes than force in corporeal phenomena. [W 104–105]

It is indeed true, however, that bodies in themselves are inert. . . . So it must be admitted that extension, or the geometric nature of a body, taken alone contains nothing from which action or motion can arise. . . . Now since these activities and entelechies cannot be modes of primary matter or of *mass,* which is something essentially passive . . . it can be concluded that there must be found in corporeal substance a *primary entelechy* or first recipient . . . of activity, that is, a primitive force which, superadded to extension, or what is merely geometrical, and mass, or what is merely material, always acts. . . . It is this substantial principle itself which is called the *soul* in living beings and substantial form in other beings, and inasmuch as it truly constitutes one substance with matter or a unit in itself, it makes up what I call a monad. For if these true unities were dispensed with, only beings through aggregation would remain; indeed, it would follow that there would be left no true beings within bodies. [L 503–504]

The pattern is to argue from the fact that there exists physical force in bodies, or that if bodies are to qualify as substances they must be active, to the conclusion that minds must be superadded or joined to bodies. It is impossible to see any argument here unless Leibniz is working within a dualist framework.

From my perspective, we can explain why Leibniz would have lapsed into a dualist framework after his programmatic statement of the mature metaphysics in 1687. The view did not stabilize until he clearly saw the basic structure of a phenomenalistic reduction of bodies to the harmonized perceptions of different substances over time. If one reads through the correspondence with De Volder, it is almost as if, under pressure from him, Leibniz "rediscovered" the mature metaphysics in June, 1704, much as pressure from Arnauld led to its original formulation in 1687.[24] I do not mean to suggest that the mature metaphysics had simply been forgotten in the interim; rather, the basic insight into the required phenomenalistic construction did not crystallize until June, 1704. The last quotation above, in which Leibniz writes of superadding or joining monads to matter, appeared in September, 1698. In a November, 1698, letter to John Bernoulli, Leibniz writes: "How far a piece of flint must be divided in order to arrive at organic bodies and hence at monads, I do not know. But it is easy to see that our ignorance in these things does not at all prejudice the matter itself" (L 512). Was Leibniz patronizing Bernoulli, or was he still in the grip of the position that monads are distributed through matter? If the latter, the reply to Bernoulli must have left him dissatisfied. Then Leibniz writes to De Volder in 1699 that "extension is... an attribute resulting from many substances existing continuously at the same time" (L 520; cf. 529); in November, 1703, and again in January, 1704, he says that bodies are "quasi-substances" (L 532, 534). The breakthrough letter of June, 1704, follows.[25]

[24]L. J. Russell, 1928, esp. p. 163, noted the parallel developments within the two correspondences.

[25]For an account of the philosophical pressures which emerged within the correspondence with De Volder, and which led to this letter, see ibid.

34. The Dynamics of Leibniz's Denial of Interaction

Through the *Discourse* and most of the Arnauld correspondence, Leibniz was working within a dualist framework. No statement of the mature metaphysics surfaces until October, 1687. Then, for lack of an account of how to reduce bodies to monads and their states, Leibniz lapsed into the dualist framework. It was not until June, 1704 that the mature metaphysics stabilized as his considered position. When do the preestablished harmony and the attendant denial of interaction emerge relative to this chronology? There is a statement of the preestablished harmony (the hypothesis of agreement, or concomitance), and of the claim that nothing external acts upon a substance, as early as "First Truths," written sometime between 1680 and 1684. Both the preestablished harmony and the denial of interaction predate the formulation of the mature metaphysics, falling within a period when Leibniz was working within a dualist framework. This suggests that although the preestablished harmony cannot be construed as a solution to the mind-body problem in the context of the mature metaphysics, nevertheless the preestablished harmony *was initially* formulated as a solution to the mind-body problem.

For this, there is ample evidence. In 1679, Leibniz writes to Malebranche: "I am entirely of your opinion concerning the impossibility of conceiving that a substance which has nothing but extension, without thought, can act upon a substance which has nothing but thought, without extension" (L 209). Here we have a statement of the mind-body problem. The continuation of the passage is of interest: "But I believe that you have gone only halfway and that still other consequences can be drawn from those which you have made. In my opinion it follows that matter is something different from mere extension." I have documented (§ 33) Leibniz's attempts to distribute minds through bodies in order to account both for the unity or substantial character of bodies, and for the existence of physical force. We can speculate that the present passage results from a temptation to allow for interaction between minds and extended matter, but not between minds and mere extended matter, by distributing minds through bodies. Obviously, such a "solution" would be unsatisfactory. The point is that the preestablished harmony and the denial of interaction were still waiting in the wings.

The following statements, dating from 1679 through April, 1687, either formulate the mind-body problem or contain closely related material:

> And when the genus is most remote, as for example, substance, we say that the things are *heterogeneous,* or different entirely in genus, as body and mind, not because they have nothing in common, since both are substances, but because this common genus is so far removed. [L 238]

> *If the diversity of soul and body be assumed, their union can be explained . . .* without the common hypothesis of an *influx,* which is unintelligible, and without the hypothesis of occasional causes, which call upon God *ex machina.* ["First Truths," L 269]

> We also see the unexpected elucidation of the great mystery of the union of the soul and the body. . . . For it is impossible to conceive that the one should have influence on the other. [*DM* xxxiii]

> Mind and body are incommensurable and nothing can determine what degree of speed a mind will impart to a body. [LA 117]

> One does not see how one can explain by what channels the action of an extended mass passes onto an indivisible entity. [LA 145]

Leibniz did recognize a mind-body problem within a dualist framework. The preestablished harmony was initially formulated as his solution to it. Thus the quotation from "First Truths" continues: "For God has equipped both soul and body from the beginning with such great wisdom and workmanship that through the original constitution and essence of each, everything which happens in one corresponds perfectly to whatever happens in the others. . . . I call this the *hypothesis of concomitance*" (L 269).

No sooner had Leibniz formulated the preestablished harmony than he generalized the hypothesis to all substances: "I call this the *hypothesis of concomitance.* This is true of all the substances in the whole universe but is not perceptible in all as it is in the soul and body" (L 269). In other words, the preestablished harmony was straightaway applied to all substances within the dualist framework. Thus he writes to Arnauld, after explaining the preestablished harmony for mind and body: "One will perhaps be more surprised to find that I deny the action of one bodily substance upon the other" (*LA* 66).

Suppose Leibniz generalized the preestablished harmony to all substances for some philosophical reason. For example, he might have felt, *given* that God has instituted a preestablished harmony between some substances, that simplicity demanded that God instituted a preestablished harmony among all substances. Alternatively, he might have felt that granting some interaction would be a threat to the preestablished harmony for minds and bodies—could not the interaction of one body with another cause the latter to be in a state that fails to harmonize with the mind with which it is united? Or both these considerations could have conspired. One can imagine various philosophical reasons for generalizing the preestablished harmony for mind and body to all substances.

This raises a horrifying possibility. The preestablished harmony is initially formulated as a solution to the mind-body problem, preferable to interactionism or occasionalism, within a dualist framework. For philosophical reasons, *given* the preestablished harmony for minds and bodies, this hypothesis is then generalized to all substances. The mature metaphysics, within which there are no extended or material substances, then emerges and finally stabilizes as Leibniz's considered view. In the transition from the dualist to the mature metaphysics, Leibniz has kicked out from underneath himself the argumentative ladder—the mind-body problem—which led to the initial formulation of the preestablished harmony. In the mature metaphysics, the preestablished harmony between substances, all of which are immaterial, then remains as *nothing but an artifact* of the earlier, dualist metaphysics. I will call this "the pure artifact" theory of why Leibniz asserts the preestablished harmony, and the attendant denial of interaction, within the context of the mature metaphysics.

This pure artifact theory, I believe, is mistaken. Leibniz generalized the preestablished harmony to all substances, at least in part, because he liked it, that is, because he found it an attractive structural hypothesis. He applied it "across the board" to all substances, not because (at least not simply because) this seemed required given that he had applied it to minds and bodies, but rather (or at least also) because he preferred the preestablished harmony as a structural hypothesis for any set of substances. Thus he was to write: "I was led insensibly to an opinion which surprised me, but which seems inevitable, and which has in fact very great advantages and very significant beauties" (L 457). And he continues: "As soon as one sees the possibility of this *hypothesis of agreement,* one sees also that it is the most reasonable one and that it gives a wonderful idea of the harmony of the universe and of the perfection of the works of God" (L 458). In part, we have here an aesthetic reaction to the intrinsic features of a hypothesis. But in addition to its "very significant beauties," the hypothesis has "very great advantages." What were these advantages? I can locate four which surface as early as the *Discourse.*

First, Leibniz appealed to the existence of the harmony between substances to provide a premise for his peculiar version of the argument from design. The argument appears in the *Discourse* as follows: "Now there is none but God . . . to be the cause of this correspondence of their phenomena" (*DM* xiv). In the Arnauld correspondence we have: "So this mutual relationship of different substances (which . . . harmonize as if they did act upon one another), *is one of the strongest proofs of God's existence* or of a common cause" (LA 147–148; cf. 92). There is an emphatic reassertion of the position in 1695: "A new proof of the existence of God can also be found here, one of surprising clarity. For the perfect agreement of so many substances which have no communication whatever with each other can come only from a common cause" (L 458). The claim that one can argue from the existence of harmony to the existence of God is often reiterated, and occurs as late as 1716 (W 350; *NE* 505, 507; *LC* v.87).

Second, Leibniz appealed to the preestablished harmony to support the figure that each substance mirrors the universe, and that spirits (rational souls) are the image of God. One substance is said to express, represent, or mirror another "when there exists a constant and fixed relationship between what can be said of one and of the other" (*LA* 144). This is insured by the preestablished harmony. Here are some quotations from the *Discourse:* "Furthermore, every substance is like a whole world and like a mirror of God or of all the universe, which each expresses after its own fashion, much as the same town is variously represented according to the different situations of the man who is looking at it" (*DM* IX); "spirits alone are made in his [God's] image... one spirit alone is worth a whole world since it not merely expresses the world but also knows it and conducts itself in it after the fashion of God" (*DM* XXXVI; cf. XXXV). In the Arnauld correspondence, Leibniz states: "there exists everywhere substances that indicate his [God's] perfection, and are as many different mirrors of the beauty of the universe" (*LA* 162). He persistently claims that all substances or monads "mirror the universe," are "so many living mirrors or so many concentrated worlds," and that rational souls are "as little Gods made in the image of God" (L 454–455, 530, 552, 579, 595, 640, 651). Such claims appear as late as 1715 (*LC* 192).

Third, Leibniz appealed to his denial of interaction between substances to show that minds have what might be called "pure metaphysical freedom." He writes in the *Discourse*: "we also see that every substance has a perfect spontaneity (which becomes liberty in intelligent substances), that everything that happens to it is a consequence of its idea or of its being and that nothing determines it except God alone" (*DM* XXXII). There is a clearer statement of the position in 1695: "There is also in it [the hypothesis of agreement] the great advantage that instead of saying that we are free only in appearance and in a manner adequate for practical purposes... , we must rather say that we are determined only in appearance and that in metaphysical strictness we are in a state of perfect independence as concerns the influence of all the other created beings" (L 458). The present theme is prominent as late as the *Theodicy*, published in 1710 (see *T* 50, 59, 63–64, 288–291, 300–301).

Fourth and finally, Leibniz appeals to the denial of causal interaction to produce a new argument for immortality.[26] The standard Platonic argument, found, for example, in Berkeley, is that since the soul is simple, without parts, and immaterial, it cannot cease to exist through corruption. Leibniz himself often appeals to the indivisibility of the soul to argue for immortality (*LA* 150; L

---

[26]More precisely, the denial of interaction makes possible a new argument for the indestructibility of the soul, a condition which Leibniz did not regard as either necessary or sufficient for the immortality of the person, though obviously connected with it in important ways. See Wilson, 1976, esp. §III, including n. 31.

454, 565, 636; W 508; *LC* 191). We have seen, however, that the mere fact that two entities interact at least constitutes a threat to the claim that the existence of the one entity does not depend causally upon the existence of the other. This threat is acute in a metaphysics (such as Descartes') in which it is the case both that the existence of a spirit at a given time depends upon the existence of some mental state or other (whether Cartesian thoughts, Berkelian ideas, Leibnizian perceptions) at that time, and that some such mental states causally depend for their existence upon certain external objects (§16). We have also seen that Leibniz recognizes the dependence of a substance upon accidents (Ch. III, n. 24). The denial of interaction undermines any external threat to the existence and hence to the immortality of a substance. Leibniz writes in the *Discourse:*

> We also see that every substance has a perfect spontaneity . . . , that everything happens to it as a consequence of its idea or of its being. . . . Now nothing gives us a firmer understanding of immortality than this independence and this extent of the soul, which shelters it absolutely from all external things, . . . hence it is impossible that changes in this extended mass which is called our body should do anything to the soul, or that the dissolution of the body should destroy what is indivisible. [*DM* XXXII; cf. XXXVII]

Leibniz writes in the Arnauld correspondence: "each individual substance or complete entity is like a world apart, independent of everything except God. There is nothing so powerful for demonstrating . . . the indestructibility of our soul" (*LA* 64). This final advantage of the denial of interaction does not receive as much subsequent play as the others, but the point is reiterated in 1695 (L 458).

We are now in a position to reject the pure artifact theory on which, in the mature metaphysics, the preestablished harmony between immaterial substances remains as *nothing but an artifact* of an earlier, dualist metaphysics. To the contrary, Leibniz liked the preestablished harmony intrinsically as a structural hypothesis, and he identified four advantages of the hypothesis. But none of these "advantages" are arguments for it. On the contrary, they are advantageous in the sense that Leibniz sees that he can exploit the preestablished harmony in offering new arguments for or new construals of the claims that God exists, that persons are created in the image of God, that persons are free, and that souls are immortal. Apart from its aesthetic appeal, his motivations for the preestablished harmony and for the denial of interaction were entirely religious. It should be borne in mind that the religious motivations which persist through to the end of Leibniz's career surfaced as early as the *Discourse*, in 1686, and hence predated the stabilization of the mature metaphysics.

The pure artifact theory is correct in one respect. In the transition from the dualist to the mature metaphysics, Leibniz had kicked out from under himself the argumentative ladder—the mind-body problem—which led to the initial formulation of the preestablished harmony, and to its generalization to all substances in turn. After the collapse of the attempt to ground the denial of interaction in the subject-predicate theory of truth (§ 31), Leibniz is unable to produce any serious direct argument for the denial of interaction. This is most evident from the quality of the argumentation in his replies on this issue to De Volder and to Des Bosses, and in section 7 of the *Monadology* (see pp. 271–272, 291, 294–296 above).

Leibniz did, nonetheless, exploit the preestablished harmony for two distinctively philosophical purposes within the context of the mature metaphysics. The first has been discussed (§ 33): in 1704, he saw that the notion could be pressed into service for the ontological purpose of reducing bodies to the harmonious perceptions of different substances over time. Second, he moved in the direction of utilizing the denial of interaction for the metaphysical purpose of constructing an account of the persistence of monads. The latter point needs explanation.

Descartes held that a mind or soul, a thinking substance$_s$, persists through changes in its accidents or modifications (HR I, 141). Leibniz agreed: "the identity of the mind is not destroyed by any modification" (L 162). It is no good to say (cf. K 156–157), however, that Cartesian thoughts or Leibnizian perceptions at different times are thoughts/perceptions of the same mind just in case they inhere in the same mind. The well-known difficulties for providing an account of the persistence of thinking substances$_s$ are compounded in Leibniz's system. This is because the lowest-grade or bare monads lack both memory and conscious experience, and

hence various standard accounts of persistence would be insuffi-
ciently general to apply to all monads.

An interesting approach to the problem emerges in the following
statements, written between 1698 and 1716:

> This law of order . . . constitutes the individuality of each particular
> substance. [L 493]

> For me nothing is preserved in things except the law itself which
> involves a continuous succession. [L 534]

> Every simple substance has perception, and . . . its individuality con-
> sists in the perpetual law which brings about the sequence of percep-
> tions that are assigned to it. [T 291]

> [God] makes them to perceive one another in consequence of the
> natures which he has given them once and for all, and which he
> keeps up only, according to the laws of every one of them severally;
> which, though different one from another, yet terminate in an exact
> correspondence of the results of the whole. [LC v.87]

Apparently, persistence is to be explicated in terms of laws of order
or laws of succession. How is this to be done? If we think of a
monad's law of succession as a mathematical formula, it seems that
each monad will have the same law of succession. This is a consequence of the preestablished harmony. How could there be a "constant and fixed relationship" between what can be said of any two
substances, and hence inter-monadic laws of coexistence for any
arbitrary time, unless the mathematical formula or law governing
the succession of each monad's perceptual states was the same?

Alternatively, some passages suggest that Leibniz identifies a
monad's law of succession with a temporal sequence of perceptual
states. Obviously, two monads can have different sequences of
states, both sequences governed by the same law, e.g., "1, 4, 7, . . ."
and "2, 5, 8, ..." But of the various perceptual states which exist at
different times, what reason is there to "unite" one pair of tempor-
ally distinct states into a sequence rather than another pair? We
want the result that the intuitively correct sequence of states gets
selected, but what is to prevent the selection of any arbitrary sequence of states (e.g., "1, 5, 8, . . ." and "2, 4, 7, . . .") as constitutive of a persistent monad?

Leibniz has all the materials for a simple, straightforward analysis
of persistence. Laws of succession construed as formulas are impor-

tant because they are causal. Of all the sequences of states which can be identified, we can pick out those that are causally connected. Let us make the following assumption: each part of the total perceptual state of a monad at time t is a (partial) cause of each part of the total perceptual state of a monad at any subsequent time t'. Would Leibniz have accepted this? The texts are silent—he does not discuss the internal structure of intra-monadic causal relations. Given this assumption, there is a remarkably simple Leibnizian causal theory or analysis of persistence: perceptual states at distinct times are states of the same monad just in case one of the states is at least a partial cause of the other. This simple causal criterion, of course, fails when applied to minds or persons in the actual world (as we believe the world to be). You direct my attention to the tree; your thought that I would be interested is a partial cause of my subsequently seeing the tree—but your thought and my visual experience are not mental states of the same mind or person. In Leibniz's metaphysics, where there is no causal interaction whatsoever between monads, such counterexamples to the sufficiency of the condition cannot arise. The success of this simple Leibnizian causal criterion depends only upon the denial of interaction between monads, and not upon the claim that there is a preestablished harmony. Were the laws of succession different for different monads, the present causal criterion would still generate the right results. The success of this criterion is therefore independent of the truth of the preestablished harmony. It is dependent upon the truth of the claim that no two monads causally interact. But this does not prevent the present account from functioning as an analysis of persistence. Leibniz writes to Des Bosses: "I do not believe a system is possible in which the monads act upon each other mutually" (L 613). Even God cannot create a system of interacting monads, though perhaps He could have created a system of noninteracting monads which fail to harmonize.

Did Leibniz ever state the simple Leibnizian causal criterion for persistence? In Bk. II, Ch. XXVII of the *New Essays*, the chapter which deals with Locke's views on identity, Leibniz writes: "An immaterial being or a spirit cannot be stripped of all perceptions of its past experience. There remain for it some impressions of all that has formerly happened to it, and it even has some presentiments of all that will happen to it. . . . This continuation and *bond of percep-tions constitutes in reality the same individual*" (NE 249–250; my emphasis). The *bond* between perceptions, as distinct from a mere continuation or sequence of perceptions, is the causal tie between successive perceptual states. Am I "reading in" the simple Leibniz-ian causal account of persistence? Leibniz wrote in 1709: "But the action proper to the soul is perception, and the nexus of percep-tions, according to which subsequent ones are derived from preced-ing ones, makes up the unity of the percipient" (L 599). The simple Leibnizian causal theory of persistence does not in any way appeal to the existence of substances or substrata in which perceptions inhere. Further, substances or substrata are not needed to account for the "unity" of a set of perceptions at a time. Distinct perceptions at a given time are perceptions of the same monad just in case there is some perception such that they are both partial causes of that perception. At this point, Leibniz was in a position to dispense with substances or substrata, at least insofar as they might seem required to provide accounts of persistence and unity.

VIII

SEVENTEENTH-CENTURY
CONTINENTAL METAPHYSICS

35. Continental Metaphysics: 1640–1715

The preceding five chapters contain a history of a philosophical genre which I call "Continental Metaphysics." The following claims are characteristic of this genre:

> Descartes denies that the existence of a mind depends causally upon the existence of any body.
> Spinoza denies that modes of distinct attributes causally interact.
> Malebranche denies that any finite or created entity is a cause of anything.
> Berkeley denies that there are causes other than volitions of spirits.
> Leibniz denies that monads causally interact.

These claims have three features in common: they deny that certain causal relations, different in each case, obtain; they are important metaphysically; and they are supported on the basis of arguments deemed to be at least demonstrative (in the sense discussed at section 3). Five major philosophers of the period were of a piece in advancing such claims. The proliferation of such claims in Europe in the seventeenth and early eighteenth centuries was no coincidence. I take Descartes, Spinoza, Malebranche, Berkeley, and Leibniz to be the leading figures in a philosophical genre, Continental Metaphysics, because each of them advances the sort of claim in question, and there are significant, historically interconnected reasons for their doing so. Let us look at the dynamics of the genre's development.

Descartes held that mind and body causally interact. It has proved extraordinarily difficult to identify an inconsistency between this claim and other theses to which he subscribed (§15). He was nevertheless responsible for the subsequent perception of the existence of a mind-body problem. This came about because he claimed that mind and body are essentially/entirely/absolutely distinct substances$_S$, that is, that the essences of mind and body have nothing in common. Descartes' purpose in putting forward this claim was not to cast doubt upon mind-body interaction, for him a plain fact of everyday experience, but rather to contribute to the argumentation for his position on immortality (§13). In asserting mind-body interaction while emphasizing the disparity between mind and body, he unwittingly ushered in the mind-body problem. He exacerbated the difficulties in the *Replies*, where he simultaneously maintains mind-body interaction and denies that the existence of mind depends causally upon the existence of body. Descartes advances the latter claim on the a priori ground that the extinction of the body is too "light a cause" to result in the annihilation of the mind.

Spinoza, for one, found Descartes' account of the relationship between mind and body such as to "excite our laughter or disgust." His metaphysics includes a sustained attempt, in the bulk of Part II and the early sections of Part III of the *Ethics*, to provide an account of the mind-body relationship that is an alternative to interactionism. The destructive component of his position, his rejection of interactionism, appears as a special case of his denial that modes of distinct attributes causally interact, a denial which is advanced on purely a priori grounds. The constructive component of his position is the psychophysical parallelism, often referred to as a "double-aspect theory," asserted at *E* IIP7.

Malebranche's occasionalism, unlike Spinoza's double-aspect theory, does not function as a solution to a mind-body problem. Malebranche denies that any finite or created entity is a cause of anything. The theory is that God is the only cause. While occasionalism generates an account of the relationship between created minds and created bodies as a special case, the claim that all created entities are causally inefficacious (that, for example, an object's physical state is not a cause of any of its subsequent physical states) seems an unlikely direction in which to generalize a mind-body problem. It is therefore no surprise that Malebranche's argumentation for occasionalism does not address any such problem. The arguments do not proceed by attempting to generalize any alleged difficulty for mind-body interaction. The arguments, all a priori in character, appeal to various claims about God (§§22, 24). Furthermore, the theory of occasionalism leaves any mind-body problem untouched; the question remains as to how the Divine mind could enter into causal relations with extended bodies (§24). The relationship between Descartes' interactionism and Malebranche's occasionalism was not that of problem and proposed solution. On the other hand, the mind-body problem did serve as the occasion for occasionalism. Malebranche could rely upon his readers' familiarity with, if not sympathy for, the claim that *mind and body* do not causally interact. Malebranche's claim that *no two* created entities causally interact looked much more plausible against this background than otherwise (§25).

Berkeley's denial that there are causes other than volitions or spirits is a liberalized version of Malebranche's claim that God is the only cause. For Berkeley, all spirits, and not God alone, have some causal efficacy (§26). This liberalization enables him to allow that the volitions of created spirits are causally efficacious with respect to the movement of their own limbs. He thereby locates human freedom in the ability of persons to do what they will, makes a limited concession to common sense, and dissociates himself from Malebranche's full-blown occasionalism according to which "it is the author of our being who executes our wills" (§27). Indeed, Berkeley derives his metaphysics from Malebranche's by allowing that some volitions of created minds are causes, eliminating material objects, and denying that created minds are directly acquainted with anything except their own ideas and mental operations (§26). The metaphysics of Malebranche and Berkeley are both occasionalist systems. The fundamental difference between them lies in the direction of the argument for the system. Whereas Malebranche argues from the existence of God to the causal inefficacy of created entitites, Berkeley argues from the causal inefficacy of ideas to the existence of (a continuously active) God (§§27–28). And Berkeley considers his arguments for the causal inefficacy of ideas to be demonstrative (§29).

Leibniz's preestablished harmony, like Malebranche's occasionalism, does not function as a solution to a mind-body problem. In Leibniz's mature metaphysics, the sole ultimate constituents of reality are monads and their perceptions. The preestablished harmony is the constructive component of Leibniz's account of the relationship between monads. The attendant denial that monads causally interact, advanced on a priori grounds and claimed to be metaphysically necessary, is the destructive component of that account. Since all monads lack parts, and are therefore unextended and immaterial, the preestablished harmony is not an account of the relationship between unextended minds and extended bodies. As Leibniz recognized, the mind-body problem is not even formulable in the mature metaphysics. He did attempt to construct a metaphysical analogue to a body by identifying a monad's "body" with the infinity of other monads which it dominates. This enabled him to write as if the preestablished harmony and the attendant denial that anything external acts upon a monad were functioning as responses to the mind-body problem (§ 32). This tactic, however misleading, was not dishonest, because Leibniz did believe that the preestablished harmony would be the best account of the relationship between mind and body within a dualist ontology. Indeed, he initially formulated the preestablished harmony as a solution to the mind-body problem. But the relationship between Descartes' interactionism and the preestablished harmony in the context of Leibniz' mature metaphysics was not that of problem and proposed solution. Rather, the mind-body problem suggested the preestablished harmony as a general structural hypothesis about the relationship between existing entitites. The preestablished harmony in turn facilitated the transition from a dualist ontology; Leibniz came to exploit the harmony in the service of a reductive, phenomenalistic, account of bodies (§§ 33–34).

It is obvious from this summary that Descartes' role in the development of Continental Metaphysics is somewhat different from those of the other figures. In denying that the existence of a mind depends causally upon the existence of any body, Descartes did advance an instance of the sort of claim which is characteristic of Continental Metaphysics. He denied that a certain causal relation obtains; the denial is important metaphysically; and it was advanced on the basis of an argument deemed to be at least demonstrative. But although he claims an interest in establishing immortality with some frequency even subsequent to the alteration of the subtitle to the first edition of the *Meditations* (§13), it must be admitted that when he produces the argument for immortality in *Replies to Objections II* he does so under considerable pressure. Descartes' denial is neither so important to him, nor so central to his metaphysics, as the respective denials of certain causal relations advanced by Spinoza, Malebranche, Berkeley, and Leibniz were to them. In this sense, Descartes is not a paradigmatic Continental Metaphysician. But since he stands as the initial figure in the genre, we should not expect, and need not claim, that he was. His principal contribution to Continental Metaphysics lies elsewhere than in the centrality of his denial to his metaphysics.

Descartes precipitated the emergence of Continental Metaphysics by forcing a perceived mind-body problem into a position of prominence. Many could not accept his claim that mind and body, substances whose essences have nothing in common, can and do causally interact. This mind-body problem provided the momentum for the entire subsequent development of the genre. Spinoza, along with any number of "minor Cartesians," responded to the problem proper by denying that mind and body causally interact; against the background of such denials, Malebranche's occasionalism acquired an air of familiarity and a measure of plausibility, even though it was not itself a response to the mind-body problem; Berkeley's qualified occasionalism was in turn derived directly from that of Malebranche; and finally it was the mind-body problem which initially stimulated Leibniz to formulate the preestablished harmony as a general structural hypothesis, one that he came to apply to an ontology within which a mind-body problem is not even formulable.

Descartes' denial that the existence of a mind depends causally upon the existence of any body probably did itself make a twofold contribution to the development of Continental Metaphysics. First, within the course of seventy-five pages of text in the *Objections and Replies*, Descartes argues as follows: on the one hand, that two substances$_S$, material and thinking, have enough in common to interact causally; and on the other hand, that qualities of material substances have so little in common with thinking substances, that changes in the former (and hence the dissolution of the body) could not cause the latter to cease to exist (§16). The artificiality of running these two arguments simultaneously must have accentuated the perceived mind-body problem.

Second, in denying that a mind's existence depends causally upon the existence of any body on the ground that qualities of material substance$_S$ have so little in common with thinking substance$_S$. Descartes provided a model for one sort of consideration (an appeal to heterogeneity) invoked by subsequent figures within the genre to support their respective denials of causal relations. Thus Spinoza ventilates his conviction that mind and body have too little in common to interact in the early propositions of Part I of the *Ethics* (§20). Berkeley, in the *Dialogues*, is prepared to argue that a material substance could not cause ideas because they have too little in common. He drops the argument only when he realizes that it would undermine his own view that volitions cause perceptions, with which they have nothing in common (§29). Finally, Leibniz, faced with the point that all monads are perceiving unextended substances, that they do have something in common and ought to be capable of interaction, proceeds to argue that they cannot interact because they "differ in nature," that is, because they do not have all their properties in common (§32). We find that wherever feasible the Continental Metaphysicians appeal to heterogeneity considerations, in assorted contortions, to support their respective denials of causal relations. In sum, Descartes' denial that a mind's existence depends causally upon the existence of any body both provided a loose sort of model for some of the subsequent argumentation within the genre, and accentuated a perceived mind-body problem. And it was the perception of a mind-body problem, stimulated in the first instance by Descartes' claim that mind and body are essentially/entirely/absolutely distinct substances$_S$, which fueled the entire subsequent development of Continental Metaphysics.

Such were the dynamics of the development of Continental Metaphysics. The Continental Metaphysicians are unified in advancing denials that certain causal relations obtain, in connection with metaphysical concerns, and on grounds they deem to be at least demonstrative. What is striking is that while each figure advanced an instance of a distinctive sort of philosophical thesis, the content of their respective claims and the motivation for advancing them are different in each case.

The motivations for the various denials are as follows. Descartes denies that the existence of a mind depends causally upon the existence of any body, in order to show that the soul is naturally immortal (§13). Spinoza's motivation in denying that modes of distinct attributes causally interact is to solve a felt mind-body problem (§§17, 20). For Malebranche, no finite or created entity is a cause of anything; the motivations for constructing an occasionalist system were to show both that there is an "immediate union" between the human mind and God, and that idolatry rests upon the false presupposition that entities other than God are causally efficacious (§25). Berkeley held that there are no causes other than the volitions of spirits. It follows as a special case that no ideas are causes. The motivation was to supply a premise for his two serious arguments (the passivity argument and the argument from the Divine visual language) for the existence of a continuously active God (§27). For Leibniz, no two monads causally interact. The motivation for this claim, and for the preestablished harmony which entails it, was complex (§34). In part, it was aesthetic. In addition, Leibniz appeals to the harmony in order to provide a premise for his peculiar version of the argument from design, and to support the figure that each substance mirrors the universe and hence that spirits are in the image of God; he appeals to the denial of interaction alone in order to show that souls have a pure metaphysical freedom, and that, for lack of any external threat to their existence, they are immortal. These early motivations may have been reinforced subsequently: it was in 1704 that Leibniz came to see that the preestablished harmony facilitated the phenomenalistic reduction of bodies (§§33–34); and at about the same time he began to perceive that the preestablished harmony enabled him to construct a simple causal account of persistence and unity, and hence to dispense with substances$_s$ altogether (§34).

The motivations for the various instances of the denial that some causal relation or other obtains are thus diffuse. In general, they relate to metaphysical issues that are especially relevant to religion. This is not true, however, in every case. Spinoza's denial was a response to the mind-body problem, and was not motivated by religious concerns. Also, Leibniz's initial motivation was in part purely aesthetic; and his denial was subsequently reinforced by its contribution to a phenomenalistic reduction of bodies, and to the formulation of a theory of persistence and unity. Furthermore, the religious motivations themselves are a diverse lot. With respect to motivations, Continental Metaphysicians fragment. But in the sense that each denies that some causal relation obtains, that each denial is important metaphysically and is advanced on the basis of arguments its author deems at least demonstrative, the differing motivations converge not only on a distinctive sort of philosophical thesis, but also on a distinctive mode of philosophical theorizing, where "theorizing" is construed to include both the content of the thesis and the character of the argumentation for it.

Continental Metaphysics is a philosophical genre circumscribed by a characteristic sort of philosophical theorizing, and by the historical interconnections which in part account for the proliferation of examples of such theorizing. These historical interconnections, however, do not include any common philosophical problem to which the various denials were a response. On the contrary, Continental Metaphysicians diverge with respect to motivation. Their convergence on a distinctive sort of philosophical theorizing is attributable, in part, to the fact that causation is relevant to the wide range of problems—immortality, the mind-body problem, union with God, idolatry, proving the existence of a continuously active God or of a designing God, freedom, and persistence—in which these philosophers were interested. And it is, I believe, attributable in part to the fact that advancing metaphysically important denials of causal relations on what were deemed to be at least demonstrative grounds came to be a standard and indeed a prominent way of philosophizing. It is worth bearing in mind that the principal texts of the Continental Metaphysicians appeared between 1641 (the *Meditations*) and 1714 (the *Monadology*). During this seventy-five year period, a highly distinctive mode of philosophical theorizing emerged and thrived in Europe, and came to be something of a philosophical fashion.[1]

---

[1]For some suggestive remarks about the role of styles in the history of philosophy, see Mandelbaum, 1977, p. 567.

36. Substance Revisited

In section 11, I offered a preliminary survey of the vicissitudes of various conceptions of substance during the seventeenth and early eighteenth centuries, and a good deal of related material has been developed in subsequent chapters. I believe that the theory presented in the preceding section can help us to explain and understand these data.

I begin with Descartes' conception of substance$_1$, and the related conceptions of substance in Spinoza and Leibniz. Recall that x is a secondary-substance$_1$ just in case it is possible that x's existence does not depend causally upon the existence of any other entity except God (§8); that x is a Spinozistic- or SP-substance only if x's existence does not depend causally upon the existence of any other entity (§9); and that monads, entities which have no parts, do not causally interact (§10). Here we have an apparent shift of interest from the capacity for causally independent existence, to the fact of causally independent existence, to the fact of a complete causal independence that precludes even causal interaction (§11).

We have seen that Descartes' substance$_1$ is not a fruitful notion within his metaphysics. It would most naturally be invoked in the course of producing arguments in support of his position on immortality. There is a simple Cartesian argument to show that a mind or thinking substance$_S$ is a secondary-substance$_1$ (§8). But what then? In considering his claims about minds listed in section 12, we saw that the least Descartes wants to show is that (8) no mind is a body. He can perhaps reach this result via a modal argument from the claim that (4) mind and body are really distinct substances$_S$, or from the claim that (3) a mind's essence (at least in part) is to think, which can itself be established by appeal to (4). I have argued, however, that the fact that a mind is a secondary-substance$_1$, that it is possible that its existence does not depend *causally* upon the existence of any other entity except God, cannot help Descartes establish that (4) mind and body are really distinct substances$_S$, that is (at least) that it is possible that a mind is not identical to any body, i.e., that it is possible that a mind's existence does not depend *noncausally* upon a body *with which it is identical* (§13). The most Descartes wants to show is that (9) a mind's existence *does not* depend causally upon the existence of any body. The fact that a mind is a secondary-substance$_1$, and hence that it is possible that (9) is true, is not going to help establish that (9) is true. In arguing for (9), Descartes had to fall back upon heterogeneity considerations (§13). If the notion of substance$_1$ is this barren, one may as well dispence with it. The most natural move is to reserve the term 'substance' in order to help formulate the result one wants to achieve: x is a secondary-substance just in case its existence does not depend causally upon the existence of any other entity except God. In these terms, what Descartes wants to show is that a mind is a secondary-substance, as just defined. Such an entity is precisely what might be called a "secondary-SP-substance" with respect to the metaphysical component of Spinoza's conception of substance: its existence does not depend causally upon the existence of any other entity except God.

Spinoza's interest was in primary-SP-substance or SP-substance proper, that is, metaphysically, an entity such that its existence does not depend causally upon anything else. Spinoza, of course, did not have his sights on the human mind and immortality in characterizing substance in this way. A standard interpretation is that his principal interest is in showing that God is the only substance in his sense, the only SP-substance. This is misleading, at the least. I have argued (§18) that in Spinoza's system any attribute is itself an SP-substance. Recall, for example, that Spinoza asserts (E IP10) that it follows immediately from the definition of 'attribute' that "each attribute of a substance must be conceived through itself"; and further that it follows by E IA4 that each attribute is in itself, that is, that its existence does not depend causally upon the existence of anything else. In other words, each attribute takes on the defining characteristics of SP-substance. Each attribute is a simple SP-substance.

Why does Spinoza want to maintain that each attribute, e.g., the attribute of extension or the attribute of thought, is itself an SP-substance, an entity whose existence does not depend causally upon the existence of anything else? The answer, I believe, is that he wants to exploit this claim in order to support his rejection of mind-body interaction: the argument at E IIIP2D to show that mind and body do not causally interact appeals to E IIP6; the argument at

E IIP6D to show that modes of distinct attributes do not causally interact appeals to *E* IP10, the assertion that each attribute is conceived through itself (§ 19). It is worth noting that prior to the demonstration of *E* IIP6, *E* IP10 is invoked in the demonstration of only one proposition, *E* IP12 ("No attribute of substance can be truly conceived from which it follows that substance can be divided"), a proposition that is itself never invoked in the course of any demonstration in the *Ethics*. Spinoza's primary reason for asserting *E* IP10 is because he believes that it can ultimately be exploited for the purposes of his rejection of mind-body interaction. So although an SP-substance is an entity whose existence does not depend causally upon the existence of any other entity, Spinoza also wants to show that certain entities, modes of extension or bodies and modes of thought or minds, do not even causally interact. Thus "the body cannot determine the mind to thought, neither can the mind determine the body to motion nor rest" (*E* IIIP2).

Against this background, it is somewhat misleading to say, as we did in section 11, that in moving from SP-substance to monads we have a shift of interest from the fact of causally independent existence to the fact of a complete causal independence which precludes all causal interaction with any other entity. This is true with respect to those entities which Spinoza and Leibniz respectively call "substances." But if we ignore the labels and attend to the properties that Spinoza in fact attributes to various entities, we see that for him modes are entities exhibiting a partial causal independence which precludes some causal interactions, interactions with modes of distinct attributes. We can think of entities as differing with respect to the extent to which they are "causally independent" of other entities. Leibniz's denial that monads causally interact, when coupled with the claim that nothing exists except monads and their perceptions (§ 32), immediately generates entities which exhibit a complete or perfect causal independence. No other entity acts causally upon a monad, and a monad does not act causally upon any other entity; it has neither "causal input" nor "causal output." Spinoza's denial that modes of distinct attributes causally interact immediately generates entitites which exhibit partial causal independence. For example, it is only other modes of extension that act causally upon a mode of extension, and a mode of extension does not act causally upon modes of any other attribute; a mode's causal input and output is restricted. Leibniz and Spinoza are both interested in identifying entities which exhibit causal independence in various degrees. In Leibniz's case, the entities which exhibit complete causal independence are themselves Leibnizian substances or monads. In Spinoza's case, some entities (modes) which exhibit partial causal independence are not themselves SP-substances, but Spinoza's principal reason for allowing that each attribute is itself an SP-substance is to establish his position with respect to the causal independence of modes of distinct attributes, and ultimately of minds and bodies.

Compared to Leibniz and Spinoza, Descartes was interested in only a weak sort of causal independence. His denial that the existence of a mind depends causally upon the existence of any body generates for minds a degree of causal independence insofar as no (changes in) body can cause a mind's existence to terminate. In other words, with respect to causal input, a mind can be acted upon by any other entity, but not by bodies in such a way as to cause the mind's termination; and with respect to causal output, there is no restriction. The fact that Descartes was interested in such a limited sort of causal independence is one symptom of the fact that his denial was not as central to his metaphysics as the denials of various causal relations by the other Continental Metaphysicians were to their systems.

I have been discussing one strand in Descartes' conception of substance, substance$_1$, together with its apparent successors, SP-substance and monads. Each of these relates to and reflects an interest in causal independence. It is important to bear in mind that while 'substance$_1$' and 'SP-substance' are *defined* in terms of causal independence (§§8–9), this is not true of 'monads'. According to the definition I extracted from the first two sections of the *Monadology*, a monad is an entity which has no parts (§10). The definition makes no reference to causal independence. But since Leibniz's denial that simple substances or monads causally interact is perhaps the most distinctive thesis of his metaphysics (§6), it was obvious all along that Leibniz's conception of substance "relates to" or "reflects an interest in" causal independence. It was equally obvious all along that monads, entities whose qualities are perceptions, are very much akin to Descartes' thinking substances$_S$.

I turn to this strand in Descartes' conception of substance, to substance$_S$, a subject or substratum in which qualities inhere. We have seen that Descartes, Malebranche, Berkeley, and Leibniz each defended the existence of thinking substances$_S$, whether in the guise of spirits or monads (§§6, 21). We have already noted in this section that for Descartes a thinking substance$_S$ exhibits a weak sort of causal independence, and for Leibniz a monad exhibits complete causal independence. As for Malebranche and Berkeley, they no more define 'substance' in terms of causal independence than Leibniz does 'monad'. But if we attend to the properties Malebranche and Berkeley attribute to thinking substances$_S$ or spirits, their interest in entities that exhibit causal independence is apparent. Malebranche's denial that any finite or created entity is a cause of anything, his theory that God is the only cause, immediately generates entities which are acted upon only by God, and which do not act upon any other entity. Here there is an asymmetry between causal output and causal input. Finite or created entities exhibit complete causal independence with respect to output, and partial causal independence with respect to input. Berkeley's denial that there are causes other than volitions is a liberalization of Malebranche's claim that God is the only cause. This fact does not result in a difference between Malebranche and Berkeley with respect to the extent to which finite or created spirits exhibit causal independence. The liberalization is principally motivated by Berkeley's desire to allow that we move our limbs ourselves (§27). If this is the only way in which volitions of finite spirits can be causally efficacious, the qualification results in no additional causal output with respect to other entities, since the "limbs" in question are just collections of ideas inhering in the spirit itself. So Malebranche and Berkeley, as well as Leibniz, are interested in entities which exhibit a degree of causal independence, though the entitites are not defined in this way. For Malebranche and Berkeley, however, the causal independence is not formulable as some simple thesis (such as "spirits do not causally interact") because the causal independence is incomplete, asymmetrical, and not applicable to all spirits (the asymmetry is precisely reversed in the case of God).

For Descartes, Malebranche, Berkeley, and Leibniz, then, thinking substances$_S$ are entities which exhibit at least some degree of causal independence. Why should it be the case that each of these four philosophers not only defends the existence of thinking substances$_S$, but also believes that such entities exhibit causal independence? Was this a historical coincidence? Was it the consequence of some common body of doctrine about substance$_S$? The correct explanation falls somewhere in between. Each of these figures had religious motivations for defending the existence of thinking substance$_S$: at the least, Descartes wanted to show that there exist minds which are not identical to bodies; Malebranche was a Catholic priest; Berkeley was a Protestant bishop; and Leibniz, whatever his private views, was bent on a scheme to unite the Protestant and Catholic churches in Europe. Further, we saw in the preceding section that each had at least some religious motivation for advancing his particular denial of certain causal relations. Now it is perfectly natural that someone who is motivated to defend the existence of souls in the first place would also have one or more of these additional religious motivations. In two cases, the additional motivations are intimately related to the desire to defend the existence of thinking substance$_S$. Descartes, at times, wants to show not only that souls exist but that they are naturally immortal, denying that their existence depends causally upon the existence of body. Leibniz also wants to show that souls are naturally immortal, and to this end, perhaps perceiving that the admission of interaction with other entities is at least a threat to the immortality of the soul ($\S\S$ 16, 34), denies causal interaction between monads. Leibniz, of course, had additional religious motivations, which conspired in the same direction. Malebranche wanted to construct an occasionalist metaphysics within which the human mind is immediately united to God; this is the motivation for the denial of causes other than God, the denial which generates the result that all finite entities, and hence spirits in particular, exhibit causal independence. The story is similar in the case of Berkeley. Had Malebranche and Berkeley not been concerned even to defend the existence of thinking substance$_S$, they certainly would not have been concerned to defend occasionalism for the purpose of undermining idolatry, establishing the existence of a God in whom "we live, and move, and have our being," etc. The point is that the religious motivations for the denials of certain causal relations which have the causal independence of various entities as a consequence are natural (though by no means necessary) accompaniments to a desire to defend the existence of thinking substance$_S$.

I turn to two subsidiary points in connection with the changing fortunes of substance$_S$. First, in the *New Essays*, Leibniz's defense of substance$_S$ in the face of Locke's attack is less than impassioned (§10). The explanation is as follows. Leibniz's monads exhibit a complete causal independence. Leibniz was in a position to exploit this feature of his metaphysics in order to formulate simple causal theories of both the persistence and the unity of a monad. For example, perceptual states at distinct times are states of the same monad just in case one of the states is at least a partial cause of the other. Leibniz was aware of the availability of such an account (§34), an account which allows us to construct a persistent monad out of perceptual states that stand in the appropriate causal relation. There is no appeal to a persistent substratum or subject in which perceptions inhere. Such substrata are at best a third wheel, and Leibniz must have perceived that they are dispensable.

Second, why did Spinoza have no use for substance$_S$? Two reasons suggest themselves. First, however one interprets his vexing claim that "the human mind cannot be absolutely destroyed with the body, but something of it remains which is eternal" (*E* vP23), it seems certain that he did not believe in immortality in any standard sense. Second, Spinoza wanted to maintain a psychophysical parallelism according to which the modes of the attributes of thought and extension comprise coordinate systems (§20). Even Descartes' texts show a sensitivity to the difficulties in a commitment to material substance$_S$ fully analogous to thinking substance$_S$ (§7), and Spinoza read his Descartes with extreme care (§§17, 19). Spinoza might well have seen an attempt to construct an ontology of substrata-in-which-qualities-inhere as at odds with his attempt to treat the system of modes of thought and that of extension as coordinate.

We can summarize as follows. There are two strands in Descartes' conception of substance. His conception of substance$_I$ is defined in terms of causal independence. His conception of substance$_S$ is defined in terms of inherence, a variety of noncausal dependence. Spinoza has no use for substance$_S$; and neither Malebranche nor Berkeley (nor for that matter Leibniz) invokes substance terminology defined in terms of causal independence. On the other hand, each Continental Metaphysician is interested in identifying entities that exhibit at least some degree of causal independence. For Descartes, Malebranche, Berkeley, and Leibniz, the causally independent entities are also thinking substances$_S$. In these cases, the religious motives which led the figures to defend the existence of thinking substances$_S$ were accompanied by further religious motives for holding that these entities exhibit some degree of causal independence. For Spinoza, whose denial of causal interaction between mind and body had no religious motivation, the entities exhibiting causal independence are attributes of simple SP-substances themselves, and the modes of those substances. All the Continental Metaphysicians were interested in establishing certain sorts of causal independence.

37. Objections from the Perspective of the Standard Theory (I)

It is of course possible that both the standard theory (§1) and my alternative are illuminating in their own ways. For example, Berkeley might be both a British Empiricist in a sense characterized by the standard theory, and a Continental Metaphysician in the sense characterized by my theory. I welcome a pluralistic approach on which there exists more than one illuminating overview of the development of modern Western philosophy. The standard theory is so powerful and pervasive that the climate has not been conducive to the formulation of alternative overview, but that is no objection to the standard theory.

I believe, however, that my theory is truer to the historical and philosophical developments within the period, that it provides a more adequate account of the interrelationships between the relevant philosophical systems. Indeed, I believe that the standard theory is radically mistaken, and I have attempted to develop a cumulative case for that thesis throughout this book. In this section and the next, I will bring together some of the principal points I have developed by considering objections to my theory which are likely to be raised from the perspective of the standard theory.

A proponent of the standard theory is likely to be disturbed by a number of features of the theory I have developed. According to the third component of the standard theory, Continental Rationalism

and British Empiricism are philosophical *movements* in the sense
that within each school shared principles are applied with increasing
rigor to a common body of problems. Continental Metaphysics does
not constitute a movement in this sense. The denials of various
causal relations which I have emphasized did not result from an
attempt to see shared principles through to their "logical conclusion" in some application. Continental Metaphysics does not exhibit the sort of dialectical development which the standard theory
attributes to Continental Rationalism and British Empiricism.
From the perspective of the standard theory, this difference will
appear a deficiency in my theory. Surely, an optimal theory about
the period should identify schools in a way which makes perspicu-
ous as much of their dialectical structure and as many of the
philosophical relationships between the systems of their members as
possible. My treatment of Berkeley as a Continental Metaphysician
is then doubly objectionable: in grouping Berkeley together with the
figures standardly classified as Continental Rationalists, I substitute
a grouping which does not exhibit a dialectical development for one
which does; and in grouping him apart from the figures usually
classified as British Empiricists, I obscure the dialectical developments within this latter school. My response is that the standard theory is mistaken in attributing various dialectical developments to Continental Rationalism and British Empiricism in
the first place. I discuss the case of Continental Rationalism in this
section, and British Empiricism in the next.

In its application to Continental Rationalism, the third component of the standard theory is typically fleshed out as follows: Descartes' admission of causal interaction between mind and body,
between two kinds of substance, was inconsistent with Rationalist
principles; Malebranche's occasionalism, Spinoza's double-aspect
theory, and Leibniz's preestablished harmony functioned in their
systems as successive attempts to solve the mind-body problem
within a Rationalist framework. In this attractive picture of their
development, the Continental Rationalists are all concerned with a
common problem, the mind-body problem, which arises within a
Rationalist framework. Is this theory correct?

It has proven surprisingly difficult to document the thesis that
Descartes' claim that mind and body causally interact was inconsis-

tent with Rationalist principles. If there was such an inconsistency, Descartes never came to recognize it. In correspondence and discussion with Elizabeth, Arnauld, and Burman, Descartes insists that causal interaction between mind and body is a plain fact of experience. He writes to Elizabeth, Hyperaspistes, and Arnauld that the mind is "corporeal" in the sense that it can affect and act upon the body. Descartes' unflinching posture is that causal interaction between mind and body is both obvious and unproblematic (§15). It seems unlikely that he adopted this position disingenuously. The ultimate objective of most of his discussion of the metaphysics of minds and bodies was to support his position on immortality (§13). The claim that mind and body causally interact does not support, and indeed, as Descartes perceived, even threatens that position (§16). He held that mind and body causally interact because he considered this to be true, and obviously so.

It is possible that Descartes was especially obtuse or blind to some inconsistency, rather than disingenuous. But what is the source of the inconsistency? I have canvassed the more obvious candidates. The strongest candidate is Descartes' claim that mind and body are essentially/entirely/absolutely distinct substances$_S$, that is, that the essences of mind and body have nothing in common (since a mind's whole essence is to think, and a body's whole essence is to be extended). Many twentieth-century commentators have seized upon this feature of the metaphysics as the source of Descartes' difficulties. His response is contained in his letter to Clerselier that is part of the *Replies:* "the whole of the perplexity involved in these questions arises entirely from a false supposition that can by no manner or means be proved, viz. if the soul and body are two substances of diverse nature, that prevents them of being capable of acting on one another." There is even a passage where Descartes foreshadows a Humean analysis of causation: "There is no reason to be surprised that certain motions... should be naturally connected... with certain thoughts, which they in no way resemble"; what matters is "the possibility of an association between thoughts and bodily motions or conditions so that when the same conditions recur in the body they impel the soul to the same thought; and conversely." Descartes simply rejects the sort of principle required to sustain the objection. I have also shown that his claim that mind and body causally interact is not inconsistent either with restrictions he introduces upon possible causal relations or with his doctrine of the freedom of the will (§15).

It is reasonable to expect, if there were some inconsistency between Descartes' claim that mind and body causally interact and some set of Continental Rationalist principles, that Spinoza would have succeeded in locating the difficulty. According to Spinoza, Descartes' interactionism does little but "excite our laughter or disgust"; his psychophysical parallelism or double-aspect theory was proposed as an alternative account of the relationship between mind and body. As the author of *The Principles of Descartes' Philosophy*, he was thoroughly familiar with Descartes' views, and I have noted specific evidence of his detailed knowledge of Descartes (§20). Does Spinoza shed light on any relevant inconsistencies in Descartes? Spinoza's informal arguments against interactionism do little to support his position (§17). His formal argument at E IIP6 to show that finite modes of distinct attributes cannot interact derives its plausibility from a suppressed premise which would generate a deep inconsistency in Spinoza's own metaphysics. Further, his formal argument at E IIIP2 to show that it follows from E IIP6 that mind and body cannot causally interact depends upon an equivocation (§19).

I doubt that proponents of the standard theory can identify in Descartes a thesis which both generates inconsistency when coupled with his interactionism, and can plausibly be appealed to in order to account for the maneuvers of the subsequent Rationalist figures. Even if there is no outright inconsistency, however, perhaps an attenuated form of the standard theory is correct. What matters is that in stressing that mind and body are essentially/entirely/ absolutely distinct kinds of substances$_S$, in stressing the radical qualitative disparity between mind and body, Descartes was responsible for the perception of a mind-body problem; how could an unextended thinking substance causally interact with an unextended thinking substance with which it has nothing in common? In these terms, the weakened standard theory maintains that each Continental Rationalist after Descartes found mind-body interactionism unacceptable, and that Malebranche's occasionalism, Spinoza's double-aspect theory, and Leibniz's preestablished harmony functioned in their systems as successive attempts to provide an adequate account of the relationship between mind and body in the face of perceived or felt mind-body problem.

My response to this weakened standard theory should be obvious. The theory is correct in the case of Spinoza, mistaken in the cases of Malebranche and Leibniz. Unlike Spinoza's double-aspect theory, Malebranche's occasionalism and, in his mature metaphysics, Leibniz's preestablished harmony, do not function as solutions to the mind-body problem (§§24–25, 32). One could try to preserve the standard theory by setting Malebranche aside and claiming that each (major) Continental Rationalist after Descartes found mind-body interaction unacceptable, and that Spinoza's double-aspect theory and Leibniz's preestablished harmony were formulated as successive attempts to solve a perceived mind-body problem.

At this juncture, there emerges a vested interest on the part of a proponent of the third component of the standard theory in defending aspects of the first component as well. The present attempt to preserve the theory requires that we set Malebranche aside—he is less important than Descartes, Spinoza, and Leibniz. This is not the sort of position one can easily refute, but there are grounds for doubt. "Importance" is presumably a matter of philosophical merit or historical influence. Malebranche's influence in the short term was substantial. Locke wrote a fifty-page essay on him; Berkeley derived the fundamental structure of his metaphysics from that of Malebranche (§21); and Malebranche's theory of causation prompted Hume's treatment of the matter in the *Treatise* (§39, below). During the same period, Spinoza was largely ignored or dismissed. It was only in the long term that Spinoza's reputation grew, as idealists, Marxists, and transcendentalists all came to see in him anticipations of their views. I suspect that his adoption by such diverse philosophical movements is a symptom of the tensions and inconsistencies in his work. As we have seen, contradictory premises are crucial to the arguments of Parts I and II of the *Ethics*, respectively (§19). This leads to the question of philosophical merit. Malebranche introduced the thesis that causal relations obtain necessarily in order to show that God is the only cause, on the ground that there is a necessary connection only between the volitions of an omnipotent being and the occurrence of whatever that being wills (§22). This was, at the least, ingenious. Malebranche's argument for occasionalism seems more coherent than anything Spinoza had to offer in support of his denial of interaction (§§17, 19). The first component of the standard theory itself requires further examination.

Suppose we do set Malebranche aside. The claim that Spinoza's double-aspect theory and Leibniz's preestablished harmony were formulated as successive attempts to solve a perceived mind-body problem is correct. The preestablished harmony was initially formulated as a solution to the mind-body problem, as an alternative to Descartes' interactionism, within a dualist ontology (§34). It would be surprising if the standard theory did not have some basis in fact, and this genetic fact about the development of Leibniz's metaphysics constitutes a part of that factual foundation. But this genetic fact provides no insight whatsoever into the function of the preestablished harmony within Leibniz's mature metaphysics. Leibniz's principal motivations for retaining the preestablished harmony as a structural hypothesis within the mature metaphysics were to provide a premise for his peculiar version of the argument from design, to establish that minds have a pure metaphysical freedom, and to produce a new argument for immortality (§34). The standard theory, in its fixation on the mind-body problem, completely obscures the function of the preestablished harmony, and the attendant denial of interaction, in the context of Leibniz's mature, considered, metaphysical system. The present suggestion perhaps preserves the standard theory, but only at the cost of considerably distorting what Leibniz was really up to, and leaving Malebranche out of the picture altogether.

A more sophisticated version of the third component of the standard theory would portray occasionalism, the double-aspect theory, and the preestablished harmony not as a common response to some single philosophical problem, but rather as consequences of some shared philosophical doctrine or doctrines. The natural suggestion would be that all three—and the attendant denials of the relevant causal relations—are consequences of some shared body of doctrine relating to substance, causation, or essence, or combinations of them. This version retains the basic idea of the standard theory, that the Continental Rationalists share principles from which fundamental aspects of their metaphysics are derived, without requiring that the principles are applied in each case to the same problems, such as the mind-body problem. It is difficult conclusively to defeat the present version of the standard theory in the absence of some detailed specification of the principles relating to substance, causation, and essence which are held to have as consequences, or are held at least to have been thought to have as consequences, the metaphysical doctrines in which we are interested. I believe, however, that we are in a position to cast substantial doubt upon the viability of this version of the theory.

It seems clear that the metaphysical doctrines in which we are interested are not derived from some shared principles about substance taken alone, without the supplementation of some body of doctrine about causation and/or essence. Suppose Spinoza could have produced some fairly direct argument, given that his attributes take on all the characteristics of SP-substances, from the fact that by definition an entity is an SP-substance only if its existence does not depend causally upon the existence of anything else, to the conclusion that modes of distinct attributes cannot causally interact. And suppose Leibniz could have produced some fairly direct argument from the fact that by definition a monad is an entity which has no parts to the conclusion that monads cannot causally interact. Spinoza and Leibniz attempt to produce just such arguments at Proposition 6 of Part II of the *Ethics* and at section 7 of the *Monadology*, respectively. Even if both these arguments succeed, they are completely different in character, proceeding from quite different definitions of 'substance'. The figures are not invoking a common definition of 'substance' which has the relevant metaphysical theses for consequences.

I also think it unlikely that the denials of causal interaction between modes of distinct attributes and between monads are consequences of Spinoza's and Leibniz's respective definitions of 'substance' together with some shared principles about the nature of causation. In the first place, although Leibniz had a good deal to say about whether or not specified entities causally interact, these pronouncements do not seem to have been supported by any serious theory about the nature of causation. Leibniz says almost nothing that could generate anything like a definition or analysis of causal relations. Negatively, he rejects Francisco Suárez's view that causation consists of an *influxus physicus*: 'influx' is a "mere word" (L 75); "this *influx* is metaphorical and more obscure than what it defines. I should think it an easier task to define the term 'cause' than this term *influx*" (L 126). But Leibniz never performs this easier task of defining 'cause'. Had he anything constructive to offer toward a definition, it surely would have emerged in the *New Essays*, in connection with his commentary on Locke's chapter *"Of Cause and Effect, and other Relations."* There Leibniz offers only the comments that Locke's definition is restricted to efficient causes, and that there is a circularity in defining causation in terms of "production" (*NE* 237).

Even if Leibniz had nothing to put forth by way of a definition of 'causation', did he not at least hold that true statements of causal relations are necessary truths or that they can be established a priori? Perhaps his position was that intra-monadic laws are necessary and/or can be established a priori, but that this is not true of inter-monadic laws. This suggestion cannot be correct. Leibniz's position is that all laws formulating relationships between states of one or more monads have the same metaphysical and epistemological status. He writes: "For as there exists an infinite number of possible worlds, there exists also an infinite number of laws, some peculiar to one world, some to another, and each possible individual of any one world contains in the concept of him the laws of his world" (*LA* 43). The best of all possible worlds is the possible world which is richest in phenomena and simplest in hypotheses or laws (L 211; *DM* v; W 92–93). In such a world, there will be a single intra-monadic law of succession applicable to all monads, and hence inter-monadic laws formulating "a constant and fixed relationship" between two substances. All laws, whether intra- or inter-monadic, have the same metaphysical status. If *all* laws are necessary truths, attributing to Leibniz the thesis that *causal* laws must be necessary truths cannot help explain why inter-monadic laws are noncausal. If all laws are contingent truths, Leibniz does not subscribe to the thesis that causal laws are necessary truths in the first place.

Leibniz of course wants to say that all laws are contingent, in the sense that their truth depends upon God's choice of the best of all possible worlds (*DM* xiii; *LA* 54–55; W 480–481). Some would argue that Leibniz cannot make room for any good sense of 'contingent truth', since it is a necessary truth that an all-perfect being exists, that goodness is a perfection, and hence that this being does choose the best of all possible worlds. On this view, Leibniz's distinction between necessary and contingent truths is at bottom epistemological: necessary truths can be established a priori in a finite number of steps; contingent truths can be established a priori, but only in an infinite number of steps (S 13; W 98–99; M 36). This leads to the result that all laws, intra- and inter-monadic, have the same epistemological status. Leibniz's view about the epistemological status of causal laws—apparently that they are demonstrable a priori, though not by humans (L 283)—cannot help explain why intra-monadic laws are causal but inter-monadic laws are noncausal.

We are considering sophisticated versions of the standard theory on which occasionalism, the double-aspect theory, and the preestablished harmony are not responses to some single philosophical problem (such as the mind-body problem), but rather consequences of some shared body of doctrine relating to substance, causation, or essence, or combinations thereof. I have argued that such a body of doctrine cannot relate to substance alone. And it appears that Leibniz has no body of doctrine relating to the nature of causation, or to the metaphysical or epistemological status of causal laws, which can discriminate between the cases of causal intra-monadic laws and noncausal inter-monadic laws. I believe that the most promising variant of the sophisticated version of the standard theory must appeal to some body of doctrine relating to essence and substance.

The best defense of the standard theory I can construct proceeds along the following lines. We stipulate that an entity is a "Rationalist-substance" or "R-substance" just in case it satisfies the metaphysical component (MC) of Spinoza's conception of substance, just in case the entity's existence does not depend causally upon the existence of any other entity. We also stipulate that an entity has a "Rationalist-essence" or "R-essence" just in case *all* its properties are essential properties. Suppose that some entity x both is an R-substance and has an R-essence. It might well seem to follow that no other entity y can act causally upon x. If y does act causally upon x, it is presumably by virtue of the fact that some state of y is causally necessary for x's being in some particular state at some particular time. Now x's being in that state at that time is just a property of x. So x's having that property depends causally upon y. Since x has an R-essence, x's existence depends (noncausally) upon its having that property. So x's existence itself depends causally upon y. This is an instance of the principle that if a (here the entity y) is a cause of b (x's having the property of being in the state in question), and c (x's existence) depends noncausally upon b, a is a cause of c as well (§ 16). But the result that x's existence depends causally upon y is contrary to the supposition that x is an R-substance. This is an argument to show that y cannot act upon x. If we suppose that y is itself an R-substance which has an R-essence, x and y cannot causally interact.

We can imagine that Malebranche, Spinoza, and Leibniz argued as follows. In the case of Malebranche, God is an R-substance that has an R-essence, whereas finite or created entitites are not; thus, by the argument of the previous paragraph, finite or created entities cannot act upon God, but there is nothing to preclude God's acting upon them (as, for Malebranche, God does). In the case of Spinoza, each attribute is an R-substance that has an R-essence, where the properties of an attribute are identified with its modes; thus, (modes of) distinct attributes cannot causally interact. In the case of Leibniz, each monad is an R-substance that has an R-essence, where the properties of a monad are identified with its perceptual states; thus, monads cannot causally interact.[2] In this way, the denials of various causal realtions which are attendant to occasionalism, the double-aspect theory, and the preestablished harmony appear to be consequences of a common body of doctrine about substance and essence.

Although we can imagine that Malebranche, Spinoza, and Leibniz produced arguments of this sort, I doubt that any of them did so. Malebranche might well have accepted the premises that God (alone) both is an R-substance and has an R-essence, but he does not argue for occasionalism from these premises. His principal (and best) argument for the claim that God is the sole cause appeals to the

---

[2]I am indebted to Alan Boon for this suggestion in the case of Leibniz. My "best defense" of the third component of the standard theory in its application to Continental Rationalism is a generalization of Boon's idea.

thesis that causal relations obtain necessarily: there is a necessary connection only between the volitions of an omnipotent being and the occurrence of whatever that being wills (§ 22). For Spinoza, each attribute does take on the characteristics of an SP-substance (§ 18), and a fortiori each attribute is an R-substance. Whether or not he would agree that each attribute has an R-essence in the sense that every mode of an attribute is an essential property of that attribute is controversial. His argument at *E* IIP6D, however, does not appeal to any such considerations. While 'essence' is defined at *E* IIDef.2, the definition is not invoked until *E* IIP10D, where Spinoza argues for the proposition that "the Being of substance does not pertain to the essence of man."

As for Leibniz, he certainly does not present the imagined argument late in his career. In the *Monadology*, for example, he attempts to extract the denial of interaction from the mere fact that monads have no parts (§ 30). If anything like the argument in question is to be found in Leibniz, the *Discourse on Metaphysics* and the correspondence with Arnauld are the places to look. In the correspondence, Leibniz writes of "individual substances" in the sense of entitites which either are true unities (lacking parts), or bear some appropriate relationship to such entitites (§ 33). He in effect stipulates that individual substances have an R-essence; an Adam who experienced other events than our Adam did would not have been our Adam (*LA* 45–48, 60–61). Did Leibniz couple this with the thesis that individuals are R-substances in order to argue that individuals do not causally interact? He *concludes* from the fact that each individual substance has a complete concept not only that nothing external acts upon that substance, but also that each individual substance is indestructible and immortal (*LA* 51, 64). Indeed, he frequently argues from the fact that nothing external acts upon an individual substance to the conclusions that an individual substance is indestructible and immortal; this was one of Leibniz's motivations for maintaining the denial of interaction (§ 34). If an individual substance is destructible, if some other entity can cause it to cease to exist, it is no R-substance; or alternatively, if an individual substance is an R-substance, it follows immediately that it is indestructible. It would have been preposterous to argue: an individual substance is an R-substance that has a R-essence; therefore, nothing external acts upon an individual substance; therefore, an individual substance is indestructible. The indestructibility of an individual substance would have been entailed by the premise that it is an R-substance taken alone (whether or not it has an R-essence)! Leibniz did not utilize the claim that an individual substance is an R-substance as a premise for his argument.

Suppose Leibniz had assumed that monads were R-substances, much as Spinoza assumed that extension and thought are attributes, and hence R-substances. When coupled with the thesis that monads, and attributes, have R-essences, this would plausibly generate the denials of interaction between modes of distinct attributes, and between monads, respectively. But what would justify the assumption that the relevant entities are R-substances in the first place? We are imagining that Spinoza assumes that the attributes of thought and extension are R-substances, Leibniz that monads are R-substances. These are very different sorts of entities: a monad is something like a proper subset of modes of the attribute of thought. There are no "rationalist" principles which even begin to tell us which entities (God aside) are R-substances. In the absence of such principles, it is difficult to see any interesting sense in which there is a common body of doctrine that has as consequences the metaphysical theses in which we are interested.

Even if Malebranche, Spinoza, and Leibniz had produced the imagined arguments, the crucial claims that the relevant entities are R-substances that have R-essences are not themselves justifiable by appeal to any shared body of doctrine. It is not as if the successive figures are applying Rationalist principles with increasing rigor through to their "logical conclusion." The most we could say is that each of these philosophers is willing to invoke the concepts of R-substance and R-essence in order to support his denial of one causal relation or another. What is more fundamental is the willingness of each of these figures to advance his denial in the first place. They all then scramble for the best arguments they can locate in support of their denials. Taking substance and essence as the central notions of Continental Rationalism has no explanatory power. In particular, it is of no help in explaining why the philosophers advanced their respective denials of causal relations, why they wanted to claim of certain entities rather than others that they exhibit some degree of causal independence. Once this is understood, it seems pointless to deny that Berkeley was a Continental figure. As with the philosophers standardly classified as Continental Rationalists, what was fundamental was his willingness to deny that some causal relation obtains.

38. Objections from the Perspective of the Standard Theory (II)

Although Continental Rationalism simply does not exhibit the principal internal dialectical developments which the standard theory attributes to it, the theory's third component still has the resources to permit the mounting of a further objection. A proponent of the theory could concede that the third component is incorrect in its application to Continental Rationalism, but maintain that British Empiricism does indeed exhibit substantial dialectical development. From this perspective, there is the objection that in grouping Berkeley apart from the figures standardly classified as British Empiricists, I obscure the dialectical developments within that school.

The third component of the standard theory is applied to British Empiricism as follows: Locke's admission of material substance was inconsistent with Empricist principles, and was rejected as such by Berkeley; Berkeley's admission of spiritual substance was likewise inconsistent with Empiricist principles, and was rejected as such by Hume. When combined with the view that the Empiricist movement proceeded dialectically largely by destructive argument, by successive ontological purifications—the elimination of material substance, and then the elimination of spiritual substance—in accord with Empiricist principles, the standard theory generates the following slogan: Berkeley's system is Locke's system minus material substance; Hume's system is Berkeley's system minus spiritual substance. Once again we have an attractive picture. Is it correct?

What are the Empiricist principles that a proponent of the standard theory might have in mind? The most obvious candidate is empiricism with respect to meanings, the claim (in Humean terminology) that every idea either corresponds to a preceding impression, or is derived from ideas which correspond to preceding impressions. What are the permissible mental operations by which ideas can be "derived" from those that do correspond to preceding impressions? Hume, officially, only allows compounding—complex ideas have simple ideas as "parts" (*Trea.* 2, *Enq.* 49). Locke is more liberal, allowing compounding or combining, relating, and separating or abstracting (*Essay* II.xii.1). In the absence of some specification of precisely what mental operations qualify as instances of "relating" or "abstracting," in the absence of specifying some determinate psychological content for these notions, what Locke holds is more of a program than a theory. As a result of this indeterminancy, Locke can perfectly well write flatly in the first edition of the *Essay* that we have "no idea" of substance in the sense of substratum or support, and later write in the correspondence with Stillingfleet that "it is a complex idea, made up of the general idea of something, or being, with the relation of a support to accidents" (§ 7). Locke's empiricism with respect to meanings is so vague that it is difficult to see how one could find any inconsistency with it in his concession to Stillingfleet, though he is, of course, inconsistent with his earlier work.

The issue of inconsistency aside, the application of the standard theory to British Empiricism does not withstand careful scrutiny. Locke brought forward two sorts of difficulties for the doctrine that there exist substances = substrata in which qualities inhere: first, it is difficult to provide any positive characterization of a substances in itself; second, it is difficult to cash the metaphorical talk of qualities "inhering" in substances, or substances "supporting" accidents. Locke illustrates these points with reference to material substrata rather than spiritual substrata, for two reasons. First, the case of material substances is more favorable for his purposes: the doctrine of a (material) substratum supporting physical extension is more problematic than that of an (immaterial) substratum supporting ideas. Second, the case of material substances is theologically less contentious than that of spiritual substances. But Locke does not restrict his conclusions to material substrata, and he explicitly contends that there is a parity between the cases of spiritual and material substances. In addition, he states that God could easily superadd a faculty of thinking to matter as to some other substance. These are not the words of someone committed to the existence of spirits.

Locke was no believer in the existence of substances$_S$ or substrata of any kind (§ 7).

The standard theory invites us to accept the following: Locke accepted both material substances = material objects which exist independently of being perceived, and which consist of a material substance$_S$ or substratum supporting physical qualities, and spiritual substances$_S$ or substrata supporting ideas; Berkeley rejected material substances=material objects which exist independently of being perceived and a fortiori material substances$_S$ (though he argued the latter point independently), but retained Locke's spiritual substances$_S$; Hume, alas, rejected spiritual substances$_S$. In fact, Locke believed in neither material substance$_S$ nor spiritual substance$_S$. When Berkeley attacks doctrines of material substance$_S$, his target is a view Locke had already demolished. When Berkeley argues for doctrines of spiritual substance$_S$, he is attempting to reinstate a Cartesian notion that Locke had already rejected (§ 7). If there are some Empiricist principles shared by Locke, Berkeley, and Hume which have the consequence either that spiritual substances=substrata could not be known to exist, or indeed that the expression 'spiritual substance or substrata' is meaningless, the Empiricist movement retrogressed when the spiritual substances$_S$ rejected by Locke were subsequently readmitted by Berkeley. What is true is that the material substances=objects which exist independently of being perceived accepted by Locke were rejected by Berkeley; the spiritual substances$_S$=immaterial substrata which support ideas accepted by Berkeley were rejected by Hume. One can summarize these developments by stating that Berkeley eliminates material substance from Locke, and Hume eliminates spiritual substance from Berkeley, only on pain of equivocating on 'substance'.

Suppose that one could somehow sustain the claim that Locke did accept the existence of spiritual substances$_S$, or at least the possibility of such. We would still have in Berkeley a reversion from Locke back to Descartes. This is evident if one compares the characteristics which Descartes, Locke, and Berkeley would be willing to assign to minds or spirits. The following points would seem uncontroversial. First, Descartes' claim that necessarily any thought inheres in some spiritual substance$_S$ was rejected by Locke on the ground that it might be matter which thinks (§ 7), but accepted by

Berkeley—necessarily, any idea exists in a mind (§26). Second, Descartes' claim that thought is essential to a mind was rejected by Locke on the ground that it is only the power of thinking which is essential to the mind (§13), but accepted by Berkeley—necessarily, a mind has some idea at every time it exists (§26); hence, "Locke seems to be mistaken w^n he says thought is not essential to the mind" (*PC* 650). Third, Descartes' argument that the soul is naturally immortal was rejected by Locke on the ground that since thought is not essential to the mind, immortality does not guarantee a conscious afterlife (§13), but is accepted and supplemented by Berkeley (§26). Berkeley is aligned with Descartes and opposed to Locke not only with respect to the existence of spiritual substances$_S$, but with respect to a large body of theory relating to the metaphysics of minds or spirits as well. Even if Locke did accept the existence of spiritual substances$_S$, the slogan that Berkeley's system is Locke's system minus material substance cannot begin to account for the Cartesian accretions to Locke's position which are to be found in Berkeley.

This is hardly the sole reason for denying that Berkeley's system is Locke's system minus material substance. If material substances, material objects that exist independently of being perceived, are deleted from Locke's system, one is left with the question of what causes ideas or sensory experiences. As we have seen, in his theory of occasionalism, Malebranche delivered to Berkeley a congenial answer to this question. If one deletes from Locke's system the material substances that are causally efficacious in producing ideas, the product would arguably lack spiritual substances$_S$, would certainly lack Berkeley's principal doctrines about spirits, and would not include any account of the causal origin of ideas. If one deletes from Malebranche's system the material substances that are causally idle, the product is precisely Berkeley's metaphysics subject to some modest qualification—principally, that a restricted class of volitions of created minds has causal efficacy since we move our limbs ourselves (§26). If one wants a slogan, the claim that Berkeley's system is *Malebranche's* system minus material substance is much closer to the truth. Metaphysically, Berkeley is much more akin to Continental figures than to Locke—his metaphysics of minds is basically Cartesian; his account of God's relation to the world is basically

Malebranchian. It is the third component of the standard theory which obscures the philosophical interrelationships within the period by insisting that Berkeley's system is a reaction to Locke.

It is open to a proponent of the standard theory to abandon the third component in its application to Continental Rationalism and British Empiricism both, while insisting on the second component: Continental Rationalism and British Empiricism, if not dialectical movements in the intended sense, are at least distinct philosophical schools. The claim would be that, whatever Berkeley's metaphysical debt to Descartes and Malebranche, grouping him together with the Continental figures nevertheless obscures some important distinction between two schools. Berkeley's affinities with Continental figures, however, are by no means confined to metaphysics. Berkeley was not especially interested in epistemology proper, but the following positions can be located in his writings. He was not concerned to reject, and indeed he explicitly accepts, the existence of innate ideas and even innate knowledge (§4). He stresses certainty, the connection between certainty and knowledge, and the virtue of intuitive and demonstrative knowledge. He claims to provide demonstrative knowledge in metaphysics—of the impossibility of material substance, of the existence of God, and of the immortality of the soul. He holds that demonstrative knowledge of morality is possible in principle (§3). In his philosophizing, Berkeley was a Continental figure. It is the standard theory which obscures his substantial debt, both metaphysical and epistemological, to Descartes and Malebranche.

More generally, it is surprisingly difficult to specify an interesting epistemological criterion which has the result that Descartes, Spinoza, and Leibniz are Continental Rationalists, and that Locke, Berkeley, and Hume are British Empiricists. Locke's attack on innateness was not directed at Descartes; Berkeley accepts the existence of innate ideas and innate knowledge; and Spinoza was silent on the matter (§4). Locke's *Essay*, I have argued, constitutes an attempt to contribute to Descartes' epistemological program by producing a theory of the general conditions under which Cartesian standards for knowledge can be satisfied, and by establishing the theoretical possibility that both truths of morality and physical laws can be known in a way which satisfies those standards.

In particular, Locke shares with Descartes the following claims
with respect to the standards, sources, structure, and extent of
human knowledge: certainty is a condition for knowledge; truths
known by intuition are perceived all at once, are self-evident, and
do not require argument; truths known by deduction or demonstration are perceived in a succession or progression, are certain but not
self-evident, and are established by arguments consisting of a series
of intuitively grasped steps; intuition and deduction or demonstration are the sole sources of knowledge, at least with respect to all
general truths; not only do propositions known by intuition not
require argument, they do not admit of argument, and in that sense
they function as the foundation of all our knowledge; demonstrative
knowledge of general or universal truths extends beyond mathematics to morality and natural science as well; and with respect to
particular truths, we have demonstrative knowledge of first-person
propositions about present mental states. Classifying Locke as a
British Empiricist obscures the Cartesian epistemology which is
central to Locke's project in the *Essay* (§ 3).

Of course, it may be possible to salvage a distinction. For example, perhaps Continental Rationalists employ a priori arguments for
the existence of God, whereas British Empiricists do not. I have a
variety of misgivings. First, I have noted that on one occasion
Berkeley writes of the necessary existence of God, and that he never
explicitly rejects the ontological argument as fallacious (§ 5). Further, I have provided an explanation of how it might have been the
case that Berkeley accepted the ontological argument, though he
did not employ it. Berkeley's principal motivation was to establish
the existence of a God who is continuously active. Both his arguments for the existence of God, the passivity argument and the
Divine visual-language argument, are designed to establish the existence of just such a God. The ontological argument, on the other
hand, in itself has no tendency to support any form of occasionalism, and thus would require supplementation. Berkeley
surely would have preferred to prove the existence of a God of the
right sort in a single stroke (§ 28).

Second, I have pointed out that while the present criterion may
seem to capture a distinction important to us, it would have seemed
much less important to Descartes, Locke, and Berkeley. The epis-

temological distinction which mattered to them is that between arguments (and hence knowledge) which are at least demonstrative, and arguments which are not. All a priori arguments are demonstrative, but not vice versa. Descartes, Locke, and Berkeley placed no premium upon those demonstrative arguments that are a priori. It was of no concern to Descartes that his principal argument for the existence of God was not a priori; similarly, Berkeley would not have thought it important that his arguments for the existence of God were not a priori, given that they are demonstrative. The present criterion obscures the epistemological constraints which mattered to Descartes, Locke, and Berkeley (§ 5).

Third, it is important to recognize that the sort of criterion under consideration emerges as the result of a retreat from more broadly based criteria, which take into account a philosopher's epistemological posture toward propositions falling within a variety of subject matters, but which fail to generate the results that a proponent of the standard theory wants to secure. The present criterion rests the Continental Rationalism/British Empiricism distinction upon philosophers' epistemological postures toward a single proposition. Such a criterion might generate the desired lists, but in doing so it functions to obscure the massive epistemological affinities between Locke (and indeed Berkeley) and Descartes. For example, the criterion has the result that Locke is a "British Empiricist," but this leaves entirely out of account his view, for example, that a priori knowledge of physical laws and truths of morality is in principle possible. It is precisely the fact that Locke held this view which required the abandonment of more broadly based criteria (e.g., is all our knowledge outside of logic and mathematics derived from reason alone?) in the first place. As a result, such single-proposition criteria do not cut very deep. On the present criterion, Kant comes out an Empiricist simply because he rejects the ontological argument. Perhaps it is the case that Kant is best classified as an Empiricist, all things considered, but so classifying him on the present basis does not begin to do justice to the complexity of the classificatory issues in connection with him. This point applies equally to the suggestion that figures qualify as British Empiricists by virtue of holding the negative thesis that reason alone (intuition and demonstration) cannot yield knowledge of the external world (§ 5). Since

Malebranche held that knowledge of the existence of the external world ultimately rests on revelation (*Eluc.* VI), he would qualify as an Empiricist, even though he persistently deprecates sense perception (*ST* Preface; 1, 14; 3, Conclusion; 6, 2, 5), and holds that metaphysics, morals, and a large part of physics are sciences, where "science" is identified with knowledge of necessary truths (*ST* 1, 3, 2; 4, 2, 3; 6, 2, 6).

Finally, just as the mere fact that a figure employs the ontological argument does not tell us much about his epistemology, it does not tell us much about his metaphysics either—only that he is prepared to grant the existence of a necessary being. I believe that my distinction between thinkers who are Continental Metaphysicians and those who are not is much more fundamental. We can think of a metaphysical system as consisting of an ontology, an account of the sorts of entities held to exist, and an account of the sorts of relations held to obtain among those entities. The relations might be, for example, ones of inherence, instantiation, resemblance, causation, and so on. The fact that a figure admits the existence of a necessary being generates a fragment of that figure's ontology. The denials of various causal relations on the part of the Continental Metaphysicians immediately generate fundamental features of their account of the relations among entities by imposing restrictions upon the causal relations or causal structure exhibited within the ontology. My theory classifies Berkeley as a Continental figure; I doubt that in so doing I obscure any sustainable and important epistemological distinction between the Continental Rationalists and the British Empiricists.

39. Hume's Attack on Continental Metaphysics

In this section, I consider the postures of Locke and Hume toward Continental Metaphysics. Locke requires only brief attention. He held that it is in principle possible to have a priori, and hence demonstrative knowledge that specified causal realtions obtain, e.g., that opium causes humans to sleep (§ 3). This is not the sort of claim that qualifies a figure as a Continental Metaphysician. Continental Metaphysicians deny that specified causal relations obtain, and the content of their denials is important metaphysically. Locke's claim is that in principle we can have a priori knowledge that specified entities do causally interact in specific ways; such knowledge is important physically. Locke did not advance the sort of claim which is characteristic of Continental Metaphysics.

Locke was a Cartesian Rationalist, but no Continental Metaphysician. His attitude toward mind-body interaction is a good example of his unwillingness to engage in the sort of philosophical theorizing characteristic of Continental Metaphysics. He consistently holds that causal interaction between mental states and matter in motion is inconceivable. We cannot conceive how motion can produce anything but motion, and how motion can produce any idea in particular (*Essay* IV.iii.6,13,28); and we cannot conceive how anything other than motion can produce motion, and how thought in particular can produce motion (*Essay* IV.iii.28,x.19). But Locke is unwilling to conclude from the fact that some causal relations are inconceivable that they are impossible—what is inconceivable to us may well be within the power of an infinite being (*Essay* IV.iii.28,x.19). Even in cases where he finds causal relations inconceivable, he abstains from denying that they obtain between the relevant entities. Locke's philosophical temperament was far removed from that of the Continental Metaphysicians.

Hume, too, was temperamentally opposed to Continental Metaphysics, but his opposition was supported by a body of philosophical theory about causation, which he stated at the beginning of section XV of Part III of the *Treatise*. The preceding section XIV treats "Of the idea of necessary connexion." Now, who was the target for Hume's attack on the view that causation requires necessary connection? It was Malebranche who stated explicitly, at Bk. 6, pt. 2, ch. 3 of the *Search*, that "A true cause . . . is one such that the mind perceives a necessary connection between it and its effect." Hume cites this specific chapter of the *Search* in a footnote in section XIV (*Trea*. 158). This is one of but three detailed citations to the works of other philosophers in the whole of Book I of the *Treatise* (*Trea*. 157, 158, 243). It must have been Malebranche's position which provided the principal stimulus for Hume's examination of causation and shaped the strategy behind his discussion.[3]

[3]Malebranche's influence upon Hume's discussion of causation was documented in detail by Church, 1938, pp. 146–161. The point receives no mention in many contemporary discussions of Hume on causation, for example, that of Stroud,

The body of theory which emerges is this: it is only through observed or experienced constant conjunctions that we can determine either (i) positively, that causal relations do obtain between specified objects, or (ii) negatively, that causal relations do not obtain between specified objects. In distinguishing the two components of Hume's view indicated by the roman numerals, I am not foisting any theory or distinction upon him. Section xv begins with the following summary statement: "According to the precedent doctrine, there are no objects, which by the mere survey, without consulting experience, we can determine [i] to be the causes of any other; and no objects which we can certainly determine in the same manner [ii] not to be the causes" (*Trea.* 173).

What was Hume's relative interest in these two components of his theory about causation? The quoted sentence is immediately followed by these remarks:

> Any thing may produce any thing. Creation, annihilation, motion, reason, volition; all these may arise from one another, or from any other object we can imagine. Nor will this appear strange, if we compare two principles explain'd above, *that the constant conjunction of objects determines their causation, and that properly speaking, no objects are contrary to each other, but existence and non-existence.* Where objects are not contrary, nothing hinders them from having that constant conjunction, on which the relation of cause and effect totally depends. [*Trea.* 173]

"Any thing may produce any thing." This follows from component (ii), that it is only through the observed absence of constant conjunctions that we can determine that causal relations do not obtain between specified objects. "Creation, annihilation, motion, reason, volition; all these may arise from one another, or from any other object we can imagine." Consider some of the permutations: (*a*) motion may cause motion, contrary to those who claim to demonstrate that there cannot be causes other than God; (*b*) motion may cause volition, and vice versa, contrary to those who claim to demonstrate that mind-body interaction cannot obtain; (*c*) motion may cause annihilation, contrary to those who claim to demonstrate that

---

1977, chs. II and III. Church considers other aspects of Malebranche's influence upon Hume at pp. 143–146. For works which emphasize interconnections between Malebranche and Hume, see: Hendel, 1925; Laird, 1932; and Passmore, 1968.

physical changes in the human body cannot cause the annihilation of the soul; etc.

Was Hume aware that component (ii) of this theory about causation has these particular applications, and, if so, was he interested in pressing these points? Here is a representative passage from I.IV.V.:

> As to what may be said, that the connexion betwixt the idea of an infinitely powerful being, and that of any effect, which he wills, is necessary and unavoidable; I answer, that we have no idea of a being endow'd with any power, much less of one endow'd with infinite power. But if we change expressions, we can define power by connexion; and then in saying, that the idea of an infinitely powerful being is connected with that of every effect, which he wills, we really do no more than assert, that a being, whose volition is connected with every effect, is connected with every effect. [*Trea.* 248–249]

So, for example, (*a*) motion may cause motion, contrary to those who claim to demonstrate that there cannot be causes other than God (cf. *Enq.* 55). And there is this:

> Matter and motion, 'tis commonly said in the schools, however vary'd, are still matter and motion, and produce only a difference in the position and situation of objects. . . . 'Tis concluded to be impossible, that thought can ever be caus'd by matter. . . .
>
> Yet nothing in the world is more easy . . . to refute. . . . We need only reflect on what has been prov'd at large, that we are never sensible of any connexion betwixt causes and effects, and that 'tis only by our experience of their constant conjunction, we can arrive at knowledge of this relation. Now as all objects, which are not contrary, are susceptible of a constant conjunction, and as no real objects are contrary; I have inferr'd from these principles, that to consider the matter *a priori*, any thing may produce any thing, and that we shall never discover a reason, why any object may or may not be the cause of any other, however great, or however little the resemblance may be betwixt them. This evidently destroys the precedent reasoning concerning the cause of thought or perception. For tho' there appear no manner of connexion betwixt motion or thought, the case is the same with all other causes and effects. . . .
>
> As the constant conjunction of objects constitutes the very essence of cause and effect, matter and motion may often be regarded as the causes of thought. [*Trea.* 246–247, 250]

In sum, (*b*) motion may cause volition, and vice versa, contrary to those who claim to demonstrate that mind-body interaction cannot obtain (cf. *Enq.* 55). And finally:

> There is no foundation for any conclusion *a priori*, either concerning the operations or duration of any object. . . . Any object may be

imagin'd to become entirely inactive, or to be annihilated in a moment; and 'tis an evident principle, *that whatever we can imagine, is possible.* Now this is no more true of matter, than of spirit; of an extended compounded substance, than of a simple and unextended. In both cases, the metaphysical arguments for the immortality of the soul are equally inconclusive. [*Trea.* 250]

So, for example, (*c*) motion may cause annihilation, contrary to those who claim to demonstrate that physical changes in the human body cannot cause the annihilation of the soul.

Of the figures I have identified as Continental Metaphysicians, Hume's claims set forth in (*a*), (*b*), and (*c*) are applicable to Malebranche's denial of causes other than God, to Spinoza's denial that mind and body causally interact, and to Descartes' denial that the existence of a mind depends causally upon the existence of the body, respectively. Hume does not identify all his targets. As elsewhere in his work, this results in part from a certain loftiness. In addition, it would have been a distraction to focus too much attention on individual figures. The sort of philosophical theorizing Hume attacks in the quoted passages was widespread, and he was not especially concerned to focus on particular manifestations of it. His tactical situation is somewhat similar to that of Locke for the purposes of Book I of the *Essay* (§4). Locke's target was a widespread doctrine of the religious and moral pamphleteers. Locke does not identify particular individuals who subscribe to it because he wants to produce a general attack, applicable to various versions of the doctrine, past and future. Hume does, however, explicitly footnote Malebranche (*Trea.* 249) in connection with his argument for (*a*). And he laments that this sort of view is "so prevalent among our modern metaphysicians" (*Enq.* 57, note 1).

In the arguments for (*a–c*) which I have quoted, Hume sometimes states that for all we can know a priori, any thing may produce any thing. But his attack is not restricted to a priori arguments in support of denials that specified causal relations obtain. I have pointed out that not all intuitive knowledge, and a fortiori not all demonstrative knowledge, is a priori; for Descartes, Locke, and Berkeley we have intuitive knowledge of the content of our own present mental states, but such knowledge is not a priori, at least in any standard sense of that term (§§3, 29). Further, the epistemological distinction which mattered to Descartes, Locke, and Berkeley was that between arguments (and hence knowledge) which are at least demonstrative, and arguments which are not (§§ 3, 5). Hume is well aware of this epistemological perspective. When he embarks on his examination of "Why a cause is always necessary" at I.III.III, he writes:

> 'Tis a general maxim in philosophy, that *whatever begins to exist, must have a cause of existence*. . . .
>
> But here is an argument, which proves at once, that the foregoing proposition is neither intuitively nor demonstratively certain. . . .
>
> The true state of the question is, whether every object, which begins to exist, must owe its existence to a cause; and this I assert neither to be intuitively nor demonstratively certain. [*Trea.* 78–79, 82]

The terms 'a priori' and 'a posteriori' do not occur in this section of the *Treatise*.

Berkeley, unlike the other Continental Metaphysicians, produced at least one demonstrative a posteriori argument for his claim that ideas are causally inefficacious: "All our ideas . . . are visibly inactive; there is nothing of power or agency included in them. . . . To be satisfied of the truth of this, there is nothing else requisite but a bare observation of our ideas" (§ 29). Here we have an a posteriori or Berkelian argument in support of a denial of a specified causal relation. Berkeley says of our ideas that "since they and every part of them exist only in the mind, it follows that there is nothing in them but what is perceived. But whoever shall attend to his ideas, whether of sense or reflexion, will not perceive in them any power or activity; there is, therefore, no such thing contained in them." Hume would grant to Berkeley that there is nothing in our ideas but what is perceived, since he holds that "all sensations are felt by the mind, such as they really are" (*Trea.* 189). Hume is prepared to generalize to the conclusion that we cannot be mistaken about the contents of any of our mental states. Thus, at I.III.I, "Of Knowledge," he asserts of resemblance, contrariety, and degrees of quality, that "these relations are discoverable at first sight, and fall more properly under the province of intuition than demonstration" (*Trea.* 70).

Against the background of his agreement with Berkeley that there is nothing in our ideas but what is perceived, Hume carefully prepares for an attack on Berkelian arguments in support of denials of specified causal relations. The relevant material is at I.III.XIV and the associated appendix. Hume begins by "observing that the terms of *efficacy, agency, power, force, energy, necessity, connexion,* and *productive quality,* are all nearly synonimous" (*Trea.* 157). He proceeds to argue that "all ideas are deriv'd from, and represent impressions. We never have any impression, that contains any power or efficacy. We never therefore have any idea of power" (*Trea.* 161). In the appendix to be inserted at this point, he extends the argument to the specific suggestion that an idea of power is derived from the activity of our minds: "Some have asserted, that we feel an energy, or power, in our own mind. . . . The will being here consider'd as a cause, has no more a discoverable connexion with its effects, than any material cause with its proper effect. . . . The actions of the mind are, in this respect, the same with those of matter. We perceive only their constant conjunction" (*Trea.* 632–633). So Hume has materials which would allow him to attack Berkeley's argument as follows: granted, there is no activity or power visible in ideas, but there is no activity or power visible in volitions either; so if your argument shows that ideas are inefficacious, it shows equally that volitions are inefficacious. (I do not want to suggest that this is a good line of attack. Berkeley would simply deny that there is no activity or power visible in volitions. Hume would probably be better advised to admit that some sort of phenomenological activity is observable through introspection, while denying the relevance of this to establishing the existence of causal relations.)

It is worth noting that although Hume develops the materials for attacking Berkelian (that is, demonstrative a posteriori) arguments in support of denials of specified causal relations, he never explicitly applies them to Berkeley. This is yet another way of raising Popkin's question (§§2, 7): did Hume even read Berkeley, and if so, did he take him seriously? Hume does make use of the materials I have discussed in "Of the immateriality of the soul": "This agency of the supreme Being we know to have been asserted by several philosophers with relation to all the actions of the mind, except volition, or rather an inconsiderable part of volition; tho' 'tis easy to perceive, that this exception is more a pretext, to avoid the dangerous consequences of that doctrine. If nothing be active but what has an apparent power, thought is in no case any more active than matter" (*Trea.* 249). Here, the final sentence makes the point that appeals to apparent power or visible activity will prove too strong for their proponents' purposes. A footnote cites "father *Malebranche* and other *Cartesians*" (cf. *Enq.* 57, note 1). Perhaps Hume did not read Berkeley. More likely, he numbered Berkeley among the "other Cartesians." I find either alternative more than congenial. What matters is that Hume developed a body of theory which he exploited for the purposes of attacking demonstrative arguments, both a priori and a posteriori, for the denial of specified causal relations.

In Part IV of Book I of the *Treatise*, Hume provides arguments against a number of manifestations of Continental Metaphysics: the views that there are no causes other than God, that mind-body interaction cannot obtain, that bodily changes cannot cause the annihilation of the mind, and that there are no causes other than volitions. Hume has prepared the ground for these arguments in Part III of Book I. I believe that his utilization of component (ii) of his theory about causation has received little attention for a number of reasons. First, the only philosopher whom he explicitly cites is Malebranche, a figure of minor importance, according to the first component of the standard theory. Second, while Hume readies the ground for the attack at I.III.XIV–XV, the applications to (a–c) and to the Berkelian form of Continental Metaphysics are drawn out in I.IV.V. The title of this section, "Of the immortality of the soul," is not such as to attract much twentieth-century interest, especially when I.IV.II ("Of skepticism with regard to the senses") and I.IV.VI ("Of personal identity") offer such strong competition for attention. Finally, most attention has been focused on component (i) of Hume's theory about causation, the claim that it is only through observed constant conjunctions that we can determine that causal relations do obtain between specified objects, because it is this component which is of principal interest from the perspective of evaluating Hume's "Empiricism."

Hume certainly does put component (i) to some use, in connection with his discussion of the representative theory of perception and the argument from design. In the course of his attack on "the philosophical system" which posits "a double existence" of perceptions and external objects, "the monstrous offspring" of the imagination and reason, a "palliative" which "has no primary recommendation, either to reason or the imagination" (*Trea.* 210–217), Hume writes:

> The idea of this relation [of cause and effect] is deriv'd from past experience, by which we find, that two beings are constantly conjoin'd together, and are always present at once to the mind. But as no beings are ever present to the mind but perceptions; it follows that we may observe a conjunction or a relation of cause and effect between different perceptions, but can never observe it between perceptions and objects. 'Tis impossible, therefore, that from the existence of any of the qualities of the former, we can ever form any conclusion concerning the existence of the latter. [*Trea.* 212]

Similarly, he writes in connection with the argument from design: "When two *species* of objects have always been observed to be conjoined together, I can *infer*, by custom, the existence of one whenever I *see* the existence of the other; And this I call an argument from experience. But how this argument can have place, where the objects, as in the present case, are single, individual, without parallel, or specific resemblance, may be difficult to explain" (*DCNR* ii). A review of Hume's attack on both the representative theory of perception and the argument from design would readily show that the appeal to component (i) of the theory about causation plays a subsidiary role in each case. By contrast, component (ii) provides the core of an attack on Continental Metaphysics. It is therefore no surprise that the summary paragraph beginning at I.III.XV should emphasize that "any thing may produce any thing."

Hume, like Locke, was temperamentally opposed to Continental Metaphysics. His claim that it is only through the observed absence of constant conjunctions that we can determine (ii) negatively, that causal relations do not obtain between specified entities, enables him to marshal a systematic attack on Continental Metaphysics. Continental Metaphysicians deny that specified causal relations obtain, claim to show that causal relations do not obtain between specified objects, by appeal to arguments which they deem to be at least demonstrative, and hence on the basis of considerations other than the observed absence of constant conjunctions. If the second component of Hume's theory about causation is correct, demonstrative arguments, whether a priori or a posteriori, to the conclusion that some causal relation or other does not obtain must fail. In other words, the second component of Hume's theory about causation has the immediate consequence that the sort of philosophical theorizing characteristic of Continental Metaphysics cannot succeed. Hume was concerned to identify and attack precisely the sort of philosophical theorizing in which the Continental Metaphysicians engaged. In section 35, I contended that Continental Metaphysics should be viewed as a philosophical genre that emerged and thrived in Europe from 1640 to 1715. Hume, writing the *Treatise* in 1734–37, recognized Continental Metaphysics as such.

BIBLIOGRAPHY

This bibliography lists works (by authors other than Berkeley, Descartes, Hume, Leibniz, Locke, Malebranche, and Spinoza) referred to in the text and notes.

AARON, RICHARD I. (1931). "Locke and Berkeley's *Commonplace Book.*" *Mind*, 40, 439–459.

―― (1937a). "Great Thinkers (X): John Locke." *Philosophy*, 12, 19–32.

―― (1937b). *John Locke.* Oxford: Oxford University Press.

ABRAHAM, WILLIAM (1969). "Complete Concepts and Leibniz's Distinction between Necessary and Contingent Propositions." *Studia Leibnitiana*, 1, 263–279.

ARMSTRONG, D. M. (1960). *Berkeley's Theory of Vision.* Melbourne, Australia: Melbourne University Press.

ASPELIN, GUNNAR (1967). "'Idea' and 'Perception' in Locke's Essay." *Theoria*, 33, 278–283. Reprinted in Tipton, 1977.

AYERS, M. R. (1970). "Substance, Reality, and the Great, Dead Philosophers." *American Philosophical Quarterly*, 7, 38–49.

―― (1977). "The Ideas of Power and Substance in Locke's Philosophy." In Tipton, 1977, 77–104.

―― (1978). "Analytical Philosophy and the History of Philosophy." In Jonathan Rée, Michael Ayers, and Adam Westoby, *Philosophy and Its Past*, 42–66. Atlantic Highlands, N.J.: Humanities Press.

BALZ, ALBERT G. A. (1951). *Cartesian Studies.* New York: Columbia University Press.

BARKER, H. (1938). "Notes on the Second Part of Spinoza's *Ethics*," Parts I, II, and III. *Mind*, 47, 159–179, 281–302, 417–439. Reprinted in Kashap, 1972.

BECK, L. J. (1952). *The Method of Descartes: A Study of the Regulae.* Oxford: Oxford University Press.

—— (1965). *The Metaphysics of Descartes: A Study of the Meditations.* Oxford: Oxford University Press.

BECK, L. W. (1967). "Kant's Strategy." *Journal of the History of Ideas,* 28, 224–236.

BENNETT, JONATHAN (1965). "A Note on Descartes and Spinoza." *Philosophical Review,* 74, 379–380.

—— (1971). *Locke, Berkeley, Hume: Central Themes.* Oxford: Oxford University Press.

BRACKEN, HARRY M. (1964). "Some Problems of Substance among the Cartesians." *American Philosophical Quarterly,* 1, 129–137.

—— (1965). *The Early Reception of Berkeley's Immaterialism, 1710–33.* The Hague: Martinus Nijhoff.

—— (1974). *Berkeley.* New York: St. Martin's Press.

BROAD, C. D. (1975). *Leibniz: An Introduction,* ed. C. Lewy. Cambridge: Cambridge University Press.

BRODY, BARUCH (1977). "Leibniz's Metaphysical Logic." In Mark Kulstad, ed., *Essays on the Philosophy of Leibniz, Rice University Studies,* 63, no. 4, 43–55.

BROUGHTON, JANET, AND RUTH MATTERN (1978). "Reinterpreting Descartes on the Notion of the Union of Mind and Body." *Journal of the History of Philosophy,* 16, 23–32.

BUCHDAHL, GERD (1969). *Metaphysics and the Philosophy of Science: The Classical Origins, Descartes to Kant.* Oxford: Oxford University Press.

CAMPBELL, KEITH (1976). *Metaphysics: An Introduction.* Encino, Calif.: Dickenson.

CASTAÑEDA, HECTOR-NERI (1974). "Leibniz's Concepts and Their Coincidence *Salva Veritate.*" *Noûs,* 8, 381–398.

CHURCH, R. W. (1931). *A Study in the Philosophy of Malebranche.* London: George Allen & Unwin. Reissued in 1970 by Kennikat Press, Port Washington, N.Y.

—— (1938)."Malebranche and Hume." *Revue Internationale de Philosophie,* 1, 143–161.

COLLINS, JAMES (1972). *Interpreting Modern Philosophy.* Princeton: Princeton University Press.

COPLESTON, FREDERICK, S. J. (1958, 1959). *A History of Philosophy,* Vol. IV, *Descartes to Leibniz,* and Vol. V, *Hobbes to Hume.* London: Burns Oates & Washbourne.

COUTURAT, LOUIS (1901). *La logique de Leibniz d'après des documents inédits.* Paris: Alcan.

—— (1902). "Sur la métaphysique de Leibniz," *Revue de Métaphysique et de Morale,* 10, 1–25. Trans. R. Allison Ryan in Frankfurt, 1972, 19–45.

CURLEY, EDWIN M. (1969). *Spinoza's Metaphysics: An Essay in Interpretation.* Cambridge, Mass.: Harvard University Press.

—— (1972). "Locke, Boyle, and the Distinction between Primary and Secondary Qualities." *Philosophical Review,* 81, 438–464.

—— (1973). "Experience in Spinoza's Theory of Knowledge." In Marjorie Grene, ed., *Spinoza: A Collection of Critical Essays,* 25–59. Garden City, N.Y.: Anchor Books.

—— (1974). "Recent Work on 17th Century Continental Philosophy." *American Philosophical Quarterly,* 11, 235–255.

—— (1975). "Descartes, Spinoza and the Ethics of Belief." In Mandelbaum and Freeman, 1975, 159–189.

—— (1977). Review of Lorenz Krüger, *Der Begriff des Empirismus. Journal of Philosophy,* 74, 184–189.

—— (1978). *Descartes against the Skeptics.* Cambridge, Mass.: Harvard University Press.

DONEY, WILLIS (1967). "Nicolas Malebranche." In Edwards, 1967, Vol. 5, 140–144.

DRURY, SHADIA B. (1978). "The Relationship of Substance and Simple Natures in the Philosophy of Descartes." In Jarrett et al., 1978, 37–58.

EDWARDS, PAUL, ed. (1967). *The Encyclopedia of Philosophy,* 8 vols. New York: Macmillan.

EWING, A. C. (1937). "Some Points in the Philosophy of Locke." *Philosophy,* 12, 33–46.

FISCHER, KUNO (1857). *Francis Bacon of Verulam: Realistic Philosophy and Its Age.* London: Longman, Brown, Green, Longman, & Robert.

—— (1887). *History of Modern Philosophy: Descartes and His School.* London: T. Fisher Unwin.

FRANKFURT, HARRY G. (1970). *Demons, Dreamers, and Madmen: The Defense of Reason in Descartes' Meditations.* Indianapolis: Bobbs-Merrill.

——, ed. (1972). *Leibniz: A Collection of Critical Essays.* Garden City, N.Y.: Anchor Books.

FRASER, ALEXANDER CAMPBELL, ed. (1894). John Locke, *An Essay Concerning Human Understanding,* in two volumes. Various editions.

FRIEDMAN, JOEL I. (1978). "An Overview of Spinoza's *Ethics.*" *Synthèse,* 37, 67–106.

FURTH, MONTGOMERY (1967). "Monadology." *Philosophical Review,* 76, 169–200. Reprinted in Frankfurt, 1972.

GARBER, DANIEL (1978). "Science and Certainty in Descartes." In Hooker, 1978a, 114–151.

GIBSON, JAMES (1917). *Locke's Theory of Knowledge and Its Historical Relations.* Cambridge: Cambridge University Press.

GINSBERG, MORRIS (1923). "Translator's Introduction" in Nicolas Malebranche, *Dialogues on Metaphysics and on Religion.* London: George Allen & Unwin.

GREEN, THOMAS HILL, AND THOMAS HODGE GROSE, eds. (1874). David Hume, A *Treatise of Human Nature.* London: Longmans, Green & Co. Green's "Introductions" are reprinted in Lemos, 1968 (though the index is omitted).

GREENLEE, DOUGLAS (1967). "Locke's Idea of 'Idea'." *Theoria,* 33, 98–106. Reprinted in Tipton, 1977.

—— (1977). "Idea and Object in the *Essay.*" In Tipton, 1977, 51–54.

GUEROULT, MARTIAL (1955, 1959). *Malebranche.* 3 vols. Paris: Aubien.

—— (1968, 1974). *Spinoza I, Dieu (Ethique, I)* and *Spinoza II, L'Ame (Ethique, II).* Paris: Aubier-Montaigne.

HACKING, IAN (1972). "Individual Substance." In Frankfurt, 1972, 137–153.

HAMPSHIRE, STUART (1951). *Spinoza.* Baltimore: Pelican Books.

HASEROT, FRANCIS S. (1953). "Spinoza's Definition of Attribute." *Philosophical Review,* 62, 499–513. Reprinted in Kashap, 1972.

HEGEL, G. W. F. (1892–96). *Lectures on the History of Philosophy.* 3 vols. Trans. E. S. Haldane and Frances H. Simson. London: Routledge & Kegan Paul.

HENDEL, CHARLES W. (1925). *Studies in the Philosophy of David Hume.* Princeton: Princeton University Press. Reissued in 1963 by Bobbs-Merrill, Indianapolis.

HICKS, G. DAWES (1932). *Berkeley.* London: Ernst Benn.

HOOKER, MICHAEL, ed. (1978a). *Descartes: Critical and Interpretive Essays.* Baltimore: Johns Hopkins University Press.

—— (1978b). "Descartes' Denial of Mind-Body Identity." In Hooker, 1978a, 171–185.

ISHIGURO, HIDÉ (1972). *Leibniz's Philosophy of Logic.* Ithaca: Cornell University Press.

JARRETT, CHARLES E. (1977). "Some Remarks on the 'Objective' and 'Subjective' Interpretation of the Attributes." *Inquiry,* 20, 447–456.

—— (1978a). "The Logical Structure of Spinoza's *Ethics,* Part I." *Synthèse,* 37, 15–65.

——, JOHN KING-FARLOW, AND F. J. PELLETIER, eds. (1978b). *New Essays on Rationalism and Empiricism. Canadian Journal of Philosophy,* Supplementary Volume IV.

JESSOP, T. E. (1938). "Malebranche and Berkeley," *Revue Internationale de Philosophie,* 1, 121–142.

JOSEPH, H. W. B. (1949). *Lectures on the Philosophy of Leibniz.* Oxford: Oxford University Press.

KANT, IMMANUEL (1781). *Critique of Pure Reason.* Trans. Norman Kemp Smith. New York: St. Martin's Press.

KASHAP, S. PAUL, ed. (1972). *Studies in Spinoza: Critical and Interpretive Essays.* Berkeley: University of California Press.

KEELING, S. V. (1968). *Descartes.* Oxford: Oxford University Press. 2d. ed.

KENNY, ANTHONY (1968). *Descartes: A Study of His Philosophy.* New York: Random House.

——— (1972). "Descartes on the Will," in R. J. Butler, ed., *Cartesian Studies,* 1–31. Oxford: Basil Blackwell.

KESSLER, WARREN (1971). "A Note on Spinoza's Conception of Attribute." *The Monist,* 55, 636–639. Reprinted in Mandelbaum and Freeman, 1975.

KIM, JAEGWON (1979). "Causality, Identity, and Supervenience in the Mind-Body Problem," in Peter A. French, Theodore E. Uehling, and Howard K. Wettstein, eds. *Studies in Metaphysics,* Minnesota Studies in Philosophy, Vol. IV, 31–49. Minneapolis: University of Minnesota Press.

KNEALE, WILLIAM (1949). *Probability and Induction.* Oxford: Oxford University Press.

KUHN, THOMAS S. (1962). *The Structure of Scientific Revolutions.* Chicago: University of Chicago Press.

LAIRD, JOHN (1932). *Hume's Philosophy of Human Nature.* London: Methuen.

LEMOS, RAMON (1968). "Introduction" in his *Thomas Hill Green's Hume and Locke.* New York: Thomas Y. Crowell.

LENNON, THOMAS M. (1974). "Occasionalism and the Cartesian Metaphysic of Motion." *Canadian Journal of Philosophy,* Supplementary Volume I, Pt. 1, 29–40. This material is reprinted, substantially unchanged, in LO, pp. 810–818.

LEWIS, DOUGLAS (1969). "The Existence of Substance and Locke's Way of Ideas." *Theoria,* 35, 124–146.

LEYDEN, W. VON (1968). *Seventeenth-Century Metaphysics.* London: Duckworth.

LOEMKER, LEROY E. (1973). "Leibniz's Judgments of Fact," "Leibniz's Conception of Philosophical Method," and "Leibniz and the Limits of Empiricism." In Ivor Leclerc, ed., *The Philosophy of Leibniz and the Modern World,* 13–28, 135–157, and 158–175, Nashville, Tenn.: Vanderbilt University Press.

LUCE, A. A. (1934). *Berkeley and Malebranche: A Study in the Origins of Berkeley's Thought.* Oxford: Oxford University Press.

⸻ (1946). *Berkeley's Immaterialism.* Edinburgh: Thomas Nelson.

⸻ (1963). *The Dialectic of Immaterialism: An Account of the Making of Berkeley's Principles.* London: Hodder & Stoughton.

MABBOT, J. D. (1973). *John Locke.* Cambridge, Mass.: Schenkman.

MACKIE, J. L. (1976). *Problems from Locke.* Oxford: Oxford University Press.

MALCOLM, NORMAN (1965). "Descartes' Proof that His Essence Is Thinking." *Philosophical Review,* 74, 315–338.

MANDELBAUM, MAURICE (1964). *Philosophy, Science, and Sense Perception, Historical and Critical Studies.* Baltimore: Johns Hopkins Press.

⸻ (1976). "On the Historiography of Philosophy." *Philosophy Research Archives,* 2, 708–744.

⸻ (1977). "The History of Philosophy: Some Methodological Issues." *Journal of Philosophy,* 74, 561–572.

⸻ AND EUGENE FREEMAN, eds. (1975). *Spinoza: Essays in Interpretation.* La Salle, Ill.: Open Court.

MARTENS, STANLEY C. (1978). "Spinoza on Attributes." *Synthèse,* 37, 107–111.

MARTIN, C. B., AND D. M. ARMSTRONG, eds. (1968). *Locke and Berkeley, A Collection of Critical Essays.* London: Macmillan.

MARTIN, GOTTFRIED (1964). *Leibniz: Logic and Metaphysics.* Trans. P. G. Lucas and K. J. Northcott. Manchester: Manchester University Press.

MATSON, WALLACE I. (1968). *A History of Philosophy.* New York: American Book Company.

MATTERN, RUTH (1978). "Descartes' Correspondence with Elizabeth: Conceiving Both the Union and Distinction of Mind and Body." In Hooker, 1978a, 212–222.

MATTHEWS, H. E. (1971). "Locke, Malebranche and the Representative Theory." *Locke Newsletter,* 12–21. Reprinted in Tipton, 1977.

MORRIS, C. R. (1931). *Locke, Berkeley, Hume.* Oxford: Oxford University Press.

NORTON, DAVID FATE (1974). "Some Anamadversions on 'British Empiricism'." Paper read to the American Society for Eighteenth-Century Studies, Philadelphia; revised version forthcoming in *History of European Ideas.*

O'CONNOR, D. J. (1967). *John Locke.* New York: Dover.

ODEGARD, DOUGLAS (1965). "Locke as an Empiricist." *Philosophy,* 40, 185–196.

O'KELLEY, THOMAS (1971). "Locke's Doctrine of Intuition Was Not Borrowed from Descartes," *Philosophy*, 46, 148–151.

PAP, ARTHUR (1958). *Semantics and Necessary Truth*. New Haven, Conn.: Yale University Press.

PARKINSON, G. H. R. (1965). *Logic and Reality in Leibniz's Metaphysics*. Oxford: Oxford University Press.

―――― (1970). Review of Curley, 1969. In *Philosophy*, 45, 342–343.

PASSMORE, JOHN (1968). *Hume's Intentions*. London: Duckworth.

PITCHER, GEORGE (1977). *Berkeley*. London: Routledge & Kegan Paul.

POPKIN, RICHARD (1959a). Review of George Boas, *Dominant Themes of Modern Philosophy: A History*. *Journal of Philosophy*, 56, 67–71.

―――― (1959b). "Did Hume Ever Read Berkeley?" *Journal of Philosophy*, 56, 533–545.

―――― (1964). "So, Hume Did Read Berkeley." *Journal of Philosophy*, 61, 773–778.

QUINTON, ANTHONY (1967). "British Philosophy." In Edwards, 1967, Vol. 1, 369–396.

―――― (1973). *The Nature of Things*. London: Routledge & Kegan Paul.

RADNER, DAISIE (1978a). "Berkeley and Cartesianism." In Jarrett, et al., 165–176.

―――― (1978b). *Malebranche*. Assen, Netherlands: Van Gorcum Press.

RÉE, JONATHAN (1975). *Descartes*. New York: Pica Press.

REID, THOMAS (1764). *Inquiry into the Human Mind on the Principles of Common Sense*. Various editions.

―――― (1785). *Essays on the Intellectual Powers of Man*. Various editions.

―――― (1788). *Essays on the Active Powers of the Human Mind*. Various editions.

RESCHER, NICHOLAS (1967). *The Philosophy of Leibniz*. Englewood Cliffs, N.J.: Prentice-Hall.

RODIS-LEWIS, GENEVIÈVE (1963). *Nicolas Malebranche*. Paris: Presses Universitaires de France.

ROME, BEATRICE K. (1963). *The Philosophy of Malebranche*. Chicago: Henry Regnery.

ROSENFIELD, LEONORA COHEN (1940). *From Beast-Machine to Man-Machine: The Theme of Animal Soul in French Letters from Descartes to La Mettrie*. Oxford: Oxford University Press.

ROTH, LEON (1937). *Descartes' Discourse on Method*. Oxford: Oxford University Press.

RUSSELL, BERTRAND (1903). "Recent Work on the Philosophy of Leibniz." *Mind*, 12, 179–200. Reprinted in Frankfurt, 1972.

―――― (1937). *A Critical Exposition of the Philosophy of Leibniz*. London: George Allen & Unwin. First edition published in 1900.

—— (1945). *A History of Western Philosophy*. New York: Simon & Schuster.

RUSSELL, L. J. (1928). "The Correspondence between Leibniz and De Volder." *Proceedings of the Aristotelian Society*, 28, 155–176.

RYLE, GILBERT (1960). "Epistemology." In J. O. Urmson, ed., *Encyclopedia of Western Philosophy*. London: Hutchinson.

SCHIFFER, STEPHEN (1976). "Descartes on His Essence." *Philosophical Review*, 85, 31–39.

SEBBA, GREGOR (1970). "What Is 'History of Philosophy'?" *Journal of the History of Philosophy*, 8, 251–262.

SIEVERT, DONALD (1975). "Descartes' Self-Doubt." *Philosophical Review*, 74, 51–69.

SMITH, NORMAN KEMP (1902). *Studies in the Cartesian Philosophy*. New York: Russell & Russell.

—— (1952). *New Studies in the Philosophy of Descartes*. London: Macmillan.

SPRIGGE, TIMOTHY L. S. (1977). "Spinoza's Identity Theory." *Inquiry*, 20, 419–445.

STROUD, BARRY (1977). *Hume*. London: Routledge & Kegan Paul.

SWABEY, WILLIAM CURTIS (1933). "Locke's Theory of Ideas." *Philosophical Review*, 42, 573–593.

TAYLOR, A. E. (1937). "Some Incoherencies in Spinozism," Parts I and II. *Mind*, 46, 137–158, 281–301. Reprinted in Kashap, 1972.

TIPTON, I. C. (1974). *Berkeley: The Philosophy of Immaterialism*. London: Methuen.

——, ed. (1977). *Locke on Human Understanding: Selected Essays*. Oxford: Oxford University Press.

WARE, CHARLOTTE S. (1950). "The Influence of Descartes on John Locke." *Revue Internationale de Philosophie*, 4, 210–230.

WARNOCK, G. J. (1953). *Berkeley*. Harmondsworth, England: Penguin.

WATSON, RICHARD A. (1966). *The Downfall of Cartesianism, 1673–1712*. The Hague: Martinus Nijhoff.

WATT, A. J. (1972). "The Causality of God in Spinoza's Philosophy." *Canadian Journal of Philosophy*, 2, 171–189.

WILLIAMS, BERNARD (1978). *Descartes: The Project of Pure Enquiry*. Harmondsworth, England: Penguin.

WILSON, MARGARET D. (1969). "Introduction" to her *The Essential Descartes*. New York: Mentor.

—— (1978). *Descartes*. London: Routledge & Kegan Paul.

—— (1979). "Superadded Properties: The Limits of Mechanism in Locke." *American Philosophical Quarterly*, 16, 143–150.

WINDELBAND, WILHELM (1901). *A History of Philosophy, Volumes I and II*. Reprinted by Harper Torchbooks, New York, 1958.

WISDOM, JOHN OULTON (1953). *The Unconscious Origin of Berkeley's Philosophy.* London: Hogarth Press.

WOLF, A. (1927). "Spinoza's Conception of the Attributes of Substance," *Proceedings of the Aristotelian Society,* 27, 177–192. Reprinted in Kashap, 1972.

WOLFSON, HARRY AUSTRYN (1934). *The Philosophy of Spinoza.* 2 vols. Cambridge, Mass.: Harvard University Press.

WOOLHOUSE, R. S. (1971). *Locke's Philosophy of Science and Knowledge.* New York: Barnes & Noble.

WOOZLEY, A. D. (1964). "Introduction" to his John Locke, *An Essay Concerning Human Understanding.* London: Fontana.

YOLTON, JOHN W. (1956). *John Locke and the Way of Ideas.* Oxford: Oxford University Press.

_____ (1969). "The Science of Human Nature." In John W. Yolton, ed., *John Locke: Problems and Perspectives.* Cambridge: Cambridge University Press.

_____ (1970). *Locke and the Compass of Human Understanding.* Cambridge: Cambridge University Press.

INDEX

Library of Congress Cataloging in Publication Data

LOEB, LOUIS E
    From Descartes to Hume.

    Bibliography: p.
    Includes index.
    1. Philosophy, Modern—17th century. 2. Metaphysics
—History—17th century. I. Title.
B801.L63   110′.9′032   80-69826
ISBN 0-8014-1289-7